BUDDHISM, POWER AND POLITICAL ORDER

Weber's claim that Buddhism is an otherworldly religion is only partially true. Early sources indicate that the Buddha was sometimes diverted from supramundane interests to dwell on a variety of politically related matters. The significance of Asoka Maurya as a paradigm for later traditions of Buddhist kingship is also well attested. However, there has been little scholarly effort to integrate findings on the extent to which Buddhism interacted with the political order in the classical and modern states of Theravada Asia into a wider, comparative study.

This volume brings together the brightest minds in the study of Buddhism in Southeast Asia. Their contributions create a more coherent account of the relations between Buddhism and political order in the late pre-modern and modern period by questioning the contested relationship between monastic and secular power. In doing so, they expand the very nature of what is known as the 'Theravada'. This book offers new insights for scholars of Buddhism, and it will stimulate new debates.

Ian Harris is Professor of Buddhist Studies at the University of Cumbria, Lancaster, and was Senior Scholar at the Becket Institute, St Hugh's College, University of Oxford, from 2001 to 2004. He is co-founder of the UK Association for Buddhist Studies and has written widely on aspects of Buddhist ethics. His most recent book is *Cambodian Buddhism: History and Practice* (2005), and he is currently responsible for a research project on Buddhism and Cambodian Communism at the Documentation Center of Cambodia [DC-Cam], Phnom Penh.

ROUTLEDGE CRITICAL STUDIES IN BUDDHISM

General Editors:
Charles S. Prebish and Damien Keown

Routledge Critical Studies in Buddhism is a comprehensive study of the Buddhist tradition. The series explores this complex and extensive tradition from a variety of perspectives, using a range of different methodologies. The Series is diverse in its focus, including historical studies, textual translations and commentaries, sociological investigations, bibliographic studies, and considerations of religious practice as an expression of Buddhism's integral religiosity. It also presents materials on modern intellectual historical studies, including the role of Buddhist thought and scholarship in a contemporary, critical context and in the light of current social issues. The series is expansive and imaginative in scope, spanning more than two and a half millennia of Buddhist history. It is receptive to all research works that inform and advance our knowledge and understanding of the Buddhist tradition.

A SURVEY OF VINAYA LITERATURE
Charles S. Prebish

THE REFLEXIVE NATURE OF AWARENESS
Paul Williams

ALTRUISM AND REALITY
Paul Williams

BUDDHISM AND HUMAN RIGHTS
Edited by Damien Keown, Charles Prebish, Wayne Husted

WOMEN IN THE FOOTSTEPS OF THE BUDDHA
Kathryn R. Blackstone

THE RESONANCE OF EMPTINESS
Gay Watson

AMERICAN BUDDHISM
Edited by Duncan Ryuken Williams and Christopher Queen

IMAGING WISDOM
Jacob N. Kinnard

PAIN AND ITS ENDING
Carol S. Anderson

EMPTINESS APPRAISED
David F. Burton

THE SOUND OF LIBERATING TRUTH
Edited by Sallie B. King and Paul O. Ingram

BUDDHIST THEOLOGY
Edited by Roger R. Jackson and John J. Makransky

THE GLORIOUS DEEDS OF PURNA
Joel Tatelman

EARLY BUDDHISM – A NEW APPROACH
Sue Hamilton

CONTEMPORARY BUDDHIST ETHICS
Edited by Damien Keown

INNOVATIVE BUDDHIST WOMEN
Edited by Karma Lekshe Tsomo

TEACHING BUDDHISM IN THE WEST
Edited by V. S. Hori, R. P. Hayes and J. M. Shields

EMPTY VISION
David L. McMahan

SELF, REALITY AND REASON IN TIBETAN PHILOSOPHY
Thupten Jinpa

IN DEFENSE OF DHARMA
Tessa J. Bartholomeusz

BUDDHIST PHENOMENOLOGY
Dan Lusthaus

RELIGIOUS MOTIVATION AND THE ORIGINS OF BUDDHISM
Torkel Brekke

DEVELOPMENTS IN AUSTRALIAN BUDDHISM
Michelle Spuler

ZEN WAR STORIES
Brian Victoria

THE BUDDHIST UNCONSCIOUS
William S. Waldron

INDIAN BUDDHIST THEORIES OF PERSONS
James Duerlinger

ACTION DHARMA
Edited by Christopher Queen, Charles Prebish & Damien Keown

TIBETAN AND ZEN BUDDHISM IN BRITAIN
David N. Kay

THE CONCEPT OF THE BUDDHA
Guang Xing

THE PHILOSOPHY OF DESIRE IN THE BUDDHIST PALI CANON
David Webster

THE NOTION OF *DITTHI* IN THERAVADA BUDDHISM
Paul Fuller

THE BUDDHIST THEORY OF SELF-COGNITION
Zhihua Yao

MORAL THEORY IN ŚĀNTIDEVA'S ŚIKṢĀSAMUCCAYA
Barbra R. Clayton

BUDDHIST STUDIES FROM INDIA TO AMERICA
Edited by Damien Keown

DISCOURSE AND IDEOLOGY IN MEDIEVAL JAPANESE BUDDHISM
Edited by Richard K. Payne and Taigen Dan Leighton

BUDDHIST THOUGHT AND APPLIED PSYCHOLOGICAL RESEARCH
Edited by D. K. Nauriyal, Michael S. Drummond and Y. B. Lal

BUDDHISM IN CANADA
Edited by Bruce Matthews

BUDDHISM, CONFLICT AND VIOLENCE IN MODERN SRI LANKA
Edited by Mahinda Deegalle

THERAVĀDA BUDDHISM AND THE BRITISH ENCOUNTER
Religious, missionary and colonial experience in nineteenth century Sri Lanka
Elizabeth Harris

BEYOND ENLIGHTENMENT
Buddhism, religion, modernity
Richard Cohen

BUDDHISM IN THE PUBLIC SPHERE
Reorienting global interdependence
Peter D. Hershock

BRITISH BUDDHISM
Teachings, practice and development
Robert Bluck

BUDDHIST NUNS IN TAIWAN AND SRI LANKA
A critique of the feminist perspective
Wei-Yi Cheng

NEW BUDDHIST MOVEMENTS IN THAILAND
Toward an understanding of Wat Phra Dhammakāya and Santi Asoke
Rory Mackenzie

BUDDHIST RITUALS OF DEATH AND REBIRTH
Contemporary Sri Lankan practice and its origins
Rita Langer

BUDDHISM, POWER AND POLITICAL ORDER
Edited by Ian Harris

The following titles are published in association with the *Oxford Centre for Buddhist Studies*

Oxford Centre for Buddhist Studies

a project of The Society for the Wider Understanding of the Buddhist Tradition

The *Oxford Centre for Buddhist Studies* conducts and promotes rigorous teaching and research into all forms of the Buddhist tradition.

EARLY BUDDHIST METAPHYSICS
Noa Ronkin

MIPHAM'S DIALECTICS AND THE DEBATES ON EMPTINESS
Karma Phuntsho

HOW BUDDHISM BEGAN
The Conditioned Genesis of the Early Teachings
Richard F. Gombrich

BUDDHIST MEDITATION
An Anthology of Texts from the Pāli Canon
Sarah Shaw

REMAKING BUDDHISM FOR MEDIEVAL NEPAL
The Fifteenth-Century Reformation of Newar Buddhism
Will Tuladhar-Douglas

METAPHOR AND LITERALISM IN BUDDHISM
The Doctrinal History of Nirvana
Soonil Hwang

THE BIOGRAPHIES OF RECHUNGPA
The Evolution of a Tibetan Hagiography
Peter Alan Roberts

THE ORIGIN OF BUDDHIST MEDITATION
Alexander Wynne

BUDDHISM, POWER AND POLITICAL ORDER

Edited by Ian Harris

Routledge
Taylor & Francis Group
LONDON AND NEW YORK

First published 2007
by Routledge
2 Park Square, Milton Park, Abingdon, Oxon OX14 4RN

Simultaneously published in the USA and Canada
by Routledge
270 Madison Ave, New York, NY 10016

*Routledge is an imprint of the Taylor & Francis Group,
an informa business*

Typeset in Times by
RefineCatch Limited, Bungay, Suffolk
Printed and bound in Great Britain by
Biddles Ltd, King's Lynn

British Library Cataloguing in Publication Data
A catalogue record for this book is available from the British Library

Library of Congress Cataloging in Publication Data
A catalog record for this book has been requested

ISBN10: 0–415–41018–5 (hbk)
ISBN10: 0–203–94749–5 (ebk)
ISBN13: 978–0–415–41018–2 (hbk)
ISBN13: 978–0–203–94749–4 (ebk)

CONTENTS

CONTRIBUTORS

Ven. Khammai Dhammasami was educated in Buddhist monasteries from his early years. He also studied Buddhism and Pali in Sri Lanka, where he obtained two MAs and an MPhil, and completed his DPhil at Oxford in 2004. He is now a trustee of the Oxford Centre for Buddhist Studies and abbot of the Oxford Buddha Vihara. His interests include *vipassanā* meditation, monastic education, and Pali and Shan Buddhist literature.

Volker Grabowsky is Professor of South East Asian history at the Westfälische Wilhelms-Universität Münster. He has specialized in the history and culture of the Tai peoples in northern Thailand and Laos. He worked at the Department of Southeast Asia Studies, Passau University (1990–94), and subsequently joined the Department of Thai and Vietnamese Studies, Hamburg University (1994–96). From 1996 to 1999, he taught traditional Lao literature as a DAAD lecturer at the National University of Laos, Vientiane. He is currently supervising a research project on 'traditional Tai polities and state formation in pre-colonial South East Asia'. His postdoctoral thesis *Population and State in Lan Na: A Contribution to the Demographic History of South East Asia* (in German) has recently been published (Wiesbaden: Harrassowitz, 2004). Together with Andrew Turton, he edited the volume *The Gold and Silver Road of Trade and Friendship: The McLeod and Richardon Diplomatic Missions to Tai States in 1837* (Bangkok: Silkworm Books, 2003).

Elizabeth Guthrie was born in 1955 in Chicago, Illinois, and moved to Dunedin, New Zealand in 1980, where she lives with her husband and three adult children. She has worked with Cambodian refugee-migrants, for NGOs as a contract researcher in Cambodia, taught English as a Second Language in New Zealand and Thailand, and is presently a tutor in Religious Studies at the University of Otago, Dunedin. In 1994, she completed a PhD at the University of Canterbury, Christchurch, New Zealand, on the history and cult of the Buddhist earth deity in Cambodia, Thailand, Laos, Burma, Arakan and Sipsong Panna (PRC).

She is currently working on a project documenting contemporary mural paintings in Buddhist temples in Siem Reap and Kandal provinces, Cambodia.

Peter Gyallay-Pap received his PhD in political science from the London School of Economics in 1990. An independent scholar and adjunct at Adams State College (Colorado), he has since 1988 worked as an education and research consultant primarily in Cambodia, including two years as a volunteer in the Khmer refugee camps along the Thai-Cambodian border. He has conducted research and published numerous articles on aspects of Buddhism and social renewal in that country.

Ian Harris was educated at the Universities of Cambridge and Lancaster. He is Professor of Buddhist Studies in the Division of Religion and Philosophy, University of Cumbria, Lancaster, and was Senior Scholar at the Becket Institute, St Hugh's College, University of Oxford (2001–4). Author of *The Continuity of Madhyamaka and Yogacara in Early Indian Mahayana Buddhism* (1991) and editor of *Buddhism and Politics in Twentieth Century Asia* (1999), he is co-founder and current Secretary of the UK Association for Buddhist Studies (UKABS) and has written widely on aspects of Buddhist ethics. His most recent book is *Cambodian Buddhism: History and Practice* (2005), and he is currently responsible for a research project on Buddhism and Cambodian Communism at the Documentation Center of Cambodia (DC-Cam), Phnom Penh.

Andrew Huxley is a barrister who used to practise in London's criminal courts. Since 1984 he has studied Burmese law in the Law Department, School of Oriental and African Studies. He has edited the books *Thai Law: Buddhist Law* (1997) and *Religion, Law, Tradition* (2002), and has published numerous articles on the subject.

Peter Koret completed his doctoral thesis at the School of Oriental and African Studies, writing his dissertation on traditional Lao Buddhist literature. Following graduation, he has taught at Arizona State University and the University of California, Berkeley. He has recently completed a book-length translation and study of the Lao poem *Leup Phasun*, and is currently working on a biography of Narin Phasit, a religious and political reformer in early twentieth-century Siam. He has written extensively on Southeast Asian literature, including, for example, 'Religion, Romance, and Politics in the Interpretation of a Traditional Lao Poem' in *Contesting Visions of the Lao Past*, edited by Soren Ivarsson; 'The Invention of Lao Literature as an Academic Subject of Study' in *Laos: Culture and Society*, edited by Grant Evans; and 'Convention and Creativity in Traditional Lao Literature' in *The Canon in Southeast Asian Literatures*, edited by David Smyth.

John Marston's interest in Cambodia began when he worked as an English teacher in refugee camps in the 1980s. He completed a doctorate in anthropology at the University of Washington in 1997. Since then he has been teaching at the Center for Asian and African Studies of El Colegio de México in Mexico City. His articles have been published in *Estudios de Asia y África*, the *Southeast Asian Journal of Social Science*, and *Crossroads: An Interdisciplinary Journal of Southeast Asian Studies*, as well as several edited volumes. He is the co-editor of *History, Buddhism, and New Religious Movements in Cambodia* (2004) published by the University of Hawaii Press.

Juliane Schober teaches at Arizona State University. Her research focuses on Theravada Buddhist practices, ritual and the veneration of images. Her publications include an edited volume on *Sacred Biography in the Buddhist Traditions of South and Southeast Asia* (Hawaii University Press, 1997), numerous encyclopedia essays, and recent articles such as 'Buddhist Visions of Moral Authority and Civil Society: The Search for the Post-Colonial State in Burma' in *Burma at the Turn of the Twenty-First Century*, edited by M. Skidmore (University of Hawaii Press, 2005) and 'Buddhism and Modernity in Myanmar' in *Buddhism in World Cultures: Contemporary Perspectives*, edited by S. Berkwitz (ABC-Clio, 2006). Her current project traces the genealogies of modern Buddhism in Myanmar.

Peter Skilling is Maitre de conférences, École française d'Extrême-Orient. Resident in Bangkok, his primary research interest is the history of Buddhism in pre-modern Siam from inscriptions, chromides, and literature. His publications include *Mahāsutras: Great Discourses of the Buddha* (2 vols., The Pali Text Society, Oxford).

PREFACE

The genesis of this collection dates back to my two-year period as Senior Scholar at the Becket Institute, St Hugh's College, Oxford, where I was undertaking research into the persecution of Cambodian Buddhists under Pol Pot. At the suggestion of the Institute's then Director, Dr Jonathan Rowland, it was agreed that I would convene a small international and multidisciplinary symposium of academics working at the interface between religion and politics in Theravada South and Southeast Asia. In due course eighteen assorted anthropologists, historians, political scientists and Buddhist studies scholars congregated for a convivial but intellectually focused three-day session of presentation and debate.

The enthusiasm and sense of intellectual community generated by the symposium suggested that at least some of the essays delivered there should be collected together into a publication. That this has taken significantly longer than first planned is something for which I, as editor, am almost exclusively responsible. Nevertheless, it is hoped that the resulting publication will complement and enrich existing work in the area. I am thinking here particularly of general studies of institutional Buddhism in the modern world, such as Bardwell Smith (1978), Bechert (1966–73), Dumoulin and Maraldo (1976), Harris (1999), Keyes, Kendall and Hardacre (1994), Ling (1993) and Reynolds (1972), as well as more geographically and culturally circumscribed works on Burma (e.g. Mendelson (1975), Sarkisyanz (1965), Smith (1965)), Cambodia (e.g. Harris (2005), Marston and Guthrie (2004), Yang Sam (1987)), Laos (e.g. Evans (1998), Stuart-Fox and Bucknell (1982)), Sri Lanka (e.g. Gombrich (1988), Seneviratne (1999), Tambiah (1992)) and Thailand (e.g. Ishii (1986), Jackson (1989), Suksamran (1977), Tambiah (1976)).

On the surface such a profuse set of references might suggest that the study of the socio-political circumstances of Buddhism in the modern world is a well-winnowed field. But this is very far from being the case. Although Buddhist studies as a discipline has grown quite rapidly in the last half-century, especially in the United States, interest in its doctrinal and textual resources, as well as in the history of its formative period, has massively eclipsed other modes of enquiry. This has been no bad thing, but when the field is observed with an eye to the future it seems a shame that the role of Buddhism in shaping the nature of contemporary Asian societies has been comparatively so neglected. Certainly the Buddhist heartlands, and Southeast Asia most particularly, manifest signs of a capacity both for astonishing economic growth, but also potential political instability, in the coming years. A better appreciation of the indigenous factors that have contributed to this paradoxical situation, Buddhism being perhaps pre-eminent, is a clear desideratum.

All that now remains is for me to thank those who have made this publication possible; namely, all the contributors and Becket Institute colleagues – Jonathan Rowland for first suggesting the idea and Raphaela Schmid for helping out with some of the practicalities of organizing the original symposium. Also the Becket Fund for Religious Liberty, Washington DC, and the British Academy for providing the funding necessary to convert ideas to concrete realities and the St Martin's College Research Development Fund for supporting the editorial process. Finally, thanks to my old Lancaster colleague John Shepherd for endless fiddling with endnotes and bibliographies, occasionally fortified with walks and beer in the Lakeland hills.

Ian Harris
Burton-in-Lonsdale
August 2006

1

INTRODUCTION – BUDDHISM, POWER AND POLITICS IN THERAVADA BUDDHIST LANDS

Ian Harris

These chapters represent an edited collection of essays, some of which were first delivered at a symposium entitled Buddhism, Power and Politics in South and Southeast Asia held by the Becket Institute, St Hugh's College, University of Oxford, on 14–16 April 2004. The intention of the event was to get the widest possible contribution from scholars working in Theravada Buddhist contexts to the debate over what constitutes a natural sphere of Buddhist political activity, with specific emphasis on the history of the last two centuries.

All religions have a political dimension. Yet, despite high-level interest in the political manifestations of the great monotheist traditions of Christianity, Islam, and Judaism, little sustained attention has been given to this crucial aspect of Buddhism, Asia's most important religion. Buddhism has exercised a significant geographic and historical presence in most parts of the continent, often for very considerable periods. It has also played a substantial role in the formation of specific states as well as in less formal ways of interpreting and informing social and political processes, and this influence has continued down to the present.

Early Buddhist sources indicate that the Buddha preached on a variety of politically related topics (Harris 1999, 1f). The importance of Asoka Maurya (268–233 BCE) as a paradigm for later traditions of Buddhist kingship is also well attested, while in China the spread of Buddhism seems to have reflected and reinforced tendencies towards social mobility and a more egalitarian ethos. So Max Weber's influential observation that Buddhism is a fundamentally other-worldly religion must be, at best, only partially true.

The extent to which Buddhism interacted with the political order in the classical and modern states of South and Southeast Asia has certainly been the subject of important regionally based studies, but there has been little scholarly effort to integrate these findings into a wider picture which might be employed as a means of illuminating relevant social and political aspects of contemporary Asian life. Given the crucial importance of this tradition in key areas of the globe, this is surprising. One factor at play here may be the complexity of the material. Indeed, the literary, doctrinal, practical and cultural manifestations of Buddhism are too complex for any individual, however learned, to do full justice to their political ramifications. Yet the time is surely ripe for the matter to be examined in a systematic manner.

It is clear that, even if in the Buddhist context politics is merely the exercise of power, the nature of such power has been conceived in radically different ways from that in the modern west. To give one fairly obvious example, Durkheim observed, long ago, that the concept of the supernatural is a modern category. Yet from the traditional Buddhist perspective, a way of envisaging the world that has survived largely unscathed into the contemporary period, power has always been something that may be exercised across the natural/supernatural continuum.

As is well known, the Buddha came from an aristocratic family and, despite the fact that he personally repudiated his right to inherit the throne by withdrawing from the world to pursue a life of moderate asceticism, he seemed to have been perfectly content to mix in the society of kings and other nobles after his enlightenment. As Craig Reynolds very aptly puts it, 'If the Buddha represents the absence of power, then he leaves a very large black hole that exerts immense gravitational forces on all those in its orbit' (Reynolds 2005: 220).

From an early period Buddhism seems to have shown a marked preference for monarchical forms of governance. Nevertheless, the tradition was not univocal in its approach to laws of succession and related matters. While the ideal of an elected king, along the lines of the legendary Mahāsammata, may certainly have been sanctioned by ancient tradition, it does not seem to have been a method of selection that fared well in the historical process. In most Theravada lands the preference appears to have been much more oriented towards the principle of primogeniture punctuated by regular and bloody conflict between competing claimants to the throne. The victor in such a contest could often compensate for the sins committed in gaining the throne by the performance of elaborate Buddhist rites, large-scale donations, and the like. In this manner, he could envisage himself sitting firmly in the tradition of Asoka, the model of all subsequently righteous Theravada rulers.

Such rulers were expected to exercise their power in accord with Buddhist principles. In return they regularly claimed high spiritual attainment. They may, for example, have been regarded as *bodhisattvas* – the eighteenth-century Burman King Alaungpaya's name means 'embryo Buddha' – or as the Buddha-to-come, Maitreya. The latter appellation often came with millennial or chiliastic connotations, and we have plenty of Southeast Asian examples of individuals who sought the highest degree of worldly power on the back of claims to be an embodiment of the future Buddha.

In line with Durkheim's previously mentioned observation, Theravada Buddhist conceptions of sovereignity did not really differentiate between 'political leadership' and 'charismatic authority' (*ibid.* 219), for the king's status was also determined by his possession of merit stored up over previous lives. But monarchical claims are only one side of the coin in understanding the relations between power and political authority. The monastic order (*sangha*) was itself perfectly capable of challenging the state when it seemed significantly out of line with Theravada virtues. Quite apart from any other consideration, the impact of large numbers of able-bodied monastics in a state of withdrawal from economic activity has done much to shape the societies and cultures of Theravada lands for centuries, and monastic law (*vinaya*) has provided the basis on which many 'larger political structures rest' (*ibid.* 225). In addition, the renunciation represented by the *sangha*, and in particular by those members of the order who undertake ascetic practices (*dhutaṅga*) at the periphery of society (Harris 2000), in the wilderness for example, is traditionally held to generate prodigious quantities of power which may then be transmitted to amulets and relics deemed to be especially convenient physical receptacles for concentrating and storing this supernatural energy (Thai: *saksit*). Possession of such special objects confers great power on their custodians, be they rulers or those who seek their overthrow. In this context, then, it is perhaps not too much of an exaggeration to suggest that a healthily functioning Buddhist polity is one in which the respective powers of king and *sangha* are held in a state of antagonistic symbiosis.

The essays in this collection engage with the ways in which Theravada Buddhism from the late pre-modern period has variously engaged with, or reacted against, a range of historical circumstances which may help to define a general concept of power conceived from a political perspective. As such, the contributors treat debates over the role of education, the evolution of a distinctively Theravada political theory, charisma, anti-colonialism and the rise of nationalism, and arguments over the proper role of political and social institutions. In addition, they seek to shed further light on the Theravada concept of security and protection, law, the acquisition of wealth, the idea of civil society, prophecy, peace-building and reconciliation, as well as the possibility of explicit Buddhist political representation and the proper forms of governance. Not unsurprisingly, the idea of monarchy is a leitmotif that runs throughout most of the collection.

Ven. Khammai Dhammasami's 'Idealism and Pragmatism: A Dilemma in the Current Monastic Education Systems of Burma and Thailand' identifies the inability of the current monastic community to find a consensus on the principal objectives of monastic education as a major problem. Traditionally, in both Burma and Thailand, the *sangha* had offered two kinds of taught curricula in their schools: one exclusively oriented towards monks, the other somewhat adapted to the needs of the wider society. As the forces of modernization and westernization grew stronger throughout the latter part of the nineteenth century, there were attempts to reform the educational system and these meant that the respective governments eventually took full responsibility for both countries' secular education needs. Yet the changes did not stop there, for monastic reformers soon began to call for an expansion of their own traditional Buddhist curricula so that they might take on board various new and potentially helpful subjects like English and mathematics. *Sangha* traditionalists in turn opposed the imposition of these unfamiliar elements, which they denoted by the derogatory term 'animal sciences' (*tiracchānavijjā*), even though mathematics, in fact, appears to have had some natural role in traditional education, particularly with reference to the semi-rote learning of Pali literature. The traditionalists' opposition to English language acquisition was further amplified by the fact that it represented the primary mode of European colonialism. Nevertheless, and especially given the pattern of Southeast Asian ordination practices, both the Burmese and Thai governments recognized the need to equip monks with a system of learning that would not hinder their prospects if and when they disrobed, and leading monastic modernizers, such as Janakābhivaṃsa in Burma and Prayud Payutto in Thailand, have worked to develop a new kind of *sangha* education that meets the unique needs of Buddhism, while at the same time being of service to both wider society and the state. These developments have led to the creation of new *sangha* universities which, ironically, particularly given the sometimes bitter disputes over the imposition of the 'animal sciences', have seen part of their goal as producing international Buddhist ambassadors with a level of education suitable for missionary work in the medium of English.

Andrew Huxley is a leading figure in the study of indigenous law in Burma. His essay entitled 'Rajadhamma Confronts Leviathan: Burmese Political Theory in the 1870s' takes the career and political writings of U Kyaw Htun and U Hpo Hlaing as its focus. Both men had been heavily influenced by the Theravada Buddhist culture from which they had emerged and both attempted to synthesize the best of indigenous political thought with elements received from the colonial power. U Kyaw Htun had started to work for the British a year before the Second Anglo-Burmese War and, despite subsequent dismissal from his post, he won the Judicial Commissioner's Prize in early 1876 for his *Essay on the Sources and Origins of Buddhist Law*. U Hpo Hlaing, on the other hand, was an aristocrat who had been a faithful servant of King Mindon of Mandalay (1853–78). Huxley applies what he terms a 'listological analysis' to key writings of both men. He shows that Kyaw Htun's *Essay on the Sources and Origins of Buddhist Law*, which includes a short analysis of Burmese political theory, represents a balance sheet between ruler and ruled. It also seeks to demonstrate that absolutism is unacceptable in the Burmese context, while the author underlines the need for due process and the rule of law. When King Mindon died, Hpo Hlaing had been a co-leader of a 'coup for constitutional monarchy', and it was in this capacity that he wrote his *Rajadhammasangaha* in 1879 to instruct the new king in the cabinet arrangements that, it was argued, should now bind him. This work of political theory addressed to a monarch on his taking the throne was both a policy statement of a *coup d'état* and strong defence of cabinet government. In the light of subsequent political developments in Burma, Huxley regrets that the distinctive political thought of U Kyaw Htun and U Hpo Hlaing was not better received.

In her essay 'Colonial Knowledge and Buddhist Education in Burma', Juliane Schober notes that colonizing forces have a tendency to impose their forms of knowledge on newly conquered territories. This takes place in many ways, one of which is in the training of suitable members of the local population to become civil servants and administrators. In Burma, the arrival of European learning gradually displaced India as the ultimate and natural source of knowledge, and marked the beginning of a new relationship between modern science and Theravada Buddhism. In an essay that touches some of the themes previously explored by Ven. Khammai Dhammasami, we discover that monastic education during the reign of King Bodawphaya (r. 1782–1819) already incorporated a variety of putatively secular subjects of Indian origin, such as astronomy, astrology, military arts, boxing, wrestling and music. But by the mid-nineteenth century, when Burmese monks began to come up against a British insistence on the teaching of science, they began a policy of non-cooperation. However, the *sangha*'s activities had unintended and far-reaching consequences, eventually giving rise to a series of millenarian resistance movements during the 1920s and 1930s. Schober also focuses on the emergence of the Young Buddhist Men's Association (YMBA) and its promotion of four national objectives: strengthening the national spirit or race (*amyo*), upholding national Burmese culture and literature (*batha*), advancing Buddhism (*thathana*) and developing educational opportunities (*pyinnya*). Among the reformers who emerged from this background were U Chan Htoon, Judge of the Supreme Court of the Union of Burma and Secretary-General of U Nu's Buddha Sasana Council, and Shwe Zan Aung, who stressed the compatibility between Buddhism and science. The essay concludes with an examination of the ways in which Burmese governments have continued to politicize education since independence, with particular emphasis on efforts by the military regime, since the 1990s, to employ monasteries in the delivery of basic education in rural areas, particularly among non-Buddhist tribal peoples, and on the strategic closure of schools and institutions of higher education as a means of preventing or quelling student unrest.

Peter Gyallay-Pap trained as a political scientist but has been personally involved in attempts to re-establish Buddhist-based welfare and educational projects in Cambodia following the tragic events of the 1970s. In his essay, entitled 'Reconstructing the Cambodian Polity: Buddhism, Kingship and the Quest for Legitimacy', he asks the question: can political science can gain a grasp of Cambodian political culture and its vicissitudes with the vocabulary and tools available to it? He responds with a fairly resounding no. Building on the insights of the political philosopher Eric Voegelin, he sees the modern Cambodian conception of political order as an allotropic arrangement in which the modern western concept of the nation has been conjoined with the older indigenous symbols of Buddhist kingship and *sangha* to create a civic religion of loyalty to the Cambodian state. He concludes that, while Pol Pot's Democratic Kampuchea (DK) '. . . could not be a more graphic metaphor of a political system that had lost its existential bearings', post-DK attempts to embed Cambodian culture and politics within the western liberal paradigm continue to be elusive. It is against this background that he suggests that it may still be possible for Cambodians to construct a modern, or post-modern, polity that does justice to a more indigenous and Theravada Buddhist political culture, and that it is only in this way that the institutions of governance will be able to gain more obvious legitimacy with the Cambodian people.

There has been a significant flowering of scholarship related to Buddhism in Cambodia since the middle of the 1990s, and John Marston is one of the leading figures in this new movement. His essay, entitled 'The Cambodian Hospital for Monks', tells the story of the establishment of a place of healing for *sangha* members in the early Cambodian Independence period which was, coincidentally, also the time when Buddhists throughout the world were celebrating the two thousand five hundredth anniversary of the Buddhist religion. It seems that the project fed into an emerging pan-Asian vision for Buddhism. Its main initiator, Khuon Nay, had a prior background as a member of the country's major political grouping, the Democratic Party, but he was also motivated by an engagement with the central Buddhist insight into life's impermanence. His fund-raising involved use of relics and his conception of the healing can be read in moderately millennial terms. The hospital was also a consciously national project with a 'civil society' dimension that linked back to both Theravada traditions of kingship and to the reformist Buddhism that had emerged during the French colonial period. Indeed, the location of the hospital some distance away from the historic and French centres of the capital seems to confirm this impression. Furthermore, Marston argues that the project's backers were able to plug into a form of spirituality that provided them with an authentically Khmer identity, while at the same time recognizing the power of western science and technology. By so doing, this unusual project of modernity was able to draw heavily on the pre-modern and indigenous so that the Khmer could validate their own culture as equal to that of the colonizers.

Volker Grabowsky describes himself as, 'an historian not specialised in Buddhist studies'. Nevertheless, his 'Buddhism, Power, and Political Order in Pre-Twentieth Century Laos' touches upon issues crucial to the understanding of how Buddhism interacted with wider Lao society in its pre-colonial past. It addresses three interconnected questions: When and how did Buddhism become the dominant religion in Lao society? How did Buddhism influence Lao conceptions of kingship? What was the relationship between the political and religious orders in pre-colonial Laos and to what extent did Buddhist monks help legitimize and strengthen political institutions? The author investigates how accurate the standard view on the diffusion of Buddhism in pre-colonial Laos is in the light of the historical evidence. He concludes that mid-fourteenth-century Cambodian influence was not a decisive factor in the diffusion of Buddhism in Lao society and that it was not until the reign of Sainya Cakkhaphat Phaen Phaeo (r. 1442–79/80), that Theravada Buddhism became the dominant religion of the ruling elites. From that time on, kings tended to abide by the tenfold royal code (*dasa rājadhamma*), build *stūpas*, manipulate relics, dedicate Buddha images, donate land to the *sangha*, and institute the practice of temple serfdom much the same as their fellow rulers in other regions of Theravada Southeast Asia. The author also discusses an interesting case of antagonistic symbiosis between ruler and *sangha* as illustrated in the career of a senior and charismatic monk called Pha Khu Phon Samek, aka Pha Khu Achom Hòm (literally, 'the learned monk whose faeces smell [good]'), following King Suriyavongsa's death in 1695.

Peter Koret's 'Past, Present, and Future in Buddhist Prophetic Literature of the Lao' offers a unique glimpse into a genre of writing hitherto largely ignored by the scholarly community. Prophetic writing effectively represents a tradition of underground religious literature which authors can reflect on the social, political and other ills of their time in a context that gives a far higher degree of protection from persecution than that allowed by alternative genres of writing. Koret divides his coverage into two sections, one dealing with materials produced in the nineteenth and early twentieth centuries, the other focusing on writings from the mid-twentieth century. Both clearly reflect the political and economic circumstances of their times, many from the former period dwelling on the suffering of the Lao and other groups under Siamese domination, and both, while fitting into a general Theravada pattern of explanation, nevertheless possess elements that might be regarded as heterodox. To give one example, the god Indra, the falsely attributed author of much Lao prophetic literature, regularly comes to the fore as an enforcer and powerful agent of righteous anger, to such an extent that the Buddha is relegated to the background as an ultimate but very remote source of justification. Nevertheless, these works tend to avoid simple solutions to present suffering whether caused by government oppression, war, foreign domination or other factors. For the Lao authors of these works, the only real solution to suffering is a fundamental restoration of the moral and orderly 'world' of the past, in line with mainstream Buddhist principles.

The Buddha's defeat of Māra (*māravijaya*), the mythological embodiment of all negativity from the Theravada perspective, has been a potent political metaphor in Southeast Asia for many centuries. The Buddha's principal ally in this incident is the Earth Goddess (*nang thoranee*) and in her 'In Defence of the Nation: The Cult of Nang Thoranee in Northeast Thailand', Elizabeth Guthrie explores that deity's association with fertility but also with more aggressive protection, which in the modern period has taken the form of the protection of the nation state. Focusing on the northeast Isaan region of Thailand, and the relatively new Khon Kaen City in particular, Guthrie traces the relationship that has grown up between Nang Thoranee and the Thai political right since the end of the Second World War. The construction of a Nang Thoranee fountain shrine in Khon Kaen coincided with a period in which the central government was trying to deal with a putative communist threat in the northeast of the country. But in the late 1990s, the earth goddess's devotees turned to her again in attempts to protect themselves from the adverse economic effects of International Monetary Fund policies towards Thailand. Some believed that she would reveal vast hidden sources of underground gold which could be used to help the nation pay off its international debts. The essay also considers possible financial corruption at the shrine itself and its inevitable decline once the country's economy began to move in a more favourable direction.

The final essay in this volume, 'King, *Sangha*, and Brahmans: Ideology, Ritual and Power in Pre-Modern Siam' is by Peter Skilling, who uses inscriptions, the *Three Seals Law Code*, chronicles, royal eulogies, and other primary materials to illuminate both the conceptions and idealizations of kingship and religion and the intricacies of ritual relations from the Ayutthaya to the early Ratanakosin periods. He argues that ritual was essential to the political functioning of the states that evolved within and beyond the boundaries of modern Thailand, and that its role in state economies and regional and trans-regional diplomacy should not be dismissed as pre-modern extravagance or despotic caprice. Indeed, the impact of ritual on royal finances was enormous, although when looked at from another perspective, the needs of ritual also influenced trade. Skilling points out that ritual in the Siamese context had a complex and hybrid nature, reflected in the Thai phrase *samana-chi-phrām*, i.e. 'mendicants, renunciants, and brahmans'. It was a cardinal duty of the king to care for these religieux, and the role of brahmans needs to be included in any examination of pre-modern statecraft in the region, for brahmans presided over royal rites and participated in ceremonies alongside Buddhist monks. While recognizing that the sources are multivocal, the essay also looks at the ways in which kings are variously described as *bodhisattvas*, Buddhas, *cakravartins*, Indra, and so on. It also covers the ten royal virtues (*dasabidha-rājadhamma*), evidence for the evolution of Theravada monastic lineages, monks as witnesses in legal processes, brahmans in literature and the classification of various religieux in the *sakdinā* system.

2

IDEALISM AND PRAGMATISM

A dilemma in the current monastic education systems of Burma and Thailand

Ven. Khammai Dhammasami

The problem

In Burma, the highest ecclesiastical body, the State Sangha Mahānāyaka Committee, wrote in its Education Report of 1981 that,

> . . . . . due to the current education system, although it is not possible to say that the efforts and intelligence of the monks and novices, who are sons of the people, are fruitless, it is, however, clear that, despite their invested effort and intelligence, the end-result is a minus, not a plus.[1]

In Thailand, Phra Prayud Payutto, whom Tambiah refers to as a 'brilliant scholar-monk', also observed the *sangha*'s education in his country in 1988 as follows:

> The present state of monastic education is similar to the sky which, although with some spots of sunshine, is in fact full of cloud. The sky is not clear. When monks themselves see the dull and overcast sky they may feel disheartened, tired and might as well fall asleep.[2]

Here the scholar-monk, Payutto refers, I believe, to various problems, for instance, the *sangha*'s gradual loss of cultural leadership; the inability of the majority of monks to relate the teaching to social problems; the uncoordinated syllabuses of various monastic examinations; shortage of teachers; the decline of Pali study (Tambiah 1976: 200; Report 1941: 11); and students being over-examined.[3]

Based on the above observations, I shall suggest that these problems are primarily caused by the inability of the *sangha*, the monastic community, to find a consensus on the objective of monastic education. To that end, I shall discuss how the argument on defining the aim of monastic education has been debated between idealists and pragmatists.

The background

The *sangha* in Burma and Thailand was the main educator of society as a whole before the 1890s.[4] Although the emphasis in monastic education has always been morality, the *sangha* until the 1890s defined the objective of its education as to serve the *buddhasāsana*, 'the Buddha's religion', as well as the society at large. In other words, it was not only to educate those who wished to free themselves from suffering but also those who had a worldly motive.

The *sangha* did well by producing two types of curricula, taking account of the needs of both the monastic order and society: one is general and the other is specialised (Bunnag 1973: 41; Zack 1977: 45–46). The general curriculum included lessons or texts on basic moral and monastic training as well as on vocational subjects current at the time. Occasionally, secular arts and sciences were integrated into the monastic curriculum, to fulfil the needs of the wider society (Wyatt 1969: 4; Rahula 1956: 161). This type of curriculum was designed and modified by individual abbots to suit the needs of their students and never adopted nationally, despite similarities in curricula between monasteries.

The other type of curriculum was for those who stayed in the monastery longer as monks and were thus more committed to the religious life. This category of curriculum was specialised, focusing entirely on the *Dhamma* and *Vinaya*, 'teaching and discipline', and it was presumed that those who studied this curriculum were committed to serious spiritual practice and would themselves one day become leading members of the order. The aim of this curriculum was to preserve the doctrine, thus the *buddhasāsana*.

However, in the 1890s, the governments of both Burma and Thailand urgently sought modern sophisticated secular education because, feeling the need to modernise since the second half of the nineteenth century, both countries wished to acquire more sophisticated 'weaponry, steamships, telegraphs, hospitals, smoke-billowing mills' (Myint-U 2000: 113) and administrative machinery. As a result, in Burma and Thailand, society as a whole began to require a more sophisticated general education, and that was not available in the monasteries.

Therefore, the king had to find alternatives to provide a better general education, that is, to send students abroad to where they could obtain such education, and to set up schools independent of monasteries. In Burma, in

1859, King Mindon (1853–1878) sent the first state scholars to St Cyr and the École Polytechnique in France. More students, some as young as fifteen, were sent to Calcutta, India, and to Europe, mainly France and England. Between 1859 and 1870, Mindon sent a total of at least seventy students abroad for western secular education. He also encouraged Christian missionaries to set up schools where western secular subjects would be taught. The first schools for laity not run by the *sangha* were set up by Rev. Dr John Marks, a British missionary, and Bishop Bigandet, a French Catholic missionary, in Mandalay (Sein 1986: 441). The king provided these missionaries with lands and financial assistance to build churches and schools,[5] where his sons, including Prince Thibaw (later King Thibaw, 1878–1885), were educated.

In Thailand, King Chulalongkorn sent students first to the famous Raffle's School in Singapore, a British colony, and then to Europe, mainly Germany and England. One of his sons, Prince Vajiravud (later Rāma VI), received his general education in England and later graduated from Christ Church, Oxford. In fact, secular schools offering western secular subjects had been first set up in the palace in the previous reign by King Mongkut (1851–1868). Mongkut was well versed in both traditional Buddhist learning and western sciences, which he had studied with American and French missionaries during his monkhood at Wat Bovonives. This secular school system was expanded by Mongkut's successor, King Chulalongkorn, in the 1890s, when he introduced secular primary education to the whole kingdom.

In fact, the monasteries had not only lacked a general system of education similar to western secular education, but also were reluctant to embrace one when it was offered to them, as would happen in the next few decades. In Lower Burma from 1866 and in Upper Burma from 1896, the colonial authorities made attempts to offer support to modernise the curriculum in the existing monastery schools (Smith 1965: 58). In 1894, the chief commissioner wrote in his report: 'Where *kyaungs* (monastic schools) exist, which are supported by the people, and in which the instruction is efficient, it is not desirable to encourage the opening of lay schools. The efforts of the department should be devoted to improving the indigenous institutions of the district.'[6] However, the monasteries were, as Matthews notes, unprepared 'to come to grips with ideological and intellectual issues associated with modernisation and foreign cultural presence' (Matthews 1999: 29). The monasteries resisted introducing additional subjects, even English and arithmetic (Smith 1965: 60). So the attempts by the British rulers to modernise 20,000 monastery schools failed.[7]

In Thailand, too, there was similar resistance to the introduction of western secular subjects. King Chulalongkorn (Rāma V) had to treat the introduction of primary education in the 1880s extremely carefully because most schools were situated in monasteries and the monks could object to the teaching of what they considered to be secular subjects. Even some of the most progressive monasteries were not always ready to embrace western secular education. For instance, Rāma V attempted to make Wat Bovonives the centre of 'relevant education in an age of progressive education' (*Prawat* 1983: 73)[8] not only 'for the whole kingdom of Siam' but also 'for other countries'.[9] The king's vision of 'progressive education' was planned and implemented by his brother Prince-Patriarch Vajirayan, who combined the study of Buddhism and the secular subjects newly introduced from the west. The Prince-Patriarch was educated in the palace secular school and later also at Wat Makutkasat, where he studied for a Pali degree. However, although under him Wat Bovonives became a teachers' training college for some time, it did not become the desired centre of learning that promoted secular knowledge guided by Buddhist philosophy for the masses. The Prince-Patriarch was the only monk there who had sufficient secular knowledge of his time and understood the needs of the kingdom. The others at Wat Bovonives and its branch monasteries were initially even reluctant to support the modernisation of the Pali curriculum introduced by the Prince-Patriarch, let alone the introduction of secular subjects. Therefore the Prince-Patriarch's initiatives, such as the teachers' training school and the Thai school at Wat Bovonives, soon came to an end.[10]

Here, there was also a radical change for the monasteries in what were considered to be secular subjects. Secular education was earlier taken by the monks to mean sciences, which were not directly relevant or even considered by some to be inimical to achieving enlightenment. These subjects ranged from astrology, medicine, healing and carpentry, the skill of the blacksmith and goldsmith, and martial arts. However, by the second half of the nineteenth century (after the lower part of Burma had been annexed into British India), secular education in Burma and Thailand came to mean the type of education which would secure those who had studied a job, a position in society, and in general the type of education to make one a good bureaucrat. In brief, people wanted a secular education system like that of the west.

When the government had taken over the educational responsibility from the *sangha* in the 1890s, this development, at least in theory, relieved the *sangha* of the need to provide education for lay society; the *sangha* could now fully dedicate themselves to studying the teaching of the Buddha. However, in practice, the government could not alone provide education to people from all parts of the country. Even as late as the 1970s in both Burma and Thailand the government's education programmes still failed to offer equal opportunity in education to the people, particularly those in rural areas, where the majority lived. For many people, education within their reach existed only in their village monasteries or in a town nearby. Indeed, recognising its inability to extend universal education to all parts of the country, the government, from the very beginning, requested the monasteries to adopt a secular curriculum to help implement a universal education policy. In Burma, the request was made by both the British colonial authorities, who ruled the country until 1948, and the government of independent Burma. However, in Burma that request was accepted by fewer than 20 per cent of the 20,000 monastic schools.[11] The reason why the majority of monastic schools refused the request was because the conservative members of the order, who had occupied important administrative positions, were against two particular developments: the monasteries teaching secular subjects; and the prospect of lay teachers teaching student monks. Indeed, in 1891 the *saṅgharāja*, or the head of the Burmese *sangha*, issued a 'circular' warning the monasteries of the pain of excommunication if any of them defied his order.[12]

Even after the rejection by the monasteries the colonial rulers continued with their attempts at persuasion. In 1939, the *Pathamapyan* Review Committee appointed by the governor, consisting of influential monks such as *sayadaws* from the Pakhokku Pali University and the deputy head of the *Shwegyin-nikāya*, the Abhayārama *Sayadaw* of Mandalay, suggested that novices should be taught arithmetic before they studied the *Tipiṭaka* (Janakābhivaṃsa 1997b: 377). This suggestion was supposed to set a precedent for certain further secular subjects in the near future. Many prominent *sayadaws* were in favour of the proposal. Unfortunately, when World War II intervened, the whole process had to be abandoned.

Soon after independence in 1948, Prime Minister U Nu (1948–1958, 1960–1962) gave some grants to monasteries to encourage them to open primary schools, which came to be known as *ba. ka* in brief or monastery schools. U Nu intended to open up to five thousand of such schools.[13] Some of the monasteries that did open primary schools were later upgraded to secondary level. These schools accepted both boys and girls. Almost all the teachers were monks. Even some teaching monasteries in big cities, especially those in deprived parts of town, were requested to open primary schools. However, the success was very minimal.

The military government that toppled U Nu in March 1962 suspended this programme about two years after it came to power. Although no official reasons were given, it was at the time believed that General Ne Win, the coup leader, wanted to get rid of as many of his predecessor's programmes as possible. Critics pointed out that Ne Win also abolished, almost at the same time, the Pali University system and the Sasana University, both of which were the brainchildren of U Nu. But the current military government, which came to power in 1988, has overturned Ne Win's ruling and asked the *sangha* to open monastery schools for lay students. So far, only a handful of individual monasteries, not the *sangha* as an institution, have responded to the request. Phaungdaw-Oo monastery high school in Mandalay is one of a few such examples.

In Thailand, too, in 1898 when the introduction of primary education to the provinces was made, King Chulalongkorn made sure that the *sangha* was involved from the outset. Prince-Patriarch Vajirayan, then the deputy leader of the *Dhammayuttika-nikāya*, and twelve other learned monks were entrusted with the task of organising the 'religion and education of the Buddhist population' and made the Mahamakut Sangha College the headquarters of national education in Thailand. Almost all schools were situated in the monasteries and monks were the teachers. However, despite the fact that they had successfully carried out the introduction of the primary education programme, Prince-Patriarch Vajirayan and the other monks soon withdrew themselves from involvement in the educational affairs of the nation. However, just as in Burma, even half a century after the introduction of primary education and after the kingdom had embraced constitutional monarchy, the Thai government continued to attempt to enlist the help of the *sangha* in providing general education to the people by setting up, in 1940, special schools, *rong rien wisaman*, in some monasteries.[14]

The special schools (*rong rien wisaman*) to educate monks in secular subjects were in addition to the existing traditional monastic courses, *Parian* and *Nak Tham*. Their aim was to provide education for the monks that was 'relevant to the modern age'. The ecclesiastical cabinet, created by the government through the amended Sangha Act of 1940, was the official organ through which these schools were set up. The introduction of special schools was popular with young monks. However, when the 1940 Sangha Act was replaced in 1961 and the *sangha* cabinet no longer existed, the ecclesiastical hierarchy, the *Mahathera Samakhom*, moved to abolish those special schools for monks.[15]

However, some young monks and novices took their own initiative by attending classes at evening schools run by the Department of Adult Education. They studied a secular curriculum in the same classes as lay students, including girls. The number of these monks is not known because the Department of Religious Affairs did not participate in the programme, and at the Department of Adult Education they were simply registered as students, not monks. The decision of the young monks to find every possible way to educate themselves shocked the senior monks, starting with the Council of Elders. Furthermore, for the monks who had taken a vow of celibacy to study in the same classroom as 'villagers (*chao barn*)', including girls, was considered socially unacceptable.

As a result, on 7 May 1963, the chairman of the *Parian* Examinations Board, Somdej Buddhaghosacārya (Pheun Cutindharo), set up a committee to reform the curriculum to accord with the vision of the state. The reform resulted in 1967 in a new form of curriculum that combined secular subjects with those existing subjects in the traditional monastic curriculum. The system started functioning in 1970 and has since become popular at the expense of the traditional *Parian Tham* and *Nak Tham* examinations. Secular subjects are emphasised because the government is concerned that when monks leave the order, which many do in Thailand, they will not be equipped with 'necessary knowledge to become valuable human resources to lay society'.[16] In fact, the aim of the study was no longer to understand the words of the Buddha and to end suffering alone, but to help develop the nation and society.

However, in Thailand, despite the introduction of some form of general education at the primary and secondary levels at the government's encouragement, conservative members of the *sangha* continued to resist the change and thus prompted a debate with those who wished to modernise monastic curricula. This resistance arose partly because the combined religious-secular curriculum now demanded was more complicated and largely unprecedented in the history of monastic education. The education programmes of the government had raised not only the standard of general education but also public expectation as to what a curriculum should consist of. This was totally different from the kind of general education the monasteries had provided up to a century or so earlier. After all, the primary education being thrust upon the *sangha* at this time was based on the model of western education, in which the *sangha* had no expertise.

Meanwhile, people, particularly in rural areas where the majority live,[17] continue to send their children, mostly boys, to the monastery for education. Indeed, recognising its inability to extend universal education to all parts of the country, the government, from the very beginning, requested the monasteries to include some western secular subjects in their curricula to help implement the government's education policy. However, for the last century the *sangha* has not shown a keen interest in helping the government. In my opinion, this is because the *sangha* has not resolved within its ranks the problem related the objective of monastic education.

The debate between the conservatives and the reformists

As to the lack of consensus among monastic scholars on the definition of the objectives of monastic education, the argument has centred on idealism versus pragmatism. The conservatives hold idealism while the reformists pragmatism. For the former the ideal life of a *bhikkhu* was to study and practise the *Dhamma* and *Vinaya*, 'teaching and discipline', aimed only at liberating himself from suffering. Part of this ideal was for a *bhikkhu*, when he could, to impart his knowledge of the *Dhamma* and *Vinaya* to newcomers into the order to ensure the continuation of the *sāsana*. However, on a practical level, the life of a *bhikkhu* was interwoven with those around him. Those who join the order may not all have had liberation from suffering as their immediate aspiration. If the number of such worldly aspiring *bhikkhus* increased, it could cause an institutional problem which would reflect the reality of the society in which the ideal *bhikkhu* lives.

The main reason for resistance offered by the conservative members of the *sangha* was, however, that the study of the secular subjects which the governments wished to prescribe for monastery schools was not appropriate for monks, and could even be considered as 'animal science', (*tiracchānavijjā*/). The rejection by the leading monks of those secular subjects, particularly English and mathematics, appears to have been made on a doctrinal basis. The Pali canon discusses some subjects (*vijjā*) or talk (*kathā*), for instance, of 'rajahs, robbers, great ministers; . . of armies, panic and battle; . . of food and drink and clothes, beds, flowers, garlands and perfumes; . . of relatives, vehicles, villages, suburbs, towns and districts; . . of women and champions; of streets and gossip at the well; . . of ghost stories, desultory and fabulous talk about (the origin of) land and sea; . . of being and not-being' as one not being 'the rudiments of the holy life. . [they do] not conduce to *nibbāna*'.[18] Some of the modern science subjects may be included in these 'animal sciences'. However, the main objection by the monks seems to have been the study of the English language (Sīlānanda 1982: 51),[19] although arithmetic has always been mentioned together with it in the debate. Not only are these two subjects not included in the 'animal science' but they had also been taught in Buddhist monasteries in Southeast Asia for centuries. And, before the British colonisation of the whole of Burma in 1885, a debate of such a kind on the study of languages, European or Indian, was unknown in either country. As such, it is doubtful if the debate over 'animal science' was ever conducted in the light of the canonical scriptures.

In Burma, it could be argued that the *sangha*'s designation of some subjects, particularly English and mathematics, as 'animal science' stemmed from the British presence in Burma. In the periods leading up to the British occupation, the *sangha* moved in a strongly nationalist direction. The Burmese monastic order came to regard the native kings as the protectors of the faith and the British as its destroyers.[20] As occupiers, the British adopted a policy of so-called neutrality towards religion (Smith 1965: 38–9, 45), refusing at the outset the traditional protection afforded by a Buddhist ruler (Bischoff 1997: 58), and ended all support for the order. (They had done the same in Ceylon (Malalgoda 1997: 183–4)). Under the British, the judicial power of the *thathanabaing*, the head of the Burmese order, was taken away (Hall 1981: 773). This was, indeed, a fundamental change for the order, and came as a blow to its influence over society, especially in education. The lack of material and moral support from the state caused the monastic educational institutions to decline, and Mandalay saw a considerable number of teacher-monks leaving the capital for other places within a few years of its fall.[21]

On the issue of designating arithmetic as an 'animal science', Janakābhivaṃsa reasoned that one could not study *Saṅkhyāvāra*, the 'chapter on numbers' in the *Paṭṭhāna*, without some mathematical skill. The *Vuttodaya*, a part of the *pathamagyi* syllabus, also requires a good knowledge of arithmetic, and the ancient *vinayadhara sayadaws*, 'experts on the *Vinaya*' themselves, he pointed out, taught arithmetic.[22] However, none of the *sayadaws* at that time suggested the incorporation of English in the *pathamapyan* syllabuses; and, this was understandable, given the strong sentiment of nationalism among the people and the *sangha* in opposition to the British.

In Thailand there was the same debate on this issue, although the country was never colonised by any European power. We do not know how it all began; but we learn that two of the most important figures in the history of Thai *sangha* education in the early twentieth century, Somdej Khemacari of Wat Mahadhatu (*Mahā-nikāya*) and Somdej Nyanavaro of Wat Thep (*Dhammayuttika-nikāya*), did not allow their students to study English on the grounds that it was 'animal science'; ironically, both were pupils of the English-speaking Prince-Patriarch Vajirayan.[23]

When the British left Burma in January 1948, the anti-colonial feeling that had clouded the debate started to subside. As it also became clear that there was no doctrinal conflict in studying English and mathematics, so the conservatives started to offer different reasons. This was that after they had studied English and mathematics, educated young monks changed their minds and left the monkhood, and this brought a great loss to the *sāsana*. This reasoning caused tremendous anxiety among lay supporters, who feared that young monks were now likely to be attracted by the good prospects for employment in the lay life.[24] In the early 1930s, Ashin Thittila (Seṭṭhila), the translator of the Book of Analysis (*Dhammasaṅgaṇī*),[25] was asked by his benefactor in Mandalay never to come to his house for alms again because he had heard that Ashin Thittila was studying English. For a monk to study English was seen as corrupt and having an ignoble aim. This perception was directed even to a dedicated monk, like Ashin Thittila, with two degrees, the *Pathamakyaw*[26] and the *Sakyasīha dhammācariya*, and already a lecturer at the famous *Phayagyi* teaching monastery at that time.

But there were also some leading *sayadaws* with a more pragmatic attitude, who tried to put the issue in perspective to allay the fears of the *sangha* and the people. One such *sayadaw* was Janakābhivaṃsa. Due to the lack of written records by others on the debate, we shall be referring to much of his work here. In one of his famous works aimed at educating lay people, *Bhathatwe*, 'The Essence of the Religion', Janakābhivaṃsa blamed 'the lack of a good foundation in monastic discipline', not the study of English, as a factor contributing to the abandonment of the monkhood: if a monk had been well trained in the *Vinaya* and lived under his teacher, he would not leave the monkhood. He argued that the first six generations of leading *sayadaws* from the Shwegyin-nikāya, including its founder Jāgara and his successor, Visuddhayon Sayadaw, had studied English. Many of them were also well versed in Sanskrit and Hindi, and with the knowledge gained from these studies they had written books on Pali grammar useful to understanding the

Tipiṭaka.[27] If these secular subjects were not taught, people would not bring their children to the monasteries any more but take them to the Christian convents where they could study more widely. If those educated at convent schools became leaders of the country, they would have little contact with or respect for the *sangha* (*ibid.*: 123, 137–8). He held responsible 'for a drop in the number of students in monastery schools the attitude of some *sayas* (*sayadaws*) that arithmetic and English are not appropriate (for a monk) to learn'.[28] He said that 'arts and science subjects that are not prohibited by the *Vinaya* should be taught (to lay people) by monks free of charge. So the monks should make efforts (to study) so that they could teach.'[29]

In Thailand some forty years later a similar argument was made by Prayud Payutto, considered as one of the leading scholar-monks in the twentieth century. In his lecture at the Mahachulalongkorn Sangha University in 1984, he said that the *sangha* had a responsibility towards individual students and the state. Individual students wished to be educated and had turned to the order for help. The quest for good education through the order by certain sections of society was a good opportunity for the order to instil Buddhist values in those students and to propagate the *dhamma*. The *sangha* also had a responsibility to assist the state in producing good citizens, because the *sangha* as an institution could not exist by itself without the support of the state. Eminent educationists such as Prince-Patriarch Vajirayan, Payutto and Janakābhivaṃsa have all believed that the *sangha*'s education should be for the *sāsana*, society and state.

Against the point that educated monks left the order once they had received a good secular education, Payutto argues that taking away an opportunity for monks to study secular subjects is not a guarantee of their not leaving the order. On the contrary, among the educated monks who had left the order, the overwhelming majority were trained in a purely religious curriculum and had no knowledge of secular subjects. That could be disadvantageous to a monk who left the order highly educated in religious scriptures and yet totally ignorant of any secular subject. He would be lost, unable to integrate into secular life. This would degrade monastic education, and thus the order, in the eyes of society.

However, there was no way that the order could prevent its members from leaving if individual members chose to do so. The *sangha* is an organisation of volunteers, which upholds the freedom of individuals to join or to leave. Instead of wasting effort in trying to prevent the unpreventable, the order, Payutto says, should concentrate on ways to provide education that would benefit both those who decide to stay in the order and those who wish to leave. If the order could help move its former members up the social ladder, not only would that help individual members, it would also bring esteem to monastic education from those who were in contact with those individuals. Not only would these individuals become better citizens, but the Order could also count on them to spread throughout society the knowledge of the *Dhamma* and *Vinaya* they had acquired as monks.

A mission or a pretext?

Meanwhile, a debate to win the hearts and minds of the people was also going on. The modernisers sought to address the lay devotees in order to allay their concerns that if they studied secular subjects more monks might be tempted to leave the order. Providing monks with both secular and religious knowledge, the reform-minded monks claimed, was essential for the promotion of Buddhism in the modern age, especially in the western world. The reformers in Burma found a sympathetic audience in the government and educated Buddhists, who considered the notion of sending Buddhist missionaries abroad, particularly to western nations who had once ruled the whole world, as a matter of national pride. In Burma, the result was the setting up of a Sangha University, officially called the World Buddhist University at the Kabha-Aye, Rangoon, where the Sixth Buddhist Council was held between 1954 and 1956. Indeed, the founding of the university was one of the many objectives of that Council.

Mendelson, who visited the new Sangha University to hear formal speeches, 'was struck by the emphasis upon missionary efforts in the English-speaking world' (Mendelson 1975: 304). 'The burden of virtually all the speeches was the need for learning English as a universal language and as the key to understanding the people missionaries would work among.' Even Janakābhivaṃsa in his argument for setting up two modern universities for the *sangha*, one in Mandalay and the other in Rangoon, saw their main purpose as producing missionary monks.[30] Any purpose other than producing missionaries would not have won from the outset the support of the people, or even the modernisers, such as Janakābhivaṃsa.

The founding of the university was not in the end successful, not necessarily because General Ne Win was determined to abolish it but rather because the *sangha* was not ready for education that combined both western and Burmese traditions. There were only eleven students from Burma, and the *sangha* was not able to participate in building up this new university or in running the administrative and academic support services. However, the university was able to inspire some of its students, small though it may sound as a consolation, to seek further education, to redress the shortcomings of their own monastic education system. But only one batch of students graduated from this university before it was closed by Ne Win.

In Thailand, the *sangha* universities, Mahachulalongkorn and Mahamakut, also initially focused only on producing missionary monks rather than enhancing academic disciplines for their own sake. This was essential to win over the hearts and minds of the prospective benefactors, and ultimately the powerful conservative members of the Council of Elders. Founded under

King Chulalongkorn in the 1890s, these two universities continued for half a century as no more than big teaching monasteries with the traditional curriculum of the *Parian*. In 1947, however, they decided to modernise their curricula in line with those of western universities. This meant that not only the format but also the subjects were to be adapted to the practice in the state universities.

However, this move to bring in secular subjects and new administrative machinery, unlike in Burma, had no backing from the government or from the highest ecclesiastical administrative body, the Council of Elders. It was rather the two biggest monasteries, Wat Mahathat and Wat Bovonives, with a traditionally close relationship with the monarchy, that took the initiative to modernise. Ironically, the abbots of the two monasteries were also members of the Council of Elders.

These two monastic universities have produced many graduates over the years without the recognition of the secular and ecclesiastical authorities. When the now most famous alumnus, Payutto, graduated in 1956, his degree was recognised neither by any of the state universities nor by the Council of Elders. Only in 1969 did the Council of Elders recognise the two universities. But the government, for its part, took no measure to support this ecclesiastical decision. So in 1973 the Council of Elders passed a motion saying that if the government were to recognise the two *sangha* universities, that would indeed be an appropriate action. However, it was not until more than a decade later, in 1984, that the government officially recognised the two universities; and the 1984 Education Act recognised only first degrees and not the two universities as institutions. (The government has since recognised master degree programmes, and recently doctoral programmes.) Here we can see that the government itself sent out contradictory messages. Although it wanted the *sangha* to help shoulder the responsibility of educating the underprivileged, it failed to give adequate support to the members of the *sangha* willing to do so.[31]

In Thailand, Payutto has summarised this problem facing the education of the *sangha*. He argued that if the government and the leaders of the *sangha* failed to give appropriate support, the *sangha* would not be able to lead the people in instilling Buddhist values into the nation. He cited examples of how the *sangha* could not teach Buddhism and Pali at state universities because their qualifications were not recognised, and argued that the higher institutions of the *sangha* themselves faced many obstacles in producing qualified teachers. He pointed out how universities in non-Buddhist countries have produced competent Buddhist scholars and how Buddhist countries themselves could not do the same. This comparison came after Payutto visited in the late 1970s some top American universities, such as Harvard and Princeton, where there has been a long tradition of Buddhist studies.[32]

In Burma, where the debate between monastic scholars on the definition of education was quiet for almost two decades, there was a sudden movement in 1980 towards providing the *sangha* with secular education through an 'up-to-date method of study'. There were two political reasons for this move. The first was the retirement of General Ne Win, who had been in power since 1962, from the post of President, although he retained the post of Chairman in the only party, the Burma Programme Socialist Party (BPSP). This meant he would no longer run the country on a day-to-day basis. The other was the government's drive to win over the *sangha* to support the controversial 'purification programme', (*thathana thant shinn yay*), of the monastic order launched in December 1979.

Seizing the moment, Ashin Vicittasārābhivaṃsa, the first monk to have been successful in the *Tipiṭakadhara* examinations, who had worked closely with former Prime Minister U Nu, took the initiative to set up two *sangha* universities. The government represented his effort as part of their 'purification programmes'. However, the government did not directly finance the project, but left that burden to the voluntary donations of the followers of Ashin Vicittasārābhivaṃsa. The two universities, one in Rangoon and the other in Mandalay, focused on the same theme: to send missionary monks abroad. The courses would be available in five major languages: English, French, German, Japanese and Chinese. In reality, however, there has been only one medium available, Burmese; and elementary English is taught in the first few years for only three hours per week by a visiting lecturer.

The setting up of the universities was very popular with the public, not only because it recaptured the spirit of the newly liberated Burma, that is to send Buddhist missionaries to the English-speaking world, but because of the calibre of the leading monk, Ashin Vicittasārābhivaṃsa, who had come first in all the then newly introduced examinations boards such as the *Sakyasīha* and the *Tipiṭakadhara*. Since then, two more *sangha* universities have been established, one by a graduate from the now defunct World Buddhist University, Ashin Ñāṇissara. He led the foundation of a *sangha* university at Sagaing in Upper Burma. For this project, he receives solid moral support from the leading *sayadaws* of the *Shwegyin-nikāya*, to which he belongs, and generous financial support from wealthy donors, who are attracted to his status as the best preacher in the country. Sayadaw Ashin Ñāṇissara continues to build on the earlier appeal of producing missionaries to go abroad. The name selected for this new *sangha* university, Sitagū International Buddhist Academy, reflects the view of the lay benefactors and the conservative members of the *sangha* as to why a *bhikkhu* may legitimately learn English and other secular subjects. Sitagū is also named after some major social welfare projects Ashin Ñāṇissara has led over the years, for instance a water scheme for all monasteries and nunneries in Sagaing; an eye hospital, the best in the country, for the *sangha* and the people; and a rice project for the monks and nuns of Mandalay, Sagaing and Mingun Hills.

The other *sangha* university, Theravada International Missionary University, was founded by the present government with the aim of sending Theravada missionaries abroad. Its name shows why the government thinks that the monks should study English. Indeed, the very reason the government set up this Buddhist institution in December 1999 was because the existing *sangha* universities lacked the capacity to teach in the English medium and the intention was to address that shortcoming. Although the government claims to have made this university a modern higher institution of study for the *sangha*, with the medium of instruction in English, there has been a shortage of English-speaking academic staff. This is not surprising, given the fact that the lecturer-monks have received their principal training in the *Pathamapyan* and *Dhammācariya* systems, which provide no teaching of English or any other European or Asian languages.

Conclusion

The debate is far from over in both Burma and Thailand. While both the idealists and the pragmatists agree that the principal aim of the monastic education systems should be to train monks in the *Dhamma* and *Vinaya*, the two sides cannot agree whether or not steps should be taken to help fulfil some of the educational needs of society by bringing in some secular subjects in monastic schools.

Today, in Burma, the curriculum in the various monastic examinations focuses exclusively and from the very beginning on the study of Pali and the *Tipiṭaka*. No English, mathematics, geography, history or social studies are offered because they are considered secular subjects.[33] As a result, even educated monks find it difficult to relate the *Dhamma* to lay people's lives.

In Thailand, too, the main curricula, such as the *Nak Tham* and the *Parian*, have remained exclusively religious. Although since 1970 there has been a new curriculum, called *Sai Saman Suksa*, with a combined religious-secular content, it seems that it has been forced on the leadership and has not been a well-thought-through policy. This curriculum has both religious and secular subjects, but too many subjects at each level means student monks do not have sufficient time to learn either Pali and Buddhism or secular subjects properly. In addition, this religious-secular curriculum has been designed neither to replace nor to complement the traditional religious systems, such as the *Nak Tham* and the Pali *Parian* curriculum. Indeed, its separate existence from these two highly regarded religious curricula suggests that the conservatives and the reformists have yet to work their differences out in defining the objective of monastic education.

Notes

1 Ministry of Religious Affairs (1981) *Naing gan daw thangha mahanayaka aphwe pariyatti simankein* [The State Sangha Mahānāyaka Committee's Pariyatti Education Scheme], Third Draft. Rangoon: Ministry of Religious Affairs: 7. All translations are mine unless otherwise indicated.

2 Phra Thepwithi (Prayud Payutto) (1988) *Thit thang karn suksa khong khana song* (Directions of the Education of the *sangha*), Bangkok: Mahachulalongkorn University Press: 9.

3 In Burma, the founder of one of the leading teaching monasteries, Ashin Janakābhivaṃsa (1890–1977) said in 1971: 'Nowadays monks and novices do not benefit spiritually from their study as much as they used to [because] the entire monastic scholarship is fixated only on formal examinations. The student's exclusive focus on the syllabuses of formal examinations takes place not only at the beginning of their monastic study, but also from halfway until the end of it.' Ashin Janakābhivaṃsa (1994) *Nan net khin ovada mya* (Records of Morning Speeches, delivered in 1971), *Dhamma byuha sarsaung*, 23–24.

4 Department of Religious Affairs (1983) *Prawat Karn Suksa Khong Khana Song Thai* (History of the Education of the Thai *sangha*), Bangkok: Ministry of Education: 16; Phra Thepwethi (Prayud Payutto) (1986) Phra phutthasasana gup karnsuksa nai adid (Buddhism and Education in the Past), Bangkok: Mahachulalongkorn University Press: 117; (1961) *Prawat Krasong Suksathikarn* (History of Ministry of Education, 1891–1961), Bangkok: Khrusapha Press: 1–2; *Thammata se zaung dwe* (A Collection of Ten Texts), Mandalay: Thammata Press, (undated): 267.

5 Gaing Tha, Shwe (1959) *Mandalay hnit taya pyi* (The Centenary of Mandalay), Mandalay: Gyi Pwa Yay Press: 216

6 *Report on Public Instruction in Burma*, 1893–94: 9–10, cited in Smith 1965: 60.

7 *Report on the National Education in Buddhist Monasteries Inquiry Committee, 1948*, cited in Mendelson 1975: 259.

8 Mahamakut University (1983) *Prawat Mahakakut ratchawithayalai nai phra boromarachupatham* (History of Royal Mahamakut University), Bangkok: Mahamakut University: 73.

9 Department of Religious Affairs (1983) *Prawat Karn Suksa Khong Khana Song Thai* (History of the Education of the Thai Sangha), Bangkok: Ministry of Education: 103.

10 (1961) *Prawat Krasong Suksathikarn* (History of Ministry of Education, 1891–1961), Bangkok: Khrusapha Press: 217, 335; Mahamakut University (1983) *Prawat Mahakakut ratchawithayalai nai phra boromarachupatham* (History of Royal Mahamakut University), Bangkok: Mahamakut University: 157.

11 *Report on Public Instruction in Burma*, 1893–94: 9–10.

12 *Report on Public Instruction in Burma*, 1891–92, Resolution: 9–10.

13 Ministry of Welfare (1958) *Phongyi kyaung pyinnya thinkyaryay mawgun* (Records of Monastic Education), Rangoon: Ministry of Welfare: 28–29.

14 Department of Religious Affairs (1983) *Prawat Karn Suksa Khong Khana Song Thai* (History of the Education of the Thai *sangha*), Bangkok: Ministry of Education: 142.

15 *Ibid*: 143.

16 *Ibid*: 142.

17 Tambiah 1976: 270–273 mentions that 85.37 per cent of 35,550,105 total population of Thailand in 1970 live in rural areas. The northeastern region where the availability of secular education is behind the other regions is described by Tambiah as 'the powerhouse of the country's sangha'.

18 F. L. Woodward (trs.) *The Book of the Kindred Sayings*, Part V: 355–356; *S* v 419–420. See also D i. 9; Vin i. 73.
19 Ashin Janakābhivaṃsa, (1979) *Pātimok bhāthāṭīkā* (Commentary on the Pātimokkha), Amarapura: Mahagandhayon Press 439.
20 The destruction, soon after the occupation of Mandalay, of the royal monastery Atumashi Kyaung Taw, where the British army was stationed, was often cited as an obvious example. Lord Dufferin, the British governor of India, in his meeting with the *sayadaws* in Mandalay in 1886 denied that the British had the intention to destroy the *sāsana*, as was rumoured among the people. The denial was among the six points he made during the meeting designed to reassure the order. See, Gaing Tha 1959: 279–280.
21 Sāsanābhivaṃsa (1998) *The Centenary of the Pariyatti Sāsanahita Association of Mandalay*, Mandalay: Pariyattisasanahita Athin: 14.
22 Janakābhivaṃsa, *op cit:* 439; Janakābhivaṃsa (1995), *Anagat thathana yay* (The Future of the *Sāsana*), Rangoon: Department of Religious Affairs, Ministry of Religious Affairs (Reprint): 371; Janakābhivaṃsa (1999) *Bhatha-thwe* (The Essence of the Religion), Amarapura: New Burma Offset Pitaka Press (Reprint): 82–88.
23 Sivarak (1976) *Sarm Somdejs* (Three Somdejs), Bangkok: Khrusapha: 3.
24 Janakābhivaṃsa (1999): 139–40; Janakābhivaṃsa (1997) *Tatbhava thanthaya* (One Life in *Saṃsāra*), Amarapura: Mahagandhayon Press, 3rd reprint: 256.
25 Published by the Pali Text Society in 1969 and reprinted in 1988.
26 *Pathamakyaw* was considered a degree at that time because the government board of examination for the *Dhammācariya* had not been set up.
27 Janakābhivaṃsa 1999: 85–88.
28 Janakābhivaṃsa 1979: 439.
29 Janakābhivaṃsa (1975) *Yup pon shin kyint wut* (Illustrated Training for the *Sāmaṇera*), Rangoon: Department of Religious Affairs: 195.
30 Janakābhivaṃsa 1995: 373–374.
31 Thepwethi 1988: 16–17, 21–24.
32 *Ibid*: 23.
33 Nor are student monks admitted to government schools to study those subjects because culturally it is not sensible for the novices and monks to sit in the same classroom with lay students. In brief, the *sangha* does not participate in the nation's education. The monks do not even teach Buddhism at government schools.

3

RAJADHAMMA CONFRONTS LEVIATHAN

Burmese political theory in the 1870s[1]

Andrew Huxley

In 1885 Upper Burma was invaded and its political and legal institutions destroyed. What possibilities thereby became lost to the world? The Indian civil servant who had lobbied most intensely for the invasion of Mandalay came to regret what he had done: 'It was a pity – they would have learnt in time.'[2] If Burma had avoided being annexed to British India, what might it have become? Thailand's recent history offers some kind of clue. The constitutional monarch of Thailand has made himself astonishingly popular over the last sixty years. If Britain had chosen to rule Burma through a client king, then a newly independent Burma in 1948 would have inherited at least one of its traditional political institutions. In this alternative universe, might Burma's political and legal institutions of the 1870s have embraced democratic and rule-of-law virtues by the 1970s? What might Burmese modernism have looked like, under a less destructive form of British imperialism? Although such hypothetical questions don't lead to any determinate answer, we can only evaluate Burmese legal and political theory by imagining an answer.

Few would dispute the centrality of law to Burmese culture. This is evidenced by Burma's having: (1) a voluminous legal literature, the three best-known genres of which were *dhammathat, rajathat* and *pyatton*; (2) a homegrown legal profession (the *shene*); and (3) a home-grown legal history (the *dhammathat* book-lists). Burma's political theory is less visible. Sometimes it is found in the *dhammathats*, mixed with rules on divorce and agricultural credit. Sometimes a whole text is devoted to it. One such political genre is the Royal Order, wherein the king can give his own account of how politics works. Others are the *myittasa* and *rajovada* genres, in which monks and ex-monks expound *dhamma* to the king. It was in the 1870s that Burmese thinkers first broke out of these genres.

My chapter focuses on the first Burmese account of politics to appear in print, and on the first to be written as the policy statement of a *coup d'état*. Hence the reference in my title to the 1870s. *Leviathan* is the epithet J. S. Furnivall gave to the Anglo-Burmese colonial state (Furnivall 1939). *Rajadhamma* denotes that part of the Pali Buddhist tradition dealing with the ethics and practice of kingship. *Dhamma* covers a spectrum of meanings from 'law' to 'necessary conditions' to 'things as they should be', but *raja* can only mean one thing. For the rest of this chapter I shall translate *rajadhamma* as 'king-law'. In the 1870s, my title suggests, Burmese political theorists had to tweak the tradition of king-law so as to better confront political theory and practice in British Burma.

I look at two Burmese politicians, one in British Burma, faithfully serving Victoria, Empress of India, and one in Mandalay, faithfully serving King Mindon of Mandalay (1853–78). U Kyaw Htun, from Arakan, got his first job with the British a year before the Second Anglo-Burmese War. He joined the British troops on their way to invade Rangoon, and was never to return home. His *Essay on the Sources and Origins of Buddhist Law* won the Judicial Commissioner's Prize in early 1876 and was published in 1877.[3] Its contents include a short analysis of Burmese political theory. U Hpo Hlaing's *Rajadhammasangaha* (written in 1879) is a work of political theory addressed to a monarch on his taking the throne.[4] Its title can be translated as 'Compendium of King-Law'. Kyaw Htun and Hpo Hlaing were political activists as well as political theorists. For the three months that his coup lasted, Hpo Hlaing was the most powerful man in Upper Burma. A few years earlier, Kyaw Htun had very nearly become the most powerful Burmese in Lower Burma, but was suddenly disgraced and sacked. The lives of political theorists illuminate their work. What Cicero did as a member of the triumvirate helps us understand his *De re publica*. That Hobbes tutored the Stuart pretender in France helps us understand his *Leviathan*. Kyaw Htun and Hpo Hlaing led lives as dangerous, and lived in times as interesting, as Cicero and Hobbes. Though my focus is on their work, I shall have to say a good deal about their lives.

King-law, the Pali Buddhist political tradition, was well over two thousand years old by the time Kyaw Htun and Hpo Hlaing wrote about it. I haven't the space to give a comprehensive history of its development,[5] but I need to describe three of the salient characteristics this body of knowledge had acquired in Burma by the 1870s. First, how it distinguished data from theory. Second, how it used lists and combinations of lists to preserve its theory. (We Europeans are so unfamiliar with organising knowledge this way that I must offer a tutorial in listology, illustrated by several examples.) Third, the *who whom?* issues: who taught this discipline to which students under what conditions? What was its seat-in-life, its sociology of knowledge? I deal with these points in the rest of my introduction. I then devote a section each to Kyaw Htun and Hpo Hlaing, before drawing some conclusions.

How does king-law distinguish between data and theory? I had better define my terms. By 'data', I mean the history of everything that has happened in the world. By 'theory', I mean suggestions as to how the data may be shaped and structured, so as to inspire answers to current problems. The canonical data-bank is largely made up of the collection of 547 *Jātaka*, many of which tell stories about kings, queens, ministers, usurpers, and princes. We normally think of the *Jātakas* as narratives, but they are more than that: they are exemplary narratives or, as lawyers put it, precedents. A monk or courtier, let us say, has to advise a king who plans such grandiose acts of merit that the country will be bankrupted. 'Don't be like Vessantara in *Jātaka* No. 547' the king will be told: 'When Vessantara gave more away than his people could stand, they threw him out.' This is no different from how European politicians use history: 'Don't be like Charles I in the 1630s. When Charles I took more tax from his people than they could stand, they threw him out.' The Burmese chronicles draw no line between the kings and queens described in the *Jātaka*, and the kings and queens who actually ruled Burmese cities. They belonged, after all, to one super-dynasty: offspring of Mahāsammata, the original and the exemplary king of this cycle of ages. Mahāsammata's history is told in the *Aggañña sutta* (Sermon on Origins), one of the two great allegories on the rise and fall of the state which are prominent within the king-law data-bank. Theory, the shaping mechanism, consists of the various 'king-law' lists with which this chapter is concerned. Such a list is designed to be memorised verbatim in Pali.[6] Pali grammar and morphology allow complex ideas to be expressed in a couple of words. Here, by way of example, is the *4 solidarities* list as generations of Buddhist students have committed it to memory: *assamedham purisamedham / sammāpāsam vajapeyyam //* We shall see later that a great deal of information is packed within these words.

A political theory that relied on a single king-law list would be like a cookbook that contained only fish recipes: we know we're going to need other cookbooks. The *4 solidarities* solve some political problems, but there are others on the menu. Each list specialises in a different range of problems, and my particular ambition in this chapter is to translate these ranges into the political terminology (*rule of law, bureaucratisation, fiscal accountability*, etc.) that my morning paper uses. Burmese political theorists expressed their individuality in choosing which lists to emphasise, just as these days our political theorists choose which topics they will cover: John Rawls said a lot about how politics should handle risk, but little about subsidiarity.[7] Pope John Paul II said a lot about subsidiarity, but little about risk. Each time a political theorist picks some lists and arranges them into a bouquet, she makes a statement about which problems are most important to her. Before I analyse the statements that Kyaw Htun and Hpo Hlaing made, I must offer a tutorial in the mathematics of the bouquet of lists, or 'list-of-lists', as I shall henceforth call it.

Buddhists combine lists in different ways. In his work on the Abhidhamma, Rupert Gethin (1992) describes matrix-like combinations where a row of 3 combines with a rank of 7 to generate 21 new possibilities. King-law uses a simpler arithmetic. The most common combinatorial device is the list-of-lists, which is based on addition. Imagine I'm a Burmese monk. Tomorrow a 10-year-old boy will join the monastery for the first time, and I have to deliver a sermon at his *shin-pyu* ceremony. To generate my sermon, I shall choose three relevant lists (but ones that have never been put together in this particular way before). As a list-of-lists, my sermon could be presented in this form:

1 12 kinds of children
2 4 noble truths
3 4 offences of defeat
3 lists of 20 items **checksum**

If I ever published my sermon, I could title it the *20 things a novice should be told at their shin-pyu ceremony*, following the useful naming convention of what I call the 'checksum' (the total of items contained in all the lists). Now let's turn to some canonical and post-canonical examples, starting with two that Gethin has discussed. At A.i.295–7 the middle way is defined as:

1 4 applications of mindfulness
2 4 right endeavours
3 4 bases of success
4 5 faculties
5 5 powers
6 7 awakening factors
6 lists of 29 items **checksum**

Checksum 29 has its own set of numerical associations. In the science of lists, these are what give 29 its own personality. There are approximately 29 days in the moon's cycle, so 29 is appropriate for those occasions which stress the calendrical or the lunar. The next personality number, 37, has spatial connotations.[8] To convert the *29 definitions of the middle way* into a checksum of 37, the list-combiners needed to add any list of eight. They chose the *Noble Eightfold Path*. Gethin rates the resulting *37 Elements of Enlightenment* as one of the most important Pali list-of-lists (Gethin 1992: 156). This process need never stop. The *Golden Pali Text* is Burma's earliest Pali document, and the earliest Pali text to have survived from anywhere in the world. It incorporates the *37 Elements of Enlightenment* into '7 lists of 88 items **checksum**'. I'm not sure what personality was attributed to the number 88 by the king and queen who dedicated this offering. It must have meant something, because after it was discovered at the last minute that two items had been omitted from the *14 kinds of knowledge possessed by the Buddha*, the two items were written in abbreviated form on the rim of the silver reliquary. Janice Stargardt comments that 'These defects were made good . . . The ritual completeness of the deposit was thus assured' (Stargardt 1995: 207–8). I'll give a final example from nineteenth-century Siam to show the list-of-lists operating in a king-law context; a work called *24 Forms of Princely Knowledge* (Gray 1886: 40). Its title derived from its checksum:

1 4 crafts
2 5 arts
3 8 merits
4 7 means of action
4 lists of 24 items **checksum**

I shall apply this kind of listological analysis to Kyaw Htun and Hpo Hlaing.

Third, and briefly, I turn to the seat-in-life issues. Who taught king-law to whom in what educational institutions? Occasionally, a *Jātaka* hints at how princes were educated. There is mention of an *atthadhammanusakamacco* (an officer who advises the king on *dhamma* and *artha*) (Gokhale 1966: 18, citing J ii 30). Elsewhere there's a list of five disciplines, which could be the syllabus he taught from: *artha* (knowledge of the conditions and causal relations), *dharma* (norms, standards of behaviour), *matra* (due measure in punishment and taxation), *kala* (knowledge of the daily timetable of a king) and *parisad* (how to treat the various classes of society).[9] As to Burma, here's a description of the syllabus of princely education in the fourteenth century, from a work written in 1780:

> After he had received the lordship of Pyinsei, Mingaung sought an education like that of other princes, in elephant and horse management, in handling a shield, in the use of bows and spears, and some instruction in the chronicles of the country and the customs and precedents in use in it, and their distinctions.
>
> (Bagshawe 1981: 51)

Prince Charles, heir apparent to the Windsor dynasty, received a not dissimilar education. Charles has learned to hunt on horseback. He spent a year at school in the Australian outback at the age of 16, so he can probably manage a kangaroo, if not an elephant. For 'bows and spears', substitute five years in the navy, latterly in command of his own ship. And for the academic stage ('the chronicles of the country and its customs and precedents'), compare Charles's bespoke degree course at Trinity, Cambridge, in British history, constitutional law, archaeology and anthropology. Imagine a Burmese tutor taking a bunch of princes through the *Jātaka* and the king-law lists. Imagine him writing up some of his better lectures for publication. Imagine some of these texts spreading through Burma's manuscript tradition. Such is the seat-in-life of the *rajovada* and *myittasa* genres.

Kyaw Htun of Lower Burma

Kyaw Htun entered the British records on 18 December 1851 (under the name 'Moung Kyaw Doon') when he was appointed a clerk in the Akyab office of Arthur Phayre, the Commissioner of Arakan. I know only two things about his life before 1851: that his parents were 'lineal descendants of the ancient Arakanese Royal Family',[10] and that he acquired perfect copperplate handwriting for both Burmese and English. I infer that he spent some years at an English-run school (perhaps a mission school) in Akyab. I don't know his age, but I'll assume that he was about 17 when he started work for the British commissioner, meaning that he was born around 1834. When the Second Anglo-Burmese War started, the British troop-ships, provisioning in Akyab, were on the lookout for trustworthy interpreters. Phayre recommended Kyaw Htun, who had been in his office a year, to Lt Col. Anstruther:

> I know his family, also that they are respectable. He has learnt English, and I think you will find him useful as a Burmese interpreter. I think Rs. 35 would be a fair amount of wages for him.[11]

He enlisted on 18 December 1852 under General Steele 'as a guide and interpreter to the British forces', and fought at Martaban and Beeling. After the war was won, Kyaw Htun moved back from the army to the Civil Service. He became clerk to J. S. Baird, the Assistant Commissioner of Prome, and spent the next decade at Prome, working his way up from Burmese writer, to assistant clerk, to treasurer, to record keeper. In September 1866, he was promoted to Extra Assistant Commissioner (EAC), 1st class, 1st grade (earning Rs.400 per month) and moved from Prome to Danubyu,[12] the fortified river port upstream from Rangoon. He was to spend the next seven years as EAC of Danubyu. Subject only to sporadic supervision by his British superiors, his word in Danubyu, and for twenty miles up and down the river, was law. The Reverend John Marks[13] records how Kyaw Htun helped out in a crisis. The premises Marks had bought at Henzada for his mission school were flooded overnight by a rise in the river.

> While waiting anxiously, and thinking what we should do, my friend Moung Kyaw Doon, the Extra Assistant Commissioner, came along, and at once solved the problem by putting a very suitable house (his own property) at our disposal, free of rent, for half a year.
>
> (Marks 1917: 114)

In 1871 and 1872, as Kyaw Htun neared the age of 40, his career prospects shone bright. Just before Albert Fytche retired as Chief Commissioner, he had agreed with Colonel Plant to propose promoting Kyaw Htun beyond the glass ceiling to Assistant Commissioner. Had it happened he would have been the first non-European in Burma to reach this level.[14] In 1872, the Chief Commissioner endorsed him to the newly appointed Judicial Commissioner as 'one of the most intelligent native officials in Burma'.[15] When the Viceroy of India came to Rangoon that year, Kyaw Htun was singled out to meet him: the Earl of Mayo awarded him a gold watch and medal. Perhaps it was a bad omen that the Viceroy was assassinated a few days later in the Andaman Islands. Within a year of hitting these peaks, Kyaw Htun's career came abruptly to an end.

The year 1873 proved to be Kyaw Htun's climacteric. He started the year well by publishing *Pakinnaka dipani kyam* ('Explanatory Treatise on Miscellaneous Topics'), a book summarising Burmese culture and history, and contrasting it with British history and institutions (Kyaw Htun 1873). He is the first modern Burmese editor of a printed work. Other Burmese publishers over the previous four years had moved text straight from one manuscript to one book. Kyaw Htun extracted and compiled the various texts he printed 'by myself'.[16] On 19 April 1873, a month before publication, Kyaw Htun received unexpected visitors – Kinwun Mingyi (one of the senior ministers to the Peacock throne) and his entourage on their way back to Mandalay from their embassy to London. Htin Aung summarises Kinwun Mingyi's diary entry:

> At 8pm the steamer stopped at Danubyu to take on firewood. Maung Kyaw Tun, the township officer, was acquainted with Major McMahon, who sent him a letter. At 7 pm he arrived and presented to the Royal secretary a copy of the ms. of a book which was being printed. The book was a comparative study of English and Burmese terms and phrases relating to history, law and taxation. He left the steamer at midnight.
>
> (Htin Aung 1974: 138)

The ambassadors took this copy of *Pakinnaka dipani* back to Mandalay, where Hpo Hlaing would have been able to consult it.[17] The British paid little attention to their protégé's work. The only review of it that I have seen in English came eleven years after publication.[18]

Meanwhile, events in Danubyu were unravelling. Six months after publication, the Judicial Commissioner (Kyaw Htun's ultimate boss) announced:

> The Judicial staff this year lost Moung Kyaw Doon, an intelligent and learned judge, but who unfortunately allowed himself to engage in speculations of trade and to adjudicate upon matters in which it was considered that he had a pecuniary interest.[19]

During the Viceroy's visit the previous year, an anonymous petition had been handed to him alleging dirty deeds in Danubyu. The petition was shunted leisurely down the system, to lodge with Kyaw Htun's immediate superior William DeCourcy Ireland, Deputy Commissioner at Henzada. Ireland spent the next nine months surreptitiously investigating affairs in Danubyu. Ireland accused Kyaw Htun of having become a rich man, worth 2½ lakhs of rupees, by skimming off the profits of Danubyu's fishing and river trade. He alleged specific instances of Kyaw Htun's involvement in robbery, sexual misconduct, and perversion of justice. An investigation by Ireland's superior, who admitted to having 'a high opinion of [Kyaw Htun]'s character',[20] acquitted him of the wilder charges, but found him guilty on count two: 'Trading, and deciding suits brought on these trading transactions in his own court in his own favour.' Kyaw Htun escaped jail by submitting his resignation on 15 November on grounds of ill-health.[21] The archives reveal that Ireland ran a one-man campaign to destroy Kyaw Htun's career, but they do not reveal his motives. Undoubtedly, the disgrace of Kyaw Htun was a significant event in British Burma. It taught Burmese onlookers that the British treated their courtiers just as capriciously as had the Burmese kings. Why endure the uncertainties of working for the British as EAC, when one could earn more money, have more independence, and enjoy higher status as a barrister or doctor?

Strange, then, that so soon after Kyaw Htun's disgrace, his second publication should be funded by the British government. In 1874, the Judicial Commissioner announced a prize of Rs.1,000 for the best essay in English on the sources and history of Buddhist law. In early 1876, he awarded the prize to Kyaw Htun and arranged for its publication as a twenty-page pamphlet in 1877. This is Kyaw Htun's *Essay on the Sources and Origins of Buddhist Law* (hereon his *Prize Essay*). It is a thoughtful summary of Burmese tradition, discussing the different ways in which one might speak of 'the sources' of law. It contains a mixture of lists and stories taken from both the canon and the *dhammathats*. I shall concentrate on what Kyaw Htun tells us in the *Prize Essay* about king-law. He presents a list of king-law lists, with checksum 28:

> The Laws binding on a King or Ruler, numbering twenty-eight in all, are the [*4 solidarities*] (*sangahavatthu*) . . . the [*3 coronations*] (*abhiseka*).
>
> (Kyaw Htun 1877: 3)

Kyaw Htun set these lists within his telling of the Mahāsammata story, making it far more explicitly a social contract than it was in the *Aggañña sutta* (see Huxley 1996: 407; Collins 1996: 42). Kyaw Htun's small print reads: everyone except Mahāsammata must obey the *5 wheel-turning precepts*, while Mahāsammata alone must obey the *28 duties incumbent on the king*. Mention of coronations leads Kyaw Htun to continue the *Aggañña Sutta* story, and by the time he finished it, he had lost his thread. He forgot to give the remaining lists, and left us with a puzzle: How shall we complete the equation 4 + 3 + n + p . . . = 28? I'll propose a solution based on three comparable texts written earlier in the Konbaung dynasty (1752–1885). The first is a lecture by a Regius Professor, addressed to foreign royalty while conducting a diplomatic mission. The lecture was delivered in the fifteenth century, but this account of it was written in 1780. The second is a classical poem written in the 1810s in praise of King Badon (1781–1819). The third is King Bagyidaw's (1819–38) appeal, in a Royal Order of 1824, for supernatural aide to dislodge the British from Rangoon. Let's look at these three from the list-of-lists angle.

In 1780, the year before the coup and counter-coup that put Badon on the throne, Shin Sandalinka wrote his *Maniyadanabon*, his edition of the wise counsels given by the courtier Minyaza to the kings of Ava in the early 1400s. How far this work can be used as a source for fifteenth-century Burma is debatable, but it is certainly a useful source on Konbaung Burma in the eighteenth century. One passage reproduces an address on king-law that Minyaza was invited to give before the King of Monland:

> O King, who are lord of all your people, if you wish to attain great honour and reputation in this present life, and if you hope to become lord of all men in the course of your successive lives in this world, you must act so as to perfect the rule of religion in your knowledge. charity, patience, enthusiasm, piety, kindness and fortitude; also you must act so as fulfil the ten royal duties of almsgiving, piety, liberality, uprightness, gentleness, austerity, self-control, mercy, patience, and consistency; you must also act so as to fulfil the four ways of helping other men, almsgiving, wise conduct, kind words and treating others like oneself. In acting thus you will win much benefit in your present and your future lives.
>
> (Bagshawe 1981: 96)

Schematically, as a list-of-lists, this lecture can be represented as:

1 7 virtues
2 10 king-law virtues
3 4 solidarities
3 lists with 21 items **checksum**

The *Rajadhiraja Vilasini* (Manifestation of the King of Kings) is a panegyric on King Badon written by the 1st Maungdaung *sayadaw* in Pali (with Burmese commentary). The *Uddesa* (*précis*) summarises chapter two, which describes Badon's 'patronage of the world' in terms of king-law lists:

> He took a constant delight in the observance of hereditary precepts, such as [the *4 solidarities*, the *7 ways not to make things worse* and the *10 king-law virtues*] and so forth.
>
> (Maung Tin 1914: 16)

The *Niddesa* (the chapter itself) leaves out the *7 ways not to make things worse*, describing instead the 5 precepts preached by the Wheel-turning Emperor in the *Cakkavattisīhanāda Sutta* (Discourse on the Lion's Roar of the Wheel-turning King). Mixing together the *Uddesa* and *Niddesa* yields the following list-of-lists:

1 4 solidarities
2 10 king-law virtues
3 7 ways not to make things worse
4 5 wheel-turning precepts
4 lists with 26 items **checksum**

My third example comes from Bagyidaw's order in 1824. It was addressed to Burma's protective spirits and asked for their help in kicking the British out of Rangoon. King Bagyidaw deserves this help because:

> Like the forefathers beginning with Mahāsammata . . . the King observes the *4 ways of a leader*, and the *10 rules of a king* so as to ameliorate the lot of the ruled. For the same reason, he had the *muddha abhiseka* coronation just like Ashoka. He made the appropriate offerings to the nats, as directed in the [*7 ways not to make things worse*] rules . . .[22]

Which yields the following list-of-lists:

1 4 solidarities
2 10 king-law virtues
3 3 coronations (implied)
4 7 ways not to make things worse
4 lists with 24 items **checksum**

Let's return to the problem Kyaw Htun has set us. How would he have completed his equation 4 + 3 + n + p . . . = 28? Here's my reconstruction in italics:

1 4 solidarities
2 3 coronations
3 4 roads not to take
4 10 king-law virtues
5 7 ways not to make things worse
5 lists with 28 items **checksum**

All of these lists occur in Richardson's bilingual edition of *Manugye dhammathat*.[23] Kyaw Htun must have regarded his copy of Richardson (with its Burmese text on the left hand of each spread and its English translation on the right) as his Rosetta stone. Writing a twenty-page essay in English is a sharp test of one's language skills, and Kyaw Htun must have been relieved to have Richardson's translations from Burmese into English available. There are, however, many other king-law lists to be found in *Manugye*. I think that Kyaw Htun chose these particular five lists as representative of the Burmese political tradition.

I have offered a reconstruction of Kyaw Htun's list-of-lists based on three Konbaung texts. I shall use other Konbaung texts to explain the current interpretation of each of the lists. I start with Kyaw Htun's account of the *4 solidarities*:

> (1.) *Thatha Maida*, meaning that he should not receive more than a tithe of the produce of the country.
> (2.) *Pooreetha Maida*, by which he binds himself to pay his servants and Army once every six months.
> (3.) *Thamapatha*, by which he is bound to assist his subjects with money, and to receive payment of it three years after, without charging interest.
> (4.) *Wahtsapayah*, or the use of courteous and fitting language; according to the age and position in life of the person addressed.
>
> (Kyaw Htun 1877: 3)

When he wrote this, Kyaw Htun had few predecessors in the Romanisation of Pali. These days (unless we fussed over diacritics), we would transliterate his four terms as *Sassamedha, Purisamedha, Samapasa* and *Vacapeyya*. Kyaw Htun's Burmese text (whatever in the quote above is not in italics) is a close translation from the Commentaries [Mp iv 69; Spk i 144]. This Commentaries passage has been translated and discussed in most of the languages of mainland Southeast Asia. Evidently Southeast Asian Buddhists found it good-to-think. I suspect that this was because the list implies a balance-sheet between ruler and ruled:

sassamedha:	income, expressed as share-of-rice
purisamedha:	outgoings, for the government and army
sammapasa:	outgoings, for farmers and merchants
vacapeyya:	respect, to be shown by the rulers to the ruled

The ruler is entitled to his tax share of the rice crop. The ruled are entitled to a redistribution of all this tax, either as wages or as loans. Everything off-balance-sheet is summed up in the word 'respect'. The ruler should use sweet language, because the ruled would like to retain some, at least, of their dignity. But why the two different categories of outgoings?

Purisamedha is the ruler's wage bill. It is the budget through which he pays his bureaucrats and soldiers. In Burmese terms, these soldiers are *ahmudan* (the higher-status villagers on the irrigation systems nearest the capital city, who were expected to form themselves into army units during the campaigning season, and could muster for self-defence at fairly short notice at other times of year). They are under a separate bureaucracy to the *athi* (the free non-servicemen who lived in villages beyond the nuclear zone, sometimes in villages that lacked an irrigation system). King Badon gives us a glimpse of how the *ahmudan* finances were organised. Soon after his accession, he ordered:

> King Alaung-hpaya, following the [*4 solidarities*], made loans from the Royal Treasury to certain Saw-bwas, Myo-zas, Thagyis, Kalans and to other officials and commoners. Some part of the principal amounts of these loans is still outstanding . . . There are also moneys that remain to be collected, from the time of my brother Sin-gu-min, from various Princes, Ministers and commoners, arising out of criminal suits brought, according to their *kamma*, against various Princes, Ministers and commoners.[24]

When the king advances money to a military commander or local ruler under his *purisamedha* budget, the recipient was under an obligation to account. In other words, he faced criminal charges 'according to his *kamma*' if the money was spent otherwise than as the king intended. The *sammapasa* section of the balance-sheet describes the king as merchant banker, and as bank of agricultural credit. Wet rice cultivation requires money or credit up front. Just to get started each year, you need to invest in compost, seed rice, and a week's hire of labour and heavy equipment. But if your crop failed last year, your credit is no good this year. The 1750s edition of *Manugye dhammathat*, associated with Alaungpaya, founder of the Konbaung dynasty, says that:

> If a person has incurred debts beyond his means of paying, and his family are unable to assist him . . . he shall make a petition to the king, who will say 'On conditions, give him an advance . . . In three years the king may take back the advances. This he may do in accordance with the [*4 solidarities*].[25]

It is in this role as lender of last resort that the Burmese king won the hearts of his *athi* population. But Badon talks as if there were a means test:

> Kings observe the [*4 solidarities*], of which *sammapasa* means that loans are advanced to the poor for three years without taking interest on them. As for loans made by other people, they might take interest on them as it is already a recognised usage.[26]

Which I read as meaning *That's just* poor *people I help, you understand. I can charge normal rates to my middle class subjects.* E Maung argues that language like this is the language of entitlement. The Burmese jurists had moved from 'moral exhortations to legal obligations binding on the ruler' (Maung 1951: 6). The Konbaung dynasty, in E Maung's view, had developed this particular king-law list into constitutional law. His view is plausible: the idea of a balance-sheet between ruler and ruled does suggest an entitlement on each of the parties doing business together. From the balance-sheet it is a short step to thinking that the ruler and the ruled owe correlative rights and duties to each other under a social contract. However, I haven't yet found a Burmese text that stresses correlativity as strongly as did the early modern European theorists.

Kyaw Htun's second list is the *3 coronations*, which he works into his account of Mahāsammata. Once the Great Elect had accepted the invitation to rule over them:

> the people poured on him the three kinds of Beet-theik, *viz*:- (1.) *Yazza Beet-theik* consecrating him King. (2.) *Manda Beet-theik* marrying him to a Queen. (3.) *Thenga Beet-theik*, confirmation or renewal of his engagement to abide by all the laws . . .
>
> (Kyaw Htun 1877: 3)

It is the third item (a Burmanisation of the Pali phrase meaning 'solidarity anointment') that connects the coronation ceremony with constitutional law. Ryuji Okudaira, in his study of the nineteenth-century Burmese sources on coronations, sees the ceremony as something like a referendum: the king asks the people to endorse the fact that he rules according to the ten royal virtues and the four solidarities (Okudaira 1994: 7, 9). Coronation European-style is an on-off validity switch at the start of a monarch's reign. But Burmese kings are encouraged to 'renew their vows' mid-reign, which gives a hitherto bad king the chance to turn over a new leaf. By choosing to undergo the *sangaha abhiseka*, a king could relaunch his career by declaring, in effect, *Now that my throne is secure thanks to my adhammic acts against potential rivals, I choose henceforth to rule according to dhamma.* The form in which he declared this was an oath to the people's representatives to rule according to *dhamma*. As Badon explained, 'Coronation means a promise on the part of the king to rule with benevolence and justice . . . placing a curse on him if he fails to do so.'[27] Mindon underwent such a coronation in 1874, twenty-two years after becoming king.[28]

A king thus constrained by his oath is, in European terminology, a *princeps legibus non solutus* ('Prince not freed from obedience to the laws'). This terminology goes back to Ulpian (the first European lawyer to have clearly distinguished between public and private law) as cited in D.1.3.31.[29] It is one of the oldest themes to survive in contemporary western discourse on politics and public law. It is, to use a single word derived from Ulpian's Latin, the *absolutism* theme.[30] Some European political theorists – Robert Filmer, Joseph de Maistre – explain that absolutism is the most rational political structure we can adopt, given the way the world really is. There were no Filmers or de Maistres in Burma under the first nine Konbaung kings. Until King Mindon (1852–78) no-one argued that kings need the freedom to act adhammically (that is, to transgress or revoke any of the traditional understandings of the king-law lists). In Part two I shall describe how Mindon systematically dismantled the *4 solidarities* section of the Burmese constitutional settlement.

At this point in his exposition, Kyaw Htun gets diverted. In my reconstruction, the next list is the *4 roads not to take* (partiality, hate, illusion and fear). In the canon these are presented as part of the causal chain that leads to suffering [D.iii.182]. It is *Jātaka* No. 22 that firmly links the list with government. The Buddha-to-be, born as the leader of a pack of wild cemetery dogs, and unjustly accused of criminal damage, exhorts a king that partiality, hate, illusion and fear are the four ways to misjudge a case. These *4 roads not to take* itemise aspects of the king's duty, when acting as a judge, to act fairly. In Europe we think of *due process* and *fair procedure* as judicial values. The *4 roads not to take* cover much the same ethical territory.

Next come the *10 king-law virtues* (generosity, morality, liberality, honesty, mildness, religious practice, non-anger, non-violence, patience and non-offensiveness), first mentioned in the canonical *Jātaka* verses [J.iii.274]. This list seems too much concerned with personal morality to be part of political theory as we understand the term. But the Burmese aren't embarrassed to admit ethics into constitutional law. This list reminds us that a Buddhist king is duty-bound to be a good king. How, then, could a tutor to the royal princes bring this list alive? I suspect that it was by linking each of the ten virtues to episodes in the *10 last Jātaka* (No. 538–547 of the Pali recension). The Burmese princes, I surmise, were taught ten different ways to be good, illustrated to them by precedents from the Stories of the Buddha's Former Births. The *10 virtues* allow some rudimentary analysis and comparison of the precedents, along the lines of *In this episode the king displayed great respect for morality, but very little for non-violence*. My aim in this article (to understand Burmese politics in European terms) becomes impossible with the *10 virtues*. I know nothing in the European tradition that specifies the particular virtues that each monarch should display. The 10-year-old princess, later to become Queen Victoria, declared simply and generically: 'I will be good.'[31]

Finally, the *7 ways not to make things worse*,[32] which appears at the beginning of the *Great Discourse of the Final Nirvana* [D.ii.75]. The special 1781 edition of *Manugye*, written in connection with Badon's accession to the throne, translates the Pali into Burmese thus:

> The king should: [1] Hold meetings and consult with his royal counsellors three times a day, [2] Tackle affairs with the application of consistent rules, [3] Only collect taxes and impose punishments which tradition allows, [4] Respect and cherish the elderly, [5] Govern his subjects paternalistically, without oppression, [6] Make the usual offerings to the Nats who watch over the capital city and the rest of the kingdom, (7) Provide for the monastic community.
>
> (Okudaira and Huxley 2001: 252)

The Konbaung authors treated items [1] and [2] as determinative of the list's character. They invoked it in relation to good governance, efficient decision-making and better bureaucracy. In 1786 King Badon proclaimed:

> It is right that the affairs of the Kingdom should not evade the [Law of *not making things worse*] . . . In accordance with the [*7 ways not to make things worse*], which rules the actions of Kings, and in accordance with ancient custom, those Ministers and officers who attend . . . the law courts will go to their proper place [therein] . . . at the first hour of the day and they will deal with whatever matters need to be dealt with for the true administration of the law . . . The Ministers . . . and petitioning lawyers will all take their places at a moderate distance from the Heir and make their reports upon whatever needs to be reported, about crime, about the affairs of the country in general and about the Religion.[33]

This seems to be what Tim Murphy, in the English context, calls 'adjudication as the mode of government' (Murphy 1991: 194). Part of this list's meaning is to reinforce a preference for presenting policy issues in the guise of legal issues. And part of it (since king-law is a subset of ethics) implies a counsel of perfection: kings should keep on searching for ever more efficient ways to govern.

At worst I've given my own summary of Konbaung political theory as it was about 1870. At best I've reconstructed Kyaw Htun's summing up of it. I'll end this first part by summarising my comparisons with European political theory in tabular form:

Table 1 Konbaung political theory as Kyaw Htun saw it, with English equivalents

4 solidarities	balance-sheet between ruler and ruled
3 coronations	absolutism unacceptable
4 roads not to take	due process; fair procedure
10 king-law virtues	[no equivalent]
7 ways not to make things worse	rule of law

Hpo Hlaing of Upper Burma

Hpo Hlaing was born in 1830 to a family that had served the Konbaung kings as staff officers for more than fifty years. His father, Yindaw Wungyi, had a reputation as a scholar and as a friend to the Europeans in the Burmese capital. However, Yindaw Wungyi was murdered by King Tharrawaddy (1838–46) in 1845. The details are disputed: either he had been complicit in a plot against the king, or he was an innocent victim of one of the king's periodic insane rages. Hpo Hlaing advanced socially after his father's death: he was adopted by two of Tharrawaddy's sons, Mindon and Kanaung, and thenceforward received a prince's education. He attended the leading teaching monasteries of the capital as a novice, and then as a monk. By December 1852, the loss of the Second Anglo-Burmese War had made King Pagan (1846–52) unpopular: Mindon and Kanaung were talked of as replacements. Pagan sent men to arrest his brothers, but they escaped to raise a revolt. He also tried to arrest Hpo Hlaing but, so the story goes, the troops who went to his monastic cell missed him, because he was up all night reciting the *Paṭṭhāna* in the ordination hall. That homage to the Abhidhamma was his last act as a monk: at dawn, he put on lay clothes and made his way to join Mindon and Kanaung. Because he gave the crucial advice that secured their victory, for the next twenty-seven years, as long as King Mindon ruled, Hpo Hlaing was a protected person. For most of that time, he served the king as minister, but occasionally he was too blunt in his criticisms and had to go into exile for a year or two. In 1871, he was exiled for maintaining that the consumption of beer in moderate quantities did not breach the precepts. In 1873, there was a more serious row, when he criticised the king to his face for giving favours to those officials who pandered their daughters to him. Mindon snatched down from the wall the very spear with which his father had killed Hpo Hlaing's father:

King Mindon: Who was executed with this spear?
Hpo Hlaing: My father the Yindaw Wungyi was executed with that spear, your Majesty.
King Mindon: Do you also want to be executed by the same spear?
Hpo Hlaing (projecting his chest towards the king): Please execute me, your Majesty.[34]

An adopted son criticises his father's predatory sexual appetites: perhaps this is as much to do with the Oedipus complex as with the good government agenda. At any rate, Mindon backed down and left the room. When the other courtiers remonstrated with Hpo Hlaing, he replied:

> If he had struck me with that spear and I were killed, that would have been worthwhile. If kings are to order what they feel like at any point, the country will be lost because of the ill deeds that will be done. If I leave that behind me as my reputation, my death will be of little benefit. It is right to be afraid of that kind of foul smell sticking in the noses of all the peoples . . . Have your say . . . That is what ministers are for.[35]

In 1879, Hpo Hlaing showed that he was prepared to risk his life in order to prevent the country being lost.

When King Mindon died, Hpo Hlaing was co-leader[36] of the 'coup for constitutional monarchy', and wrote *Rajadhammasangaha* to instruct the new king in the cabinet arrangements that would now bind him. The plotters kept control of Mandalay for three months, running the country from their headquarters in the Southern Royal Gardens, having installed one of the weakest of Mindon's children, the 20-year-old Thibaw Prince, onto the throne.[37] They drafted an oath of office for him to swear that invoked three of the king-law lists and the *sassamedha* tax's upper limit of 10 per cent, before saying:

> There is the oath of allegiance twice administered to ministers and officers. They shall meet and talk and decide rules that would stand the test of time and remain good for several generations to come. Once they had decided the rules, people should abide by them.[38]

Thibaw was being asked, as I understand it, to cede legislative sovereignty to his Council so that they could draw up a formal constitution. As far as we know, Thibaw took the oath without demur (and, perhaps, without understanding). All government functions were reorganised into fourteen ministries. Hpo Hlaing headed the new *Sassamedha* department, which gave him sole authority to authorise payment from the Treasury. By controlling all government expenditure, he, in effect, controlled the government, though Kinwun Mingyi was the oldest and most prominent of the ministers involved.

The coup was defeated when Thibaw managed to win the support of an army commander. On 13 February 1879, units of the Household Guard under the Yanaung Myoza's command arrested Hpo Hlaing and two of the other coup leaders. Hpo Hlaing was sacked from court, but escaped death or imprisonment. He used his retirement to add to his reputation as an author. Previously he had translated Ampère's textbook on chemistry from French to Burmese (*Pyinthit Dat kyan*), and developed a Morse Code for the Burmese alphabet to use on Kanaung's newly installed telegraph line. Between 1879 and his death in 1883, he wrote his popular book on medicine and health *Udobhojana Sangaha*, and wrote *Mahasu Jātaka*, a Burmese summary of Sanskrit works on divination. With the possible exception of the Ledi *sayadaw*, Hpo Hlaing was the most prolific Burmese author of the late nineteenth century. It is his *Rajadhammasangaha* (*Compendium of King-Law*) that concerns us. U Htin Fatt produced his revised scholarly edition of the *Compendium of King-Law* in 1978. His seventy-six-page introduction describes and discusses all the known textual and epigraphic evidence of Hpo Hlaing's career. I have drawn heavily on Htin Fatt's work, and owe an equally large debt to Euan Bagshawe, who has made his translation of the Htin Fatt edition of 1978 available to all for free.

Hpo Hlaing had divided the ninety-four pages of *Compendium of King-Law* into three parts, respectively thirty-one pages, thirty-eight pages, and sixteen pages long. At the end of each part he summarised its content in traditional Burmese deadpan style. Part 1 ends:

> In this section the [*7 ways not to make things worse*]
> and other rules that are to be followed by kings and their ministers
> the book named *Rajadhammasangaha* sets out.[39]

His three summaries reveal nothing of his authorial intentions. That, I take it, was the point. The longer it took Thibaw to discover what was going on, the easier for the conspirators to prosper. Hpo Hlaing has, I think, written a muddled book when he was quite capable of writing a clear book. He did so by slavishly following Burmese genre conventions. The closer *Compendium of King-Law* resembled earlier works in the *myittasa* and *rajovada* genres, the better the chance that the young Thibaw king would skim through it without realising its revolutionary import. The plotters needed all the help they could get, and Hpo Hlaing's *hide it in the small print* strategy might have bought them a few extra weeks. As a result, Hpo Hlaing emerges as Burma's first ironist. He wrote the *Compendium of King-Law* entirely within Burmese genre constraints, but did so ironically, that is, in full appreciation of the muddying effect that strict adherence to genre could have.

Let's examine the structure by way of its Parts and Sections:

Table 2 The structure of Hpo Hlaing's *Compendium of King-Law*

Part 1:
(1–6) *7 ways not to make things worse* (as the People of the West);
(8–13) *4 solidarities* (as the People of the West)
(14–15) *3 motives leading down* (Burma's population decline),
(16–18) *2 motives leading up* (leading to a 2×2 Burmese deontology)
(19–24) *4 rules for here and beyond* (as the People of the West),
(25–6) *5 winning arguments* and *4 ways for people to do what they're told*

Part 2:
(1–7) *Three Birds Jātaka* (the West on implementation)
(8–10) *10 royal virtues* (plus sticks and carrots debate)
(11–18) *7 ways to beat an enemy*
(19–22) six more random lists
(23–27) *Art of War* sections
(28–36) five more random lists, interspersed with:
(32) another *Art of War* section
(31, 33, 36) the revolutionary manifesto

Part 3:
(1–6) *Singalovada sutta*
(7) *7 types of wife*
(8–12) *Singalovada sutta*

Coda: Hpo Hlaing's autobiography in Pali verse, followed by an auto-commentary in Burmese

If one omits the last two sections from Part 1 (the *5 winning arguments* from *Narada sutta* and the *4 rules for defeating inferiors* from the *Dhammapada*), Part 1 makes much better sense. From beginning to end, the argument would become a sociological and political comparison between Burma and 'the people of the western countries'. The first six sections contain his revolutionary theory, and the last five his Weberian analysis of the motivation behind western capitalism. Perhaps Hpo Hlaing tacked on the two lists of s25–6 to ensure that, despite its strong start, Part 1 ended on an anticlimax?[40] Or perhaps he was making up the numbers? If the list-of-lists analysis influenced him (and nowhere does he even hint that it does), then the extra two lists might have arithmetical significance. Here's the schema:

Part 1:	8 lists contain 34 items
Part 2:	16 lists contain 116 items
Part 3:	13 lists contain 65 items
	37 lists of 215 items **checksum**

I am not aware of any special personality attached to the number 215. But 37, as we have seen, connects with space, with protection, and with the 37 nats, who may be invoked for protection against most threats. The *Compendium of King-Law* is a book about how Burma may be protected from Britain.

What are we to make of the book's tripartite structure? Why are the 37 lists divided into three parts? Htin Fatt gives an answer that is of considerable jurisprudential interest:

> . . . after dealing very elegantly with the question of rights in the first part of the book, in the second and third parts he went on to demonstrate the duties mutually incumbent upon the rulers and those who accept their rule.[41]

Hpo Hlaing, in Htin Fatt's reading, understood the social contract between ruler and ruled in terms of correlative rights and duties, and used this relationship to provide the structure of his book. I remain agnostic. To my eyes, the contents of Hpo Hlaing's three parts are distinguishable as follows:

Part 1: Morality for kings
Part 2: Techniques of governance
Part 3: Rules for the Buddhist laity

The first two parts concern the ruler; the third addresses the ruled. Part 1 deals in moral generalisations; Part 2 in institutional particulars.

How do we know which of the 37 king-law lists in *Compendium of King-Law* Hpo Hlaing thought most important? That the book is, fundamentally, a comparison between Britain and Burma suggests a likely answer. He explicitly singles out four areas (three lists and one theme) as being the areas in which the British have worked out a political ethics superior to the Burmese. The first two of the lists are old friends:

> Because . . . they give the greatest importance to the [*4 solidarities*] . . . the peoples of the West stand out for their prosperity . . . Since the [*7 ways not to make things worse*] have been observed, the peoples of the western countries are at present the most advanced of all lands.[42]

The third list, which I call *4 rules for here and beyond*, has not, as far as I am aware, previously appeared in any Burmese work of king-law. It is from the *Alavaka sutta* [S.i.213] wherein the Buddha answers ten questions put by the earth-destroying demon Alavaka. Alavaka asked him 'What strategies hold good both in relation to this world and the next?' The Buddha answered with this list: '[1] *sacca* truth, [2] *dhamma* learning, [3] *dhiti* purposeful energy, [4] *cāga* charity.' I think that Hpo Hlaing has searched the vast repertoire of canonical lists for one that best expressed his understanding of what had prodded Europe into modernity. That which Max Weber identified as a certain combination of Puritan attitudes, Hpo Hlaing identifies as the *4 rules for here and beyond.* Of these four, it is *dhiti* that most interests him. We can have all the technological knowledge in the world, he says, but unless we exert ourselves, nothing will get made.[43] Part of the western mindset that encourages purposeful energy is a fixation with time-keeping:

> Thus the peoples of the West, recognising . . . that failing to keep properly to time brings loss, and punctuality brings profit, do not go beyond a promised time and, so that work may be done quickly, make use of telegraph lines, steam ships and steam trains . . . Everybody – women, men, important and unimportant people, all carry watches so as not to miss an appointment.[44]

These are the three lists in which Burma lags behind Britain. Fourth comes a theme: that Burma's government institutions are weaker than the British, in that Burma is unable to get its policy intiatives enforced at lower levels of the bureaucracy. In Burma, though government tells its minions what the new policy is, they find ways to delay its implementation:

> If in a major project you speak without meaning it, you will get much blame . . . The peoples of the western countries know that speaking the truth and keeping faith bring great benefits, while untruth is a great fault . . . Whatever they have agreed in joint consultation to enact into law cannot be begged off, there are no exceptions and the law is so enacted[45]

Since he talks in terms of promise-keeping, it is possible to read this passage as extolling the virtues of sticking to agreements. But in context, I think he is talking about bureaucrats who agree the king's new policy to his face, but subvert it behind his back. This is one of two explanations offered by Hpo Hlaing as to why the Burmese state is weaker than the British state. The other explanation is that the mid-levels of the bureaucracy travel the *4 ways not to go*: 'since a bias might be introduced by bribes or presents and by the status of people involved in the action.'[46] Government by king-in-cabinet will automatically put an end to such difficulties:

> What one man does not know another will; when one man has feelings of hate, another will not; when one is angry, another will be calm. When people have agreed in a meeting and preserve their solidarity, there will be no need for fear . . . [When] people conduct their business in an assembly there is no way in which the [*4 ways not to go*] can be followed.[47]

The checks and balances involved in cabinet government will cancel out each individual's bias, duress or ignorance. These are the final words of the *Compendium of King-Law*, and they sound like an anticipation of Jürgen Habermas. The Burmese minister and the German professor both believe in the disinfectant powers of decision-making by committee. But they differ over democracy: Habermas is in favour, and Hpo Hlaing was not. Hpo Hlaing wanted to move Burma from absolute monarchy to rule by an oligarchy of courtiers and generals. He belongs with the barons at Runnymede, not with the conventioneers at Philadelphia. If his two explanations overlap, we may substitute the *4 ways not to go* for the 'weak state' theme, in order to present Hpo Hlaing's analysis of how the people of the western countries excel as a list-of-lists:

1 4 solidarities
2 7 ways not to make things worse
3 4 rules for here and beyond
4 4 ways not to go
4 lists of 19 items **checksum**

I don't attach any significance to the checksum: I believe that here, at the heart of what Hpo Hlaing had to say, he was no longer guided by numerological considerations. These four lists happen to be what the data (the comparison between Britain and Burma) threw up. Hpo Hlaing's analysis of modernity is itself modern.

It remains to interpret what Hpo Hlaing says about these four lists. The *4 solidarities* would cause difficulty to anyone writing about it in the 1870s. Mindon had systematically dismantled that whole chapter of Burma's constitutional understandings whose heading was the *4 solidarities*. Kyaw Htun, observing Upper Burma from down-river in Danubyu, put it thus:

> Since [Mahāsammata's time], up to about 12 years ago, the several Kings and Rulers contented themselves with one tenth of the revenues of the country, but the present Sovereign of Burmah introduced a system of paying his servants, and abolished the tithe system.
>
> (Kyaw Htun 1877: 2)

King Mindon changed the currency of the tax system from rice to cash. In 1857, he imposed a poll tax, named the *sassamedha* tax, at three kyat per household. It rose to five, and then to ten kyat per household after 1866. Thant Myint-U has calculated that this 'vast change in the working of political power' imposed a severe drag on the most dynamic parts of Upper Burma's economy (Myint-U 2001: 115, 124). In respect of the *4 solidarities*, it was Mindon who was the revolutionary. Hpo Hlaing, inaugurating the post-Mindon era, had to decide whether this bit of the tradition has been irretrievably ruined, or whether it could be reconfigured to present needs. His attempt at reconfiguration was to shift the name *sassamedha* from the tax to the central treasury department that he headed. As to the *7 ways not to make things worse*, Hpo Hlaing merely added some detail. Like his predecessors, he thinks of the list in terms of optimising the daily procedures for cabinet government. He adds four checkpoints for successful meetings:

1 The time and place of meeting to be circulated in advance
2 An unfinished meeting to adjourn to a fixed date
3 Follow the agenda. Let everyone have their say.
4 The final decision should be made public, and should pursue consensus.[48]

These help us achieve 'discussion, leaving out individual prejudices, aiming for agreement'.[49] Finally the *4 roads not to take* concentrate on the institutional advantages that comes with well-conducted cabinet government:

> As has been said on the [*7 ways not to make things worse*], if a number of people get together for any sort of action, there can be no question of following the [*roads not to take*] way.[50]

As I did with Kyaw Htun, I shall try to summarise Hpo Hlaing's core message in tabular form, with European equivalents:

Table 3 Konbaung political theory, as Hpo Hlaing saw it, with English translation

4 solidarities	budget under cabinet control
7 ways not to make things worse	institutional cabinet government
4 rules for here and beyond	motivation of western modernity
4 roads not to take	epistemological cabinet government

Conclusion

Two of Hpo Hlaing's Burmese readers differ as to the extent of his debt to western thinking. Tin Ohn reads *Compendium of King-Law* as showing that: 'Burmese intellectuals were fully aware of the world outside their own country and were quick enough to appreciate the new ideas.'[51] Htin Fatt concedes that Hpo Hlaing was enthusiastic about some of the political ideas arriving from western countries. However:

> We cannot say that it follows from this that it is only a book that copies western ideas; in it the author compares the past with the present, the old with the new, western notions with eastern, in his search for objectivity.[52]

If you're a Burmese proponent of cabinet government, as Hpo Hlaing was, does that make you un-Burmese? If you covet the strong government that westerners have achieved, are you thereby betraying your eastern roots? Did the *Compendium of King-Law* so revolutionise the Burmese political tradition as to catapult itself outside that tradition as Kyaw Htun and his contemporaries understood it? We are now in a better position to assess the different emphases of Tin Ohn and Htin Fatt. In relation to Table 3's first, second and fourth lists, we can make a direct comparison between Burmese king-law as presented by Kyaw Htun and by Hpo Hlaing. Mindon's monetarisation of the tax system had destroyed a long-entrenched part of the Burmese constitutional settlement. Certainly, Hpo Hlaing's treatment of the *4 solidarities* is a new approach to the theme, but the old approach was already dead. In this respect Hpo Hlaing was a revivalist rather than a revolutionary. In respect of the *7 ways not to make things worse* Hpo Hlaing was a traditionalist: the details he added were well within the parameters set down by Burmese tradition. In respect of the *4 roads not to take*, he gave an epistemological twist to the Buddhist analysis of natural justice. Decisions reached after full discussion by a well-briefed cabinet were likely to be better (meaning purged of more of the *4 roads not to take*) than decisions reached in other ways. This does introduce something new into the previous Burmese discourse on the *4 roads*. In relation to this list and this list only, Hpo Hlaing does choose to bend the tradition he inherited into something new.

There were two big might-have-beens in relation to Upper Burma's governance. Hpo Hlaing's coup of 1879–80 might have succeeded, and *Compendium of King-Law* become the official ideology of Mandalay's constitutional monarchy. Or Viscount Dufferin and Randolph Churchill might have accepted Kinwun Mingyi's proposals of 1886 and installed a constitutional monarchy in Mandalay. In the first case, Upper Burma might have been able to evolve through the twentieth century as a nominally independent state, like Thailand. In the second case, Upper Burma might have been subject to indirect colonial rule, as were the northern Malay states. I concede that we cannot know whether these might-have-beens would have brought a better future for the Burmese. But looking at Burma as it actually was in 1948, and as it is in 2007, it is hard to imagine that things could have turned out worse.

Notes

1 My thanks to Patricia Herbert, Euan Bagshawe, Michael Charney and John Okell, for their help in researching Kyaw Htun and Hpo Hlaing.

2 Charles Crosthwaite, cited in Harvey (1932: 439).

3 Kyaw Htun (1877).

4 Hpo Hlaing (1979). Euan Bagshawe's translation (2004) of the whole text is available at http://www.ibiblio.org/obl/docs/The_Rajadhammasangaha-print.pdf

5 For an excellent guide to the first millenium of its history, see Steven Collins (1998).

6 Note the interesting ambiguity in the Pali word *mātikā*. It can refer to each item in a list: 'Monks, there are these eight *mātikā* for the removal of robe-privileges . . .' [V.i.255]. And it can also refer to the list as a whole: the *Pātimokkha*, which is a list-of-lists comprising 227 items, is commonly referred to as the *mātikā* of the second half of the *Vinaya*. If you know the list, it's because you have learned all its items by heart, and can reproduce each one verbatim.

7 'Subsidiarity' meaning which levels of government are appropriate to handle which problems.

8 That is, 32 quarters of the compass + 4 options in the third dimension + the point where the observer sits.

9 The five Pali nouns are in A.iii.151. The information in brackets is from the Commentary [Mn P.iii.283]. See Gokhale (1953: 162).

10 India Office Library Records [henceforth 'IOLR'], P4/36 November, citing Col. W. Plant's letter to Albert Fytche, June 1871.

11 IOLR, P4/36 November.

12 Kyaw Htun spelled it 'Donabyoo' on the front of his *Pakinnaka Dipani Kyam*.

13 Born into the Jewish faith in London's East End. Spent most of his life as an Anglican missionary in British Burma. For a few eventful years, he ran an Anglican church and school in Mandalay.

14 IOLR, P4/36 November, Plant to Fytche, June 1871.

15 IOLR, P3/37, 18 March 1872.

16 John Okell's translation of a manuscript letter (Kyaw Htun to Col. Ardagh) bound into the SOAS library copy of *Pakinnaka Dipani Kyan*.

17 Though I have not yet found conclusive proof that he did.

18 Emil Forchhammer, Rangoon's Professor of Pali, said that it 'recommends itself for the fair judgment which the author displays in the selection and arrangement of the material, and in the omission of all, or, nearly all, that a European critic would condemn as emanating from national idiosyncrasies' (Maung Tet Pyo (1884), General remarks by Dr E. Forchhammer, Professor of Pali and Government Archaeologist, British Burma: 1–2).

19 IOLR, V/24/2233: Judicial Commissioner's Report for 1873: 49.

20 IOLR, P4/36 November.

21 IOLR, P4/35 November, inclosing a medical certificate dated 14 November from J. Lamprey, Surgeon-Major HM 67th Regiment, Rangoon, attesting to Kyaw Htun's impaired vision.

22 ROB 24–5–1824. Than Tun justifies this date (the manuscript has 15–7–1817) at: Than Tun 1984–90: VII:109–10.

23 The *10 royal duties, 4 solidarities and the 7 ways not to make things worse* all appear in a single passage offering reasons why the king should not be a sexual predator (Richardson 1896: 181). The *4 roads not to take* are enumerated (without their collective name) as characteristic of the seven types of incompetent judge (Richardson 1896: 157). The *3 kinds of coronation* are given their collective name in the book's opening pages (Richardson 1896: 7). Richardson adds an enumeration taken from a named manuscript source ('Benga R'heo's Book, letter su.'). Unfortunately, we do not know who Benga R'heo was. If *Manugye* was indeed Kyaw Htun's source for the *3 coronations*, he has used it critically. *Manugye's thaga* becomes *thenga* in the *Prize Essay*, with the implication that this kind of coronation connects with the *thenga taya leba* (the *4 solidarities*).

24 Badon's ROB of second waning day of Kahson 1144, quoted in U Tin (2001: 304).

25 Richardson (1896: 109).

26 ROB 28–1–1795 s.56.

27 ROB 18–3–1796, Than Tun's English summary.
28 Htin Fatt, *Introduction*, trs. Bagshawe (2004: 58ff) (see Hpo Hlaing 1979). This ceremony was designed by Hpo Hlaing, along lines indicated in his *Decisions of King Mahasammata*, written two years before. Htin Fatt was unable to find a copy.
29 Ulpianus *libro 13 ad legem Iuliam et Papiam: Princeps legibus solutus est: Augusta autem licet legibus soluta non est, principes tamen eadem illi privilegia tribuunt, quae ipsi habent.*
30 See, as representative of a much larger literature: Esmein (1913), Daube (1954), Simon (1984).
31 http://www.royal.gov.uk/output/Page1699.asp.
32 Pali *aparihāniya*, literally meaning 'connected with whatever causes non-decay'. Buddhists believe that things will naturally get worse. What deserves special attention are the few things that can reverse the downward trend.
33 RoB 14th waxing day of Tazaung-hmon, 1148, quoted in U Tin (2001: 314).
34 My paraphrase of Htin Fatt, *Introduction*, trs. Bagshawe (2004: 56) (see Hpo Hlaing 1979).
35 Htin Fatt, *Introduction*, citing the Hmawbi Sayadaw Theingyi, trs. Bagshawe (2004: 56) (see Hpo Hlaing 1979).
36 Kinwun Mingyi, Hkanbat Wungyi, and Yeinangyaung Wungyi were the other important figures in the coup.
37 On one account, they would have preferred to enthrone the Nyaungyan Prince, but he had taken sanctuary inside the British Residency, which refused the Kinwun Mingyi's formal demand for their delivery. See: Aung San Suu Kyi (1990: 43). Thibaw Prince had learned English and cricket at Rev. Mark's Anglican school in Mandalay, before shifting to a more traditional education at the Bagaya *kyaung*.
38 ROB 12–10–1878, Than Tun's summary of the Burmese text.
39 *Rajadhammasangaha*, trs. Bagshawe (2004: 119) (see Hpo Hlaing 1979).
40 There seems to be more obfuscation in Part 2. The agenda for the institutional implementation of the coup is to be found in s31, 33, and 36. But these sections are hidden within a deliberate muddle of lists from a military manual, along with a random handful of king-law lists.
41 Htin Fatt, *Introduction*, trs. Bagshawe (2004: 75) (see Hpo Hlaing 1979).
42 *Rajadhammasangaha*, trs. Bagshawe (2004: 103), 94 (see Hpo Hlaing 1979).
43 *Ibid.*: 117.
44 *Ibid.*: 123.
45 *Ibid.*: 122.
46 *Ibid.*: 92.
47 *Ibid.*: 174.
48 *Ibid.*: 92.
49 *Ibid.*: 89.
50 *Ibid.*: 174.
51 Tin Ohn (1963: 90).
52 Htin Fatt, *Introduction*, trs. Bagshawe (2004: 70) (see Hpo Hlaing 1979).

4

COLONIAL KNOWLEDGE AND BUDDHIST EDUCATION IN BURMA

Juliane Schober

> *Faith and power must always, however uneasily, take a stance toward one another. The polity, more than most realms of human action, deals obviously with ultimate things.*
>
> (Bellah and Hammond 1980: iv)

Education has long been associated with power and privilege. To this, one may add the role of religion in education. Taw Sein Ko, the eminent scholar of Burmese history and culture and Superintendent of the Archeological Survey (1918–19) observed categorically that 'education divorced from religion is of little value'.[1] Indeed, it is difficult to negate the role of religious education in the formation of the self, in shaping moral values and even in promoting social change from colonial hegemony to national sovereignty. And there is perhaps no better vantage point to explore the intricate connections between knowledge, religion, and power than in the contexts of colonial education.

Education is a tool for mediating diverse, and at times contradictory, bodies of knowledge concerning culture and world-view, modernity and tradition, politics and religion, and temporal and ultimate visions of reality. It helps shape conceptual structures of knowledge used to negotiate the fluctuating boundaries of experience in the encounters of traditional and modern societies, such as colonial Burma and colonizing Britain. This is particularly apparent at those moments in history when colonial reforms of education seek to integrate divergent bodies of local knowledge. Education therefore also plays a role in shaping cultural notions of identity, national belonging, and religious reasoning.

Colonizing forces tend to impose their forms of knowledge on newly conquered territories by training local populations to become civil servants and administrators in the colonial regime (Cohen 1996: 1–15). Colonial education claims to convey objective facts through the rational methods of modern science and technology. The curriculum and language of instruction in colonial education are significant instruments in the consolidation of foreign rule (Altbach and Kelly 1991: 1). It teaches what Cohen calls colonial forms of knowledge that comprise subjects such as historiography, geographic surveys, ethnic practices and beliefs, surveillance, and so on. The colonial state itself becomes a theatre for 'experimentation, where documentation, certification, and representation were . . . modalities that transformed knowledge into power' (Dirks in Cohen 1996: xi).

This essay casts into relief cultural and historical locations at which particular forms of knowledge can open access to power, while other forms of knowledge lose relevance in the political context of the time. By focusing on colonial knowledge and Buddhist education in Burma, I do not intend to privilege any particular education, policy, or curriculum. Nor do I seek to describe Burmese Buddhism as 'compatible' with or 'hostile' to rationalism, modernity, or secular knowledge. Instead, I hope to locate debates about education within colonial histories to highlight selectively cultural dynamics that motivate the continuing politicization of education in Burma. Secular subjects were not novel to the monastic curriculum in Burma. During the reign of King Bodawphaya (r. 1782–1819), monastic education incorporated what might loosely be termed secular subjects of Indian origins, including astronomy, astrology, military arts, boxing, wrestling and music (Mendelson 1975: 151). Yet, in the mid-nineteenth century, when Burmese monks encountered the colonial stipulation to include the teaching of science as an instrument of colonial power, they largely refused to cooperate with British education policy. My essay begins by describing the cultural contexts in which the monastic opposition to teaching modern subjects emerged, especially to mathematics, geography and drawing. The *sangha*'s refusal was motivated largely by reactions against the colonial threat to monastic authority, autonomy and ethics. The *sangha*'s position on educational reforms proved to have unintended and far-reaching consequences, and eventually gave rise to millenarian resistance movements against colonial rule, such as the Saya San Rebellion during the 1920s and 1930s (Schober 1995).

A second focus is the emergence of nationalism advocated by the Young Buddhist Men's Association (YMBA), which was in many ways a colonial organization. Founded in 1906, it was the first civil organization to raise awareness about national identity. Its members were primarily products of colonial education and included many of the country's post-independence leaders. The YMBA's nationalist agenda focused in large measure on matters of education. It advocated standards for instruction in secular subjects in rural areas, while, at the same time, promoting government support for instruction in religious and vernacular subjects like Buddhism, Burmese language and classical literature in public schools where modern, secular subjects and instruction in English formed the core of the curriculum.

Next, the discussion shifts to modern efforts to construct a fundamental Buddhist rationale that encompasses and foreshadows modern science and to missionize Buddhism among sympathetic western audiences in the 1950s and 1960s. Here, a modern Buddhist discourse appropriates, seemingly without contradiction, scientific rationalism, perhaps the hallmark of modern western education. In this context, colonial knowledge is again subordinated to a universal, yet modern Buddhist cosmology. The essay concludes with a brief delineation of the ways in which Burmese governments have shaped public debate about education since independence. Particularly noteworthy in this regard are efforts by the military regime, since the 1990s, to employ monasteries in the delivery of basic education in rural areas and particularly among non-Buddhist tribal groups. Restrictions imposed on access to education under military rule have motivated pro-democracy forces in Burma to bring to the attention of the international community the widespread need for education in shaping the future of civil society.

Colonial and cultural knowledge

To a significant degree, the Burmese experience of modernity commenced as a colonial project. The encounter of what is now called 'traditional Burmese culture' with historical forces that would link this country's future to modernizing innovations was motivated by the concerns of colonial administration and propelled by particular historical conjunctures in this unfolding development. Together, these forces eventually eclipsed traditional cultural values, institutions, and life-ways.[2] The collapse of traditional institutions, initially only in Lower Burma and, after 1886, also in Upper Burma accelerated the restructuring of Burmese society in the advent of modernity.[3]

Colonial rule in Burma effectively dislodged military or secular power from its Buddhist world-view in which it had been traditionally embedded. By separating practical, physical and secular power from its Buddhist foundations, the British followed a deliberate policy of non-involvement in the religious affairs of the colony. This diminished colonial authority in the views of traditional Burmese Buddhists, who expected the British to act like righteous Buddhist rulers (*dhammarāja*). At the same time, colonial rule introduced alternate access to power that until then had not been a conceptual possibility in Burmese cultural knowledge. British rule promoted the rationalization of the state, modern values and western education, and created administrative structures that furthered the economic and political goals of the empire (Schober 2005).

The British encountered in Burma a firmly established and entirely different system of formal education, with a relatively high rate of literacy among the general population. Colonial sources report that basic literacy rates exceeded those of India and matched those of Italy, Ireland and North America in the mid-nineteenth century. Yet, British and Burmese notions of education were not commensurate. Colliding world-views and political projects characterized debates about educational policy, access and reforms of education. Education remained a contested issue throughout colonial and national history, informing national identity, politics and religion, and serving as flashpoints around which Burmese leaders rallied and mobilized public opinion in the struggle for independence. From the British perspective, the purpose of colonial education was to produce local administrators trained to implement the colonial project. Colonial knowledge was primarily secular in its orientation, although Christian missionaries played significant roles in delivering a curriculum infused with a Christian ethos. It presumed an ideology of cultural evolution that legitimated colonial rule over native peoples and obligated colonizers to take on 'the White Man's Burden' and educate the colonized. In this western view of enlightenment, modern man was able to master human progress through scientific rationalism. The 1854 British Dispatch on colonial education echoes these sentiments (Bagshawe 1976: 28–29). Accordingly, the government's objectives for education in India were to bring about intellectual and moral improvement; ensure the supply of government servants, and safeguard the expansion of trade. It was intended to produce an appreciation for 'European knowledge' by teaching about the arts, sciences, philosophy and literature of Europe. English was to be taught already in the elementary grades along with vernacular literacy. Under the authority of colonial departments of Public Instruction, reforms of local school systems were undertaken and institutions of higher education were to be developed. Private and missionary schools observing these government regulations would receive government funding.

The purpose of formal education (*batha*) in pre-colonial Burmese culture was intrinsically religious. Education properly belonged to the domain of Buddhist monks and monastic learning. Its premise rested on a Buddhist understanding of the world wherein all phenomena, be they social, political, cultural, are constituted by karmic action and regulated by the Universal Law, the *dhamma*, the Buddhist Truth. Religious and other ultimate concerns encompassed secular and temporal matters (*lokiya*) that were ultimately meaningful only to the extent to which they were linked to notions of Buddhist morality. Humans were not in control of nature, but subject to it through the Universal Law. Practical or vocational knowledge was imparted primarily through contextual learning and mostly in informal settings. Buddhist knowledge is also intensely personal and the insights it entails are believed to lead to moral perfection (*nibbāna*). Such knowledge is embedded in lineages of monastic teachers that can be traced, at least in principle, to the pristine time of the Buddha.

Colonial rule and the demise of traditional Buddhist education

In response to a growing European mercantile presence encroaching upon its southern coast regions, the Court of Ava had followed the cultural mode of its predecessors by retreating inward and temporarily moving the court from Ava across the Irrawaddi River to Amarapura, near Sagain (Stewart 1975: 32ff). Embedded in the Burmese retreat was a fateful misapprehension of European global trade networks and the political power protecting the colonial enterprise. Although intermittent efforts to become familiar with European knowledge and technical capacities had been initiated during the reign of King Bodawphaya, the Kingdom of Ava was, by all accounts, at the political and cultural apex of an imperial Theravada polity whose ruler styled himself to be 'The Master of the White Elephant' and 'The Lord of all Umbrella-Bearing Chiefs' (Myint-U 2000: 53). Through the aid of Barnabite missionaries and Father Sangermano, the King of Ava requested the papal court in Rome in 1723 to provide access to western knowledge, explaining that 'many teachers and technicians were needed'.[4] While the Portuguese had initiated some Christian missionary education along Burma's southern coastline since 1600, western education was carried out primarily by Roman Catholic and American Baptist missionaries well into the first half of the nineteenth century (Ba 1964; Kaung 1931, 1960a, 1960b, 1963). The Reverend J. E. Marks, of the British Society for the Propagation of the Gospel, established St James College in Rangoon in 1885, following several years' residence in Mandalay during the 1870s. Thant Myint-U credits two members of the Burmese elite, the Myoza of Myawaddy and the Prince of Mekkaya, as pioneering a renaissance of local scholarship during the 1830s and 1840s affecting:

> . . . many and diverse fields of knowledge, including geography, astronomy, history and the natural sciences. The arrival of European learning also displaced India as the ultimate and natural source of outside information, and marked the beginning of a long relationship between modern science and Theravada Buddhism.
>
> (Myint-U 2000: 101)

In 1824, the British commenced the first of three wars that eventually led to the annexation of Burma in 1886. The First Anglo-Burmese War (1824–1826) served to protect mercantile interests of the British East Indian Company in the region and was declared against the Kingdom of Ava and King Bagyidaw (r. 1819–1837), the reigning monarch of the Konbaun Dynasty. A significant milestone of the colonial project, however, had been achieved in 1826, when British land surveyors completed a map of the geographic boundaries of the Kingdom of Ava (Myint-U 2000: 101).

Access to formal education in pre-colonial and early colonial Burma continued to be largely shaped by a pre-modern, cosmological Buddhist mentality and its cultural values. Religious education and literacy were products of that mentality, and a monastic career was the primary venue for gifted young men to realize educational goals and join the ranks of the literati. Prior to the First Anglo-Burmese War (1824–1826), literacy was acquired through the study of religious subjects and firmly rooted in the monastic mission to preserve the *dhamma*. Scholarship and teaching were natural extensions of a religious vocation. Formal education was concerned with 'general principles' and timeless, ultimate knowledge. Its study was accessible through the institution of the *sangha*, the teaching practices of monks, and through knowledge engraved in palm leaf manuscripts that were catalogued according to Theravada classifications and housed in monastic libraries. Taw Sein Ko notes that basic multiplication was taught in monasteries alongside the study of classic texts (Taw Sein Ko 1913b: 228). Khammai Dhammasami (in this volume) also points to the use of basic mathematics as an aid to memorizing Pali texts. The monastic curriculum further incorporated subjects such as Burmese traditional law, history, astrology, military skills and archery, taught by court Brahmins of primarily Manipuri descent to children of the elite (Myint-U 2000). In dynastic times, too much erudition among commoners entailed the risk of raising suspicion about a potential incursion of power and possible revolts against royal power.

Buddhist monasteries functioned as primary educational institutions providing basic literacy for Burmese young people. British surveys taken in the mid-nineteenth century confirm that monastic education was firmly established throughout the country.[5] Most males spent some time as students (*kyaun:tha*) or novices residing in the monastery where daily routines made study of the *dhamma* a central focus. Other male students attended monastic instruction, but continued to live with their families. Taw Sein Ko (1913: 224) bemoans the fact that the education of girls was generally left to 'untutored masters', as teaching young girls was considered beneath the 'holy dignity' of monks and viewed as 'unnecessary' by much of the population. By 1869, however, slightly more than 5,000 girls, who were not permitted to attend monastic schools, enrolled in 340 lay schools located in homes set aside for instructional purposes in some of the larger villages. However, attendance at these home schools was intermittent, instructional periods were shorter, and educational expectations were less rigorous.[6]

Monastic examinations sponsored by kings offered monks access to higher levels of education since at least the seventeenth century in Burma (Spiro 1970: 362). Following a hiatus after the fall of Mandalay in 1886, the British Government reinstituted Pali examinations in 1895 (Taw Sein Ko 1913b: 248). Scholarly achievements were honoured with monastic titles and continue to be rewarded today. A curriculum of four levels, *pahtama-nge*, *pahtama-lat*, *pahtamak-gyi*, and *pahtama-gyan*, led to the higher levels of Buddhist learning. Education began with simple recitation and memorization of the Burmese alphabet, religious liturgies (the Three Refuges, the Precepts, the Eightfold Noble Path, etc.), and formulae of homage and protection. At higher levels, Pali language instruction complemented the memorization of increasingly extensive selections of canonical texts taken from each of the three baskets.[7] In addition, monks were also taught the *Maṅgala sutta*, the *Lokanīti* with its astrological focus, the *Dhammanīti and Rājanīti*.[8] Cultural knowledge was therefore found in monks as the embodiment of Buddhist learning and in the palm leaf manuscripts housed in monastic libraries of local communities that served as repositories for textual study.

Monks were expected to lead a life that was withdrawn from and above worldly affairs (Mendelson 1975: 157). Monastic teaching styles affirmed cultural expectations that one may not challenge the authority of monastic teachers. Senior monks like local abbots tended to assume teaching roles and hence enjoyed considerable authority and respect. They instructed students in traditional methods such as reading aloud in unison and recitation from memory and seldom offered explanations or interpretations of the materials studied. As questioning a monastic teacher might be perceived as a challenge to his authority, students would seek answers from parents and others in the lay world. The work of interpreting or filling in gaps in basic religious knowledge occurred mostly outside the *sangha* in the larger social circles of the family.

Monastic education in nineteenth-century Burma relied mostly on scarce copies of palm leaf manuscripts as the major material repositories of textual knowledge. In her study on the local diversity in Buddhist learning in north-eastern Thailand, Tiyavanich (1997) notes the advent of printed materials helped facilitate concurrent reforms to standardize the monastic curriculum. In the absence of detailed research on diverse Buddhist traditions in Burma during the nineteenth century, we may nonetheless surmise that the introduction of print similarly served to standardize a heterodox tradition and a diverse monastic teaching curriculum. In 1864, Bishop Bigandet, the Vicar Apostolic of Ava and Pegu, was instrumental in producing the first printed version of the Burmese *Tripitaka*.[9] Although print culture flourished in Burma relatively late, we can point to several hallmarks of an incipient print culture. The first English newspaper, *The Moulmein Advertiser*, began publication in 1846, serving the commercial interests of the East India Company and its local representatives.[10] By 1852, Rangoon had emerged as the centre for printing and publishing,[11] and by 1874, the *Yadana Neipyidaw* became the first newspaper published in Burmese in Mandalay, King Mindon's (r. 1853–1878) capital in Upper Burma.[12] Printed textbooks became available only after the British sought educational reforms in the 1870s. In his exhaustive study on books in Burmese used in the curriculum, Bagshawe (1976) notes the impoverished literature on modern subjects available to schools.[13] Moreover, the availability of printed materials in Burmese developed at a relatively slow pace. The growing cultural currency of colonial bodies of knowledge in print continually challenged the viability of monastic education, for which few printed materials were used.[14]

Soon after the First Anglo-Burmese War, the British government began to develop educational policy for its Indian colonies. Subsequent educational reforms during the late nineteenth century profoundly shaped the colonial and national history of Burma. British policy to remake education in its colonial rationality met with strong resistance among the *sangha*, as most monastic schools refused to integrate western, secular subjects into the curriculum taught at monastic schools. Indeed, disdain for local canons of knowledge was expressed by the chairman of the Committee on Public Instruction, Thomas Macaulay, who announced that:

> . . . (w)e have to educate a people who cannot at present be educated by means of their mother tongue. We must teach them – our own language . . . We must form . . . a class (of) interpreters between us and the millions we govern; a class of persons, Indian in blood and color, but English in taste, in opinions, in morals and in intellect.
>
> (cited in Rives 1999: 122)

Against such pronounced objectives of the colonial project, the proposal made by Sir Arthur Phayre, the British Chief Commissioner, in 1866 appeared liberal and progressive.[15] His educational reforms envisioned a collaboration between government institutions and Burmese monastic schools. Phayre's goal was to ensure that colonial knowledge, so central to the concept of a modern government, be taught through the existing infrastructures in Burmese Buddhist monasteries. He sought to persuade the *sangha* to integrate modern subjects, including arithmetic and geography, into the existing monastic curriculum. His proposal offered financial incentives to Buddhist monasteries to compensate monastic teachers, to employ government-certified lay teachers to teach modern, secular subjects at monastic schools, and to extend stipends to students.

The cultural chasm between Buddhist learning and colonial knowledge soon became apparent as British conservatives and the Burmese monastic patriarch both responded negatively to Phayre's proposal. It was unpopular among British conservatives because they saw it as contravening the Anglo-Indian government's policy not to become involved in the religious affairs of colonies. Similarly, few monastic schools responded to Phayre's initiative, and the implementation of educational reforms was slow. In 1866, an education department was established by the local government and a plan for building a public education system was inaugurated. By 1871, five years after Phayre's initiative had been launched, only forty-six monastic schools were authorized under the government's policy. Two years later, in 1873, 'the number of authorized monastery schools had risen to 801' (Ono Toru 1981:

111), a considerable proportion of approximately 3,438 monastic schools in Lower Burma alone (Smith 1965: 59). By contrast, only 112 lay schools had registered with the government by 1873.[16]

The slow acceptance of British education policy in Burmese monastic schools was complemented by a concurrent and rapid increase in demand for colonial education. Eager to promote its agenda of colonial subject formation and train potential recruits for the Indian Civil Service, the colonial government determined to increase its support to existing Christian missionary and secular government schools. The demand for colonial education, with English as its medium of instruction, also increased rapidly. This trend was amplified after the annexation of Upper Burma in 1886.

Following the British annexation, the Taungdaw Sayadaw was the monastic patriarch or *thathanabain* who had been appointed by Thibaw, the last king of the Konbaun dynasty. Although he resided in Mandalay, he assumed at least nominal authority over the entire Burmese *sangha*. When he passed away in 1895, the office was left vacant until 1903, when the British confirmed his successor, the Taunggwin Sayadaw, who resided in Rangoon. Census and registration figures during the final decades of the nineteenth century make clear that Phayre's plan to involve monasteries in the delivery of secular education subjects proceeded very slowly, and with considerable resistance from the *sangha* until it was finally abandoned in the vernacular Education Committee report of 1924 (Mendelson 1975: 159). The *sangha*'s objections to Phayre's attempt to deliver a modern secular education through existing monastery schools centred on what would have amounted to a colonial redefinition of monastic authority.[17] The monks did not want to be accountable to the colonial government concerning their roles as teachers and resented British interference in what the *sangha* perceived to be concerns internal to its organization. There was also resistance to accepting the presence in the monastery of government-certified lay teachers who had been commissioned with the instruction of secular subjects, and there was some perception that the presence of lay teachers in monastic schools constituted a threat to monastic authority. In 1891, the *thathanabain* explicitly prohibited monastic schools from implementing the colonial education curriculum, specifically the teaching of arithmetic and geography.[18] The presence of lay teachers on monastic grounds was not permitted. Emissaries were sent out to reinforce these orders with local abbots, who were enjoined not to employ government-certified lay teachers (Smith 1965: 59). For the most part, the *sangha* stood its ground throughout the decade-long vacancy in the office of its patriarch, refusing to assume a monastic role in colonial education reforms. However, a few monasteries, especially in Lower Burma, showed at least nominal participation in the reforms by registering with the government and by accepting government school books and other forms of support. It was not until 1909 that a new *thathanabain* in his letter to the Director of

Public Instruction indicated his willingness to assume a neutral position on this issue, affirming his intent to work towards a resolution in matters of mutual interests by delegating the decision to participate in the colonial education project to local abbots.[19] He stated that the acceptance of money granted by the government to monks constituted a breach of *vinaya* rules as the notion of 'results grants' and 'salary' was unsuitable for Theravada monks, who may not accept money or work for pay. He further objected to certain proposed subjects as unsuitable for monastic study. Indicating his flexibility on some subjects proposed in the Education Code, he objected firmly to instruction in drawing, and especially the drawing of maps.[20] He found the idea of starting education in kindergarten 'quite unsuitable' and concluded by stressing that:

> Special rules should be framed for the guidance of monastic schools, and the indigenous curriculum should be adopted with such modifications as are necessitated by circumstances. In other words, *only such subjects should be taught as are consistent with the tenets of Buddhism.*
>
> (Taw Sein Ko 1913b: 268 – emphasis added)

The *sangha*'s response to Phayre's proposal proved detrimental to the future of monastic education in colonial Burma. Over the three decades of relative prosperity and stability between 1891 and 1918, there was a rapid increase in secular government schools and a concurrent decline of government-recognized monastic education throughout all of Burma.[21]

The British saw the lack of Buddhist collaboration as undermining the colonial project to educate a new class of civil servants. Christian missionary and government-funded schools soon attracted talented, ambitious youths for whom instruction in English and western knowledge provided new opportunities and life-ways. With profitable opportunities in the economy and in colonial administration afforded by a modern education, missionary and government schools soon recruited bright and ambitious young Burmese.

This trend was especially pronounced in towns and urban centres, which further deepened the cultural divide between urban and rural areas that already characterized Burmese colonial experience. In contrast to pre-colonial Burma, where elites sought out monastic teachers and mentors, monastic education was relegated to the cultural and political backwaters in rural areas, where monastic schools instructed rural youths with less ambition or talent. This further weakened the intellectual vitality of Buddhist institutions in colonial Burma. Monastic authority continued to be diminished by a rise in lay meditation and lay religious education in the aftermath of the decline of Burmese traditional culture. In short, the trend away from monastic education created economic, cultural and intellectual divisions between British educated colonial elites and those who remained confined to a pre-colonial Buddhist rationality.

The impact of colonialism and modernity on traditional Burmese culture was not confined to monastic education. The British conquest of Upper Burma was devastating to traditional life-ways and to social, cultural, political and economic institutions (Myint-U 2000). Colonial rationality and practice had dislodged secular uses of power from the Buddhist cosmology that traditionally encompassed it. The colonizers looted and burned Mandalay Palace, the seat of power in Upper Burma. They exiled the Burmese King, Thibaw (r. 1878–1885) to India, and relocated the Lion Throne, the seat of royal power, to the Calcutta Museum. Mandalay Palace itself was transformed into a British military garrison, Fort Dufferin, and Rangoon, the mercantile centre of Lower Burma, now assumed still greater political and economic importance. Though diminished in its influence and cultural vitality, the institution of Buddhism, as embodied by the *sangha*, nevertheless emerged as the only traditional institution to survive colonization.

The *thathanabain*'s refusal to allow monastic schools to become conduits of colonial knowledge diminished the political and cultural relevance of the *sangha*. Monastic leaders seemingly had not anticipated the historical and political consequences this decision would hold. Nor did they foresee the utility colonial knowledge held for an emerging class of Burmese civil servants. Living within a world-view in which Buddhist rationalities encompassed practical knowledge, the *sangha* could not foresee the authority colonial knowledge would acquire within a modern way of living. From the perspective of a traditional *sangha*, practical, applied and vocational subjects traditionally had been taught in the informal contexts within the worldly realm. Technical and practical education therefore did not fall with its educational mission.

The patriarchal decision indicates more than a Buddhist rejection of secular rationalism and colonial knowledge. It constituted a defence of monastic education as rooted in the *vinaya* and, more generally, a defence of the monastic status *vis-à-vis* a colonial regime that had shown scant respect for Buddhist monasticism. This stance placed the *sangha* in opposition to the colonial regime, and eventually created an arena for resistance against colonialism, secular power and knowledge. It located early Burmese anti-colonial resistance movements within a pre-modern Buddhist context. Increasingly, the *sangha* as an institution and monks as political actors became focal points of anti-colonial resistance around which Burmese national identity was affirmed and articulated through millennial movements and other forms for neo-traditional Buddhism.

The *thathanabain*'s fateful refusal of Phayre's proposal undermined monastic authority as the source and embodiment of knowledge in the future. The vacuum created by the disjuncture between Buddhist knowledge and colonial education opened venues for cultural innovations of authority by Burmese lay teachers.[22] Mendelson comments that the *sangha*'s retreat from modern education transformed Burmese Buddhist practice and gave rise to new lay associations:

> The loss of the educational role, formerly the exclusive role of the monk, has had profound effects upon the Sangha's place in modern Burmese society. The movement to place education into secular hands was a legacy of colonialism that left a vacuum in Burmese life, for the specifically Buddhist nature of the traditional learning process was lost in the transfer to lay schools. Lay associations, formed in the realization of such a loss, attempted to promote Buddhism to make up the difference . . .
>
> (Mendelson 1975: 161)

Colonial education and the rise of nationalism

The Young Men's Buddhist Association (YMBA) was that kind of lay organization that spoke to the popularly felt need among urban and middle-class Burmese at the time to enhance lay authority in religious matters. Perhaps indicative of a popular disenchantment with modern life-ways, the YMBA championed a modern rationalism and an educational agenda centred on Buddhist and vernacular canons. It was an urban, colonial organization that aimed to instil nationalist sentiments based on Buddhist principles through mass education and public schools. It emerged independently from its Sri Lankan namesake in Rangoon in 1906 as a religious, cultural and welfare-oriented organization that served as an umbrella structure for a variety of disparate groups (Taylor 1987: 177). The *Buddha Batha Kalyana Yuwa Athin* (Association to Care for the Wholesomeness of Buddhism), as it was known in Burmese, was explicitly modelled after modern organizational and social objectives of the Young Men's Christian Association. In particular, it aimed to imitate the YMCA's organizational form, and use of print materials to mobilize the public and mass education 'crucial to the development of a Burmese nationalist organization' (Taylor 1987: 162). It initiated an organization to mobilize nationalist sentiments across Burma, and its agenda was largely articulated around issues of education.

During its early development, the leadership of this Buddhist society was decidedly pro-colonial. Both mirroring and reacting to the secular values British colonialism had introduced, the YMBA initially adopted a civil and religious charter that championed the project to define Burmese Buddhist identity in contradistinction to the British elite. Implementing its charter to uplift Burmese society in religious, social, cultural and economic ways, the YMBA promoted four national objectives: namely to strengthen the national spirit or race (*amyo*), to uphold a national Burmese culture and literature (*batha*), and to advance Buddhism (*thathana*) and education (*pyinnya*). The last two items bear particular relevance to this discussion. Support for a national language (*batha*) resulted from the fact that 'knowledge of Burmese literature [had] almost died out among the educated Burmese classes and . . . Burmese speech tended to be confined to rural areas and the domestic sphere . . . [A]t the beginning of the twentieth century, the greatest number of Burmese students studied in Europe' (Bečka 1995: 399; Sarkisyanz 1965: 108). English had become the language of use, knowledge and instruction among the Burmese colonial elite. Burmese language and literacy were insufficiently taught, as the teaching of Burmese literacy and literature was located in monastic education. Yet, the educational and cultural decline of the *sangha* was pervasive and the declining knowledge of classical Burmese literature also entailed a decline in cultural and religious values.

A reformed, modern perspective on Buddhism (*thathana*) pervaded the YMBA's mission. To reduce the economic burden in rural areas, the YMBA petitioned the government to exempt monastic land from taxation (Maung Maung 1980: 4). They discouraged traditional Buddhist rituals associated with ostentatious spending such as funerals, weddings and novice initiations. They encouraged moral self-reform among their fellow Burmans (Bečka 1995: 40) and advocated the prohibition of intoxicants, including liquor and tobacco.

The YMBA undertook many initiatives on education (*pyinnya*) to promote a modern educational system that incorporated instruction in Burmese and in the fundamentals of Buddhism. Concerned about the pervasive influence of western education on Burmese national identity,[23] it promoted schools where Buddhism was part of the curriculum and sought government funding in parity with colonial support for Christian missionary schools (Singh 1980: 30–31). It petitioned for the appointment of a Minister of Buddhist Affairs and for instructors of Buddhism (*dhammakatika*) to teach religious fundamentals in public schools. The YMBA further wanted national schools where Burmese was the medium of instruction. It also agitated for compulsory basic education enforced by the government in rural areas and support for examinations in mathematics in rural schools (Maung Maung 1980: 5). Aware of the declining relevance of monastic education in shaping Burma's future, the YMBA pursued a religious and modern educational orientation, implicitly acknowledging its preference for modern schools that incorporated religious instruction by lay teachers over traditional monastic education. The history of this organization thus represents significant modern conjunctures of colonial and Buddhist education from which a spectrum of nationalist movements would develop.

Educating westerners: the scientific discourse about the *dhamma*

In the late nineteenth and early twentieth centuries, rational and scientific discourse was the primary lens through which orientalists and western converts gained an understanding of the Buddhist *dhamma*. In Burma, as elsewhere in the Theravada world, Buddhists engaged in the project of educating colonizers about the Universal Law (*dhamma*) and history of the dispensation (*thathana*) by using a 'scientific' discourse that appealed to western audiences. Their efforts were successful amongst two kinds of western audiences, namely colonial orientalists in the late nineteenth century and western converts to Buddhism by the mid-twentieth century. For the colonial scholar engaged in the discovery, classification and enumeration of Buddhist doctrines, texts and histories, this rationalist discourse confirmed their goal of defining the pristine origins of the tradition (Hallisey 1995). A rational system of ethics, structured by causality, held a strong appeal for western converts. Both of these projects displayed an intuitive affinity between Buddhist philosophy and western intellectual inquiry and seemed to imply an unqualified affirmation of modern rationalism in Buddhist terms.

A variety of modern Buddhist teachings may be adduced to support this contention and several modernist Buddhist organizations developed to bridge this divide.[24] In a lecture delivered in 1958, the Honorable U Chan Htoon, Judge of the Supreme Court of the Union of Burma and Secretary-General of U Nu's Buddha Sasana Council, addressed a *Conference on Religion in the Age of Science* in Star Island, New Hampshire, in the following way:

> Scientific knowledge has shown itself not only negative towards dogmatic and 'revealed' religion, but positively hostile to it . . . In the case of Buddhism, however, all the modern scientific concepts have been present from the beginning. There is no principle of science, from biological evolution to the general Theory of Relativity that runs counter to any teaching of Gotama Buddha.
>
> (Chan Htoon 1958: 29)

Similarly, U Shwe Zan Aung (1871–1932) published an essay in the *Journal of the Burmese Research Society*[25] that explored the relations between Buddhism and science. He asserted that Buddhism, while never departing from its original canonical texts, encompassed scientific discoveries, past and future, in the way a philosophy of science foreshadowed scientific discoveries. In support of his contention, Shwe Zan Aung pointed to shared comparative and analytical methods, and rules of criticism, between the two bodies of knowledge. Both encouraged the study of phenomena and both rely on observation as a method, with the Buddhist cultivation of insight as the highest form of observation. He asserted that Buddhism proclaims generalizations of the highest order, such as the theory of ceaseless flux, the theory of *kamma* and the theory of causality. Hence, Buddhism is held to have foreshadowed many modern sciences such as psychology, geography, astronomy and geology, cellular biology, chemistry, etc. His discussion likened key concepts in each scientific discipline to a corresponding Buddhist notion. Asserting that Buddhist explication proceeds sometimes allegorically, he even likened Mount Meru to the axis of the Earth and the North Pole to the desired abode of gods. He concluded that Buddhism was undogmatic and universal, and that its philosophy underlies all of science. Thus, in the Buddhist education of western converts, the Universal Truth of the *dhamma* frames the modern discourse of science, rational inquiry and secular knowledge.

Buddhism and education in post-independence politics

The tension between traditional Buddhist and modern colonial knowledge created a legacy of contestation in the Burmese struggle for national identity. The rejection of colonial knowledge in monastic education in the late nineteenth century portended lasting effects and eventually contributed to a politicization of education in the Burmese public sphere, where educational policy has been pivotal since the advent of the colonial project. Student strikes have been important junctures in the struggle for national independence in Burma.[26] State support for religious education, and especially for Buddhist education, proved to be a deciding factor in the collapse of U Nu's government in 1960.

Disputes between the *sangha* and the democratic government of U Nu over the place of the religious education for non-Buddhist Burmese nationals precipitated the military take-over in 1962, ending more than a decade of parliamentary democracy and the way to 'Burmese Buddhist socialism'. As Prime Minister of Burma from 1948 to 1962, U Nu promoted the Sixth Buddhist Convocation (1952–1958) to revitalize Buddhist institutions and practices, to lend religious legitimation to his political office, and to control the public influence of the *sangha*. However, U Nu's government was coming under increasing pressure from the *sangha* to institute Buddhism as a state religion. Following lengthy and complex negotiations, a constitutional amendment was passed to adopt Buddhism as the state religion in August 1961. As the State Religion Act defined non-Buddhists as second-class citizens, ethnic and religious minorities were alienated from the nation-building project. Negotiations between U Nu's government and the *sangha* finally collapsed over state support for non-Buddhist religious education in public schools, despite U Nu's significant support for Buddhist institutions and causes. Although U Nu accommodated *sangha* demands for Buddhist instruction as part of state-funded, public education, he failed to secure the *sangha*'s acceptance of educational rights for non-Buddhist minorities. Although the government supported Buddhist education in public schools, monastic leaders refused to accept policy provisions for non-Buddhist minorities that would have entitled them to offer religious instructions on private property with non-government funds (Smith 1965). As negotiations failed, the military usurped the political vacuum in a move that weakened not only Buddhist institution but all forms of education in Burma for the remainder of the twentieth century. Against the background of complex tensions between the government and ethnic separatists, the educational demands of the *sangha* had again emerged as pivotal forces in the project of nation-building, subject formation and modernization.

The collapse of U Nu's government ushered in decades of military rule, economic deprivation and cultural isolation. Ne Win's government and its successor regimes continued to politicize education through the strategic closure of schools and institutions of higher education, appealing to a national need to prevent or quell student unrest. Students at Rangoon University emerged as leaders in the popular uprising in 1988. The failures of educational policy and practice, and particularly of the prohibition against teaching English in public schools during the 1970s, intensified Burma's isolation during Ne Win's regime. While teaching English has been reintroduced into the public school curriculum, the present regime continues to restrict access to higher education. In the 1990s, the government augmented again the role of Buddhist monasteries in delivering basic education, especially among non-Buddhist tribal minorities.

Since then, various civil rights advocates, including the Human Right Documentation Unit of the National Coalition Government of the Union of Burma (NCGUB) and Aung San Suu Kyi have appealed to the international community to promote education at all levels in Burma, arguing that four decades of military rule have had a negative impact on quality and access to education in Burma.[27] The lack of government support for education, they argue, has disastrous effects on basic human rights, including political participation in shaping civil society and public health care. Restricted access to education, particularly to higher education, has indeed become a major hurdle in the development of modern civil society in Burma. Nonetheless, the enduring cultural value of education for many Burmese is attested by the numerous private schools in towns and cities that opened in an effort to compensate for the state's restrictions to education.

Conclusions

The cultural history of education in colonial and independent Burma is not a continuous narrative that distinguishes consistently between modernity and tradition, secularism and religion, rationalism and Buddhist cosmology. My aim in this essay has been to show that the unfolding of this history defies categorical distinctions that contrast religious values in education with modern knowledge and secular rationalism and, instead, focuses our attention on conjunctures deeply embedded in cultural contexts. Religious and nationalist concerns weave through the project of education during the colonial period and the independent nation state in complex and often fragmented episodes that link the agendas of local actors with the cultural trajectories of institutions and the concerns for the greater good of civil society. Education, it seems, is always someone's project. Our attention therefore must focus on the cultural and political contexts and audiences at specific moments, when educational values and policy emerge as pivotal agents of social change, profoundly shaping the course of Burmese colonial and national history.

I began this essay with the assertion that the Burmese encounter with modernity began as a colonial project in which knowledge and education offered pivotal access to power and wealth. Implicit in this assertion are also questions about the present conditions of modernity, Buddhism and civil society. Recent studies on Buddhism and the nation state in Sri Lanka contend that the modern nation state represents a continuation of the colonial project (Abeyesekara 2002; Scott 1999). Similar arguments can be made concerning the moral authority of the modern Burmese state that appeals to neo-traditional Buddhist ritual to legitimate a military elite in power, particularly in the absence of a national constitution. In analogy to its colonial history, the Burmese *sangha* is similarly locked into a continuing dynamic of co-optation by and resistance to modern state power. The monastic role in public education continues to be multifaceted, ranging from state-mandated meditation retreats for civil servants to the critical engagements with the needs of modern civil society socially engaged Buddhists have undertaken. There can be no doubt, then, that Buddhism in Burma, like religion in contemporary western and Middle Eastern societies, inserts itself into the public sphere in ways that challenge received understandings of modern education as a rational and secular project.

Notes

1 Taw Sein Ko (1913b: 242). See Edwards (2004b) for an insightful appraisal of Taw Sein Ko's role in brokering local and colonial knowledge.

2 See Myint-U (2001) and also Cohen (1996), Furnivall (1943), and Moscotti (1974).

3 Jan Bečka (1995: 127, 210) points out that, prior to 1886, Lower Burma referred to the southern regions under British administration, namely the Irrawaddi Delta, Pegu, the Tenerassim and Arakanese districts, while Upper Burma designated territories under the control of the Mandalay court. Following the British annexation in 1886, Upper Burma comprised the administrative division of central and northern Burma, such as Magway, Mandalay and Sagain.

4 Rives (1999: 106). Bishop Calchi, Vicar of Ava and Pegu and Bigandet's predecessor, began to compile a first Burmese dictionary that later provided Judson with the foundation for his own dictionary work.

5 Ono Toru (1981: 108) reports that a British survey taken in 1869 counted nearly

3,500 monastic schools in Lower Burma alone, with nearly 16,000 resident monks and almost 28,000 lay (male) students enrolled.

6 See Ono Toru (1981: 108–9). Sein Ko (1913b) reports some concern among the British about the restricted access and lack of quality education for Burmese girls.

7 Mendelson (1975: 367) lists Buddhist texts used for study at each of the progressive levels of monastic examination, beginning with basic *vinaya* rules and progressing to include studies of Pali grammar and selected canonical texts from each of the three baskets, including the *Abhidhamma*.

8 These Burmese texts, mentioned as part of the monastic curriculum by Sein Ko (1913b: 230), contain ethical and moral instructions on matters of lay life, law, and government. For a detailed discussion, readers may consult the compilations of *Burmese Manuscripts* by Bechert *et al.* (1979–1985).

9 Royal Orders of Burma, AD 1598–1885, Part Nine AD 1853–1885, Than Tun (ed.) Kyoto: Center for Southeast Asian Studies, Kyoto University, 1989: XX.

10 Bečka (1995: 166) states that the Maulmain (sic) Chronicle commenced publication in 1836.

11 According to Cuttriss (1960: 45, 47), the *Rangoon Chronicle* commenced publication in 1853 and was renamed the *Rangoon Times*, a bi-weekly paper, in 1858.

12 See Bečka (1995: 166). An English gloss would be 'The Mandalay Citizen', referring to the city's classical name, Yatanaboun.

13 The first book printed in Burmese, *Alphabetum Barmanum*, was a Burmese grammar published in Rome in 1776 by Bishop Percoto, a Italian missionary and recognized authority on Pali and Burmese (Rives, 1999: 109).

14 Mendelson (1975: 158) writes that in '1867–1868, only 41 monastic schools were using the new textbooks, and only 91 students nominally studying them. In 1868–1869 . . . 170 books were distributed and 82 pupils were studying them.'

15 Sir Arthur Phayre (1812–1885) resided in Burma from 1834 onwards. He was Chief Commissioner from 1862 to 1867 and headed several missions to Mandalay between 1862 and 1866.

16 See Ono Toru (1981: 108, 109). Ono Toru reports that, according to a 1869 government census, 15,980 novices and 27,793 students attended 3,438 monastic schools in Lower Burma, while 5,069 students attended village-based lay schools. Mendelson (1975: 159) reports that, in 1891, there were 2,343 monastic schools and 757 registered lay schools, whereas in 1938, the numbers had shifted to 976 monastic schools and 5,255 lay schools. The most comprehensive account is found in Furnivall (1943: 25–30). While the specific statistics differ in various sources, they concur in demonstrating a trend of decline in monastic education and a disproportionately greater growth in demand for a curriculum delivered in English.

17 *Report on Public Instruction in Burma*, 1891–1892, Resolution, pp. 9–10; Upper Burma, pp. 12; 24; 35–36; 43–44 and 48–50.

18 It is noteworthy that already in April of 1855, two 'American missionaries, Kincade and Dawson, presented King Mindon with history and arithmetic books written in Burmese', according to the *Royal Orders of Burma* (Part Nine, p. xvi). It is unclear why the instruction of arithmetic, given its general level of abstraction and potential affinity to mathematical calculations employed in astrology and related Indian forms of knowledge, should be especially objectionable to the Buddhist *sangha*.

A plausible explanation may be its application to geography and colonial land-surveying techniques. Modern conceptions of geography were in clear contradiction with traditional Buddhist cosmology. It not only formed the conceptual foundation for a Buddhist understanding of the structure of the universe, it also formed the basis for calculating astrological constellations to foretell the future.

Astrological signs also informed military formations in battle. Given such radical divergence from received ways of conceptualizing universal order, it is not surprising that Buddhist monks would object to the teaching of modern geography and drawing techniques, such as those used in land surveys.

19 Taw Sein Ko (1913b: 263–268) offers insightful minutes of a meeting in August 1911 attended by the *thathanabain* and his council, representatives of the Education Department and the Commissioner of Mandalay, Colonel Strickland, and his entourage.

20 Cohen (1996) notes the important place modern land-surveying techniques held within colonial knowledge, for they were central to the colonial project. In contrast, traditional Buddhist cosmology imagined the geographic order of the universe in entirely different terms, with Mt Meru at the centre and surrounded by gigantic walls that contained the Southern island on which human beings were thought to live. For a particularly helpful discussion of Burmese cosmological representations, see Herbert (2002).

21 See Cady, (1958: 179), where he writes concerning all of Burma: 'In 1891–1892, government-recognized monastic schools numbered 4,324 compared to 890 lay schools. The numbers were: 3,281 monastic to 1,215 lay in 1897–1898; 2,208 to 2,653 in 1910–11; 2,977 to 4,650 in 1917–1918. Lay schools were obviously taking over.'

22 Taw Sein Ko's discussion (1913b: 249–253) of cultural debates concerning appropriate demonstrations of respect for lay teachers aptly illustrates the ways in which the authority of lay teachers was initially contested.

23 This was brought on in considerable measure by the rush towards the economic benefits of a modern colonial and secular or Christian education. It was also a reaction to the malaise that characterized monastic education and its retreat to rural areas and, finally, the decline in educationed expectations and levels of performance, and resulted from the monastic refusal to integrate scientific subjects into education, particularly geography and mathematics.

24 Among them can be listed the Young Men's Buddhist Association (YMBA), the Mahasi Meditation movement, U Ba Thein's Meditation Center, the World Peace Congress, the Buddhist Peace Fellowship, the Mahabodhi Society, and others.

25 See *Journal of the Burma Research Society*, 8(2): 99–106 (1918).

26 As student strikes primarily revolve around issues of secular education, they have been largely left out of this discussion.

27 See, for instance, the *Burma Human Rights Year Book 2002–2003: Rights to Education and Health*, Human Right Documentation Unit, NCGUB (www.burmalibrary.org/show.php?cat=333).

5

RECONSTRUCTING THE CAMBODIAN POLITY

Buddhism, kingship and the quest for legitimacy

Peter Gyallay-Pap

Cambodians have since World War II endured an array of short-lived regimes unmatched by any Asian country in number and intensity.[1] The most recent attempt to start anew, with the second post-war Kingdom of Cambodia, was carried out with massive United Nations intervention in the early 1990s as Cambodia became the only Asian party-state to shed its communist mantle following similar reversals in Eastern Europe and the former Soviet Union. Comparable political reconstruction challenges were faced following the overthrow of the millenarian Khmer Rouge regime by the Vietnamese army in early 1979 (People's Republic of Kampuchea); the fall of the pro-American republican regime in 1975 (Democratic Kampuchea); a *coup d'état* followed by the deposition of the monarchy in 1970 (Khmer Republic); an authoritarian monarchy (first post-war Kingdom of Cambodia – revised version) two years after gaining independence from indirect French rule in 1953; and an interregnum of French-sponsored parliamentarism after 1945 (first post-war Kingdom of Cambodia). One could go further and mention the tumultuous changes during World War II that affected all of Southeast Asia; the strains of Cambodia's accommodation with colonial France, preceded in turn by the interregnum of King Ang Duang's rule in 1847–60, when Cambodia regained its sovereignty after centuries of unstable rule marked by internecine struggles linked to territorial encroachments by neighbouring Siam and Vietnam. Political stability has not been a hallmark of Cambodian history, modern or pre-modern, but the post-World War II attempts to establish a modern, or post-traditional, polity, as its victims especially in the 1970s bear witness, have been especially tragic.

My main task in this essay is to explore why Cambodia has not evolved into the modern, democratic nation-state that its new elites, including the young King Sihanouk, aspired to after the war. What is it about Cambodia's political culture that has impeded development towards a goal to which post-war leaders, whether of the left or right, have given and continue to give so much lip-service? For all these new regimes foundered, most on the chrysalis of political legitimacy. Delving into this seemingly elusive task, however, begs the question of how political science can gain a grasp of Cambodian political culture and its vicissitudes with the vocabulary and tools available to it. How can political science begin to make sense of the heavy cultural and historical baggage that shapes questions of politics in post-traditional Cambodia? For all post-war regimes sought, willy-nilly, to justify their existence and authority to rule through appeals, or reactions, to the cultural and political cloth of both Theravada Buddhism, here understood as a localized articulation of a wider Indian-derived religion and civilizational culture, and the people-centred kingship that has been tied to it.

An entry point we can readily identify are three constants that have run through the flux of post-Angkorian Cambodian political history, namely, the Buddhist monarchy, the Theravada *Sangha* (community of monks), and the village-based society of ethnic lowland Khmer, who to this day comprise between 80 and 85 per cent of Cambodia's population. These three elements are again embedded, after the turmoil of the 1970s and 1980s, as the official symbols – 'Nation', 'Religion', 'King' – of the modern Cambodian polity that emerged after World War II. In this essay, I use a deconstructed reading of this triune symbolism, first articulated in the mainland Theravada countries by the Sandhurst-educated Thai King Wachirawut (1910–25), where the modern western concept of nationalism was conjoined with the older indigenous symbols of kingship and *Sangha* to create a civic religion of loyalty to the nation. This nationalist discourse only entered the Cambodian vocabulary in the 1930s through a small coterie of western-educated and -influenced individuals who, in claiming to speak for the Khmer people, assumed the reigns of political power after World War II (cf. *infra*, n. 32). The point I wish to make here is that, for political scientists in particular, any discussion of political legitimacy in Cambodia that neglects to factor in these constituent elements, of which the village community/societal structure is fundamental in terms of its dependence on the existence of the other two (Kalab 1976: 155), risks being irrelevant.

Political science, legitimacy, and Cambodia

The problem of the extreme volatility of post-war Cambodian politics has as a phenomenon received scant attention among political scientists. The remarkable paucity of political science studies on Cambodia (the sub-field of international relations being a minor exception), given the social and political catastrophes that have beset the country, is due only in small part to Cambodia having been sealed for decades from independent scholarly inquiry.[2] A more cogent reason is intractability. Political scientists have as a scholarly community simply lagged behind cultural anthropologists, social and cultural historians, students of religion, and other social science scholars in developing approaches conducive to understanding non-western societies and conceptual systems on their own terms.[3] Various neo-positivist methodologies, while subject to recent challenges in several areas of social science discourse, still largely prevail in a political science as yet incapable of acknowledging them as products of the collective self-understanding and language of a western industrial bourgeoisie.

In this essay, I draw as a corrective on work done in contemporary political theory, understood here as an activity of experientially grounded inquiry, or as Sheldon Wolin once felicitously put it, of critical 'reflection grounded in experience'. Political theory as a vocation in political science, whose most radical exemplar may be Eric Voegelin (1901–1985), is not empty conjecturing or opining about how human beings organize themselves in society but is, rather, a hermeneutical or noetic 'attempt at formulating the meaning of (a society's) existence by explicating the content of a definite class of experiences (and whose) argument is not arbitrary but derives its validity from the aggregate of experiences to which it must permanently refer for empirical control' (Voegelin 1952: 64). One attribute of such inquiry is that it does not subordinate theoretical relevance to method, where disciplines are organized around certain *a priori* principles rather than the content-area being investigated. While this doesn't mean rejecting the systematic results that studies based on *a priori* epistemologies produce, one must be aware of their limitations. For political science, it means going beyond the (neo-Kantian) 'phenomenalist interpretation of politics in terms of calculative reason, rational action, contract, and consent' (Cooper 1999: 166). A more inclusive theory of politics requires 'an examination and analysis of the full breath of the realms of being in which human beings participate' (*ibid.*: 7). For example, in place of a positivist theory of the state based on an aprioristic concept stipulating juridical content, invariably in the form of western constitutionalism, a more adequate theory of the state is one whose 'systematic center is located . . . in the fundamental human experiences that give rise to the phenomenon of the state' (Voegelin 2001: 5).

As a counterpoint to phenomenalist rationality, critical political theory entails exploring and analysing the natural conditions of the human being, including experiences of non-rational modes of being and thought that are responsible for human culture. It allows for a process of critically clarifying modes of being as expressed symbolically in myth, ritual, stories, cultic actions, sacred texts, language, and the like (Cooper 1999: 167). As an ontological philosophical anthropology in the Schelerian sense (i.e. showing the human person's position in and towards the whole of being), it includes in its ambit the religious or spiritual dimensions that had been separated out from positivist social science. In this respect, concepts such a 'motivating centre', 'ordering spirit', or form or foundation are more critical to understanding political society than any isolated examination of doctrines such as sovereignty, contract theory, or, for that matter, legitimacy.[4] Moreover, such a philosophical anthropology integrates various modes of human experience rather than splitting them into such familiar dichotomies as culture and nature, mind and matter, heredity and environment, spiritual and secular, religious and political, subjective and objective (Cooper 1999: 170).[5] Central for the validity of this approach is expanding the range of evidence beyond the self-understanding of western society. Voegelin built on Weber in insisting on the importance of mastering non-western sources and acquiring a wider-ranging comparative knowledge. For how else can we appreciate France's projection of enlightened reason in the eighteenth-century context into a legitimizing source for her *mission civilisatrice* in Indo-China as amounting to the imposition of 'reason' on other people whether they were convinced of its reasonableness or not (*ibid.*: 347)?

A starting point for most discussions on legitimacy in western political discourse has been Weber's classification of three alternative claims – rational-legal authority, traditional authority, and charismatic authority – where the former ineluctably trumps the other claims on grounds that the conventionalization of social life, itself a product of the disenchantment of the world, requires the impersonal and rational procedures of a bureaucratic, territorial state (cf. Connelly 1984: 8f.). Political scientists and others have accordingly charted the progress of charismatic authority becoming routinized into traditional authority which, in turn, under the impact of western science and secularism, gives way to rational-legal authority, implicitly accepted as the most differentiated, advanced form of legitimacy (Schaar 1984: 104–105).[6] In his *New Science of Politics*, a volume of lectures devoted to the question of representation, Voegelin (1952) posits alternative classes of differentiation where the question of representation may be linked to that of legitimacy. He begins by distinguishing between elemental and existential representation. The former refers to the internal organization or formal structures of a political society, such as a written constitution, which corresponds to Weber's notion of rational-legal authority. The problem with elemental representation is its confinement to an external description of the representation of political society, avoiding if not ignoring the manifestation of human being in political institutions. Existential representation addresses this problem by dealing with the relation of the power-state to the community substance, or society. A human society here is not merely an external observable fact to be studied and treated like natural phenomena but, rather, a 'cosmion of meaning' that is illuminated from within by its own self-interpretation through which it is able to articulate itself for action in history. Such social articulations are the existentially overriding problem from which an understanding can emerge of the conditions under which representative institutions develop. We can arrive at an understanding of a society by critically clarifying the symbols, which are independent of social or political science, through which a given society interprets the meaning of its existence. A key criterion for legitimate political order is one where this social articulation is embodied in the form of a state through its institutions, irrespective of where a society may be on Weber's developmental time-line.

Voegelin does not stop here but distinguishes another level of representation. His third level of differentiation raises the notion of political society as also being a representative of something beyond itself, namely of a transcendent or cosmological truth. Until the advent of the modern secular nation-state, political societies, including those in Asia, were organized as empires that understood themselves as representatives of such truths. Cosmological representation is the self-understanding of society as the representative of a cosmic order through the mediation of a ruler king. For Southeast Asia, cultural anthropologists (e.g. Heine-Geldern, Tambiah) and historians (e.g. Coedès, Mus) were independently confirming Voegelin's more general finding that 'one uniformly finds the order of the empire interpreted as representative of cosmic order in the medium of human society. The empire is a cosmic analogue, a little world reflecting the order of (the cosmos)' (*ibid*: 54).

This imperial symbolism is not confined to political societies representing the truth of a transcendent or cosmic order. Voegelin points out that Marxist states had a similar structure, merely replacing the truth of cosmic or transcendent order with the truth of a self-willed, historically immanent order in the form of an ideological second-reality construction where nature, society, and politics are entirely de-divinized. Liberal-national symbolisms with their inherent imperial ambitions (the primacy of the impersonal market and the ethnic principle) are another if more attenuated example of an historically imagined, immanent order (cf. Anderson 1983). I raise but leave open the question of whether all immanentist political constructions lack legitimacy. Marxist-Leninist regimes, whose power emanated from the people in name only while rejecting *a priori* any authority beyond itself, certainly suffered in this regard from a legitimacy problem. More importantly, my argument in this essay is that the notion of a political society in the existential (including in the differentiated cosmological truth) sense has in the case of Cambodia not been superseded except in outward form by the elemental representation of the modern western state model adopted after 1945. To help make this case requires a digression for a political culture, the Cambodian, where the past is a more of a foundation for the present than we may choose to think.

'Allotropism' as a condition of post-traditional Cambodian politics

After some one hundred and fifty years of exposure to and, since World War II, direct elite engagement with modernity, Cambodia, along with other non-western societies in greater or lesser degrees, exists as a political society in what may be described as 'allotropic' form, that is, having a variety of new features or physical properties though essentially unchanged in form or substance.[7] Etymologically, 'allotropic' comes from the Greek *allotropos*, or form in another manner, and allotropy, a term used in chemistry, denotes a variation of physical properties without change of substance. I use the term to describe a non-western political system whose leaders have knowingly, unwittingly, or ineluctably appropriated western cultural materials as a means of legitimizing its external existence as a modern nation-state while its body politic remains more or less unchanged.

I choose the descriptor allotropic as an alternative to syncretistic, a term often used to describe Southeast Asia's belief system and social order. Syncretism refers to mixing and blending various conceptual systems on a basis of tenets that are considered common to all, an attempt at sinking differences to effect union between such systems. But the term has not been helpful in understanding Southeast Asian societies from a Southeast Asian point of view and reveals little about the social realities of a particular culture or lifeworld (*Lebenswelt*). A better tool for clarifying how indigenous, or local, cultures in Southeast Asia responded to foreign cultural materials has been Wolters' (1982) localization concept.[8] In adopting this conceptual tool for his anthropological work in Southeast Asia, Mulder (1996: 18) describes how, in the localization process, 'foreign elements have to find a local root, a native stem onto which they can be grafted. It is then through the infusion of native sap that they can blossom and fruit. If they do not interact in this way, the foreign ideas and influences may remain peripheral to the culture.' While Cambodia's political system has in fits and starts, since World War II in particular, assumed the trappings of an imported secular liberal democracy, not to mention the immanentizations of communism (also western-derived) in the 1970s and 1980s, these foreign elements, unlike the earlier Indic or even Chinese materials, have arguably yet to find a local root for a successful graft.

How, then, can political science gain at least a tentative grasp on Cambodian political culture in terms of a Cambodian self-understanding of its social and political existence?

Specialists are familiar with formulations of Indic statecraft in the classical states of Southeast Asia in general and the Angkorian empire in particular, as well as the Theravada Buddhist polities that followed on the mainland.[9] The classical political system was organized in a *mandala* form of concentric circles around an *axis mundi* represented by Mount Meru, the cosmic mountain around which sun, moon, and stars evolve, and which served as the magic centre of the empire.[10] As a rule, the royal palace occupying the centre of the realm is identified with Mount Meru, where the king, court, and government enact cosmic roles governing the four parts of the kingdom corresponding to the four cardinal points.[11] The Angkorian cosmic state was intimately bound up with the idea of divine or (more precisely) semi-divine kingship and in its dominant Brahmanic form, the so-called god-king (*devarāja*) was considered an incarnation of a god, usually Śiva, or a descendant from a god or both.[12] In the Mahayana Buddhist conception, it was the Bodhisattva *Lokeśvara*, or the 'Lord of the Universe', that inhabited the central mountain from which the empire extended to the horizons of its experience. The theory of divine incarnation or, more accurately, sanction served to justify the legitimacy of the ruler king.

Compared to the work of more than three generations of (mainly French) Indologists, less work has been done on the subsequent Theravada Buddhist conceptions of power, authority, and political rule in mainland Southeast Asia, which is of more direct interest to us. We know that much of Brahmanic cosmology was carried over and absorbed into the new faith and that Buddhist concepts were interpolated from Hindu concepts of kingship. But in a formal sense, as Theravada Buddhism supplanted the Hindu-Mahayana Buddhist belief system between the thirteenth and fifteenth centuries, it rejected the Angkorian and pre-Angkorian theory of divine sanction as justification for rule and replaced it with the doctrine of *kamma* and religious merit. As a human being who through exemplary behaviour merited the right to rule, the Theravada ruler king was seen as the best person to uphold the Buddhist teachings and law through the practice of the ten royal virtues, *dasarājadhamma*, enumerated in the Pali canon. What is less sufficiently recognized or explored in the literature is the soteriological aspect of the new faith in terms of its social and political impact. If the Hindu-Mahayana Buddhist symbolisms were court-centred and did not penetrate in palpable ways to the village level, Theravada Buddhism as a religion of the people extended the goals of the 'state' by providing for the redemption of humanity. It sought to transcend the inequality of an attenuated caste-based system by evoking the concept of a quasi-egalitarian 'community' in the symbol of the *Sangha*. It was in this sense revolutionary, arguably setting loose a social transformation in mainland Southeast Asia that added a grassroots vigour to the political structures it inherited, a vigour that, as Thion (1988: 3) claims, has extended into our time (cf. Benda 1969; Bechert 1967: 223–4; Leclère 1974 [1914]: ch. 9).[13] In the Theravada Buddhist king, birth was replaced by the virtue of the *dhamma*, the law of nature to which the ruler was also subject. The post-Angkorian king was no longer a *devarāja*, but righteous ruler, or *dhammarāja*, a moral human being who, ruling in a personal way, was considered a father to his people, assuring their happiness by respecting the Buddhist laws (Gour 1965: 23). In the eyes of the common people to whom this new faith appeared to have a particular appeal, a king who did not adhere to the *dasarājadhamma* was considered unworthy to rule and would lead his kingdom to ruin.

This political conception was not stripped of its older cosmological moorings, but derived from the mythological Buddhist and possibly pre-Aryan Indian cosmological theory of the *cakkavattin*, or the wheel-turning, world-pacifying universal monarch. The *dhamma*, or law of nature, was a universal doctrine symbolized by the sacred wheel, or *cakka*. In Buddhist cosmology, the *cakkavattin*, the legendary temporal ruler counterpart of the Buddha, was a wheel-turning cosmocrator who created the just society based on and by embodying the ten royal virtues. Pali canonical texts refer to the relationship between the Buddha and *cakkavattin* as the 'two wheels of the Dhamma' (cf. Reynolds 1972). The Theravada tradition thus constructed 'kingship in the image of the Buddha and Buddhahood in the image of the king with power as the key denominator' (Swearer 1995: 92).[14]

This source of political authority in Theravada societies derived not only from the *cakkvatti* ideal, but also very likely from the *Mahāsammata*, or 'Great Elect' principle prescribing election of a ruler king through a consensus of people calling for order in an otherwise theft-ridden (lawless) society. This principle, as put forward in the *Aggañña Sutta*, appears to postulate a Buddhist social contract theory of the origins of kingship and political society that is deserving further attention by social and political researchers (Tambiah 1976: 483; cf. Collins S. 1998: 448–451). It is plausible that the Theravada monks who came to inhabit the village-based cultures of the Southeast Asian mainland between the eleventh and fifteenth centuries adopted this contract theory in view of the importance Theravada Buddhism places on assemblies and traditions of monks electing their own abbots. These ecclesial structures may in turn have shaped political and social structures of pre-colonial Cambodia, which we know were highly decentralized and where village headmen in Cambodia, Thailand, Laos and other possibly Theravada lands were elected consensually by the people. Such elections were as a rule effected through the medium of socially prominent villagers and elders associated with the monastery (*wat*), mimicking, as it were, the election from below (and/or horizontally) of abbots in Theravada *wats*.[15] Until the French reforms, the royal capital in pre-colonial Cambodia had little more than a strong symbolic hold on the people, exercising administrative control only over an area a few days' walk from the royal palace. Although the king as judge meted out punishment, including for capital offences, 'his judicial and legislative powers were henceforth [i.e post-Angkor] far from being absolute' (Gour 1965: 25). The quasi-autonomous royal princes governing the provinces exercised more direct control over village life, responsible in most cases for collecting the ten per cent tithe of their harvests to the king and exacting corvée labour, a practice exercised with more frequency the closer one lived to the centre. While these mandarins, no more or less than the Theravada kings themselves, at times abused their authority, villagers nonetheless enjoyed relative autonomy in regulating their lives after fulfilling their obligations to their king, who, prior to France's introduction of private property in the first decades of the twentieth century, 'owned' the land they tilled.

After the fourteenth century, the new Theravada Buddhist kings modelled themselves after the *cakkavattin* as well as its first historical exemplar, Emperor Asoka, the third-century BC Mauryan ruler in India who converted to Buddhism (Gombrich 1994: 9; Tambiah 1976: 482). Asoka, repulsed by the military carnage in which he took part that led to his conversion, not only approximated the ideal of the *cakkavattin* in his just policies and benevolent rule, but also established the social and political validity of the Theravada tradition at the Third Buddhist Council held in his capital, Pataliputta, around 247 BC. He thus became the first historical ruler to found a state on Buddhist principles. In Suvannaphumi, or 'golden peninsula' as Southeast Asia was then known, some sixteen centuries later, the Buddhist *Sangha* served as the titular if not *de jure* legitimizer of political authority; in return, the king, many of whom bore Asoka, *dhammarāja*, or *paramarāja* (highest/perfected ruler) in their royal title or name,[16] was the duty-bound protector (*varman*), patron, and when necessary, purifier or reformer of the *Sangha*. A symbiotic relationship of separated but conjoined powers was thereby created between these two institutions, with which villagers' lives were intertwined. This religio-political dimension bonded the society into a single Buddhist political community 'in the sense that the consciousness of being a political collectivity (was) tied up with the possession and guardianship of the religion under the aegis of a dharma-practicing Buddhist king' (Tambiah 1982: 132).

Misuse of these Buddhist principles of rule and humane behaviour were not few or far between, due in part to weak succession laws (royal succession in Cambodia was not heredity but determined through election by a crown council) that were invitations to both royal rivals and usurpers. Equally, if not more important, the exercise of royal power in an imperfect world frequently obliged the ruler, as a warrior and judge, to commit acts of violence incompatible with the model of virtuous and ascetic life imposed on members of the *sangha*.[17] Given the tension between these two realms, monks not infrequently served as moral checks, direct or discrete, on abusive royal power. The symbiosis between the political power of the monarchy and spiritual power of the *Sangha* was attenuated by a not unhealthy tension between the two (Collins, S. 1998: 35, 415, 496).

We have thus far looked at the question of religious 'power' and political authority from the perspective of the higher, scripture-based religious traditions imported from India into the life-world of pre-modern Cambodia. We can thus far agree in this context with Steven Collins (1998: 31) of the usefulness in seeing 'both "politics" and "religion" . . . as complementary and overlapping varieties of civilizational articulation, spread in the (largely) unchanging prestige language of Pali, structuring the time-space continuum in which human life was both lived materially and construed in authoritative traditions of representation.' Both the conception of the cosmic role of kingship in Southeast Asia and Voegelin's more general view of cosmological empires are also confined to historical civilizational structures tied to the higher 'book' religions. To this must be included the 'something else' alluded to by Wolters (cf. *supra*, n.8), namely the dimension of the indigenous folk base that not only represents a pre-existing example of cosmological structures of consciousness, but also the local stem, as it were, onto which foreign materials *cum* civilizational structures are grafted. This realm, of both local (indigenous) and localized (indigenized) supernaturalism, is the world of magic forces and spirits which, while not connected with statecraft in the imperial sense, are nonetheless expressions of sacred power that to a large degree remain embedded in the consciousness of Khmer and neighboring peoples to form an important part of what we call a society's political culture. Mulder (1996: 21–24) describes the most fundamental religious practice in Southeast Asia as a relationship with power that 'is located in the nature/supernature in which human life is embedded' (p. 21). In its indigenous form, it is concerned primarily with individual potency, protective blessing, and protection from danger and misfortune. At the same time, localized supernaturalism has been grafted to this indigenous tradition through appropriation of ancient Brahmanic (Vedic) and Tantric cosmological elements.[18] Whether these cosmological structures of consciouness, local or localized, are concentrated or manifested in (Brahamanic) deities, saints, guardian spirits, the recently deceased, or potent objects, they remain a part of the human situation and everyday life that constitutes 'religion' in Cambodia and the neighbouring Theravada lands. How this manifests itself politically has been expressed in what Mulder, focusing on Thailand (Siam), ascribes to the 'Thai-ification' of religion and the 'Thai-ification' of Indic thinking about statecraft. He states that the tension between Theravada Buddhism and the so-called animistic practices in Thailand

> was resolved by appropriating those elements of the Buddhist doctrine that are compatible with animistic thinking and basic human experience. As a result, the institutional and ritual expression of Thai religion appear to be very Buddhistic indeed, but its characteristic mentality is not so much interest in their Theravada message of moral self-reliance as in auspiciousness, worldly continuity, and the manipulation of *saksit* (supernatural 'sacred') power.
>
> (*ibid.*: 5)

As a consequence, Buddha images become seats of such power and the practice of merit-making becomes what Charles Taylor (2004: 56) calls acts of 'human flourishing', the invoking or placating of divinities and powers for prosperity, health, long life, and fertility, or, inversely, protection from disease, dearth, sterility, and premature death – not to mention the invoking of propitiatory spirits to help deflect anger, hostility, or jealousy. May Ebihara (1966: 190), the first American to conduct anthropological fieldwork in Cambodia (in 1959–60), drew a similar distinction in stating that 'while Buddhism (could) explain the more transcendental questions such as one's general existence in this life and the next, the folk religion (gave) reasons for and means of coping with or warding off the more immediate and incidental, yet nonetheless pressing, problems and fortunes of one's present existence.' If the highly demanding life of the ascetic virtuosu as the paradigmatic Buddhist life was a calling for the few, respect for and/or fear of spirit world entities was 'virtually universal among the villagers . . .' (*ibid.*).

The political significance of what modern political scientists and commentators (not to mention Buddhist literalists) have described and often dismissed or ignored as local 'superstitions' is a field that remains open for further study and interpretation. Mulder (1996: 20), for one, claims that the powerful indigenous *saksit* represents the core element, or cosmic energy, that fuses and articulates 'the great traditions of Theravada Buddhism and Indic theory of state with the ordinary practice of life and the mentality that animates it'. He points to this powerful yet morally exemplary core as physically represented in the royal palace *cum* temple complex in Bangkok. In a similar vein, Tambiah (1976: 484–85) argues that Buddhist concepts such as merit and *kamma* and magical concepts of power do not exist as separate, discrete entities, but, rather, 'comprise a set or domain related according to mutuality, hierarchy, and tension. . . . . Thus instruments such as amulets and verbal formulas . . . are not necessarily seen as working in defiance of the laws of merit-demerit and of karma but within their limits and "with the grain" of merit . . .' This integration of collective cosmic rituals produced a 'theatre' state where the king was a focal point in 'the building of conspicuous public works whose utility lay at least partially in their being architectural embodiments of the collective aspirations and fantasies of heavenly grandeur . . . (thereby) providing the masses with an awe-inspiring vision of cosmic manifestation on earth as well as providing the rulers with an ideal paradigm to follow in their actions' (*ibid.*: 487).[19]

What we may draw from the above is that moral-cosmological ordering principles, made transparent through an array of beliefs, myths, and symbols through which the people ritually participated, were the in-forming signatures, or 'spiritual form', of pre-modern Cambodian political society. This home-grown conception not only did not abruptly end in 1945 but, if challenged and transformed, is still with us as a major factor in the equation of what constitutes Cambodian political culture. As things go, recent scholarship has only begun the task of an empathetic clarification of the practice of Theravada Buddhism as a complex moral-cosmological conceptual system, where a close fit exists between political rule, the (cosmological) structure of being, and the ethical norms that shape and govern behaviour (Hobart and Taylor 1986: Introduction, cf. Becker and Yenogoyan 1979: Foreword).

Representation and legitimacy in modern Cambodia

This integrated, socially embedded political universe began to fray under the weight of the ninety-year French protectorate, during which time the cultural seeds for a modern nation-state were planted by a handful of Khmers equipped with western secular educations (Népote 1979; cf. Edwards 1999, 2004a). But France's colonial presence in Cambodia as well as Laos caused, in the end, only light structural damage on the traditional culture compared to Vietnam, Cochin-China in particular, where modernizing measures were introduced with more vigor.[20] For the first forty years of the protectorate, until the end of King Norodom's reign in 1904, French reforms remained largely on paper, passively resisted by the monarchy, *Sangha*, and villagers. The separateness of existence between ruler and ruled, a feature common to traditional Southeast Asia, nonetheless belied the totality, or 'single, unified world' (Osborne 1997: 52) inhabited alike by kings, courtiers, monks, merchants, peasants, fishermen, and petty traders. The relative calm in Cambodia was interrupted only by a two-year open rebellion against centralization measures in the mid-1880s led by the provincial governor-princes. The clash of ontological versus deontological (viz., immanentist) political cultures, as described in a recent Southeast Asian social history text (Steinberg 1987: 217), which may well apply to King Norodom's reign, appeared unbridgeable inasmuch as:

> the main function of the [Theravada] ruler was to *be*, symbolizing in his person an agreed-on social order, a cultural ideal, and a state of harmony with the cosmos. The new colonial . . . governments existed primarily to *do*, providing themselves with a permanently crowded agenda of specific tasks to accomplish. They felt, by older Southeast Asian standards, a peculiar need [moral obligation] to tidy up casual and irregular old customs, to bring uniformity to the numerous small, local societies in their jurisdictions, to clear paths for economic 'progress,' to organize, reform, and control.[21]

The French accomplished more with Norodom's successors, kings Sisowath (1904–1927) and Monivong (1927–41), but not merely because they were more pliant. After World War I, having recognized the deceptive strength and relative unmalleability of the political culture, France opted to de-emphasize her assimilationist policies in favor of working more with and through the indigenous institutions representing the traditional culture. She sought in fact to strengthen these institutions as a means through which to effect reform, thus opening a fissure to allotropism. Major French reforms included the privatization of land and the establishment of a new administrative unit in the *khum* (sub-district) that expanded the colonial state's taxing authority and administrative reach to the grassroots level.[22] Among more culturally sensitive reforms was the upgrading, rather than the supplanting, of Cambodia's *wat*-based primary education system.[23] During the period, political society as represented by the two wheels of the *dhamma*, while subjected to bureaucratic-rationalization pressures, remained largely intact as most

Khmer elites evinced little interest in entering this new world. The French were obliged through World War II to depend mainly on Vietnamese to staff the middle and lower echelons of the state administration. Nonetheless, under the separate influences of the École française d'Extrême Orient and the Thommayut reform sect of Theravada Buddhism from Siam initiated by King Mongkut IV, the *Sangha* hierarchy bifurcated into modernist (*samay*) and traditionalist (*boran*) wings. The former, small though influential, gradually assumed authority with French support in urban centers (principally Phnom Penh) and became committed to purging Buddhism of its mythopoeic 'accretions' in the name of a purer, more rational and scripturally based Buddhism while also centralizing monastic administration (cf. Harris 2005: ch. 5).

The making of an allotropic political system also began to emerge with the appearance of a small liberal-nationalist movement in which some monks educated in the Higher School of Pali Studies, founded in 1922, played a not insignificant role. The main leader of this movement, Son Ngoc Thanh, was a French-trained lawyer who in the mid-1930s began to appropriate Buddhism for a budding nationalist agenda through the agency of the Buddhist Institute. The Institute was established on French initiative in 1930 as an instrument designed in part to advance a more rational, print-based form of Buddhism and in part to seal off Thai cultural-political influence in order to strengthen loyalty to French Indo-China. When Thanh was implicated in a monk-led nationalist demonstration against French rule in July 1942, his main organ, the *Nagaravatta* newspaper, was suppressed and the Institute's program curtailed. Pro-Japanese during the war, Thanh fled to Tokyo from where he helped form, with King Sihanouk, a Tokyo-backed royal government in March 1945 that sought to end French colonial rule. By August, while serving as foreign, then prime minister of this short-lived regime, he had become a republican and was again implicated, this time in an abortive insurrection against King Sihanouk. Captured and imprisoned in Saigon by the British as the French were returning to re-impose their rule in Indo-China, Thanh was to bob up and down in right-wing Cambodian politics through 1975.

If Siam's modernizing elites, more copious and prudent, were able to usher in western reforms over a period stretching several generations, Cambodia's shift from a traditional to allotropic polity was relatively abrupt and, given the turmoil that has accompanied the process, remains unsettled. Since the political upheavals of the World War II years, Cambodia remains in search of an existentially representative political system capable of mediating, if not reconciling, a problematic power structure with a conservative political society. The remainder of this essay focuses on contrasting two post-war regimes that provided at least a semblance of extended stability and peace: the *Sangkum Reastr Niyum* (People's Socialist Community) between 1955 and 1970, and the post-communist regime functioning under a restored constitutional monarchy from 1993 to the present. My main interest here lies in: a) how these allotropic polities sought (or are seeking) to strike a 'compromise between old and new conceptions' (Heine-Geldern 1956: 16), while b) addressing the underlying tension between existential representation and political authority.

Sangkum Reastr Niyum (People's Socialist Community)

While Thanh languished in a Saigon prison (until 1951), his followers were among the first of a new bourgeois elite of intellectuals who, following the restoration of French rule in 1945, embarked under French tutelage to establish a multiparty democracy in Cambodia. In a political culture that had not previously known political parties, they joined forces with the newly formed Democrat Party established by other Cambodian returnees from France led initially by Prince Sisowath Yuthevong, a returnee from more than ten years of study in France. The party's base of support consisted of younger Khmer intelligentsia assuming control of the state apparatus, the reform (*samay*) wing of the main Mohanikay Buddhist sect, and supporters of the militant nationalist Issarak movement. Its emblem was an elephant's head with three lotus flowers representing the monarchy, Buddhism, and the people, the latter now re-imagined as embodying the values of a modern nation-state. With French assistance and the endorsement of the young, equally reform-minded King Sihanouk, this new elite initiated a reform process that quickly tipped the Cambodian political balance in favor of a French-modeled parliamentary regime governed by a majority party or coalition. Following the 1946 election for a constituent Assembly, the victorious Democrat Party-led government drafted a constitution the following year that, if closely modeled on the 1946 constitution of the Fourth French Republic, attempted to blend the new and the old by preserving elements of customary law and the monarchy. The constitution was anchored in the individual rights doctrine of France's Declaration of 1789, with law itself now defined as an expression of the national will (Article 17). At the same time, Buddhism was proclaimed the religion of the State (Article 8) and Article 21 declared that 'all powers emanated from the King', a departure even from the popular sovereignty principle of the new constitutions of Laos (1947), Thailand (1949) and other Southeast Asian states. The same article stipulated, however, that the king's powers were to be 'exercised in the manner established by the present constitution', creating an ambiguous separation between essential power as embodied in the king and the exercise of those powers. The constitution, which was effectively a pact negotiated between the twenty-three-year-old king and cautiously republican-minded representatives of the Democrat Party, had the legislature become the defining power organ of the new regime (Gour 1955: 49).

The equivocal nature of the new constitutional monarchy led, ineluctably, to a political standoff between a government run by an artificial political grouping endowed with formal power but little or no legitimacy and a legitimate king vested with powers that were highly circumscribed. Parliamentary government ran into an impasse when a workable association between the republican-minded dominant party and a monarch who remained the preponderant personality in the political life of the country could not be achieved (Preschez 1961: 129). The peasant electorate came to perceive the urban-based parties as factions breaking up the unity of a political culture and system where even the concept of a legitimate opposition, central to the functioning of a parliamentary system, was absent. A former colonial official *cum* political scientist who witnessed the unfolding tragicomedy described the new political climate as 'a proliferation of parties, factionalism, usury among the elites, the paralysis of power (that) led everywhere, or nearly so, to political disorder; social, ethnic, or linguistic conflicts; and economic impotence or stagnation' (Philippe Devilliers in his preface to Preschez 1961: vii). The necessarily messy nature of democracy notwithstanding, there was, to state the obvious, little 'in Cambodia's previous experience to prepare it for the sudden introduction of an alien political system' (Osborne 1973: 45).[24]

By 1955, the king, who was reaching his political maturity and seeking to distance himself from French tutelage after having successfully negotiated Cambodia's formal independence, applied a systemic corrective. Spurred in part by delegations of villagers petitioning him to assume direct rule and in part by his undisputed popularity for having single-handedly ended colonial rule, he exercised the royal mandate by supplanting the parliamentary system. He created a form of semi-direct rule through a 'community of national union', a supra-party royalist movement to which he appended the modern word symbols 'People's Socialist Community' (*Sangkum Reastr Niyum*). Arguing the time had come for him to turn his attention from the independence struggle to the development of the country, and in view of the elections mandated by the 1954 Geneva Accords, Sihanouk abruptly abdicated in favour of his father in order to be able to carry out this mission. In entering the political fray, he declared the time had come 'to put an end to a situation in which the powers of government were concentrated in the hands of a small group of privileged, who one could in no way say represented the true interests of the people who they in fact exploited' (quoted in Preschez 1961: 58). Inured by the prevailing rhetoric of democracy, his goal was to transfer power such that the people themselves could exercise it more directly. Candidates to the national assembly would henceforth only be individuals from the countryside with at least three years of unbroken residence in a sub-district (*khum*), a requirement that proved difficult to realize. In practice, Sihanouk's rule was authoritarian (I use this term in a traditional, not pejorative sense) and highly personalized, using his new-found freedom of action to establish, unlike former monarchs, direct contacts with the people, whether in the provinces inaugurating schools and development projects or in the bi-annual direct democracy national congresses held on the sacred Men Ground adjacent to the royal palace.[25]

The organization and goals of the Community as spelled out in its statutes reveal how Sihanouk sought to re-create a traditional polity now re-mythologized by conflating it with the language of national unity, progress, the fatherland, democratic socialism, and popular sovereignty. He was able to adapt these new language symbols into restatements of the older symbiotic relationship between the people, the *Sangha*, and the personal rule of the monarch as the pinnacle of power:

> *Article 3:*
>
> [The *Sangkum*'s] organization is devoted to the formation of a cadre of volunteers constituted for common action, disinterested and with solidarity, in order to realize the Union of the children of the Khmer Fatherland (*Patrie*), a union compromised by the proliferation of Political Parties, as well as of the birth in Cambodia of a true egalitarian and Socialist Democracy, and, finally, of the return of the Fatherland to its past grandeur. The Community will seek to assure this return by giving a true sense to the Trinity: Nation-Religion-King, this Trinity (being) unable to survive and render service to the Fatherland without its state institutions returning to search for its inspiration next to the mass of the Little People and functioning under the real control, direct and permanent, of the latter, and for the purpose of their real and permanent interests. . . .
>
> *Article 4:*
>
> Our Community is the symbol of the aspirations of the Little People, who are the Real People of Cambodia, our much-loved Fatherland. . . .
>
> Our Community defends the National Unity through the return to the good traditions that shaped the grandeur of the Country in its glorious past. These traditions are the Communion of the People with their two natural Protectors: Religion and the Throne.
>
> Our Community means to promote the *Reastr Niyum* Regime that must give to the True People – to the large mass of the Little People that symbolizes the Khmer Nation – the Sovereignty, the National Powers to enable the direct, and simultaneous, exercise at the *Khum, Khèt* (provincial) and *Pratés* (national) levels in conformity with the spirit of the Constitution and the arrangements foreseen by the Project of Reforms

> bestowed and conceived for the People by *Preah Bat Samdech* NORODOM SIHANOUK.
>
> (Sihanouk 1955: 2–3; my translation from the French)

In a metaphor used on more than one occasion, Prince Sihanouk, who acquired the unique royal title of *Preah Upayuvareach* (lord prince as former king), evoked the twin pillars of the Buddhist monarchy and *Sangha* to sustain and accord legitimacy to a new progressive regime that was simultaneously an affirmation of a traditional polity:

> Cambodia may be compared to a cart supported by two wheels, one of which is the state and the other Buddhism. The former symbolizes power and the latter religious morality. The two wheels must turn at the same speed in order for the cart, i.e., Cambodia, to advance smoothly on the path of peace and progress. . . .
>
> (quoted in Zago 1975: 111)

The legitimizing principle, or glue, for the new national regime was a thinly constructed 'Buddhist socialism'. The term, socialism, was, clearly, conceived not in Marxist, social democratic, or even Maoist terms, but according to the egalitarian and democratic principles of Theravada Buddhism (Yang Sam 1987: 13f.; Bechert 1966: 183–84 and 1967: 250–58). Although both Premier U Nu in Burma and President Bandaranaike in Sri Lanka were also propagating ideas of Buddhist socialism from the mid-1950s, Sihanouk appeared to be less influenced by these latter-day *dhammarājas* than by pragmatic politics. The legitimizing role of the *Sangha*, which remained an autonomous, if weakened, institution during the *Sangkum* (Bektimirova 2003),[26] was indispensable to achieving his goals. Conjoining political and religious motives was both traditional and useful. He drew his principal rationale for Buddhist socialism from the social welfare concerns of the heralded Mahayana Buddhist King Jayavarman VII (1181–1220) and of Asoka, models both of good conduct and national development. Through much of the 1960s, Buddhist socialism served both internal and external ends, the former as a model for bringing about a just, prosperous, and peaceful society, the later as a justification for his policy of neutrality, peaceful coexistence, and the independence and territorial integrity of the country (Zago 1975: 111–12; Harris 2005: 144f.).

It would be remiss to interpret Sihanouk's appeals to tradition 'as a purely artificial device, . . . since the very frequency with which the appeals (were) made suggests a view of history in which the realty of the past is perhaps more apparent that is the case in contemporary western society' (Osborne 1966: 6). That Sihanouk's appeals to tradition were not purely instrumentalist in the machiavellian sense is suggested by his acts of piety and patronage of Buddhism. Unlike his three predecessors, he ordained as a monk for short periods in 1947 and 1963. Although no King Ang Duang in terms of closely working with and relying on the advice of the *Sangha* or an U Nu in terms of conviction, he, among other acts of patronage, founded the first Buddhist high school (*lycée*) for monks, named after his father King Suramarit, as well as the Preah Sihanouk Raj Buddhist University, which was established in 1954 before the formal opening of any secular universities. He also revived non-Buddhist rituals such as the ancient royal practice, enacted on the Men Ground, of the 'ploughing of the sacred furrow', a fertility rite symbolizing the defloration of virgin soil prior to the rainy season.[27]

Prince Sihanouk succeeded through much of the *Sangkum* period in absorbing and outmaneuvering the political parties, including through elections.[28] His efforts at building a traditional consensus while simultaneously embracing modernity, including and especially economic development, brought about more than a decade of peace, relative political stability, and economic growth. But these successes in fashioning one of the most original allotropic polities in perhaps all of Asia began, after the mid-1960s, to be overtaken by events in the region as well as events of Sihanouk's own undoing. Harem politics and dealing with political opponents in unseemly ways, while contradicting Buddhist teachings, were, however, no exceptions to the concubines and uses of violence that historically accompanied the rule of warrior-class Southeast Asian Buddhist monarchs.[29] The escalating Indo-China war emboldened both the left- and right-wing Khmer nationalists who, with their foreign backers, compromised Cambodia's neutrality and drew the country into the maelstrom of war and social upheaval.

Second Royal Government of Cambodia (1993 – present)

Within a week of his overthrow in March 1970, Prince Sihanouk appealed through broadcasts from Beijing for the Khmer people to rise up against the American-backed putchists by joining forces under a royal resistance movement with the Khmer Rouge, who at the time numbered approximately 2,000 cadres and fighters.[30] The coup and ensuing civil war, marked by a North Vietnamese invasion countered by South Vietnamese and, for a spell, American troops as the fledging republican regime itself began massive mobilization,[31] led to enormous confusion, anger, and unrest in the largely apolitical and a-nationalistic peasant society.[32] For the peasants, the absence of a sovereign ruler meant 'lack of effective communication between the celestial powers and the world of men; without him you have complete chaos' (Ponchaud 1989: 176) and many of them, in the eastern half of the country in particular, actively heeded their sovereign's call. The Khmer Rouge leaders, disguised mandarins manipulating royal symbolisms while playing into the peasants' pre-existing distrust of central government, 'were to ride the wave of this powerful rural opposition' and mould the peasantry into a fighting force that led to the 'most savage onslaught ever launched against a peasantry', in this case by the republican Lon Nol forces and its sponsors (Thion 1993: 43).[33] The scenario – a) of a 'naïve' peasantry loyal to a sovereign who was protector of their faith and the legitimate upholder of a social order in tune with cosmic order, b) manipulated by a band of French educated millenarian ideologues, c) pitted against a mechanized army of putative city dwellers (many them wearing amulets and talismans) who were d) armed, trained, and manipulated by a naïvely ignorant western power – could not be a more graphic metaphor of a political system that had lost its existential bearings. In severing all ties with kingship, the republican regime also 'lost its chance, not only to unify the country, but to gain legitimacy. even among the mass of urban dwellers' (*ibid.*: 125).

The Khmer Rouge period epitomized, homologically, what Camus expressed in his *L'Homme revolté*: that for totalitarian regimes, in their moral nihilism, mass murder became the only sign or manifestation of the sacred possible in a de-divined nature, society, and polity. In seeking to create a new world that signified a moral inversion of Buddhism, Khmer Rouge cadres claimed in their puritanism to have even surpassed the discipline of monks, who, as members of a 'parasitical' class and the greatest single obstacle to building their utopian society, were eliminated through forced disrobing and/or death by execution, starvation, and disease.[34]

Following Vietnam's overthrow of the Khmer Rouge regime in January 1979, *wat*, not state much less party, structures spontaneously re-emerged to spearhead the recovery process. *Wat* committees led by surviving elders worked informally to assume primary responsibility for the country's rehabilitation and reconstruction efforts well through the 1980s (Löschmann 1991; Yang Sam 1987: 86–87; personal communication from Yi Thon, who travelled with PRK authorities to many provinces in 1979–80). As the Vietnamese-installed People's Republic of Kampuchea (PRK) in Phnom Penh gained control of the countryside, its representatives joined and began to direct the work, and resources, of the *wat* committees. The practice of Buddhism remained tightly controlled by the party-state until the late 1980s, when the PRK, obliged to address the legitimacy problem, began to court Buddhism. Initially, the regime created holocaust monuments and sponsored Buddhist rites at killing fields to evoke a cult of the dead associated with the restoration of Buddhism. It also allowed and at times assisted local communities with materials to rebuild their razed or damaged *vihears* (sacred sanctuaries) (Keyes 1994: 66, cf. Yang Sam 1987: 79–82; Harris 2005: 190–200).

When the Vietnamese troops withdrew in 1989, triggering a peace process sponsored by the international community, the legitimacy issue became a more paramount concern. The PRK, renamed the interim State of Cambodia (SOC), was faced with the need to placate the peasantry. In de-collectivization measures short of giving up ownership of the land, the regime granted usufruct rights to people cultivating land and transformed the collective labor production solidarity groups (*krom samaki*) into more traditional mutual aid solidarity groups (Frings 1994: 51–52). Buddhism was restored as the state religion; restrictions were lifted on both monk ordinations under the age of fifty and the previously set limit of four monks per *wat*; and a detested *wat* tax was rescinded. Accompanying these legal changes, the ruling party, renamed the Cambodian Peoples Party (CPP) in anticipation of internationally supervised elections, engaged in increasingly numerous ceremonial public displays of courting Buddhism. Setting the pace in January 1989, Premier Hun Sen, in an unprecedented gesture, prostrated himself before the head monk at his native *wat* in Kampot province and used the occasion to apologize for his government's past "mistakes towards religion" (Hiebert 1989: 36).[35] A month after the signing of the Paris peace accords in October 1991, the CPP skilfully orchestrated Prince Sihanouk's (viz., the 'King's') triumphal return to Cambodia, symbolizing the end of a second civil war between a Sihanouk-led resistance coalition government backed by the West (and which held Cambodia's United Nations seat) and the Soviet and Vietnamese backed PRK/SOC regime.

In spite of a sustained campaign of pre-election intimidation and violence by supporters and agents of the SOC regime, the UN-sponsored 1993 elections resulted in a surprisingly clear-cut CPP loss to the royalist party. Some 24,000 UN troops, police, and personnel (whose presence had its own set of positive and negative social consequences) and an adroit UN radio campaign assuring voters of a secret ballot helped guarantee the freest and fairest election that Cambodia has known before or since. The UN Transitional Authority in Cambodia (UNTAC), 'which committed itself to taking complete control of a foreign state in order to create, *ex nihilo*, what amounted to a new social contract for its citizens' (Lizée 2000: 10), contented itself with the illusion of a successful exercise in multi-party liberal democracy as called for in the Paris agreements. What is perhaps closer to the truth, all but a small fraction of the voters cast ballots not for any of the two dozen contending parties than with their feet for a) peace and, not unrelated to this, b) the return to power of their savior-king. The royalist FUNCINPEC[36] party won the election not by dint being a political party preferred over others based on rational voter calculations than by virtue of a poster and ballot containing an image of the King's son, party leader Prince Norodom Ranariddh, which bore a striking resemblance to Sihanouk in his younger *Sangkum* days.[37]

During the peace negotiations and subsequent UNTAC election period, neither the international community, represented by the five permanent members of the UN Security Council, nor the four Cambodian political factions (PRK/SOC regime on the one side and an uneasy resistance coalition of royalists, Khmer Rouge, and the Khmer People's National Liberation Front led by former a prime minister, Son Sann, on the other)[38] who signed the Paris agreements envisaged a restored monarchy much less one that would return Sihanouk to the throne. Sihanouk himself thought in terms of becoming a non-royal head of state unaffiliated with a party. In the election aftermath, as if needing a reminder, a rare consensus materialized between the Cambodian players, with Son Sann as president of the constituent assembly playing a pivotal role, that 'the constitution should provide for a king' (Brown and Zasloff 1999: 199). The ensuing Constitution of thirteen chapters and 139 articles again prescribed a liberal democratic and pluralist system with a sharper separation of legislative, executive, and judicial powers (Preamble, Article 1, Article 51) and, in a departure from earlier constitutions, a strong emphasis on human rights (Chapter VI) drafted in western legalese. It bore a resemblance to both the 1947 constitution and the views of the Cambodian drafters' American (and one French) advisors (cf. Brown and Zasloff 1999: ch. 6). The powers and authority of the monarch were diminished from the 1947 constitution, with power no longer emanating from the king but the western popular sovereignty principle (Article 51); the monarch's principal role as head of state was to serve as 'a symbol of unity' and the continuity of the nation (Article 8).[39]

The constitution notwithstanding, a pseudo-*Sangkum* authoritarian regime has emerged since 1993 whose center of power lies with a self-perpetuating PRK/SOC/CPP elite that at best tolerates political parties at the margins. If the former East European and even Soviet communist parties were able to relinquish control and become one among several contending political parties, in the case of the Cambodia, the former communist party never considered relinquishing control of the state apparatus as an option. When the CPP balked at the 1993 elections results, Sihanouk brokered a face-saving coalition government run by two prime ministers, Prince Ranariddh and Hun Sen, which co-existed uneasily until 1997, when the latter ousted the former in a violent coup. The CPP has used subsequent elections to gradually seal (legitimize) its monopoly of power under the eyes of a Cambodia-fatigued international community acquiescing to strongman rule as the price of stability. This form of allotropism as an outcome should come as no surprise for a political society that abhors the insecurity of a vacuum provoked by factional politics, which is how partisanship continues to be perceived in Cambodia. The problem, however, is that in spite of external recognition/legitimacy accorded by a weary international community, the CPP-led government is beset with a lack of internal legitimacy that renders its authority to rule synthetic at best. It commands a thin veneer of elemental and, more importantly, only such existential representation as it is able to mine in instrumentalist ways from the monarchy, *Sangha*, and people.

Wary nonetheless of its legitimacy problem, the regime has since 1998, following elections whose campaign and immediate aftermath were protested in the media and streets, resumed a policy of courting, appropriating, and manipulating Buddhist and royal symbolisms while attempting to cut a populist image.[40] The official patronage of Buddhism, once a principal royal prerogative, is a widespread practice of not only the CPP, which has tended to favor wats claiming cosmo-magical powers, but also other parties and politicians. For example, Premier Hun Sen and his family have through donations rebuilt virtually the entire complex of Wat Weang Chas (old palace *wat*), a *wat* permeated with magical powers that was once part of the royal palace complex in the ancient capital of Oudong. Located some 35 kilometres northwest of Phnom Penh, it has since the 1990s has become a favoured pilgrimage site for Cambodians and foreign tourists. 'By taking over the old royal palace at Oudong, Hun Sen is defining himself as the legitimate successor of the old Khmer kings of Oudong' (Guthrie 2002: 68). His patronage of the *wat*, which includes an associated Pali school, links him to the last king to occupy Oudong, the revered Ang Duong, who initiated a notable Buddhist revival from Oudong in the mid-nineteenth century. The apparent thriving of the *wat* lends visible proof of Hun Sen's good karma, personal power, and merit.[41] The power he and other politicians seek to access through, in particular, *wats* with cosmo-magical histories is *boramei* (Pali: *pāramī*), which as a Buddhist technical term means 'mastery', 'supremacy', 'highest', or 'perfection', as in the formal royal titles adopted by many Khmer and other Theravada kings *(paramarāja)* (cf. *supra*, p. 79). The indigenous meaning of the term, however, as Guthrie (2002: 70) points out, also means 'sacred force', 'magical power', or 'energy', identical or akin to the supernatural *saksit* in Siam/Thailand (and Laos) cited above.

The return of symbolic rituals associated with cosmo-magical consciousness is not confined to modern politicians seeking to appropriate royal prerogatives. Ritual aspects of the Khmer court, together with their officiants, the Brahman court priests (*baku*), were restored with the monarchy in 1993 (de Bernon 1997). Among these include popular festivals associated with ploughing of the sacred furrow rite, revived after twenty-four years in May 1994, and the annual pirogue regatta during a water festival held in November, when current of the Tonlé Sap river reverses its flow, 'thereby symbolically liberating the waters of the Tonlé Sap and the *nagas* (serpents) whose benevolence assures the proper irrigation of the rice fields' (*ibid.* p. 52).[42] The Hun Sen regime, a majority of whose senior members reached their political maturity during the 1970s and 1980s, has been obliged to sustain the monarchy in return for the king's bestowal of 'neo-traditional legitimacy to the (ruling) Cambodian People's Party' (Kershaw 2001: 98). The manner in which the CPP has successfully courted and co-opted the royalist FUNCINPEC party since the 1998 election has solidified its image as the sole purveyor of legitimate power in a kingdom that does not lightly suffer political division. King Sihanouk, not known among his faults for having forsaken his sense of independence and unpredictability as a royal personality, nonetheless remained a thorn for an entrenched ruling élite preferring a monarch that would reign at its pleasure. In October 2004, citing health reasons, Sihanouk cleverly played his cards in forcing the government's hand by again dramatically abdicating, this time in favour of his son, Sihamoni. This manoeuvre preserved, at least in principle, the independence and symbolic power of the monarchy as an (existentially representative) institution that serves, in effect, as a people-oriented counterbalance to a discordant political class.[43]

As for the relation of the people to Buddhism, we can note that its revival, begun cautiously during the PRK regime, was a largely spontaneous village-based and -driven phenomenon through much of the 1990s. Villagers accorded priority to repairing or rebuilding their *wats* and, after 1988 in particular, ordaining their sons.[44] Not unlike instances after the early 1990s of micro-credit recipients donating their loans to their *wats* (to the exasperation of international donor agencies), recovery of their sacred integrative ground, coupled with the practice of merit making, was considered more important by villagers than material reconstruction and development needs. In spite of and in response to the upheavals of the previous decades, traditional patterns of social and religious interaction, if manifested in new ways or forms, have gradually re-emerged in post-conflict Cambodia (Aschmoneit 1996; Ledgerwood 1996; Collins, W. 1998; Ebihara 2002; Marston and Guthrie 2004).[45] These patterns have since 1989 included reconstructions of the cosmo-magical dimension of the Khmer understanding of the structure of reality. It has, for example, rekindled the debate begun in the first decades of the twentieth century between the modern (*samay*) challenge to the ancient cosmological (*boran*) tradition within Cambodian Buddhism. This has generated a tendency especially among the governing elites to seek anointment, or *boramei* power, from the *boran* tradition, however opaquely practised and understood (Marston 2002; Harris 2005: 221–224).

The revival of Buddhism has not come without unexpected costs, of which the most notable has been the politicization of the *Sangha*. The weakness and subservience of the *Sangha* hierarchy to the power structure since 1979 period has been noted. If village-based Buddhism benefited from a relatively free rein between 1989 and 1997, there is evidence since of the regime seeking to restrain the relative autonomy of Buddhism at the village level. By the mid-1990s, the traditional practice of head monks elected by the monks in individual *wats* re-emerged,[46] and the *Sangha* had begun to play an increasingly 'decisive role' in the society (Bektimirova 2003: 3). But the years since the 1997 coup have seen pressures on the *wats* to tow the political line, which has led to tensions and splits within and among *wats*. The UN's uninformed insistence in 1993 on the right of monks to vote, in spite of muted opposition voiced within the *Sangha* at the time (Harris 2005: 2004), invited a climate of partisanship *cum* factionalism among monks within a *wat* or, in the presence of strong head monks, between *wats* aligned with any of the two or three largest parties. Given the large majority of monks favoring the opposition parties (which since 1998 has increasingly become a moot point), the CPP, whose velvet glove control of society through the state apparatus extends to the village level, has exerted pressure directed not only at reigning in monks but also, and more importantly, delivering villagers' votes at election time.

Tactics have included informing villagers that a vote for an opposition party is a vote against the Buddha or, in another thinly veiled threat, that an omniscient Buddha knows for whom one's ballot is cast. Another reported form of intimidation disseminated through the *wats* were casual warnings that the country would again revert to civil war if the CPP lost the election.[47] Since 1998, the CPP has dexterously worked the electoral politics machine to its advantage, winning all elections by increasingly wide margins. It has lost only in the country's one major urban centre, Phnom Penh, representing 8 or 9 per cent of the population, where a secret ballot seemed assured by a greater sense of voter anonymity, voter sophistication, and the watchful presence of the international community and media.

Some concluding thoughts

Analysing the relationship between Cambodian society and its governing structure through the medium of the country's political culture raises old questions in a new, or different, light. Among them are: Who is to govern?; What is representative government?; and What constitutes political authority? In reviewing Clifford Geertz's *Negara: The Theatre State in Nineteenth Century Bali*, political theorist Quentin Skinner noted that the western 'inherited tradition of political analysis may now be serving to inhibit rather than clarify our understanding not merely of alien cultures but also of our own' (quoted in Wolter 1982: 97). It is outside the scope of this essay to digress on this issue beyond, briefly, picking up a thread in my introduction and making reference to the phrase 'structures of consciousness' used above. In the last mature decades of his work, Voegelin developed a theory of human consciousness wherein so-called structures of consciousness, 'concrete consciousness of concrete persons', are seen as integral parts of the structure of reality, including political reality. In his meditative essay on 'What is Political Reality?', Voegelin (2002: 341–412) maintained that concrete human beings order their existence in accordance with their consciousness, where that which is ordered is not merely their consciousness, but their entire existence in the world. 'Consciousness is the experience of participation, namely, of man's participation in the ground of being' (*ibid.*: 373). A corollary of this reality of participatory knowledge for a theory of politics requires addressing the problem of political organization on the basis of the entire existence of human beings in society (*ibid*: 398f.). The formal systems approach of modern political analysis denies in its reductionism the reality of what Victor Turner and other students of ritual have demonstrated, namely, that the sacrality of social life is what renders that life intelligible. As the mounting evidence of anthropologists, archeologists, students of comparative religion, and others enters the public domain, political analysts are invited to become familiar with aspects of culture that have been invisible to them because of their theoretical blinkers. Moreover, as things have turned out in the century since Weber, myth and religion, rendered meaningful or intelligible through participatory ritual, are not, with the exception of parts of the West (Europe in particular), dying epiphenomena of a coming secular age where political legitimacy is tied to an impersonal, rational-bureaucratic state.[48]

Already in the early 1950s, as Cambodia was achieving its independence and embarking, with other post-colonial states whose elites were trained in the metropoles, on the path of becoming a modern nation-state, Voegelin cautioned a West and the international institutions through which it acted in the world as unintentionally generating disorder 'through its sincere but naïve endeavor of curing the evils of the world by spreading representative institutions in the elemental sense to areas where the existential conditions for their functioning were not given' (Voegelin 1952: 51).[49] He stated that such 'provincialism, persistent in the face of its consequences, is in itself an interesting problem for the scientist' in so far as the 'odd policies of western democratic powers (are) symptomatic of a massive resistance to face reality, deeply rooted in the sentiments and opinion of the broad masses of our contemporary Western societies' (*ibid.*). In the context of an anthropological study on the problem of communication across diversity, Becker (1979: 1) questioned why western science approached other conceptual systems as lacking 'some essential ingredient of our own', seldom if ever using non-western conceptual systems as 'models of the way the world really is, as versions of wisdom. Or as correctives of pathologies in our own system'. Comaroff (1994: 301) confirms that religion and ritual remain crucial in the life of so-called modern nation-states in communities in Asia and elsewhere. 'They urge us', she states, 'to distrust disenchantment, to rethink the *telos* of development that still informs the models of much mainstream social science.'

If as I have sought to demonstrate above the western liberal paradigm continues to elude Cambodian culture and politics, it is not unreasonable to ask at this juncture whether it is only a question of time, patience, and persistence before a country like Cambodia can be brought, with the encouragement and assistance of an international community that continues to run on European time, reason, and logic to accept the reasonableness of this model of political organization.[50] Is there no alternative but for so-called traditional and post-traditional societies to pass through the 'fiery brook' of modernity and embrace its dominant political form, liberal democracy? If the answer remains no, we are left with the pleonast asking whether 'it is possible to establish the conditions for legitimate and sustainable national governance through a period of benevolent foreign autocracy' (Chesterman 2005: 1), whether by a single power or the international community. Henry Kamm, who pessimistically concluded that Cambodia 'is past helping itself' (1998: 251), is not alone in advocating such an unimaginative western-centric view.

If there is an alternative, one has to ask if it is possible for Cambodians to construct a modern, or post-modern, polity that does justice to its political culture, where the institutions of governance have legitimacy with the people. Heine-Geldern (1956: 16) rhetorically asked the impossible in the mid-1950s: whether there was any possibility of indigenous moral-cosmological conceptions 'becoming the basis of future constructive developments'. Practically, he called for a better 'compromise between old and new conceptions (where) the outward expressions of the old ideas could easily be kept in tact and gradually filled with new meaning without in the least impairing educational and material progress' (*ibid.*). Are there any international precedents? Among the Eastern European countries since the collapse of communism, only in Poland can we point to a Catholic *communitas* that is to a degree represented in the governing structure; as such, the country has become a thorn in a secular-liberal European Union in search of a moral compass capable of listening to its grassroots. In North America, we find a stronger example in the experience since the 1970s of tribes and first peoples rebuilding institutions of their own design, frequently bypassing the conventional treaty process established by the US government and Canada. While this exercise in genuine nation-building and indigenous governance has a common key in a return to culture and tradition, and is not as a rule accompanied by a written constitution (but reliance on the institution of a council of elders), individual native nations have been creatively dealing with the process in ways unique to them.[51] In Africa, we have the largely (non-fundamentalist) Muslim country of Mali, which divested itself of a vaguely Marxist-Leninist dictator in 1990. She has since developed a fledgling democracy whose most striking feature, apart from discretely bypassing French tutelage, 'is its success in drawing [an unchauvinistic] intellectual and spiritual sustenance from an epic past, and actively incorporating homegrown elements, such as decentralization' (Pringle 2006: 39).

These cursory examples suggest successful adaptations of the concept of allotropism I have invoked to describe the constancy of indigenous cultural underpinnings, or structures of consciousness, uneasily coexisting in more or less artificial modern state structures. In the case of Cambodia, Népote (1979: 784f.) held that a 'harmonious complementarity' between the 'indigenous-traditional' and 'foreign-modern' developed in the first half of the twentieth century under, ironically, French protection. This ostensibly healthy allotropism was broken in mid-century, he argues, as political society bifurcated into modernizing national elites entrusted with power and a powerless conservative populace buffeted and manipulated by, and ineffectually resisting, change.[52] The process that led to the two forms of post-war allotropism discussed in the essay – the *Sangkum* (1955–1970) and CPP (1993-present) periods – hints at a pattern. From 1) tumult (World War II/the anti-colonial struggle and the Khmer Rouge period) to peace in the form of 2) liberal democracy directly or indirectly imposed by an outside power, which is followed by 3) an authoritarian self-correction. The elemental representation of 2, bereft of existential representation, was bound to fail and lead to 3. In both instances, the self-corrections were motivated by the disintegrative effects of a perceived Cambodian factionalism masquerading as a multiparty system unequipped to govern based on power-sharing arrangements, including implied acceptance of the concept of legitimate opposition, while also cut off or alienated in palpable ways from the basic symbols of Cambodia's political culture.[53]

One difference from the immediate post-war period is that while multiparty democracy had a chance to unfold in the late 1940s and early 1950s before its replacement by the personal rule of the (abdicated) monarch, the same process was stopped in its tracks when the CPP balked at the 1993 elections results and refused to cede power, regaining undisputed control after the 1997 coup. A more critical difference is that in place of a perceived legitimate monarch filling the political void in 1955, a reorganized post-communist power elite lacking legitimate authority filled the same void in 1997. The legerdemain of the monarch in creating a quasi-traditional polity wrapped in modern language symbols was replaced by the legerdemain of an ex-communist strongman wrapping himself in legitimizing royal and religious symbols to create, in this case, a new type of allotropic polity: a *Sangkum* shorn of legitimacy wherein the monarchy, *Sangha*, and people have been used less to buttress national ideology or development goals than power and its perquisites for their own sake.

While criticized by his political opponents on the left and right and by western observers for having quashed liberal democracy through the personalization of power, Prince Sihanouk's version of Cambodian allotropism nonetheless passed the test of existential representation more than the marred parliamentary system it replaced and the regimes that have followed. As such, the *Sangkum* as a model is deserving of further study by a political science capable of coming to grips with the 'severe disadvantages of a political system that used western forms without the support of any political traditions that could easily accommodate themselves to the practices and institutions of the West' (Osborne 1973: 114). Such an avenue of research could map out, as in Kershaw's (2001: 6) study of monarchy in Southeast Asia, the dimensions of 'synthetic institutional asset' and 'authentic traditional values' where the latter is seen, as in this essay, both in terms of an 'authentic reality' experienced by the people and a 'doctrine' manipulated by modern elites for legitimizing purposes. I have tried to demostrate that allotropism as a conceptual tool in the context of a political theory where symbols in theory correspond to symbols of reality may be one framework through which the problem of social and political order in Cambodia can be re-examined. Such a project is likely to reveal that for an allotropism to be workable, a political regime and its institutions be authentically invested with that quality of 'givenness' that Geertz associated with primordiality (in Keyes *et al.* 1994: 5). In this context, the cultural gestalt of a so-called traditional polity may also be explored, heuristically or otherwise, by a political science concerned with the problem of western (and westernizing) societies bereft of community in the ontological sense, that is, of people participating in a system of meaning informed by principles of order whose source lies outside intramundane time. For individuals and communities will invariably continue to strive, *pace* Max Weber, to enter that magic garden where the relation between the world as it is culturally experienced and politically conceived actually coincides.

Notes

1 In revising this essay, I wish to thank Ian Harris, Peter J. Optiz, and Frank E. Reynolds for their obliging and helpful comments.

2 In a volume on 'political legitimacy in Southeast Asia' (Alagappa 1995), there was apparently no-one qualified or interested in covering Cambodia.

3 For an excellent, culturally sensitive compendium of articles on social aspects of Buddhism and religion in Cambodia, written by humanities scholars who began specializing on Cambodia in the 1990s, see Marston and Guthrie 2004.

4 In a similar vein, Geertz (2000: xii), as a critical cultural anthropologist, acknowledged a debt to Wittgenstein's notion of ' "forms of life" ' as 'the complex of natural and cultural circumstances which are presupposed in . . . any particular understanding of the world . . .'

5 Kapferer (1988) provides related insights on the usefulness of an ontological approach in his understanding of the cosmic logic of Sinhalese Buddhist myths, legends, and rites as an ontology explicating 'the fundamental principles of a being in the world and the orientation of such a being toward the horizons of its experience' (p. 79). Ontology here defined is not a 'property of the psyche independent of history', but a dynamic process 'of the constitution of form or being-in-existence' in time and space, a conception and approach that is neither essentialist or psychologistic (p. xix). I thank George Schöpflin for bringing this source to my attention, and Barry Cooper for having read the first two sections of this paper.

6 Schaar (1984: 106) maintains that contemporary social science has even 'failed to appreciate the precariousness of legitimate authority in the modern states because it is largely a product of the same phenomena it seeks to describe and therefore suffers the blindness of the eye examining itself'.

7 I define 'modernity' in generally sceptical terms, with Taylor (2004: 1), as 'that historically unprecedented amalgam of new practices and institutions (science, technology, industrial production, urbanization), of new ways of living (individualism, secularization, instrumental rationality); and new forms of malaise (alienation, meaninglessness, a sense of impending social dissolution).'

8 He demonstrated, referring to the Angkorian and pre-Angkorian eras, how the influx of Indic culture (Brahmanism, Buddhism, Indian mores and customs) retreated into local cultural statements, fitting one way or another into new contexts by the 'something else' in the local cultures responsible for the localizing process. In architecture, the classic example of how Indic foreign materials were absorbed and retreated into local cultural statements are, of course, the striking temples of Angkor Wat.

9 Those specialists are invited to skip this section of the paper (to p. 79) or correct shortcomings of my condensed interpretation.

10 Although the cosmic city in its Angkorian architectural manifestation assumed the square form, the idea of the circular form of the Hindu and Buddhist cosmologies nonetheless holds (Heine-Geldern 1956: 4, n.3).

11 In classical Cambodia, Heine-Geldern (1956: 10) points out that the temple and not royal place formed the centre of the capital, and thus the Mount Meru of city and empire. In Theravada Cambodia, the royal palace assumed this function (Népote 1990: 100–107).

12 Both Kulke (1978), an Indologist relying on epigraphic evidence, and Pou (1998), a Khmerologist using a socio-linguistic approach to epigraphy, question earlier held assumptions by Coedès (1968) and others about the divine nature of Angkorian kings. They have demonstrated that the god (Śiva) was lord of the universe/cosmos, sovereign over the king, who was lord of the earth, 'each one responsible for the sphere he managed, in a perfect macro-microcosmic system, thus standing as the main pillars of a [Hindic] *dharma*-ruled world' (Pou 1998: 2).

13 Harris (2005: 26–28) urges caution in characterizing Theravada Buddhism as a grassroots movement 'spread through a previously neglected rural environment'.

14 Collins, S. (1998: 474), while not questioning the symbiosis between the monarchy and *Sangha* implied here, questions whether the wheels of the Buddha and *cakkavattin* are parallel in that it 'misses much of the tension and competition' between the 'ideological (sic) power' of the monastic order and the 'political-military power' of the kings, whose rule was not infrequently accompanied by the use of force.

15 For a mid-1950s description of such an informal village headman election in Cambodia, see Zadrozny (1955: 310–311). For the *cakkavattin* and *Mahāsammata* as sources of 'mimetic empowerment', see Swearer (1995: 72–91).

16 See, *passim*, the *Chroniques Royales du Cambodge*, 3 vols, redacted and translaed by Mak Phoeun (1981 and 1984) and Khin Sok (1988) published by the École Française d'Extrême-Orient (Paris).

17 For the moral ambiguity of a Buddhist ruler, enjoined to 'renounce the world', to either embrace an ethic of absolute values or adopt an ethics of reciprocity, 'in which the assessment of violence is context-dependent and negotiable', see Collins, S. (1998: 419–23) and *passim*, ch.6.

18 cf. Bizot (1976: Introduction). The sources of healing power, for example, of traditional Khmer healers (*kruu*), who inhabit all villages and whose power lies outside the Buddhist *wat*, are drawn on the one hand from orthodox Buddhist doctrine and cosmology and, on the other, from older Brahmanic, Vedic (including Ayurvedic healing rituals) and Tantric influences merged into local folk customs (Eisenbruch 1992: 290, 309). Unlike western medical practice, traditional healers are not concerned solely with the patient or the patient's ailment in isolation, but with the ritual space of the community and, by extension, the three worlds of humans, deities (above), and demons (below) that constitute the cosmological structure of being: 'The *kruu* makes no distinction between what has to do with the patient and the what has to do with the society. The ritual work of the *kruu* aims at restoring the relative order and harmony of these two axes' (*ibid.*: 312, cf. 289–90).

19 In an earlier work, Tambiah (1970: 263) described the relationship of spirit cults to Buddhism as 'not simple but complex, involving opposition, complementarity, linkage, and hierarchy.' For a royal reconstruction of Buddhist, Brahmanic, and local supernatural rituals in the Khmer lunar calendar devised by the 'renaissance' King Ang Duong (1847–60), see Yang (1990: 75–81); cp. Chandler (1983).

20 Ironically, while republican France chose to retain the institutions of the monarchy and *Sangha* in Cambodia and Laos, the British imperial monarchy dealt fatal blows to the Buddhist kingships, while simultaneously endeavouring to disestablish Buddhism, in Burma and Sri Lanka.

21 The sense of quiescence suggested here is belied by what Népote (1984: 89–91) refers to as administrative and other reforms undertaken taken by Khmer rulers

from the late eighteenth century, with King Ang Eng, through the reign of King Monivong, principally in reaction to the Siamese and Vietnamese intrusions and the French occupation. These initiatives, which drew on a long pattern of earlier cultural exchanges within the region, were tantamount to a localized 'modern redefinition of Cambodian society' that served to prepare the country to deal with the modern (in the western sense) world. These dynastic reforms, including and especially those of King Ang Duang from 1847 to 1860 as well as King Norodom in the last twenty years of his reign, were enacted in the context of the old symbolisms. Mention of King Norodom's four requirements of traditional learning, Buddhist and non-Buddhist, for service in the court, as uttered upon rejecting a job applicant in 1895, is cited in Osborne (1969: 242, 345 n.1). Leclère's lengthy turn-of-the-century account of Buddhism in Cambodia (1899a), based on informal field observations and interviews among learned Buddhist informants, is couched in Buddhist and non-Buddhist cosmological, including cosmogonic, language. Regarding Khmer cosmogony, see Bizot (1980) for an explication of a Buddhist origin myth and initiation rite. For the Brahmanic influence on Khmer administrative law, see Leclère 1899b. For a lucid commentary of Indic law and its animating idea, *dharma*, as diffused in Southeast Asia, see Geertz (1973: 195–207).

22 Unlike in Vietnam (and post-1993 Cambodia), the introduction of private property into Cambodia did not lead to the creation of a rich landholding class (cf. Delvert: 1961: 488f.). Similarly, the introduction of the purely administrative *khum* did not become a frame of reference among the people that the more mythically-laden terms *phum* (village) and *srok* (country, district) retain to this day.

23 By contrast, the French succeeded in eliminating Vietnam's Confucian-based education system, especially in the southern provinces of Cochin-China, by the first decade of the twentieth century.

24 Gour (1965: 65) states that 'the political parties . . . did not represent more than a surface agitation, having no rapport whatsoever with the public opinion of the masses (who were very sensitive to insecurity). They did not reflect in anything the profound desires of the Khmer people with whom they were not in direct contact.' The savvy 1946 election strategy employed, in an instrumentalist sense, by the Democrat Party in the provinces was to recruit *achars*, influential lay elders presiding over the practical affairs of Buddhist *wats*, 'whose election represented, on the part of the electors, more a traditional social and religious reaction than a real political choice consciously favoring the program of the Democrats' (*ibid.*: n.2).

25 The term *men* is a Khmer vernacular variant of 'Meru'. The peoples' congresses held on the Ground, which was also ritually used as the royal cremation site and for ploughing the sacred furrow (cf. *infra*, n. 27), were a 'theatre' of democratic political participation.

26 In his pragmatic openness if not zeal to modernize, Sihanouk, perhaps also pressured by the new governing elite sensitive to international expectations, gradually stripped the *Sangha* of its control over primary education.

27 Through the power of his royal anointing (*apisek*) of the Ground, where he places the earth in relation with the cosmos, the king derives legitimacy in the Khmer mentality from his power to give fertility to the soil (written communication by François Ponchaud).

28 Heder (2002) claims that no election in Cambodia since 1947 had been lost by the party or power in control of the state apparatus. He states that the French, who still held the reins of administration in 1947 Cambodia, facilitated the Democrat Party's victory (p. 2). That said, there was no need for Sihanouk to rig elections held during the *Sangkum* years.

29 For accounts highlighting nefarious aspects of Sihanouk's character and rule, cf. Chandler (1991) and Osborne (1994).

30 Sihanouk maintains the relatively insignificant Khmer Rouge joined his royalist liberation movement, not *vice-versa*, before gaining the strength to co-opt it.

31 The ousted monarchy had left a force of 34,000 marginally combat ready and equipped men, about one-half the number of registered monks and novices in 1969. By mid-1972, there were 200,000 men in arms.

32 Broad-based appeals to nationalism were ineffective as this new credo did not extend beyond the small intellectual urban class. 'Chauvinistic appeals to the preservation of Khmer "race" or "blood"', while launched by Sihanouk and fully exploited in the 1970s by coup leader Lon Nol and the Khmer Rouge leadership, 'failed to transcend the educated class. The related manipulation of the image of the "hereditary foe," the Vietnamese, also failed to produce spontaneous action or commitment' (Thion 1993: 127).

33 Serge Thion, a secondary school teacher in Cambodia in the late 1960s, was a *Le Monde* correspondent 'embedded' with the Khmer Rouge in 1972, the only western observer to have visited a Khmer Rouge zone and survived before their victory in 1975.

34 For more on the Khmer Rouge 'tendency to reconfigure and reemploy Buddhist symbolism and modes of thought' (Harris 2005: 184), cf. *ibid.*: 181–89.

35 Since 1989, the number of officially registered monks increased from some 6,000–8,000 to more than 60,000 today. There were 65,000 monks and novices residing in 3,369 registered *wats* in 1969, when the population of Cambodia was approximately seven million. The current number of monks reside in just over 4,000 *wats* in a country whose population has surpassed 14 million. Although the number of monks today represents a decline relative to the population, it attests, given the circumstances, to the ongoing vibrancy of Buddhism as a force in Cambodian society.

36 A French acronym for Front Uni National pour un Cambodge Indépendent, Neutre, Pacifique et Coopératif.

37 On election day in Battambang's Maung Russey district, I witnessed inside a large, earthen floor schoolroom serving as the polling place a portly *yay* (grandmother) squinting her eyes while turning a confusing election ballot paper, utter in a clear, disarmingly perplexed voice for all to hear, '*Samdech niw ay nah*?' (where is the Lord Prince, that is, 'King' Sihanouk). That, for most Khmers, seemed to capture the election moment.

38 The Khmer Rouge withdrew from the Paris peace process in 1992 to resume its struggle until running out of steam, including and especially through defections of leaders to the government, by 1998, the year Pol Pot died.

39 Lao Mong (2002), taking issue with Sihanouk's lame responses to pleas over the years to be a more active monarch, gives the prerogatives and powers of the king in the constitution a more muscular interpretation.

40 For an account of post-election mass demonstrations, confined for the most part to Phnom Penh, led by monks and students that turned violent in August-September 1998, see Harris (2005: 216–19). Hun Sen the populist has been a regular feature in the Khmer media criticizing or haranguing the government and its corrupt ways (one source has described the regime as an 'authoritarian kleptocracy') in language that may not be entirely duplicitous.

41 In 1971, a youthful Hun Sen joined the Khmer Rouge in response to America's saturation bombing campaign, rising to the level of commander until his defection to Vietnam in 1977 and return behind Vietnamese forces in January 1979 (Kiernan 1996: 370–71). He has ruled Cambodia since the early 1980s.

42 On October 4, 2003, while watching the national television channel over steamed chicken and rice in a restaurant a few blocks from the royal palace, I witnessed in real time the king's swearing in after a long political standoff of the new national

assembly members. In a ritual known as *bhịk tịk sampath* (drinking the water of the oath), traceable to the reign of Sūryavarman I (1002 to 1050 AD), all leading politicians including the premier, Hun Sen, attired in *chaang kbeń*, a white jacket over a royal red silk kilt passed back between the legs and tied in the small of the back, one by one prostrated themselves before the king and then the two Buddhist supreme patriarchs before drinking a vial of lustral water sacralized and administered by the *baku* priests. Supreme Patriarch Tep Vong administered the loyalty oath (to the 'nation'), which the responding parliamentarians chanted in unison. (Re the water oath, cf. Hansen 2004: 45–46)

43 For years prior to this surprise move, the CPP had impeded Sihanouk's proposal for enabling legislation governing the role of the Crown Council, the organ constitutionally responsible for electing a new king within seven days of the death of the king. The CPP, it was commonly known, held a majority of the votes on the Council, including the Buddhist Mohanikay order's Supreme Patriarch (*sanghareach*), Tep Vong.

44 Bektimirova (2003) reports that while the official number of monks in the mid-1980s was set at 6,000, there were nearly twice as many non-registered, or illegal, monks – approximately 11,000 – most presumably males under the legal age limit of fifty for ordination.

45 William Collins, a cultural anthropologist who conducted field work with a team of Khmer researchers in Battambang and Siemreap provinces in 1996–97, reported on the distinction made by informants, principally those with 'high levels of Buddhist learning', between *aanaa'cak* (or *roat amnaac*), referring to 'government power', and *putthea'cak*, or 'Buddha power'. The distinction is not equivalent to the western dichotomies of church and state or even sacred and profane, but expresses, rather, a tension between 'an external force that tries to organize action and to enforce obedience to rules on the one hand, and an internal force that gives rise to conduct and promotes adherence to principles on the other hand' (1998: 19–20).

46 Personal communication from Ven. Yos Hut (2003).

47 Apart from my limited footnotes there are no documented studies beyond patchy press and oral accounts of these practices; as such, the scope and intensity of systematic political intimidation of villagers through the *wat* structure since 1997 remains plausible conjecture. While working with a dozen *wat* communities in two districts of Battambang province during 1992–93, in the run-up to the UN-sponsored elections, I saw no evidence of the government party or any political party setting up shop in a *wat*. By contrast, two days before the national commune elections in February 2002, I by chance encountered at Kandal province's Tbeng commune, some forty kilometres southeast of Phnom Penh, a not inconspicuous CPP pre-election meeting in a *wat*. Officials had assembled at least twelve local authorities (along with four district policemen, one armed) in a building marked with a large CPP banner within a *wat* compound festooned with CPP banners, bunting, and other festive decorations. Except for a small number of children, no villagers or monks were within sight.

48 If the myth of the modern state, a universal Idea that Hegel reified in end-of-history terms as the last word in political organization, has since the mid-twentieth century waned in the western consciousness, the corollary myth of a commercially grounded liberal pluralism, and its exportability, has not. In the wake of America's recent Cold War victory, history, in the otherwise thoughtful neo-Hegelian terms of Fukuyama (1992), appeared to be reaching its final synthesis, and the Idea was 'post-historical' liberal democracy, the pluralist paradigm for state building.

49 Referring to Southeast Asia, Heine-Geldern (1956: 16) stated that a) for the 'vast

mass of the common people, grown up in the old traditions, . . . the modern ideas of democracy and [elemental] representative institutions mean little or nothing,' and b), in what is now a prophetic statement for Cambodia, that 'a sudden complete break of cultural traditions has almost always proved disastrous to national and individual ethics and to the whole spirit of the peoples affected.'

50 Ponchaud (1990), a Catholic missionary in Cambodia since the 1960s equipped with a keen understanding of Khmer culture, offers an example of the below-the-radar durability, if recently shaken, of Cambodian culture. In a culture where locals ascribe to the axiom that 'to be Khmer is to be Buddhist', he is good naturedly non-plussed by the fact that, after 450 years of evangelization, the Buddhist Khmers have with very few exceptions not taken to Christianity – unlike larger or smaller segments among the Vietnamese, Malaysians, and Koreans and, much earlier and as a special case, the Tagalogs. (The jury is still out on a massive campaign since the mid-1990s by American Protestant evangelicals to Christianize the Khmers.)

51 Sovereignty, or genuine participatory self-rule, has been the starting point. According to Cornell and Kalt (1998: 205), '[t]he trick is to invent governments that are capable of operating effectively in the contemporary world, but that also match people's ideas – traditional or not – about what is appropriate and fair.'

52 It deserves to be noted, as Népote (1979: 777) does, that the calamities that beset Cambodia since mid-century did not 'emanate from social classes that were the most disfavored and/or remained closest to the traditional models (small farmers, the religious elders, holders of traditional knowledge, etc . . .), but rather those classes that were the most "evolved" . . .'

53 As part of the rapid post-World War II modernization, the modern secular education system introduced in the 1950s and 1960s led to what Népote (1979: 784) called 'the creation of an increasingly important nucleus of "detribalized" young people who no longer recognized themselves in their cultural context, their hierarchy, and their political symbolism.' These disoriented, disenchanted, and for the most part unemployed *neak cheh-dung* ('capable-informed ones') became what he called the 'social detonators' of Cambodian society and politics as, together with their younger teachers and mentors (many of them French *gauchists* doing alternative military service as teachers), they attached themselves with fervour, in many cases successively, to the rebellions that overthrew the monarchy in 1970 and the republican regime in 1975 (Osborne 1973: 72, 92; Delvert 1979: 747). Those who came of age at that time and survived are today in their political maturity, many as leaders of the regime or the thirty-eight other parties that ran in the 2003 election.

6

THE CAMBODIAN HOSPITAL FOR MONKS

John Marston[1]

It is not unusual to find academic reference to the Christian roots of such modern Western conceptions as individuality or rights, or the Weberian thesis that the historical roots of capitalism lie in the Protestant ethic. Nevertheless, one rarely finds references to links between religion and the institutions of Western modernity in actual practice. This is related to the fact, explored by Casanova (1994), that in many Western countries modernization entailed the development of a secular sphere, with religion increasingly defined as a "private" issue. Civil society, by this logic, is by its very nature secular, as is the modern nation-state. To this we may contrast Chatterjee's description (1986) of societies responding to colonialism, where there is often a pattern of finding in spirituality a source of identity which allowed them, while recognizing the power of Western science and technology, to validate their own cultures as equal to that of the colonizers. In this context the revitalization of religion, sometimes entailing its own "modern" transformation, can be very much part of a modernizing process, however ambiguous that modernization may be.

My essay here examines the project of the building of a hospital for monks in Cambodia at the moment of the country's independence. My interest in this topic, which grows out of more general research on Cambodian religious building projects, is the seeming incongruity of the combination of "traditional" and "modern" elements. It is my hope that in this juncture of the traditional and the modern we can find something significant about the post-colonial project in Cambodia.

The monks' hospital was the brainchild of a jurist named Khuon Nay, who in late 1949 established what was called in French the "Societé d'Assistance Médicale aux Religieux Bouddhique", whose main goal was the creation of the hospital. Khuon Nay had in 1946 been one of the founding members of the Democratic Party,[2] one of Cambodia's first political parties and an important political force in the years immediately prior to independence; the Party was a strong advocate of nationalism and independence, and attracted key progressive members of the French-educated Cambodia's elite of the time. Cambodia had been encouraged by the Japanese to declare its independence in March 1945; although within months Japan was defeated and the French had officially returned as a colonial authority, its position could never be quite the same. A new constitution called for a national assembly and the creation of political parties, thus authorizing the existence of the new Democratic Party. Its slogan, "Use the Elite to Serve the King and the People" (Chandler 1991: 30) perhaps captures some of the spirit that motivated the building of the hospital. It is also significant that the Party had strong links to the leadership of the Buddhist Sangha and actively drew on networks of lay Buddhist leaders. Khuon Nay played a prominent role in Cambodian politics precisely in the period of the Democratic Party's efflorescence, serving as the President of the High Council from 1948 to 1950 and president of the National Assembly from 1951 until it was dissolved by King Sihanouk in January 1953. During this period he also, at different times, headed various ministries.

As a prominent Democrat, Khuon Nay would have been close to Suramarit, the king's father and an advisor to the party. His links to the royal family were also underlined by his marriage to Princess Sisowath Soveth, the older half-sister of Sisowath Kossamak, Suramarit's wife and the king's mother.

The association in support of a monks' hospital was created precisely at the time that Khuon Nay was conspicuously a public person, while Cambodia was still a colony of France and Sihanouk was still king, a time of a flurry of political activity anticipating independence. Actual construction began in February 1953, soon after Sihanouk had dissolved parliament, and during the month Sihanouk left for France to lobby for independence. By the time the hospital was completed, in 1956, the country was independent and Sihanouk had abdicated the throne to play a more active political role, setting up a movement called the Sangkum Reastr Niyum, which quickly overshadowed and replaced all other parties, including the Democrats. Sihanouk's father Suramarit became king and the hospital was named after his queen, Preah Kossamak Hospital. Khuon Nay, by this time 65 years old, kept heading the organization that raised funds for and administered the hospital, and was still living nineteen years later, when the country fell to the Khmer Rouge.[3]

Why was the hospital built? In the text of a speech dated 25 January 1950, Khuon Nay gives three reasons. The first is the most poignant. He states that he began thinking about the hospital:

> because I have been struck with great sorrow, the sorrow of being separated from younger associates[4] and friends who I loved greatly with all my heart. Illness and death came to rob me of them, causing me to grieve and feel great anguish. I would like to be free from the whole cycle of lifetimes full of suffering.
>
> (Khuon 1950)[5]

These are ideas basic to Buddhist philosophy and ground the hospital and Khuon Nay's personal involvement in it in a deeply Buddhist perspective on life. Those hearing the speech would surely have been reminded that only eleven days earlier Ieu Koeuss, a prominent Democrat and the President of the National Assembly, had been assassinated – a death that echoed the death, in 1947, of Prince Sisowath Yuthewong, the founder of the Party, both of a generation younger than Khuon Nay. As a Cambodian political figure, Khuon Nay already had reason to be reminded of the transience of human endeavour.

The other reasons stated were also based on Buddhist teachings. He spoke of the great merit to be gained by the gift of medicine, citing the case of the *arahant* Bākula Thera living at the time of the Buddha who, because of distributing medicine in a previous lifetime, lived 160 years completely without illness; the speech was, after all, designed to remind contributors that their donations would generate great merit for themselves, and an expression of Khuon Nay's own aspirations to merit.[6] Finally, Khuon Nay stated his fear that monks and novices receiving health care in hospitals for the general public, where they were under a single roof with women, were in violation of the disciplinary rules of the *Patimokkha*.

It should be noted that it is far from clear that a monk staying in a hospital for the general public would always be in violation of the *Patimokkha*; nevertheless, a hospital exclusively for monks would have facilitated the maintenance of monkly routine and discipline during periods of hospitalization. One of the advantages of the hospital was that it included a small *preah vihear* (the central ritual building of a Cambodian monastery or *wat*) consecrated with ritual boundary stones (*sīmā*). This meant that the hospital and its grounds could function officially as a *wat*, and that monks could legitimately stay there the length of a rainy season retreat. It also meant that it could legitimately be the destination of a *kathin* ceremony, the annual ceremony whereby monks' robes and other donations are brought in procession to a *wat*.

Khuon Nay's 1950 speech, emphasizing Buddhist principles, did not bring out the aspects of the hospital which were innovative: 1) the fact that, like any modern hospital, it entailed systematization of health care on a large scale, with the assumption that this kind of systematization could and should be extended to the monkhood; 2) similarly, the fact that the hospital project implicitly affirmed that the tradition of the monkhood could and should interface with modern technologies of medicine; 3) finally, the fact that the hospital project was consciously *national* in scale. The hospital did not fall under the purview of either of the two monastic orders, the Mohanikay or the Thommayut, but involved the cooperation of both under an administrative committee with the symbolic patronage of the king. From the beginning, the project was conceived as connected to the king and the royal family, while, to the extent that it relied on contributions by the mass of the Cambodian population, it also had a populist dimension.

The very creation of a formal organization is significant in a society that had only recently begun generating social groupings which fell in the middle ground between those of the royal government and the type of local organization which served a *wat* or a village. (Although a Buddhist Association and various secular organizations were formed in the late 1930s, Cambodia never developed anything remotely comparable to the YMBA in Burma [Edwards 1999, 2004].) Khuon Nay's association was to this extent part of a movement in the direction of "civil society" – although it is significant that the organization existed "under the high patronage of the king", as well as the fact that its goals and principal activities could be compared to the more *ad hoc* community-level groups that are formed to organize *kathin* ceremonies.[7] The Societé d'Assistance Médicale aux Religieux Bouddhique was officially registered, with its rules and regulations published in both Khmer and French.

At the inauguration of the hospital, Khuon Nay stated that its cost had totalled 12 million riel. Of this 3.5 million had come from "the Cambodian people", 6.5 million had come from the government, and 2 million from foreign aid (*Kambujā Suriyā* 1956a: 390). Foreign aid included, from France, the donation of some equipment and the supply of medical personnel, but consisted in large part of the donation of medical equipment by the United States, eager to bring the newly independent country into its sphere of influence (Agence Khmer Presse 1956).

One of the earliest fundraising activities took place in October 1952, when two relics from India, one of the Buddha and one of the *arahant* Mogallana, were brought to Cambodia, paraded through Phnom Penh with great pomp and ceremony, and displayed for one week at the *preah vihear* on the grounds of the Royal Palace. At this time, "tens and hundreds of thousands" viewed the relic, and monks, ministers of the government, and the general Buddhist public made offerings totalling 1,667,300 riel. Of this, 900,000 were to go towards the monks' hospital and 200,000 were to go towards the construction of a stupa in front of the railway station designed to contain a Buddha relic (*sakyamunichediy*) (Jā Gān and Un' Sou 2000; Institute Bouddhique 2001: x, xi).

Whatever else the building of the hospital may have been, it was a very public event, if only because Khuon Nay had sufficient public profile to make it so. Early on the campaign to build the hospital was endorsed by the National Assembly. Its fundraising campaigns, the beginning of construction, and the inauguration of the hospital are recorded in Khmer and French-language newspapers and news service reports, and the latter in articles in the most prestigious journal of Cambodian culture of the time, *Kambujā Suriyā*.

As such, it coincides with a handful of other events that focused public attention on the role of Buddhism at the moment of independence: the establishment of a Buddhist University in 1954 (Sam 1987: 26); the publication of a fifty-volume Khmer translation of the Buddhist scriptures (the culmination of a project begun in 1930) (Institut Bouddhique 2001: 218), and the building of the Sakyamunichedi in front of the railway station to house a Buddha relic.

The latter two events, in particular, occurred in 1957, which in Cambodia was the year 2500 of the Buddhist calendar. Since Buddhist scriptures are popularly interpreted to say that the Buddha of the future, or the Maitreya, will arrive 5,000 years after Gautama Buddha entered nirvana, the year 2500, as the half-way mark, known as the Buddha Jayanti, was considered especially auspicious. This auspiciousness was accentuated by the fact that four Theravada Buddhist countries, including Cambodia, had recently achieved independence. Probably the momentum of the occasion initially generated the Sixth Buddhist Council in Rangoon, a two-year event which was timed to end on the occasion of the Buddha Jayanti as celebrated in Burma, in 1956. Both Sihanouk and Chuon Nath, Cambodia's most senior monk, visited Burma at the time of the Council.

There was a sense of the dawn of a new Buddhist era. One of the key books published on the occasion of the celebrations in India stated, "It is believed that this anniversary will bring about a great revival of Buddhism and universal peace throughout the world" (Bapat 1956: 53–54). Sarkisyanz quotes a prominent Burmese editor telling him, in 1952, that, ". . . there is some belief even here that the 2500th anniversary of the Mahaparinibbana of the Buddha will mark a great Revival of Buddhism and there is some feeling that the 'Golden Age' for which all men long, may dawn with this" (1965: 207). This new era was symbolized, among other things, by the fact that relics of the Buddha that had been in British possession were being returned to Buddhist countries, such as the one designated for the new Sakyamunichedi. The introduction to a book published by the Cambodian Buddhist Institute on the occasion of the 2500 BE celebrations even suggested that Sihanouk fulfilled the role of the prophesied Preah Pat Dhammik (Institut Bouddhique 2001: v).[8]

In each of the four newly independent Theravada countries, the coincidence of independence and a new Buddhist era meant the emergence of movements to involve Buddhism in social agendas (Gombrich 1988; Sarkisyanz 1965; Stuart-Fox and Bucknell 1982). This was also true in India, where Dr Ambedkar used the occasion of 2500 BE (celebrated in India in 1956) to organize the ritual conversion to Buddhism of thousands of members of the untouchable caste. Celebrations in Thailand included the release of political prisoners; Reynolds notes that "the occasion also gave progressive activists and writers an opportunity to celebrate May Day 1957 and nudge history forward" (Reynolds 1987: 34). Earlier in the year a leftist party had also been founded in Burma, named after the future Buddha Maitreya (Sarkisyanz 1965: 207).

The 2500 BE celebrations in Cambodia, focused especially on the installation of the Buddha relic in the new Sakyamunichedi, were organized on a grand scale, bringing together thousands of monks and lay people and deeply capturing the imagination of the public. Unlike other relics in Cambodia, this was not associated with a specific *wat*, but a central public place in the capital of the new nation.[9] The festivities were doubtless the most massive celebration to that date of what was being defined as the spirit of the new country, at this moment dramatically celebrated as a *Buddhist* country.[10] It is not surprising that, on the agenda for visiting Buddhist dignitaries were tours of the one-year-old monks' hospital.

The preface to a book published by the Buddhist Institute on the occasion of the 2500 BE celebrations starts with a reference to the Buddha which emphasizes his healing characteristics:

> The Buddha is a *vecchea kru* (a doctor/teacher *over* doctors) in the world. He has provided remedy: the moral philosophy which christened the humans of the world, suffering from disease of the heart and soul *(khang pleu chitt)*, the defilement of desire (*tanha*) – and provided cure, in accordance with his vocation, before entering *nirvana*. There remains only Buddhism – as a teacher instead of the actual Buddha – up until the present time.
>
> (Institut Bouddhique 2001: I)

Later in the preface there is an extended discussion of how events taking place in Cambodia, and the 2500 BE celebrations, relate to a prophetic text, the *Puttumneay*, and it is striking how this is interpreted specifically in *medical* terms.[11]

> Whoever is able to live at the halfway point of the religion and has fulfilled the injunctions of *dharma* on three points – 1) by not threatening his/her father or mother, and thus destroying the Buddha, 2) by not stealing the possessions of others, 3) by never killing or destroying life – this person will have great well-being, for there is the prophecy that, in the future, a golden mountain and a mountain of silver, crystal, bracelets of cat's eye gems, and *sourikan* will arise, and among all humans there will be no more diseases. When it is time to die, death will come at the end of one's life. Does this mean that, in the near future, this will really occur in our Cambodia? Because we have seen some of this dimly starting at the present time – namely that in our country, the two-year projects for dike construction, both general projects and those for the pier at the ocean-front in Kampong Som – all could be regarded as mountains of gold and silver for all Cambodians. One should note that all these dikes can permit Khmers to farm rice during two seasons in one year, and that the planting of crops will generate increases, and the production that will be born from the Khmer earth (*preah thorani*) will be carried by

> way of the ports of the Khmer fleet to be sold in world markets, bringing gold and silver to Cambodia to the extent of meeting the heart's desire of the Cambodian people.
>
> Not only that, Khmer health organizations have received great amounts of aid in the form of effective remedies from the health organizations of the world, in order to do away with the diseases of the people, and can relieve the disease which our nation has believed cannot be cured. We see that the truth appears little by little in sequence; one should regard it indeed as the truth.
>
> (Institut Bouddhique 2001: vi)

I have found no concrete evidence that the building of the monks' hospital was *planned* to coincide with the Buddha Jayanti, but the implications of passages like this, and the fact that Buddha relics were used to raised funds for it, is suggestive. What is clear is that, at this particular historical moment, the hospital was used as evidence that Cambodia was a Buddhist nation and a distinguished if not even auspiciously marked member of the community of Buddhist nations.

A sermon given on the one-year anniversary of the hospital emphasizes this point:

> [The association was formed] in order to build a separate hospital for monks in a way that was appropriate to the honor of a Buddhist country . . . And this hospital for Buddhist monks, precisely in the form you see here, was born out of the spirit of compassion of benefactors, both from among the monkhood and the lay community, from the entire kingdom, demonstrating that our Cambodia has a generous heart well-filled with *dhamma* in Buddhism, flowing with willingness (*satthea*) to generate the signs of *dhamma*, such that it may be seen clearly that it is no less than any other Buddhist country.
>
> (Pang Kāt' 1957: 6)

The movement to build the monks' hospital reflected a particular strand of Cambodian Buddhism. Since the 1920s, there had been a major division within the Mohanikay Order between traditionalists (the ancient or *boran* tradition) and reformists. The latter were at the time called Dhammakay, a term which emphasized the degree to which they drew on elements from the Thommayut as well as the Mohanikay tradition; at the present time, the reform movement is generally simply remembered as the "modern" or *samey* practice (Marston 2002).

The reform movement is most commonly associated with two scholar monks, Huot Tat and Chuon Nath, who rose to greater and greater prominence within the Cambodian monkhood (Edwards 2004; Hansen 2004). At the time of independence, Huot Tat was the head of the Pali school and Chuon Nath was the Mahanikay patriarch. Chuon Nath, in particular, is enshrined in Cambodian national consciousness as the icon of the great monk, an image that probably has less to do with awareness of his contributions as a scholar or a reformer than the fact that his prominence crystallized at the moment of independence. (Many *wats* at the present time which consider themselves "traditionalist", and thus theoretically in opposition to the reforms that Chuon Nath promoted, still display his picture prominently.)

One should keep in mind that many of the reforms promoted by Chuon Nath and Huot Tat now seem somewhat arbitrary, and they were important not so much because they were truly more faithful to Buddhist principles. as they claimed, or because they were inherently "modern" in any absolute sense, as because they came to *define* what at that moment was considered modern in Cambodian Buddhism. They thereby in effect demarked categories within Cambodian Buddhism, giving direction both to those who supported them and those who opposed them.

Sources of tension between traditionalists and modernists had to do with the pronunciation of chants, the details of rituals, and ways of wearing robes. More profoundly, perhaps, they had to do with modes of instruction for monks – whether that of a disciple at the feet of a master or students seated at desks in a modern classroom, and the principle of whether Pali chants should be learned by rote and recited in the original language, or, instead, there should be systematic instruction in Pali and translation into Khmer. Reformists were devoted to the principle that the textual tradition of the Buddhist scriptures should provide the basis for all practice and tended to reject texts and rituals that had no clear scriptural foundation. They believed that, by eliminating extraneous non-scriptural elements, one could arrive at a form of Buddhism consistent with modern science and technology.

The Buddhism of the reformists was also one that interfaced well with colonial administrative structures – and a locus of opposition among traditionalists was that it was associated too much with the French. We might add that the vision of Buddhism promoted by the modernists was one that could easily interface with the Buddhism of other countries, some of which were undergoing similar reforms.

The prominent public events associated with Buddhism which took place near the time of Cambodian independence were all very much projects promoted by Chuon Nath and associated with his vision of Buddhism. This is especially obvious in the case of the creation of the Buddhist University and the publication of the Khmer version of the Tripitaka. While to a Western observer, the enshrinement of a Buddha relic seems less "modern", it was also a project enthusiastically promoted by Chuon Nath and was in its own way a product of his vision: in sharing the body of the Buddha, Cambodia demonstrated that it was an integral part of the body of international Buddhism.

I see the monks' hospital as intimately associated with this strand of reformist Buddhism. Chuon Nath was one of the figures closely identified with the project from the beginning and may have been the person to originally give the idea circulation in Cambodia. In a 1950 speech he mentions having seen a hospital for monks in Laos and praised it upon returning to Cambodia. The idea of a hospital for monks suggests a vision of Buddhism consistent with science and technology and which, in more general terms, was not afraid of innovation. It also represented a vision of Buddhism operating on a national level and in a strong degree consistent with the systematization of the monkhood as an institution. It was a symbol of Cambodian Buddhism that could be represented to the larger Buddhist world, even, perhaps, something that other Buddhist countries could look to as a model. Khuon Nay's emphasis that the monks' hospital would help make the disciplinary practice of monks consistent with Buddhist scriptures is also very typical of the reformist way of looking at Buddhism, which gave stress to scriptural validity over tradition.

Pamphlets with the articles of incorporation of the Societé d'Assistance Médicale aux Religieux Bouddhiques were published in 1950 and 1954, apparently for fundraising purposes. The covers of the Khmer versions of the pamphlets had illustrations of the planned hospital. The 1950 picture, drawn before construction had actually begun, was an idealized building in a classical European style, vaguely antiquated, with its Greek columns in front of a box-like three-storey building with curtained windows; a pair of monks standing in discussion in front of the building convey an iconic, school-book quality. Perhaps the most Cambodian element of the building is a pyramid-like pointed roof rising above the box-like structure, pinnacled with a small turret.

The 1954 picture, published when the building was actually under construction (and during the year Cambodia achieved independence), resembles the final building and was probably based on the architect's drawings. The building is bigger and more self-consciously modern in design – even, perhaps, "heroically" modern. A flag now appears conspicuously on the roof of the hospital. The artist no longer thought to include pictures of monks on the grounds; the picture to that extent is less human in scale. The religious element of the hospital is instead depicted by an angel-like male deity (*devata*) in royal garb who hovers over the hospital at the pinnacle of a rainbow. From his hands fall written Khmer syllables which with difficulty can be seen to fit together in expressions of blessing: "May you have no disease, no suffering, and be happy"; "Long life, good complexion, happiness, strength . . ."[12] The sequence of the two pictures suggests that the hospital was conceived more and more in terms of a heroic modernity; even so, that modernity was consciously linked to spirituality.

On the occasion of the inauguration of the hospital, the Minister of Public Works, Meas Yang, made the very measured statement that, "This handiwork, added to many other handiworks completed since the Khmer people have achieved independence, proves clearly our value and demonstrates once again that our country has indeed entered a new era" (*Kambujā Suriyā* 1956b: 493–494).

One should not exaggerate the modernity of the building in architectural terms. It was not in the same category as what would be called the New Khmer Architecture, which flourished soon after this, and was closely associated with the work of the architect Vann Molyvann, who would combine with great sophistication a modernist aesthetic with motifs from ancient Khmer architecture; the hospital was a much more modest project.[13] What it had in common with the New Khmer Architecture was that it was an imposing new building in a heretofore undeveloped part of the city, which seemed to capture the momentum of the construction of the newly independent country.

Some of the later buildings associated with the Sihanouk period would be in the vicinity of the hospital. A 1967 article in French, quoted by Sihanouk in 1969, lists the hospital as one of the glorious buildings lining the road from the airport to the centre of town.

> The traveler, pressed for time, must think that this concentration of beautiful edifices is nothing but a façade, and that it provides an imaginary view of what is inside the wrapping paper. But that is nothing of the case, because one observes after a short time that the whole capital reflects the same concern for beauty and equilibrium.
>
> (Sihanouk 1969)

New construction near the airport since the 1980s means that the hospital is no longer easily visible from the road. But one can imagine that part of the effect of the building in the 1950s and 1960s was that of a glistening modern building situated at some distance from the road behind well-gardened grounds.

The hospital also, obliquely, demonstrates the relation between kingship and socio-political developments in the country. Sihanouk's political movement, established in 1955, was called Sangkum Reastr Niyum, which translates roughly as "Popular Socialist Community". From the beginning, Sihanouk stressed the idea of a socialism existing in interdependence with monarchy. While some might say the modernization entailed in socialism was undermined by its link to monarchy, one might also, more from the perspective of Sihanouk, say that what was being worked out was a peculiarly modern permutation of monarchy. In 1965, Sihanouk had written an editorial for the review *Kambuja* called "Our Socialist Buddhism" which would be later published as a pamphlet by the Cambodian Ministry of Information. The original article was composed a few months after Sihanouk had broken diplomatic relations with the US, and in part represented the gesture of declaring that Cambodia's path was neither that of the US or of communism, both of which he criticized at length. The editorial was also a way of recalling the Sangkum Reastr Niyum path of development up to that point and framing its accomplishments in Buddhist terms.

Much like Khuon Nay's 1950 speech, it spoke of the Buddhist recognition of the universality of human suffering and of a socialist obligation to address suffering. The "socialist" effort to resolve the problem of suffering was very much conceived in terms of the bounty and the generosity of the monarchy.

The editorial drew heavily on a book by Alexandra David Neel, who had written, using strikingly militaristic images, that "Buddhism is a school of stoic energy, of resolute perseverance and of very special courage, the aim of which is to train 'warriors' to attack suffering."[14] Sihanouk wrote that:

> Transposed to the plan of our national politics, such a doctrine makes of us 'warriors,' convinced and energetic, fighting for our national ideology, which is, in regards to internal politics, the fight against under-development, against social injustice, the raising of our people's living standard, their happiness, and their *joie de vivre* in fraternity and concord.
>
> (Sihanouk 1966: 8–9)

In the essay, Sihanouk makes scattered references to Asoka as the model of Buddhist kingship, such as when he quotes Neel that, "On the pillar which Emperor Asoka had constructed for the edification of his subjects, one reads: 'I consider the well-being of all creatures as a goal for which I should fight," and adds his own comment: "It is the goal of the Sangkum" (Sihanouk 1966: 19).

More striking, perhaps, are two other analogies. Sihanouk makes reference to the story of Prince Vessantara, the immediate previous incarnation of Gautama Buddha, who embodied the perfection of generosity to the extent that he was willing to sacrifice all his possessions and his family. The analogy hints that Sihanouk himself was a Vessantara figure (an idea which, taken to its logical extremes, would also make him a *bodhisattva*). What he actually states is that the Cambodian people have been generous to Sangkum Reastr Niyum projects because of the example of Vessantara.

> The foreigner must come to know that 80% of our schools and infirmaries and a large percentage of our other accomplishments are nothing but the generosity – I should rather say the Buddhist charity – of innumerable admirers of Vessantara.

The other analogy he draws on is the Angkorean King Jayavarman VII – a patron of Mahayana Buddhism and the ancient Cambodian monarch most associated with Buddhism in popular Cambodian consciousness. The model of Jayavarman VII – a world conqueror who, depicted iconically in meditation, was also a world-renouncer – is a theme running throughout the Sihanouk period. In addition to being Buddhist, Jayavarman VII was also the Angkorean king most massively engaged in building projects. In 1969, Sihanouk would liken the building projects completed in the Sangkum Reastr Niyum period to those of Jayavarman VII, calling Phnom Penh "the new Angkor Thom" (Sihanouk 1969). In the 1965 editorial, Sihanouk uses Jayavarman VII to explain Buddhist socialism, citing the ancient king's numerous temples and monuments, his thousands of kilometres of roads and canals, and his hundreds of *hospitals* (Sihanouk 1966: 8; emphasis mine). What I would like to emphasize is the degree to which the vision of a new and "modern" society was constructed to echo the iconography of Cambodian Buddhism.

In a provocative recent article about Cambodian kingship in relation to the icon of the leper king, Ashley Thompson (2004) argues that, since the time of Jayavarman VII (and the inscriptions know as the Hospital Edicts), kingship, by means of its association with Buddhahood and its metonymic extension to the body of the population, has been associated with healing. The physical and moral well-being of the king is intrinsically tied to the physical and moral well-being of the kingdom. The Hospital Edicts use imagery of war to describe the king's *conquest* of suffering and disease. This association between kingship and healing, she argues, extends to the reign of Sihanouk. The public emphasis in the 1950s and 1960s that the hospital projects of Jayavarman VII paralleled Sihanouk's own projects supports, to a degree, the thesis that this idea was operative in Cambodian popular consciousness and adds a dimension to the "modernity" of these projects.

The monks' hospital was completed early in the period of the Sangkum Reastr Niyum, and we cannot assume that all the ideas in the pamphlet on Buddhist socialism were fully developed at that time. The hospital project did anticipate Sihanouk's vision of socialism in the degree to which it was presented as a combination of popular will and royal patronage. Speeches at the inauguration credited to Sihanouk the fact that there were government donations to the hospital and the arrangement of foreign aid in its support. We do not know whether these speeches reflect his active involvement in the project or simply the fact that at the time the social body was so deeply associated with kingship that all public projects tended to be seen as in some sense Sihanouk's handiwork.

What we do know is that, already, at the time of the hospital dedication, speeches depicted the building of the hospital as in the tradition of Jayavarman VII. The representative of the Thommayut Order stated on the occasion, "Buddhism in our country has encountered a glorious resurgence. One can almost compare it with the glorious growth [of Buddhism] in the era of Jayavarman VII – simply because our king is a Buddhist of the highest order"[15] (*Kambujā Suriyā* 1956: 394). The representative of the Ministry of Religion cited a famous quotation of Jayavarman VII when he stated:

> The building of this hospital for monks is an indication that it was in accordance with the policies of the government headed by the prince [Sihanouk], under the sovereign authority of the king and the queen, who have continuously had the desire to eliminate illness among monks and eliminate illness among the people – because the illness of the people is the illness of the king.
>
> (*Kambujā Suriyā* 1956)[16]

One more regional hospital for monks would be built in Takeo in 1957, and an infirmary was built on the premises of a large Phnom Penh *wat*, Wat Mahamontrey, at around this time. After that, as far as I have been able to determine, the idea seems to have lost momentum. Sihanouk would not, in fact, be known for sponsoring the building of Buddhist temples or schools.[17] If we see the hospital as a *gift* to the *Sangha*, so much in the Theravada tradition of generating merit, no similar pattern would emerge. What would be more characteristic of the Sihanouk period were "gifts" to the *people*. Initially, many such projects supported with foreign aid, such as the Soviet aid towards the construction, near the monks' hospital, of the Soviet-Khmer Friendship Hospital; they later represented significant civic mobilization. The monks' hospital, and a medical school building completed the year before near what would be the site of the Sakyamunichedi, did anticipate the fact that there would be much hospital construction during the period of his political power. A US report from the late 1960s states that:

> . . . many of the new medical facilities are reported to have been built largely by popular subscription and with labor furnished by the people of the village or district. Reports of civic participation come from official sources, and there is corroborative evidence that people in urban areas have contributed substantial sums toward the building of hospitals and that villagers furnish volunteer labor in building their local infirmaries.
>
> (Munson *et al.*, 1968)

This was part of a campaign organized by Sihanouk. According to Martin (1991: 74), the project began in 1964, when Cambodia was rejecting US aid. "The state supplied iron to reinforce concrete; villagers had to supply sand and bricks and do the construction work." As she describes it, the programme was very successful in terms of the sheer numbers of buildings constructed, but had a Potemkin village quality in remoter provinces, since there was no money for medicine or furniture. She describes how communities would borrow medicine and furniture from the capital or nearby towns for the inauguration ceremonies, then ship them back. Certainly there was an element of theatre to Sihanouk's projects of "modernity". It is interesting that this theatre of hospital construction consciously cultivated parallels with the reign of Jayavarman VII.

In conversations with people in Phnom Penh at the present time, I have found a widespread belief that the monks' hospital was built under the direct sponsorship of the Queen, Sisowath Kossamak, for which it is named, even though I have found no documentary evidence of her involvement. This reflects, I believe, a tendency of popular Cambodian conception to forget institutions of civil society as such, and to conceive of projects from that period instead as part of a general royal mandate.[18] It may also reflect the fact that donations to the monkhood by high-ranking women have particular cultural resonance.

I have so far been able to find very little information about the actual running of the hospital, how it was different from other hospitals, or what impact it had on the Cambodian monkhood. One of the current administrators of the hospital says that before 1975 it primarily treated cases of tuberculosis or of complications related to tuberculosis. In addition to monks, a few lay persons received treatment in the hospital, perhaps lay ritual specialists (*achar*) closely associated with Buddhist *wats*; they were housed on the ground floor so they would be at a lower level than the monks. Khuon Nay's granddaughter recalls that his younger brother, Khuon Kim Seng, was the principal doctor. "He lived within the premises with the whole family in a wooden house built near a lotus pond".[19] (The pond circled the hospital as a sort of a moat. The house was outside the wall behind the hospital, near a small bridge connecting the hospital grounds to the outside.) There were apparently at times some foreign medical personnel working at the hospital. A French-language booklet giving the internal regulations of the hospital states of the nurses that:

> Their role is the same as that of nurses in other hospital establishments, with, however, a small difference in regards to the status of the patients. Here, in fact, it's a question of monks who are ill, toward whom it is necessary to comport oneself with great tact, patience, and consideration. In a word, it is necessary to know how to treat them with particular respect and deference, while nevertheless not neglecting discipline and internal regulations.
>
> (Hôpital des Bonzes 1956: 4)

A 1964 fundraising booklet states that the hospital received 2 million riel a year from the Cambodian government, but that this had to be supplemented by money pledged by donors on an annual or monthly basis, and fundraising through the selling of flowers and plants. Appeals for funds were regularly broadcast on holy days (*thngay sel*) on the national radio (Kaev Sāret 1964: 6–7).

In April 1975, the Khmer Rouge evacuated the population of Phnom Penh to the countryside and in the course of the Pol Pot period, practically all Cambodian monks were forced to disrobe. The monks' hospital would never again be a hospital for monks *per se*, although it was apparently used for medical purposes during the Pol Pot period and would be one of the first hospitals to be put to use after the fall of Democratic Kampuchea.

In the People's Republic of Kampuchea period, the hospital was opened again for the general public with the name April 17 Hospital. It was not until the early 1990s that it would again be called Preah Kossamak Hospital. Around this time one of the most senior Cambodian monks, Ven. Oum Sum, once closely associated with Chuon Nath, made two separate attempts to set up hospital units for monks, both doomed to close after short period of time. When he travelled to the US with Mohanikay patriarch Tep Vong, money donated to them was earmarked for two projects, one of these a building for monks at the Calmette Hospital.[20] This building was constructed later that year, but soon diverted by the hospital to other uses, although a sign still identifies it as the monks' unit, and a plaque acknowledges the contributions of Cambodian-Americans.[21] Ven. Oum Sum later, in 1994, organized the construction of a small hospital/infirmary on the grounds of his own *wat*, Wat Mahamontrey, under the authority of municipal health authorities. Municipal health staff proved reluctant to work at the unremunerative hospital for monks, and this also fell by the wayside, with the building converted to a monks' residence at the time of Ven. Oum Sum's death. These incidents perhaps demonstrate that a hospital for monks, originally so much associated with new-found independence and the project of modernity, cannot capture public imagination and support in the way it could before the war.

The most vivid reminder of Preah Kossamak Hospital's past is a miniature *preah vihear* that still stands on the grounds, a stone building with Angkorean-style decorations built on an elevated platform of land. After a period of use as warehouse in the 1980s, it was returned to its original religious use. When I visited it in the summer of 2003, it was being used by a small group of female and male lay ascetics, six *doun chi* and four *ta chi*. They said they resided in the vicinity of the *wat* and had for the past four years been coming here to do meditation during the rainy season. Every other day they receive instruction by a monk from a *wat* associated with Ven. Sam Bunthoeurn, a charismatic meditation teacher who was assassinated the previous year under circumstances that remain unclear. A portrait of Queen Kossamak is situated conspicuously in conjunction with the principle shrine to the Buddha, and the lay ascetics tell me that she was the principal donor of the hospital. I was struck by the great beauty of the small temple and the calm sense of spirituality it evoked in relation to the hospital grounds, the larger hospital building, and the small group of women and men in retreat. Later I learned that, among patients in the hospital, it is still believed to have great healing power.

Conclusions

The significance of the monks' hospital lies in the fact that it is so quintessentially a product of the period of Cambodia's independence and the way the project of modernity was conceived at that time. What I would want to emphasize is the degree to which that project of modernity was imbued with references to what might sometimes be called Cambodia's "pre-modern" culture: to kingship and Buddhism and the mobilization of personal networks. Insofar as we can generalize about Cambodian religious building projects, we can see that some of the same concerns that inform neo-traditional religious movements I have written about elsewhere also inform state-sanctioned projects very much labelled as "modern".

These issues have wider relevance in that they parallel processes that were taking place in other Theravada Buddhist countries at the same time, especially insofar as countries newly emerging from colonialism were redefining themselves as Buddhist countries, and in different ways making the attempt to adopt types of reformed Buddhism consistent with specific visions of modernity. My research suggests that these issues were more salient in Cambodia than is acknowledged in the standard histories of the period. In particular, I see the Buddha Jayanti festivities in Cambodia, with their parallels with what was happening in other Buddhist countries, as much more significant than has generally been recognized.

Notes

1 Research for this essay was supported by a grant from the Center for Khmer Studies with funding from the Luce Foundation. My thanks to Michele Thompson for encouraging me to pursue this topic.
2 Personal communication, Julio Jeldres, 6 Feb. 2004.
3 Personal communication, Dina Nay, 10 Feb. 2004.
4 The word used here, *koun chau*, literally "children and grandchildren", could refer either to offspring or those serving under him.
5 Unless otherwise indicated, translations are mine.
6 One reference to the long life of Bākula Thera is the *Bākula Sutta* (M. iii. 125). See Malalasekera (1983: 261–2).
7 Edwards (1999) indicates that many of the associations formed in Cambodia in the 1930s had fundraising goals. She suggests that in addition to the fundraising activities of Cambodian *wats*, these organizations may have drawn on the model of Chinese self-help and fundraising associations, which probably existed in Cambodia since the late nineteenth century. Some Chinese fundraising was for hospitals.
8 The prophecies of the coming of a dhammically powerful king, who will usher in an era of millennial greatness, should be considered as separate from prophecies

of the coming of the Maitreya, although in practice the two concepts sometimes blur, with the implication that Preah Pat Dhammik will lead the way to the coming of the Maitreya.

9 The relic was in 2003 moved to a huge newly constructed stupa at the old capital of Oudong. Various reasons are given for the transfer to a new location. The general consensus was that the site in front of the railway station was not auspicious, perhaps because of prostitution in the vicinity, and that this may have affected Cambodia's history since independence.

10 The celebrations were in May. Osborne (1994: 105) and Chandler (1991: 91–2) describe how in July 1957 Sihanouk resigned as prime minister and went into a retreat for two weeks at a wat on Phnom Kulen, assuming a white robe and a shaved head and announcing his permanent withdrawal from public life. While Osborne attributes this to Sihanouk's "physical and emotional exhaustion", and both authors see the immediate precedent to this as political wrangling within the National Assembly, the conjunction with the Buddha Jayanti is probably more significant than they acknowledge.

11 Scholarly work on the *Puttumneay* has been done by Smith (1989) and de Bernon (1994, 1998).

12 My thanks to Sath Sakkarak for helping decipher the messages in the shower of syllables.

13 Personal communication, Helen Grant Ross, 14 Feb. 2004. One source for information on Vann Molyvann is Reyum (2001).

14 Ian Harris (personal communication, 22 Jan. 2005) suggests that David Neel may have been influenced by the vitalistic ideas of Julius Evola.

15 This refers to King Suramarit.

16 The actual quotation in the Hospital Edicts, as given by Thompson (2004: 97) is: "The illness of the body of the people was for him the illness of the soul – and that much more painful: for it is the suffering of the kingdom which makes the suffering of kings, and not their own suffering."

17 Personal communication, Helen Grant Ross, 14 Feb. 2004. Nevertheless, it is clear that he participated frequently in their ritual dedication.

18 The idea that Queen Kossamak sponsored the building of the hospital is also stated in Sam (1987: 9).

19 Personal communication, Dina Nay, 9 Feb. 2004.

20 Because of the US trade embargo at the time, the funds had to be sent to Cambodia via an NGO, the American Friends Service Committee, which was licensed by the State Department for humanitarian activities in Cambodia. I accompanied the two monks during the Washington State segment of their visit and visited the site of the hospital building under construction later that year. Details of the financial arrangements were clarified for me in personal communication by Susan Hammand of US-Indochina Reconciliation Project (12 Jan. 2004) and Dave Elder of American Friends Service Committee (22 Jan. 2004).

21 Guthrie (2002: 63–4), drawing on field research by Sek Sisokhom, makes reference to the monks' hospital project at Calmette. Although the total picture remains far from clear, her data do give some indication that the decision to use the building for patients other than monks generated controversy at the time.

7

BUDDHISM, POWER AND POLITICAL ORDER IN PRE-TWENTIETH CENTURY LAOS*

Volker Grabowsky

The history of Lao Buddhism is a subject that still awaits greater scholarly attention. Though Buddhist rites and practices in contemporary Laos have been analysed from a historical perspective by Archaimbault and from a social-anthropological aspect by scholars like Archaimbault (1980), Condominas (1998), and Zago (1972), we lack a comprehensive study of the diffusion of Theravada Buddhism in Laos and of its relationship with the pre-colonial political order. However, as an historian not specialised in Buddhist studies I would like to touch upon three problems that I consider crucial to the understanding of the political role of Buddhism in pre-twentieth century Laos. First, when and how did Buddhism become the dominant religion in Lao society? Second, how did Buddhism influence Lao conceptions of kingship? This question is directly related to the interrelation between the political and religious orders in pre-colonial Laos. Third, to what extent did Buddhist monks help legitimise and strengthen political institutions?

First of all, I have to define the geographical and cultural scope of what we call 'pre-colonial Laos' since the 'geo-body' of modern Laos is doubtless the product of a political discourse which dates back to the late nineteenth century when the colonial power of France encountered Siam. When defining 'pre-colonial Laos' as the region under the political control and/or cultural influence of the Lao kingdom of Lan Sang (1353–1707/13) and her successor states, we have to be aware that the borders of Lan Sang had been subjected to constant changes over the centuries and were not conceptualised in any modern sense. Moreover, large areas in present-day northern Laos did not belong to the kingdom of Lan Sang but had been under the influence of other Tai polities (such as those of the Tai Lü and the Tai Yuan) and of their respective religious traditions. On the other side, the bulk of the Khorat Plateau, which is the nowadays northeastern Thailand, was an integral part of Lan Sang. It is this region, instead of the Lao People's Democratic Republic, where four fifths of the Lao speaking people are living today.

Diffusion of Buddhism in Laos

According to a standard view shared by most scholars of Lao history, Theravada Buddhism came to the Lao lands, quite lately, in several waves: The first wave started shortly after the founding of the Lan Sang kingdom by Fa Ngum (r. 1353–1373/74), an exiled prince from Müang Sua (Luang Prabang), who unified the politically fragmented Lao-inhabited areas of the middle Mekong valley with the military support of his father-in-law, the ruler of Angkor (Phanya Nakhòn Luang). At the request of his daughter, the Khmer king sent a religious mission to Luang Prabang to help Buddhism take root in Lan Sang. This mission brought monks from Cambodia and Sri Lanka along with a complete collection of Pali texts, including the Tipitaka, and two sacred Buddha images to the Lao capital. Thus Buddhism first entered Laos from the South and strengthened Khmer influence on Lao culture. A second wave of Buddhism reached Lan Sang from the North in the mid-fifteenth century. Following a period of political turmoil, which lasted more than one decade, King Vangbuli (r. 1442–1479/80) forged close religious and political ties with his western neighbour Lan Na, which at that time had developed into a major centre of Buddhist learning in Southeast Asia, under King Tilok (r. 1441/2–1487). The 'Lan Na school' of Buddhism was reinforced during Phothisarat's reign (1520–1547/48). Phothisarat who married a princess from Chiang Mai sent a mission to Lan Na in 1523 to bring back copies of the entire Buddhist canon, other religious texts, and to invite learned monks to gather at a great monastic council in Luang Prabang. This event marked the third wave of disseminating Buddhism, which resulted in a deep and penetrating embodiment of Buddhism in Lao society. How accurate is this standard view in the light of the historical evidence?

1 The only evidence suggesting a southern origin of Lao Buddhism is the *Nithan Khun Bulom* (NKB), 'The Legend of Khun Bulom', the earliest version of which dates back to the reign of King Visun (r. 1501–1520), i.e. the early sixteenth century. It says that the two senior monks dispatched by the Khmer king, Phra Pasaman and Phra Maha Thera Cao Thep Laṅkā, founded close to the southern section of the ancient city wall of Luang Prabang two monasteries, which were named after their respective founders. Both monasteries are now deserted and no archaeological evidence has been discovered to support the assertion that Buddhism was spread to Luang Prabang via Cambodia in the mid-fourteenth century. In a recent paper Michel Lorrillard, representative of the École française d'Extrême-Orient at Vientiane, stresses the 'completely artificial nature' of the narration in NKB referring to the religious mission sent by the Khmer king in 1359 as it

establishes 'links with various similar literary traditions' found in the Tai-Lao world.[1] Shrinking back from totally refuting the NKB narrative as mere fiction, Lorrillard (2003: 9) proposes that it might rather reflect the collective memory of a pre-Lao past of early forms of Buddhism that had flourished in the middle Mekong valley generations before the arrival of the first Lao immigrants. Closer attention deserves an idea raised first by Tatsuo Hoshino (1986) and later elaborated by Amphay Doré (1987). Hoshino argues that three or four different accounts about the spread of Buddhism in Laos were mixed up in NKB (Hoshino 1986:147). Whereas Fa Ngum and his Khmer wife Kaeo Keng Nya promoted a 'Lamaist' inspired form of Buddhism that had spread to mainland Southeast Asia during the first half of the fourteenth century under Mongol-Chinese influence, a rival 'Theravada Buddhist school' was introduced, or at least supported, by Fa Ngum's second wife Kaeo Lòt Fa, a princess from Ayutthaya (see Doré 1987: 678–681). Martin Stuart-Fox speculates that it was not until Kaeo Keng Nya's death in 1368 and the arrival of the Siamese princess 'that adherents of an invigorated Sri Lankan school of Theravada Buddhism then dominant in Sukhothai and Ayutthaya finally gained the upper hand' (Stuart-Fox 1998: 53). Though this hypothesis is by no means convincing, it seems that different 'schools' of Buddhism were contending for religious supremacy in Lan Sang during the second half of the fourteenth century. All 'schools' faced an obstinate opposition from the traditional spirit (*phi*) cults, the vehemence of which is testified in NKB. At the time when Fa Ngum had returned to Luang Prabang:

> [. . .] all the people of Meuang Lān Xāng worshipped [only] the Phī fā, Phī Thaen, Phī Phoh, Phī Mae (*ie. paternal and maternal spirits*). Worse, they did not know the virtue of Phra Buddha, Phra Dhamma, and Phra Sangha. Moreover, they like to show off their precious stones (*ie. amulets*), their daring, lances and swords.
>
> (Souneth 1996: 193)

Fa Ngum's own half-hearted support of Buddhism and tolerance of animist practices might have contributed to the king's deposition and sending into exile in 1373/74.

2 Vangbuli whose reign (1442–1479/80) marked a long period of political stability was the first Lao king who ascended to the throne under a name of Pali origin, namely Phanya Sainya Chakkaphat (Jaiya Cakkavattin) Phaen Phaeo. The title *cakkavattin* (Skt: *cakravartin*) means 'universal monarch' and this exhibits the ruler's ambition to build up a powerful Buddhist kingdom. He was an exact contemporary of King Tilok of Lan Na (r. 1441/2–1487) and King Trailok of Ayutthaya (r. 1448–1488), whose official titles also referred to the *cakkavattin* ideal of a universal Buddhist monarch. Vangbuli probably had cultivated good relations with both neighbouring kings who were waging a long and bitter war over the control of the Sukhothai-Si Satchanalai region.

Stuart-Fox emphasizes the political and religious ties between Lan Sang and Ayutthaya, which were 'particularly close' as 'is evident from the lavish gifts dispatched by kings of Ayutthaya on the occasions of both his coronation and cremation' (Stuart-Fox 1998: 64, cf. Souneth 1996: 236–237: Sila 1964: 43, 46). Though it seems quite plausible that the Siamese ruler paid special respect to Phanya Sainya Chakkaphat Phaen Phaeo because he was the son of King Sam Saen Thai's Siamese wife, Nang Kaeo Lòt Fa, this alone is not sufficient evidence for any significant Siamese influence on the Lao political and religious order. The 'Lan Na factor', however, was much more important. In early 1449, the Tai principality of Nan, a former ally of Sukhothai, was subdued by troops from Chiang Mai. A subsequent Lao attempt to seize Nan from Lan Na failed, and in border skirmishes that flared up several years later the Lao forces lost out again. (See Wyatt and Aroonrut 1995: 81–83.) Thereafter relations between the two kingdoms, now close neighbours, seem to have continuously improved. The incorporation of Nan into the Lan Na polity promoted, in the long run, manifold exchanges between Lan Na and Lan Sang. Military support of Lan Na to repel strong Vietnamese forces, who had invaded Lan Sang in 1478 and even temporarily occupied her capital, was crucial for the very survival of the Lao kingdom. Though refuted by the Lao chronicles,[2] contemporary Chinese sources confirm that the Lao Prince Cao Sai succeeded his father Sainya Chakkaphat Phaen Phaeo, who had apparently been killed during the war, under the name of Suvanna Banlang as King of Lan Sang (in 1480) with the help of King Tilok of Chiang Mai.[3]

It was obvious that from that time on Lan Na's political as well as cultural influence on Laos had intensified. The prestige of Chiang Mai did not depend on the military factor alone; just one year before the Vietnamese invasion of Lan Sang the eighth official Buddhist council was held at Vat Cedi Cet Yòt in Chiang Mai with the purpose of producing a new recension of the Tipitaka. Although doubts about the nature of this council exist (see Swearer and Premchit 1978: 30–31) – no account is found in the Lan Na chronicles – and we don't know whether monks from Lan Sang had attended it at all, it certainly contributed to the spread of the 'Lan Na school' of Buddhism to neighbouring countries, such as the eastern Shan region, Sipsòng Panna, and Laos. Two of the oldest dated Buddha images, found so far in the Lan Sang cultural area, are from the 1480s and they resemble images from northern Thailand. An inscription at the pedestal of a Buddha image of bronze kept at Vat Sisaket, Vientiane, dated 'Saturday, the twelfth [waxing] day of the third month, C.S. 852, a *kot set* year' (22 January 1491), is the earliest known sample of the Lao Dhamma script,[4] the Mon-derived religious script of Lan Na which spread in the second half of the fifteenth century throughout the 'Greater La Na cultural area' (including the Lü and Khün inhabited areas east of the Salween river). During the reign of King Visun (1501–1520), Suvanna Banlang's younger brother, the religious influence of Lan Na continued.

3 Donald K. Swearer and Sommai Premchit characterize Tilok as the monarch of Lan Na who 'best exemplifies efforts to build a single moral community unified on the sociological level by a common religious institution', a Sangha who, despite royal support for the new Sīhala Nikāya (headquartered at Vat Pa Daeng), integrated different Buddhist sects. Thus, the groundwork for the 'golden age' (Thai: *yuk thòng*) of Buddhist scholarship in Lan Na during the reign of Müang Kaeo (1495–1526) was laid. Lao rulers tried to emulate their Tai Yuan counterparts. The famous Lan Na chronicle *Jinakālamālīpakaraṇaṃ* (Jkm.), composed by Bhikkhu Ratanapañña between 1516 and 1527, reports that in 1523 the king of Lan Na offered Visun's son and successor, Phothisarat (r. 1520–1548) sixty volumes of the Pali canon and other gifts:

> On the full-moon day itself, he (i.e. King Müang Kaeo) made lavish gifts of monastic requisites including pairs of fine robes of the Elder Devamaṅgala together with his followers and sending with him the Tipiṭaka consisting of sixty volumes[5] he despatched him to the King of the city of Dasalakkhakuñjara, 'City of a Million Elephants' (i.e. Luang Prabang), in order to convert him.
>
> (Ratanapañña 1968: 183)

What does the phrase 'in order to convert him' (*pasāda jananat kaṃ pesesi*, literally: 'in order to produce faith in him') mean? As Buddhism had already been the religion of the state and the ruling elite for generations, this phrase certainly does not indicate a completely new 'conversion'. It refers rather to the introduction or re-introduction of a new religious order to Lan Sang where Buddhist heterodoxy and pre-Buddhist beliefs were still dominant. Could it be that King Phothisarat introduced the orthodox Sīhala Nikāya of Vat Pa Daeng to Lan Sang to purify and unify the Lao *Sangha* along the model of Chiang Mai? Probably, he did so under the influence of his principal wife who was a daughter of King Ket Klao of Lan Na (r. 1525–1538) (Ministry of Education and Culture 2000: 177). In 1527, Phothisarat ordered 'to stop the misguided worship of Phī Yāv, Phī Heuan and Phī Seua whose shrines are in the houses of the people and the great shrine of Sob Dong'.[6] The propagation of the cult of sacred Buddha images, the construction of monasteries under royal patronage and the donation of land and people to support these monasteries increased under the reigns of Phothisarat and his successor (see details in the following section). Lorrillard observes that since 1527 the sacred Dhamma script appears on Lao steles along with a secular script that is almost identical with the northern Thai Fak Kham ('Tamarind pod') script. He arrives at the conclusion that:

> [. . .] All these inscriptions, which bear a very strong mark of northern Thai culture, are royal inscriptions commissioned by Phothisarat

> (Phothisalalat) and Setthathirat (Setthathilat), who were the first Lao sovereigns to appear in epigraphy during their lifetimes. It can be seen very clearly that the Lao lands, which had already been reached by a form of Buddhism originating in Lan Na during the fifteenth century, experienced a second wave of Buddhism in the sixteenth century. This later movement differed rather significantly from the first, in that it was based both on more orthodox practice and on a more evolved textual tradition. The introduction of the Tham script is clearly associated with the appearance of Pali language traditions which probably had previously been unknown.
>
> (Lorrillard 2003: 5)

Though Phothisarat and his son and successor Setthathirat (r. 1548–1571) were pious kings who took every opportunity to demonstrate their devotion to the universal values of Buddhism, heterodox beliefs, including the *phi* worships, survived; and in times of political and social crises, even experienced a revival, as was the case in the nineteenth century. Despite the fact that Buddhism had taken firm roots in Lao society when the first Europeans arrived at the court of King Suriyavongsa (r. 1633/38–1690/95) (see de Marini 1998 and Lejosne 1993), large segments of the population in Lan Sang, notably the indigenous 'Kha' peoples, still adhered to non-Buddhist beliefs. Furthermore, the southern provinces of present-day Laos were only peripherally, if at all, touched by Buddhism at that time.[7] Buddhism was spread with the southward migration of the politically dominant ethnic Lao. This migration reached the areas south of Saravan and the interior of the Khorat Plateau not earlier than the late seventeenth century. The founding of Champassak by Lao dissidents from Vientiane (in 1713) furthered the 'Lao-isation' and 'Buddhisation' of the South. I will discuss this subject in the last section.

Lao kingship and Buddhism

All the kings of Lan Sang, at least since King Sainya Cakkhaphat Phaen Phaeo, emulated the ideal of the righteous Buddhist monarch (*dhammarāja*) and many of them claimed to be at least formally the status of *cakkavattin* or universal conqueror. However, not all acquired the reputation to live up to that ideal. Some of those Lao kings who are remembered and eulogized in Lao historiography because of their outstanding political and/or religious achievements – such as Visun, Phothisarat, Setthathirat, and Suriyavongsa – included the titles *dhammikarāja, dhammavaṃsa*, or *dhammadevo* in their official names. A righteous king had to abide by the *dasa rājadhamma* (tenfold royal code)[8] and several other moral codes as they are stipulated in the *Khamphi Pha Thammasat Luang*, an ancient Lao customary law text. Moreover, as moral principles he has to follow strictly the thirty *pāramī*, i.e. the ten

Buddhist virtues,[9] each to be attained in three stages of spiritual perfection, which a Bodhisattva achieved on his way to Buddhahood. In 1566, Setthathirat built the That (Dhātu) Luang, 'the great stupa', in Vientiane in order to reinforce the *dhammarāja* concept as the foundation of Lao kingship. Tracing the origins of the new ritual centre of Lan Sang back to the days of King Asoka, the NKB reports:

> When Phra Jaya Jetthādhirāja Chau lived in Meuang Candaburi, [he] built the Mahā Cedī over the 'Pulima Dhātu' which was first built by Phrayā Srī Dhammasaokarāja. Then [he] built thirty Samatingsa Pāramī to surround this stupa. He gave a lot of offerings and countless [pieces of] glassware to worship the Phra Sālīka Cedī. Indeed, when Phra Jaya Jetthādhirāja Chau occupied the throne, [he] abided by [the Dasarāja]dhamma, [and] enjoyed the friendship of Phrayā everywhere.
>
> (Souneth 1996: 258)

As Souneth Phothisane observes, the central spire of the That Luang represents Mount Meru, the axis of the world in Buddhist cosmology, but it also symbolizes the *cakkavattin*. The thirty smaller surrounding *stūpas* represent thirty tributary *müang*. The control over many vassal states was one important factor to prove the king's claim that he did indeed possess such qualities.[10]

According to Lao Buddhist theory, a king's legitimacy was derived from a superior store of merit that he had accumulated over many previous existences. The king had to increase his store of merit in his present life by doing good deeds, notably by making donations to the religious order and constructing or repairing Buddhist monuments. Almost all Lao kings since the times of King Visun founded monasteries or built *stūpas* as visible manifestations of Buddhist kingship. King (Sai) Setthathirat is a case in point. In 1560, when the king was probably already preparing for the transfer of the royal capital to Vientiane (accomplished in 1564), he still ordered the construction of a splendid monastery in Luang Prabang, situated at the confluence of the Khan and Mekong rivers: Vat Siang Thòng Vòlavihan.

> *Vat Siang Thòng Vòlavihan*: The monastery, housing at present more than fifty monks and novices, occupies the site at the confluence of the Mekong and the Nam Khan rivers where two nāgas are thought to have their residence. The two shrines dedicated to the two nāgas were preserved at Vat Siang Thòng until recent times. The monastery also played an important role in royal ceremonies. A stairway leads from the Mekong to the entrance of the monastery, and it was there that important visitors entered the town before being received by the king. Mosaics on the rear of the *sim* and surrounding buildings depict scenes from Jātaka stories and the famous classical epos Sin

> Sai. One mosaic also shows the magnificent flame-of-the-forest tree (*Rhinacanthus nanitus*), called Ton Thòng in Lao, which is believed to have once grown nearby and from where one part of the old name of Luang Prabang, Siang Dong-Siang Thòng, derives. In fact, Siang Thòng comprised the peninsula at the confluence of Mekong and Khan River. Siang Dong ('Town at the Dong River') is situated in the southern section of present-day Luang Prabang.[11]

Luang Prabang was to maintain her position as 'a place of Buddhism and of the three gems', as Lao chronicles emphasize, but the new capital needed also a powerful religious symbol to lend legitimacy to the new political and ritual centre of the kingdom. Such a symbol was That Luang which the king built after the model of the Cedi (Cetiya) Luang of Chiang Mai. This *stūpa*, by far the largest one in the country, is revered to this day as one of the most important religious symbols and as 'the central symbol through which the nation remembers itself' (Evans 1998: 41).[12] Furthermore, That Luang, situated at the highest point (of Vientiane next to the National Assembly), is the place where the That Luang festival (*ngan bun that luang*) is held in November of every year. Grant Evans reports that the That Luang festival was promoted as a national festival under the Royal Lao Government in the 1950s, and 'it became the time for swearing an oath of fealty to the king at Vat Ong Tue' (ibid.: 42), a monastery in the centre of Vientiane founded by King Setthathirat.

The sacredness of That Luang was backed up by the popular belief that it has been built on the site of an ancient stone pillar (*sao hin*) once erected by King Asoka and containing relics of Lord Buddha. According to the *Nithan Urangkhathat*, there was an old prophecy saying that the sacred stone in Candaburī (Vientiane) would one day become the site of an important religious centre.[13] By fulfilling this prophecy, Setthathirat linked his new royal capital with the very origins of Buddhism.

There are many more cases showing that other Lao kings acted in a similar way. In 1816, King (Cao) Anu of Vientiane, who was a Siamese vassal at that time, initiated the work on Vat Sisaket, which is a jewel of Lao architecture. It differed from other Lao monasteries both in style and the costs spent on its construction. When the monastery was completed on 6 May 1824,[14] King Anu ordered the engraving of a stone inscription to eulogize the construction of the monastery and its founder. The king is here called Phra Bun Sai Settha Thammikarat, 'the meritorious ruler Sai Settha, the righteous king' (ibid.: 53). The founding of Vat Sisaket has to be seen in the context of Cao Anu's aspirations to regain full independence from Siam. His attempt seven years later to unify the Lao lands under his leadership, however, failed and ended in the almost total physical destruction of Vientiane and the end of autonomous rule in central Laos.[15]

Apart from the construction of religious monuments, Lao kings gained political legitimation by promoting the worship of sacred Buddha statues and footprints of the Buddha (*phra phutthabat*). Lao chronicles, such as the NKB and the Urangkhathat, tell us of how the Buddha left his footprint at sacred sites in each important *müang*. In Lan Sang such sites were considered the centre of their respective *müang*; and people believed that *stūpas* for relics had to be built on places tha the Buddha had once visited. Footprints of the Buddha were designed to override the power of sacred sites associated with pre-Buddhist spirit cults. Due to the symbolic links established between Buddha's footprints and the nearby religious monuments built for housing his relics, these sites became places of pilgrimage throughout the kingdom of Lan Sang.[16] Thus, a cult of the *müang* centred on the worship of Buddhist relics replaced the spirit cults and thereby legitimised the power and territorial rights of the king.

The worship of sacred Buddha statues played likewise an important role of reinforcing Buddhist kingship. Two of these statues are in particular regarded as the Lao royal palladia. One statue is the Emerald Buddha (*phra kaeo mòrakot*). The Emerald Buddha was a famous statue that was found in 1464 near the town of Chiang Rai and then, twenty years later, established in a monastery under royal patronage in Chiang Mai. First it was the palladium of the Lan Na kings, and after Setthathirat's accession to the throne in Chiang Mai (1546), it became the royal symbol of two kingdoms – Lan Na and Lan Sang – united under one rule for a short period. On his way back to Luang Prabang (1547/48), Setthathirat took the Emerald Buddha to Luang Prabang and established it later at Vat Hò Pha Kaeo in Vientiane. Like a 'winner's trophy', the sacred statue was removed to Siam by King Taksin's victorious armies in 1779. It is now kept in the Thai Royal Palace in Bangkok.[17] Until today, among normal Lao citizens the loss of this single prestigious Buddha statue arouses much stronger nationalistic resentments against their western neighbours than it is the case with regards to the loss of the territories on the west bank of the Mekong River.

The second statue under discussion is the famous Pha Bang Buddha image, which became the focus of a state cult after King Visun had moved the statue from Viang Kham (in Vientiane province), where it had been housed since the days of King Fa Ngum (r. 1353–1373/74), to Luang Prabang. Visun built in the early years of his reign a richly endowed temple to house the statue. The monastery was called Vat Visun after its founder but is better known as Vat Mak Mo ('water melon temple') for the shape of its *stūpa*.[18] Worship of the Pha Bang as the palladium of both the kingdom and its ruling dynasty dates from that time. It was in front of the Pha Bang image that governors and vassal rulers took oaths of allegiance to the king. Such a ceremony is described in a ritual text entitled 'Great sermon of tributary rulers' (*kan suai saban luang*), which probably refers to the reign of King Visun. Among the *müang* of which their governors (*cao müang*) had participated in that oath-taking ceremony are Champassak and Si Khotabòng (present-day

Savannakhet) in the south, Vientiane, Loei and Dan Sai in the centre, and Sam Nüa, Müang Phukha and the land of the Lamet in the north (Doré 1987: 733). The Pha Bang cult provided a focus for royal support of the religious order, in return for the legitimation of the king as a *dhammarāja*. The cult effectively reinforced the institution of Buddhist kingship (see Stuart-Fox 1998: 72).

Lao kings saw themselves and their subjects as having definite places within a well-defined Buddhist cosmological order. They tried to regulate their kingdom according to the principles that they believed to be in harmony with that order. The *dasa rājadhamma* (Lao: *thotsa latcatham*) defines religious donations (*dāna*) as the first and foremost task of a king. One of the most meritorious acts a Buddhist monarch could perform was the allocation of land to monasteries and the donation of people to provide services of various kinds for these monasteries. A survey of Lao inscriptions from the Lan Sang period (c. 1353–1707/13) shows that the vast majority of them almost exclusively deal with religious matters, notably monastic endowments. Such royal donations, called *kappana* in Pali (a term Lao inscriptions seldom use), could comprise:

1 Manpower:

 a senior abbots (*thera*);
 b monks (*bhikkhu*) and novices (*sāmaṇera*);
 c *saṅghagārī* (those responsible for the administration of laypersons attached to the monastery);
 d temple serfs (*kha okat* or *khòi okat*[19]).

2 Land:

 a the monastery grounds (*rattanakhet* or *phutthakhet*);
 b the area surrounding the monastery, space of the nearby village (*khamakhet*);
 c rice fields (*na canghan*) of the temple serfs.[20]

Let us begin the discussion with the donation of land: Lao inscriptions distinguish between the *rattanakhet* (P: *ratanakhetta*)[21] and *khamakhet* (P: *gāmakhetta*), on the one hand, and the so-called *na canghan*, on the other hand. Whereas the former were donated by both the king and powerful high-ranking aristocrats, the donation of the latter seems to have been limited to the privilege of the king. However, this thesis is based on the twofold assumption that the *na canghan* were never donated alone but only together with temple serfs and that the king held the exclusive right to remit people from corvée labour and the payment of taxes to the state (Thawat 1984: 157–158). We know from Lan Na inscriptions that before the reign of Müang Kaeo (1495–1526), ambitious governors donated both land and manpower to monasteries so as to accumulate religious merits and concurrently to increase their political reputation. Later, they first had to ask the king for permission and religious endowments were made in the names of kings alone (Rawiwan 1982: 122). Unlike the Lan Na inscriptions which frequently record large numbers of donated temple serfs, sometimes comprising whole villages (see Grabowsky 2004: 56–58) and even their names being mentioned, the Lan Sang inscriptions place particular emphasis on the size of the endowed lands, while the donation of manpower is more implicitly mentioned by prohibitions to use the *khòi okat* (as well as the crops from the *na canghan*) for purposes other than religious. Potential violators were intimidated by curses such as the following one which appears in the final lines of an inscription engraved on the pedestal of a Buddha image of bronze (kept at the National Museum, Khòn Kaen):

> If someone is full of greed and comes to violate[22] this royal edict, this person will be on fire in hell[23] for four lifetimes. Don't be ambitious and insolent. Don't be daring and violate the stipulations of the royal edict.[24]

The status of *khòi okat* was hereditary; the obligations a temple serf had to fulfil were also valid for his or her descendants.[25] Lao customary law *Khosarat* stipulates that *khòi okat* who had abandoned their duties and placed themselves illegally under the protection of a nobleman in another locality would have to be sent back to their original monastery, as soon as their new master had found out their real identity.[26] No person of high rank had the right to use *khòi okat* for his own service. In the inscription No. 2 of Vat Daen Müang (Phon Phisai district, Nòng Khai province), dated 1535, it is stated that '[concerning] the plantations and rice-fields of the country (*ban-müang*), the betel nuts, the coconut and sugar plantations, and the serfs (*khòi*) who [are employed] by the monastery and the monks, a man called Mui and Lung Phanya Can have dripped water [expressing the wish] that all those who take [the fruits of the land and the serfs] away for the [benefit] of the *cao* (king) and the *khun* (nobles) have to return them. Don't let them perform corvée labour' (Thawat 1984: 238). This text obviously refers to a previous donation to the same monastery made in 1530.[27]

It ought to be stressed that both the Buddhist *Sangha* and the king took advantages of endowments to important monasteries. Though neither in Lan Na nor in Lan Sang the *Sangha* seemed to have been a big landowner, as was the case in Sri Lanka, the endowments certainly enhanced its reputation. The king on the other hand secured an effective means to increase his religious prestige as well as his political influence beyond the region close to the capital. Through this means he profited from the monopoly of religious foundations that he, *de facto*, held.[28] The king succeeded in consolidating his role as *thammikarat*, and at the same time in weakening potential rivals because the loss of workforce to the monasteries could mean for the regional rulers a serious decrease in their demographic basis. The king imposed a network of loyal religious institutions on a system of potential centrifugal forces. A rare description of the donation of temple serfs is given by the Genoan priest Father Giovanni Maria Leria who had stayed in Laos for several years in the 1640s, i.e. during the early part of King Suriyavongsa's long reign. His memories were later recorded by Giovanni Filippo de Marini, another Genoan priest with experiences in the Far East:

> [The king] always pays them (i.e., the monks) the greatest honor possible. Indeed, as soon as he observes a monk he greets him first by raising his right hand, which is the signal of respect and civility most used in this country. He makes slaves of his vassals and destines them to the service of their temples in payment for the tribute that they owe him. Sometimes he has evacuated villages and entire quarters in favor of monks and obliged those who lived there to maintain and supply the monasteries in their area, which these poor unfortunates accept with reluctance and by coercion as they have then to deal with insatiable people whom one can never fully please, insolent in their demands and importunate when they receive what is given to them and authoritarian in the orders they prescribe, so that those who know them well, would rather become slaves and serve others than to depend on the monks while not losing their freedom.
>
> (de Marini 1998: 64)

This statement is, of course, full of prejudices the Catholic priests held against Buddhism, and especially against the Buddhist clergy. It is doubtful whether living conditions for the temple serfs were really so unbearable that they preferred anything else rather than working for the monks. On the contrary, there is evidence showing that temple serfs, in general, were very proud of their special status,[29] which, however, did not always prevent them from being recruited in the military service,[30] as it could be argued that fighting against a foreign invading force contributed to the defence of Buddhism (see Thawat 1984: 152).

Another aspect related to the donations of land and manpower to monasteries is of an economic nature. The Thai historian Dhida Saraya sees a close connection between religious donations and the expansion of settlements in the region of today's Thailand. Noting that the endowments, known as *kappana* (or *kalpana*), were 'associated with both Hinduism and Buddhism', she argues that the rulers of Dvāravatī and Lopburi, later also the ruler of Sukhothai, had attempted to expand their territories into previously mostly unpopulated new land by means of donating land and labourers to Buddhist monasteries.[31] In Lan Sang, as in Lan Na, new religious centres and the supporting villages received from the monarchs often generous material advantages, which gave them a quasi-model character. Thereby they could attract more settlers so as to reclaim additional land for cultivation in the region and to establish additional villages. In this way, the newly developed regions prospered. Since in general the king as 'ruler of the land' (*phracao phaendin*) possessed the privileges of such a donation, the founding of monasteries, the expansion of settlements, and the consolidation of the royal sphere of influence developed hand in hand with one another.

It is unknown when exactly the tradition of royal endowments of monasteries in Laos began. The earliest evidence found is mentioned in an inscription dated 1530, i.e. in the reign of Phothisarat (1520–1548). From the rather incomplete corpus of Lao inscriptions, we can conclude that most royal donations occurred during the reigns of Setthathirat (1548–1571) and Suriyavongsa (1638–1695). In the early eighteenth century, this tradition was apparently interrupted, probably due to the political instability, which prevailed after the division of the Lan Sang kingdom into three separate entities and the decline of royal authority as a result of it. There is a hiatus of almost one century until a short-lived revival of monastic endowments under the reign of Cao Anu (r. 1804–1829). The last epigraphic record is from 1811, when the ruler of Vientiane donated land and temple serfs to the Vat Hò Pha Kaeo (Si Chiang Mai district, Nòng Khai).[32] From then on, the Lao lands on both banks of the Mekong River became increasingly exposed to Siamese influence, politically as well as culturally, and the institution of an independent Lao kingship – with the partial exception of Luang Prabang – ceased to exist.

The relationship between the religious and the political order

As mentioned above, the Lao *Sangha* had many privileges from the monarchy, which in return was legitimized by a supportive *Sangha*. The relationship between the religious and the political orders was in fact based on mutual benefits. Going back to the reign of Sainya Cakkaphat Phaen Phaeo (1442–1479/80), we can observe that the king of Lan Sang reinforced the religious legitimation of his rule by appointing new abbots in two prominent monasteries of Luang Prabang. The two abbots were given exalted titles, such as *dhammasenā* and *saṅghasenā* (Hoshino 1986: 195). The influence of the *Sangha* increased steadily. After the withdrawal of the Vietnamese invasion forces in 1479, the reconstruction of the destroyed country was discussed jointly by the king's ministers and monks from five important monasteries in Luang Prabang (Souneth 1996: 233–234). On several occasions the Supreme Patriarch played a crucial role in nominating new kings. This happened, for example, in 1591, when a delegation of senior monks led by the Supreme Patriarch[33] went to Pegu to ask the Burmese king, as Lan Sang was a Burmese vassal state at that time, to appoint Pha Nò Müang (Nò Kaeo Kuman) as the new ruler of Vientiane (Souneth 1996: 276). Both in lending support to a pretender to the throne and in rescinding its backing, the Buddhist clergy was able to gain political power as well. A case in point is the political upheaval following King Suriyavongsa's death. In this crisis a senior monk called Pha Khu Phon Samek took up a prominent position.

Who was this monk? How did it happen that he could play a very important role in Lao politics at a turning point in the country's history? Apart from oral histories, various versions of the *Champassak Chronicle* provide rather similar accounts of Pha Khu Phon Samek's role as one of the founders of the kingdom of Champassak in 1713.[34] He was born around 1631 in Yasothòn (northeastern Thailand), an area where, at that time, ethnic Lao lived in close neighbourhood with Mon-Khmer-speaking indigenous peoples. A legend that associates him with the founding of Phnom Penh at a later stage of his life might hint at his non-Lao, possibly Khmer, ethnic background. As a novice he impressed a senior monk in the capital with his outstanding intelligence and amazing capacity to memorize whole volumes of sacred scripts. The novice's fame spread throughout the kingdom and caught the attention of King Suriyavongsa, who supported his later monastic career. Entering the monkhood first at Vat Phon Samek (near Vientiane), the young monk was soon given the prestigious title 'Pha Khu' and thus received his popular name. Pha Khu Phon Samek combined a strict observation of the Buddhist moral precepts and a profound knowledge of the religious scripts, which he learned perfectly by heart, with the alleged possession of supernatural powers. This might have explained the charisma he reputedly possessed. In the early 1690s, Pha Khu Phon Samek was the most popular and widely revered monk in Laos. The only surviving Lao manuscript of the *Champassak Chronicle* reports:

> By observing moral commandments and monastic discipline, Than Phakhu reached the levels of the [six] *aphinnya*[35] [and] the eight *atthasammabat*;[36] he possessed abundant merits (*puñña*) and perfections (*pāramī*); he was able to accomplish everything he wished. All people revered him. About his spittle, which was left in a spittoon, or even his urine and faeces, [people also] said that they smelled good. Known under the name of Pha Khu Phon Samek a number of people called him Pha Khu Achom Hòm (literally, 'the learned monk whose faeces smell'). He was praised under different names by different people. The King of Vientiane wished to become an attendant [of Pha Khu Phon Samek].[37]

In 1695, King Suriyavongsa passed away without leaving an heir. Phanya Müang Can,[38] the highest-ranking minister, seized the throne and paved the way for a long period of political turmoil in Lan Sang. The Lao chronicles are contradictory and inconsistent on the events during the two decades following Suriyavongsa's death as Lorrillard has demonstrated (Lorrillard 1995: 215–224). If we follow the historiographical tradition of the South, it appears that Phanya Müang Can's downfall, only six months after he had usurped royal power, was brought about by a lack of popular support and opposition from influential figures of the Buddhist clergy. Pha Khu Phon Samek is given credit for lending tacit support to the usurper's opponents. To avoid a direct confrontation with Phanya Müang Can, the charismatic abbot of Vat Phon Samek led 3,000 of his followers, among them Princess Sumangkhala, who was one of Suriyavongsa's daughters and pregnant at the time, out of the capital to the south. 'Wherever, they stopped on his way downstream', says the That Phanom Chronicle (*Nithan Urangkhathat*), 'great numbers of devotees volunteered to join them on their journey' (Preuss 1976: 66). At That Phanom (Nakhòn Phanom) the monk and his followers stopped to repair the ancient and most sacred reliquary; through this meritorious act the dissidents linked their uncertain political future with the perceived glorious Buddhist past of the country.

The refugees finally reached the region of Champassak where they settled down with the permission of the town's female non-Lao governor Nang Phaen. The *Champassak Chronicle* says that this governor, a devout Buddhist, asked Pha Khu Phon Samek to take over the administration of Champassak in order to facilitate Buddhism throughout her entire territory. The monk did not refuse and thus gained control of both secular and religious affairs.[39] After a certain period of time, in 1713, Princess Sumangkhala's son was crowned as King of Champassak under the royal name Cao Sòi Sisamut Phutthangkun.

At least parts of the founding story of Champassak appear fictitious. In particular, the story of the two female rulers – Nang Phaen and her mother Nang Phao – preceding Sòi Sisamut's reign seems sheer legendary, as Archaimbault (1961: 530–536) has testified. It may, however, reflect the 'hybrid' origin of Champassak, namely as a polity where Lao Buddhist settlers from the North intermingled with a strong pre-Buddhist Mon-Khmer substratum. Should we interpret Pha Khu Phon Samek as a symbol for a long-term cultural process in today's southern Laos which may have started some time in the late seventeenth century, and after one or two generations had transformed this formerly predominantly non-Lao and non-Buddhist region into a constituent part of the Buddhist Tai-Lao world?

As a direct descendant of King Suriyavongsa, who was the last fully recognized ruler of Lan Sang, Sòi Sisamut linked Champassak with the rest of the Lao world. Thus, the kingdom of Champassak could repudiate the image of a 'renegade province' and claim to be one of the three successor states of Lan Sang, on a par with Vientiane and Luang Prabang. Royal lineage alone, however, was not sufficient to consolidate political power in the South. The young king needed the charismatic monk Pha Khu Phon Samek to reinforce his moral standing. In the town of Champassak, the capital, Sòi Sisamut built Vat Luang Mai, 'the new main/royal monastery'. This monastery was the symbol of Buddhist kingship focusing on the concepts of righteous king (*dhammarāja*) and universal ruler (*cakkavattin*).

On close reading, the *Champassak Chronicle* reveals the importance attached to Pha Khu Phon Samek for the religious legitimation of secular power and for defining the territorial extent of the kingdom. The chronicle describes how the monk led his many followers to seek a suitable place for settlement and finally established a new *müang*. Together with his disciples, he prayed for auspicious signs, which would show the Lao migrants the land of their destiny. All these episodes render strong support to the legitimation of kingship. Furthermore, Pha Khu Phon Samek had a reputation for possessing supernatural powers that could make him even invisible.[40]

As was discussed above, sacred Buddha images were used to legitimate royal power. Pha Kaeo Phalik, a beautiful Buddha image made of pure crystal, was found by two brothers of 'Kha', i.e. non-Lao, origin. They took the image as the effigy of a small human being. This shows that their community was still untouched by Buddhism. The Pha Kaeo Phalik image was later enshrined in a *stūpa* in the town of Champassak. This happened still during the reign of Sòi Sisamut. Thereafter, the Pha Kaeo Phalik was revered as a state palladium, the symbol of prosperity of Champassak.[41]

Even though the 'Kha' were the indigenous people of southern Laos, they often migrated to other places. They moved because of their special connection with the local spirits. A number of the 'Kha' population from Ban Sompòi Nanyòn, where the Crystal Buddha had been discovered, left their home village and settled next to the city of Champassak as they were needed by King Sòi Sisamut to serve as serfs of the Crystal Buddha (*kha pha phalik*).[42] Furthermore, they were also required when sacrificial ceremonies or traditional festivals were held.[43]

Traditionally, a monastery was not only the residence of Buddhist monks and novices, but was also a centre of education. Learned men who sometimes took over the position of village headman used to be former monks or novices, in other words Buddhist-educated men. Therefore, the founding of monasteries by a king increased his religious merits and thus was an indicator for the legitimacy of royal rule. By donating parts of their property to the *Sangha*, the kings would expect that the people considered them as generous and benevolent. Thus the people would respect and praise such righteous monarchs. The *Champassak Chronicle* (Vat Citsavang version) does not fail to mention that Sòi Sisamut (r. 1713–1737) built at least two monasteries for Buddhist monks.[44] One of his later successors, Cao Kham Suk (r. 1863–1900), who was already a Siamese vassal, founded the monastery of Vat Nyuttithammathalalam.[45] All these activities ought to be considered as fulfilments of the duties of a ruler relying on Buddhism for political legitimacy.

Concluding remarks

Theravada Buddhism came to Laos later than in any other country of mainland Southeast Asia. Contrary to the assertion of traditional Lao historiography it was not the Cambodian influence of the mid-fourteenth century that had a decisive impact on the diffusion of Buddhism in Lao society. It was probably not earlier than the mid-fifteenth century, starting with the reign of Sainya Cakkhaphat Phaen Phaeo (r. 1442–1479/80), that Theravada Buddhism became the dominant religion of Laos, at least among the ruling Lao elite. The most influential Buddhist wave reached the Lao kingdom of Lan Sang via Lan Na. The cultural, religious, and political relations between the two kingdoms intensified in the sixteenth century; and after the incorporation of Lan Na into the Burmese sphere of power, Lan Sang even became the heir of Lan Na's erstwhile flourishing Buddhist culture. In the Lao lands the new religion spread with the southward migration of the Lao people and reached the interior of the Khorat Plateau and today's southern Laos only by the late seventeenth and early eighteenth centuries.

Lao kings took the concepts of righteous king (*dhammarāja*) and universal ruler (*cakkavattin*) seriously. As in neighbouring Lan Na, but unlike Ayutthaya, royal donations of land and manpower to monasteries were widespread in Lan Sang. Such religious endowments demonstrated that a monarch lived up to the expectations of Buddhist kingship. The Buddhist *Sangha* thus held a privileged position in traditional Lao society and was in times of political crises even able to intervene in the secular realm. Lao customary law texts, such as the *Kotmai Khosarat*, were inspired by the rules of monastic discipline (*vinaya*). Thus, the monks' advice would have been appreciated in the decision of law cases. The borders between the secular, political sphere (*āṇācakra*), and the religious order (*buddhacakra*) were more fluid than it is the case today.[46]

What has not been discussed in this essay but deserves special attention is the transformation of the religious order during the period of Siamese domination (i.e. since 1778/79). We can deduce that the gradual loss of political sovereignty and, more decisively, the social disruptions following the destruction of Vientiane (in 1828/29) had precipitated the decline of royal control of the Buddhist order.[47] The millenarian revolts that shook Laos in that period are certainly associated with these fundamental changes.[48] This, however, would have to be discussed separately.

Notes

* I am grateful to Foon Ming Liew for helping me to polish up my English and giving me her comments on the draft version of this essay. My thanks are also extended to Bounleuth Sengsoulin for allowing me to make extensive use of his MA thesis on the *Champassak Chronicle*, Citsavang Version. I also would like to thank Michel Lorrillard for his acute remarks on my essay and providing me with some of his unpublished work on the history of Lao Buddhism. However, the responsibilities for the statements contained in this essay remain with the author.

1 Lorrillard (2003: 2). In fact, the mention of a huge entourage, including astrologers and craftsmen, accompanying the monks and Brahmins from Angkor to

Luang Prabang, resembles the Mon Princess Cāmadevī's procession from Lavo to Hariphunchai, where she founded a Buddhist kingdom in the eighth century, according to a Lan Na chronicle of the fifteenth century.

2 According to the NKB (Souneth 1996: 234–235), King Phaen Phaeo abdicated in favour of his son, who alone expelled the Vietnamese.

3 The *Mingshi Gao* ('Draft of the History of the Ming Dynasty') (chapter 189, p. 34a) reports. 'In the year Chenghua 17, [6th month, renzi] (1481), Li Hao (r. 1459–1497), [the King of] Annam, commanded 90,000 barbarian soldiers (*man bing*), constructed three routes through the mountains, and marched his troops to conquer Ailao (the Lao people) and then proceeded to the territory of Laowo (Laos), killed the father, the Pacification Commissioner, Dao Banya of Lanzhang (Cao Phanya of Lan Sang), [and his] two sons, three persons [in all]. The youngest son, Paya Sai (Phanya Sai or Cao Sai), turned to Babai (Lan Na) for support. The Pacification Commissioner [of Babai], Dao Lanna (Cao Lan Na, i.e., Tilok), dispatched troops to escort [Phanya Sai] to Jingkan (Chiang Kham).' (*Mingshi Gao* [Draft of the History of the Ming Dynasty], edited by Wang Hongxu, Wan Sitong *et al.*, completed in 1723 (repr. 1973, 5 vols, Tokyo; 1985, 7 vols, Taipei.)) Quoted after the translation of Liew n.d.: 100.

The claim laid by the Royal Chronicle of Ayutthaya that the Siamese king (personally?) 'granted that Phraya Sai Khao be anointed as the King of Lan Chang' does not appear credible. Quoted from Cushing (2000: 17).

The Luang Prasoert version ('Phraratcha phongsawadan krung si ayutthaya chabap luang prasoet' [The Royal Chronicle of Ayutthaya, Luang Prasoet Version] 1963. In *Prachum phongsawadan* [Collected Chronicles], Part 1, Vol. 1, pp. 141–171. Bangkok: Khurusapha: 138) says : 'In the year [*cula*]*sakkarat* 842, the year of the rat (B.E. 2120), the king of Lan Chang (Sang) passed away and Phaya Sai Khao was enthroned as the new King of Lan Chang.'

4 See Hoshino (1986: 216). The inscription is published in Gagneux (1975: 81–83). Michel Lorrillard argues that the inscription was dated according to the Chiang Mai calendar (which differs by exactly two lunar months) because the script was clearly 'Tham Yuan' and the Buddha image thus of Chiang Mai provenance. Lorrillard proposes 24 November 1490 as the corresponding date of the Julian calendar (Lorrillard, personal communication, 29 April 2004). Moreover, this day was a *ruang rao* day mentioned on line five of the inscription. (Note that *rao* is only barely legible whereas we have a lacuna for *ruang*.) However, 24 November 1490 falls on a Wednesday, not a Saturday (*wan sao*) as the inscription clearly states on line 3. From my point of view, the 'Tham Yuan' style of the inscription does not necessary imply that the Buddha image was originally produced in Lan Na. A dating according to the Lao calendar is only contradicted by the fact that 22 January 1491 was a *kot san* day, but the following day – 23 January 1491 – was indeed a *ruang rao* day. This slight deviation may be attributed to a calculation error of the scribe.

5 N. A. Jayawickrama, the translator and editor of the English-language version, comments: 'There is no such division of the Tipiṭaka and the phrase can equally be translated as "with sixty volumes (treatises) and the Tipiṭaka. See Ratanapañña (1968: 183, fn. 3).

6 NKB, Souneth (1996: 249). Cf. Piyachat Sinthusa-at (1997) *Sangkhom lan chang tangtae plai phutthasattawat thi 21 thüng ton phutthasattawat thi 23* [The society of Lan Sang since the end of the twenty-first until the beginning of the twenty-third Buddhist century]. MA thesis, Thammasat University: 77.

Lieberman (2003: 259) observes that '[a]s late as the second quarter of the 15th century a king of Chiang Mai, to the scandal of monastic chroniclers, revered shamans while sacrificing cattle to the spirits of trees, rocks, and mounds.' As to epigraphic evidence for Photisarat's edict see, for example, the inscription no. 2 of Vat Daen Müang (Lorrillard 1995: 365–367).

7 The Chronicle of Attapü (*Phongsavadan Müang Attapü*) claims that the 'Kha' peoples in the south got closer contact with the Lao civilization in the early 1570s when King Setthathirat retreated to the south in the face of a Burmese attack on Vientiane. Legend says that Setthathirat disappeared in Attapü but did not die as he was rescued by the local Kha tribes who accepted him as their leader. Setthathirat remained immortal in the eyes of his people. They were waiting for him, like the Germans in the Medieval Age were waiting for Kaiser Barbarossa to return and establish a new empire. In 1579, a native from Attapü claimed that he was the reincarnation of King Setthathirat. As a man who claimed to possess magical power (*phu wiset*), he gathered many followers whom he sent to conquer Vientiane (see *Phongsavadan Müang Attapü* [The Attapue Chronicle]. Composed by Maha Butdi Sakdavong, BE 2491, 20 December 1949, transliterated from Lao Buhan into modern Lao script by Volker Grabowsky, October 1997).

8 The *Khamphi Pha Thammasat Luang* defines the tenfold royal code as follows: '1. *dāna* – making donations; 2. *sīla* – abiding by the five or eight religious precepts; 3. *paricāga* – giving up of [one's own] belongings, elephants, horses, clothes, gold and silver, and donating it to the *sena-amat* (i.e., high-ranking officials) and close friends; 4. ājava (<ajjava>) – rectitude; 5. *maddava* – gentleness to elderly people; 6. *ak{k}odha* – freedom from wrath; 7. *avihiṃsa* – refraining from harassing the population; 8. *khanti* – having patience; 9. *sacca* – sticking to the truth and not accepting lies; 10. *avirodha* – no violation of ancient royal customs, rules and traditions. See Aroonrut Wichienkeeo *et al.* (1986) *Khamphi phra thammasat buran* (*kotmai kao khòng lao*) [Phra Thammasat Buhan: An ancient Lao law text]. Bangkok; Samlit Buasisawat (transcr.) (1993) *Khamphi thammasat luang: kotmai buhan lao* [*Thammasat Luang*: A Lao customary law text]. Vientiane. Cf. Ministry of Information and Culture 2000: 177.

9 The 'ten Buddhist virtues' are *dāna* [donation], *sīla* [religious precept], *nekkhamma* [renunciation], *paññā* [wisdom], *viriya* [courage], *khanti* [patience], *sacca* [honesty], *adhiṭṭhāna* [praying], *mettā* [mercy] and *upekkha* [equanimity].

10 See ibid.: 385–386. As to the construction and the meaning of That Luang, see Lorrillard (2004), the so far most detailed and authoritative study on this subject.

11 Pha One Kaeo Sitthivong and Volker Grabowsky, 'Comprehensive List of Monasteries in Luang Prabang', in Berger (2000). This account is based on oral traditions. Lorrillard points out that no original Lao source mentions the construction of Vat Siang Thòng in 1560.

12 That Luang is visible as a central symbol on the Lao national emblem as well as on present-day Lao bank notes.

13 See Kham Campakaeomani (1994) 'Phrathat luang wiang can' [The great stupa of Vientiane]. In *Phrathat cedi wat samkhan lae phrakhru yòt kaeo phonsamek* [Important stupas-monasteries and Phrakhru Yòt Kaeo Phonsamek], pp. 1–13. Chiang Mai: Social Research Institute, Chiang Mai University: 2.

14 The construction works had started already five years earlier, and the first date mentioned in the inscription of Vat Sisaket, 4 March 1819, probably marks the beginning of the works. See Lorrillard (2002: 4). As to the dates mentioned in the stone inscription on the founding of the monastery, cf. Can Inthuphilat (1994) 'Phra khru phonsamek rü yakhru khi hòm' [Phrakhru Phonsamek or Yakhru Khi Hòm]. In *Phrathat cedi-wat samkhan lae phrakhru yòt kaeo phonsamek* [Important stupas-monasteries and Phrakhru Yòt Kaeo Phonsamek], pp. 85–99. Chiang Mai: Social Research Institute, Chiang Mai University.

15 Accidentally, Vat Sisaket was the only major religious building that escaped the Siamese pillage of 1828.

16 See, for example, Buddha's footprints at Luang Prabang (Phusi), Vientiane (Phon San), and That Soeng Sum (Sakon Nakhòn, northeastern Thailand).

17 According to one legend, in 1464 lightning struck at a figure of a Buddha made of gypsum in a pagoda in Chiang Mai. The figure broke and a sitting Buddha made from one whole piece of jade came to light. The Emerald Buddha first found its home in Chiang Rai and from 1486 onwards in Chiang Mai. Since then it was a sort of palladium, a function, which it also served after 1548 in Laos until the Siamese, suppressing the uprising of Cao Anu (1828), brought it to Bangkok, where today it is still placed in Wat Phra Kaeo in front of the royal palace. On the history of the Emerald Buddha until it was brought to Luang Prabang see, for example, *Tamnan pha müang kaeo* [The Chronicle of Pha (Müang) Kaeo]. Vat Si Sai Mun, *tambon* Nòng Còm, *amphoe* San Sai, Chiang Mai, SRI 80.047.05.019–019, 25 ff°. The title of this manuscript from Vat Si Sai Mun (San Sai, Chiang Mai) is a bit misleading as it is not about the reign of King Müang Kaeo (r. 1495–1526) but concerns the 'journey' of the Emerald Buddha image (*pha kaeo*).

18 The Pha Bang (Pra Bang) is said to have originated from Sri Lanka from where it came to Cambodia. The Khmer king gave that golden image portraying Lord Buddha standing with both arms raised forward at the elbows, palms facing outward, to Fa Ngum, his son-in-law, in order to promote Buddhism in the newly founded Lao kingdom of Lan Sang. The precious Buddha image, only 50 centimetres tall, was worshipped as a state palladium and should later give the royal capital of Siang Dong-Siang Thòng its new name under which it is still known: Luang Prabang, 'Royal [City] of the Pha Bang'. The Pha Bang image was transferred several times during the last centuries reflecting the vagaries of Lao history: Vientiane (1563), Thonburi (1778), Bangkok (1781), Vientiane (1782), Bangkok (1828), and finally back to Luang Prabang (1867).

19 Also known as *kha phra yomsong* or *lek vat*.

20 Adapted from Thawat Punnothok (1984) *Silacarük isan samai thai-lao: süksa thang dan akkharawitthaya lae prawattisat* [Northeastern Thai inscriptions of the Thai-Lao period: Epigraphical and historical studies of the Northeast]. Bangkok: Thammasat University Press: 153–154.

21 In several Lao inscriptions also called *khet phra rattanatrai*.

22 *Mang*, literally 'to destroy, to annihilate'.

23 *Abai* (P: *apāya*), literally 'places, states or conditions of suffering'. It refers to one of four rebirths where there is no hope of progress or of escape.

24 Thawat (1984: 364). The inscription is dated 'the seventh day of the waxing moon of the second month in the year C.S. 1155' (Wednesday, 8 January 1794).

25 See Thawat Punnothok (1999) 'Kha okat phrathat phanom' [The temple serfs of Phrathat Phanom]. In: *Saranukrom watthanatham phak isan* [Encyclopedia of Thai Culture: The northeastern region], Vol. 2, pp. 488–492. Bangkok.

The monastery containing the *stūpa* of That Phanom, one of the most important religious monuments of Lan Sang, had up to 3,000 temple serfs. See Preuss (1976: 58).

26 See Saowani Phannaphop (1996). *Süksa wikhrò kotmai khosarat nai thana thi pen ekkasan thang prawattisat* [An analytical study of the *Khosarat* law as an historical document]. MA thesis, Sinakharinwirot University: 54, 433.

27 See Inscription No. 1 of Vat Daen Müang, in Thawat (1984: 230–235). Compare similar prohibitions in numerous other inscriptions.

28 Lao inscriptions mention very few exceptions. An important one is the donation of Mae Cao Kham Haeng to Vat Saensukhi-aram (Vientiane province) made in

1603. See inscription G 3/34 N° 108 dated 'seventh day of the waning moon of the tenth month, C.S. 973', i.e. Wednesday, 28 September 1611 (Gagneux 1975: 191–192).

29 Thawat Punnothok (1999) mentions the so-called Bun Sia Kha Hua, a merit-making ceremony performed until the present day on the eighth day of the third month (Lao calendar) of every year by the descendants of a village whose ancestors had been temple serfs of Vat That Phanom (Nakhòn Phanom province). The obligations of the temple serfs had ended more than two centuries ago when Siamese rule spread to the Khorat Plateau.

30 See, for example, the inscription of Vat Si Suphana-aram (Nòng Khai), dated Tuesday, 4 March 1567. Thawat (1984: 261–264).

31 See Dhida (1982: 155–158). Dhida (ibid.: 157–158) emphasizes 'that there was a basic belief concerning land and territorial spirits regardless of religion, which made people donate primarily as a means of gaining merit. This notion corresponds with Paul Mus's idea about the belief in the relationship of land and territorial spirits that played an important role in the expansion of the chief's authority and rights to land. This basic idea spread among the peoples and left some traces in the practice of donating land to religion.'

32 This inscription, dated 'Wednesday, the second day of the waning moon of the fifth month in the *sanga* year (i.e. year of the horse), CS. 1172 [10 April 1811], is published in Thawat (1984: 381–392). Eade (1996: 129–130) argues convincingly that Thawat misread the digit '5' as a '4' as this would change the corresponding Western date to 11 March 1811, which is a Monday.

33 Called Maha Saṅgharāja Cao Khu Hong Kham, which means literally, 'Supreme Patriarch, teacher in the golden hall'.

34 Pha Khu Phon Samek's life is discussed in the *Champassak Chronicle*, Citsavang version, ff° 4/1/1–15/1/2. Cf. Bounleuth (2004: 18–37). A well-written synthesis of the various accounts of Pha Khu Phon Samek in the *Champassak Chronicle* and orally transmitted traditions is Can Inthuphilat (1994) 'Phra khru phonsamek rü yakhru khi hòm' [Phrakhru Phonsamek or Yakhru Khi Hòm]. In *Phrathat cediwat samkhan lae phrakhru yòt kaeo phonsamek* [Important stupas-monasteries and Phrakhru Yòt Kaeo Phonsamek], pp. 85–99. Chiang Mai: Social Research Institute, Chiang Mai University.

One finds a short biography of the monk in the That Phanom Chronicle (*Nithan Urangkhathat*) where he is credited with the respiration of the sacred *stūpa* of That Phanom, notably its spire. See Preuss (1976: 65–67).

For other accounts of Pha Khu Phon Samek's life, see Phraratcha Prichayanmuni (1970) *Theraprawat* [Biography of senior monks]. Nakhòn Phanom: Cao Khana Nakhòn Phanom: 1–20; and Toem Wiphakphotcanakit (1987) *Prawattisat isan* [A history of the Northeast]. Bangkok: Thammasat University Press: 34–47.

35 Very deep knowledges: 1) supernatural power; 2) all-hearing ability; 3) extrasensory perception, reading the mind of another; 4) ability to remember previous incarnations; 5) clairvoyance, all-seeing ability; 6) ability to eliminate evil thoughts or emotions, cessation of desire.

36 Attainment in the practice of Buddhist meditation.

37 *Champassak Chronicle*, Vat Citsavang version, ff° 5/1/4–5/2/2. (Bounleuth 2004: 20–21).

38 In the various versions of the *Champassak Chronicle* called Phanya Müang Saen.

39 *Champassak Chronicle*, Vat Citsavang version, ff° 10/2/3–11/1/1. (Bounleuth 2004: 29–30).

40 'Than Phakhu then was praying [for his safety] "With the power of the good deeds (*deśa pāramī*) being performed in the past existences, [I] would help human

beings (*panna sat*) to avoid danger. [I] prayed to the Gods (*thepphacao*) for protecting people in this time." Then, Than Phakhu could conveniently lead [his] families [of laity] to escape from danger. See *Champassak Chronicle*, Vat Citsavang version, ff° 8/1/1–8/1/2. (Bounleuth 2004: 32).

41 *Champassak Chronicle*, Vat Citsavang version, ff° 16/1/2–16/2/4. (Bounleuth 2004: 39–40).

42 For details, see *Champassak Chronicle*, Vat Citsavang version, ff° 17/1/1. (Bounleuth 2004: 40).

43 For details, see *Champassak Chronicle*, Vat Citsavang version, ff° 12/1/4. (Bounleuth 2004: 32).

44 For details, see *Champassak Chronicle*, Vat Citsavang version, ff° 11/1/2, 11/1/3 and 15/2/1. (Bounleuth 2004: 30, 37–38).

45 *Champassak Chronicle*, Vat Citsavang version, ff° 41/1/3–41/2/1. (Bounleuth 2004: 79–80).

46 Piyachat (1997: 79) even proposes that 'Buddhism [. . .] received a role to support the secular realm (*āṇācakra*) to a large extent until it appeared as if the *buddhacakra* and the *āṇācakra* were inseparably linked with each other'.

47 Bechert (1967: 268) mentions that equally disrupting were the raids of the Chinese ('Hò') marauders in 1872/73 and 1887.

48 As to a discussion of the millenarian revolts, notably the uprising of Cao Hua Sa Kiat Ngong (1817–1819) and the so-called 'Holy Men uprisings' (*kabot phu mi bun*) of 1901/02, in the Lao lands since the late eighteenth century see, e.g., Nonglak Limsiri (1981) *Khwam samkhan khòng kabot hua müang isan ph.s. 2325–2445* [The importance of the uprisings in the northeastern region, AD 1782–1902]. MA thesis, Bangkok: Silapakorn University; and Toem (1987: 491–516).

8

PAST, PRESENT AND FUTURE IN BUDDHIST PROPHETIC LITERATURE OF THE LAO

Peter Koret

Whereas the topic that is most prominently treated in prophetic literature of the nineteenth through twentieth centuries is not surprisingly the future, a study of its content reveals that in that future the authors are very much talking about the present, and that that present is very much given meaning by their preoccupation with the past. Prophetic literature, therefore, can serve as an important source of information in the construction of both a cultural and intellectual history of Lao-speaking people, and more generally a study of the effect of modernization on traditional Theravada Buddhist cultures in Southeast Asia. In our approach to prophetic literature, we will examine prophetic works in the context of a) the literary tradition out of which they originated, and b) the historical circumstances under which they were composed, out of which arose the specific set of concerns that literary expression was made use of to address. We will examine both prophetic literature from the nineteenth through early twentieth centuries, which anticipated modernization and its consequences, and prophetic works from the mid-twentieth century onwards, in which the consequences that were anticipated in earlier works very much dictate the concerns that a traditional style of writing is made use of to express.

Part One: Prophetic works of the nineteenth through early twentieth centuries

In contemporary studies of traditional culture in Southeast Asia (both by westerners and Southeast Asians), the perspective of the writers – and the style that is made use of in the presentation of that perspective – is very much a product of the modernization of which they write. One important aspect of prophetic works is that in contrast and in counter-balance to modern studies of the past, prophetic works can be understood as 'studies' of the future as seen from the perspective of the past by literary composers whose very duty was to preserve that past from the threat of that future.

Buddhist prophetic literature of the nineteenth through early twentieth centuries presents a picture of the world based upon the belief in a Buddhist era of five thousand years following the enlightenment of the Buddha. As time grows increasingly distant from the appearance of a Buddha on earth, Buddhist teachings gradually deteriorate, throwing the world into a state of great turmoil. Prophecy of the decline of Buddhism is not original to the Lao, but can be traced back to the *Tripiṭaka*. Indeed, one of the most popular works of Lao Buddhist prophecy, *Khwam Fan Phanya Patsen* (The Dreams of Phanya Patsen), is based upon a canonical Jātaka tale. Prophetic works of literature depicting the decline of Buddhism are also widespread among neighbouring Southeast Asian groups, including, for example, the Tai Yuan (i.e. people of Lan Na), the Thai, the Khmer, etc.[1] Similar to the use of the framework of canonical Jātaka tales in the composition of traditional Lao literature, the conventions of Buddhist prophecy were adapted by the Lao and came to take on a variety of traits reflective of Lao society in their adaptation.

Literary and historical context to prophetic literature

In order to make sense of Lao works of Buddhist prophecy, we first need to understand the sense that they make in the context in which they were created, i.e. as a form of literature. Whatever unique characteristics they may possess within their own category, that category only exists as part of the larger literary tradition, in the context of which it was meaningful. Traditional literature provided the composers with a pre-existing framework of conventions with which to record their thoughts in writing, and the audience with a familiar 'vocabulary of expression' with which such thoughts could be understood and appreciated. It was very much this literary background, both in the conventions of literary expression and the social context in which such expression was customarily presented to an audience, that gave the literature its power as a means of communication.

Both the similarities and differences between traditional and prophetic works of Lao literature need to be understood in the context of the social and historical environments that led to their creation.[2] From the fourteenth through late seventeenth centuries, Lan Sang was a powerful and prosperous kingdom that united Lao and other groups under a single rule. Similar to other Southeast Asian kingdoms during the same period, Theravada Buddhism played an important political as well as religious role as an institution. The power of the temple was at times comparable to that of the monarchy, which was dependent upon religious legitimization in its governing. The significance of literature in Lan Sang largely rested upon its efficiency as a medium through which the temple could communicate its teachings.

Literature in Lan Sang owes its origins to two primary sources: a) the cultural influence of the neighbouring kingdom of Lan Na, from which the Lao borrowed many of their stories, conventions in the telling and performance of the stories, and the scripts in which the stories were recorded, and b) a tradition of regional oral poetry and story-telling that has predated and continues to exist to the present day side-by-side with the written tradition. One of the most important literary imports from Lan Na was the specific relationship between literature and the temple, and the precise ways in which the literature defined its religious identity. On one level, a fundamental objective of literature in Lan Sang was to teach Buddhist practices that were expected to be followed by laymen, such as the observance of the Five Precepts, support of the temple, etc. On another level, the responsibility of literary works was the maintenance and preservation of the 'world' from one generation to the next, which included, for example, conventions to be followed in everyday life, performance of the monthly rites (known as *Hit Sip Saung* – 'Annual cycle of events that are mandated by custom'), which were necessary to avert disaster and assure the prosperity of the community, a prescribed code of interaction between people and groups of people based upon established social hierarchies, an understanding of man's place (and his proper duties) within the world in which he lived, etc. None of these teachings in any way contradicted the notion of literature as a religious tradition, for the conventions were not legitimized and given value within a modern nationalist framework as being part of a precious and secular 'Lao heritage', but rather through the way in which they were traceable back to the 'religious' realm of the past in which they were sanctified by the Buddha, the Lord Indra, and various Tai deities.

In the late seventeeth century, Lan Sang split into three smaller states as a result of internal rivalry among its nobility. The lack of unity within the kingdom, and the weakened conditions that it engendered, were to ultimately prove fatal to the Lan Sang royalty and their aspirations for power in the region. The bitter conflict between the kingdoms that formerly comprised Lan Sang was ultimately to be exploited by the kingdom of Siam, which desired to extend its influence, while at the same time fearful of the assistance that independent Lao kingdoms might provide to their enemies, the Burmese. Vientiane was invaded and sacked by the Siamese in the early 1820s after a war between Siam and Vientiane that was to have disastrous consequences for the Lao. Following the defeat of Vientiane, the Siamese significantly increased their control of the region, and implemented deportations of an unprecedented scale in which people were forcibly settled in Northeast and Central Thailand. Despite Siamese expansion, however, prior to the late nineteenth century Siamese control was largely exercised indirectly through local elites who continued to rule following traditional Lao administrative practices. At the same time, Siamese culture did not make great inroads into the region. All of this was to drastically change, however, with the threat of

French colonial expansion. The territory that comprised contemporary Laos was annexed by the French at the end of the nineteenth century. Fearful of further expansion by the French and British, King Chulalongkorn radically reformed the administration of outlying regions of the country. In Northeast Thailand, the local elite were replaced by administrators and administrative practices brought in from Bangkok, and vigorous attempts were made to instil in its inhabitants a Siamese identity. Such change, however, did not go uncontested. In the late nineteenth and early twentieth centuries, millenarian movements spread throughout the region, which can be interpreted as a result of both the social and cultural upheavals in the region, and the exploitation of those upheavals by members of local elites whose interests were directly threatened by the process of change.

During this period, literature in the traditional mould continued to be produced and performed. Indeed, there is even evidence to suggest that the majority of literary works in the Lao language that have come down to us were produced during the nineteenth century.[3] At the same time, however, from the late nineteenth century onwards, the unsettled conditions of the period also provided the impetus for the creation of a type of literature that was very different from previous works. The literature of prophecy can be understood as a reflection of and reaction to the social and political turmoil of the nineteenth and twentieth centuries, which brought about new demands in the preservation of the 'world' that was a traditional subject of literature. In traditional literature, not only was the preservation of traditional society a primary objective in its composition, the very preservation of those traditions was, in and of itself, undertaken in a traditional manner. The conventional nature of the style that was made use of in literature was not only considered practical as a result of its proven track record (i.e. it had worked in the past), but also legitimized as a part of the past that it attempted to preserve. In contrast, as a result of the radical changes in society, composers were forced to recognize that traditional approaches could no longer successfully achieve their desired ends. As a result of the late stage of the Buddhist era, the authors commonly declare that a) new diseases have arisen that have never before been seen, and b) old types of medicine have grown ineffective in the treatment of the very same diseases that they had once cured.[4]

Prophetic works composed during this period are widespread in Lao-speaking regions, and can be found throughout northern, central, and southern Laos, and Northeast Thailand. In my own research I have uncovered a total of roughly twenty works, which are by no means exhaustive. Whereas the majority of Lao literary works are composed in poetic form, the great majority of prophetic works are recorded in a prose form known as *Nitsay*, a writing genre in which Pali texts are (or supposedly are) translated into Lao.[5] In previous writings, the sole reference that I have found to this type of literature is in relationship to its connection with the above-mentioned millenarian movements and the political objectives of its instigators. It is important, however, to emphasize that whereas some of the works were indeed made use of (and perhaps specifically created) by such movements, and the identity of their composers shared certain similarities with what we know about figures within these movements, the category of works in general can be understood less as being deliberately orchestrated by certain groups or individuals than as the outcome of the cultural environment under which such movements were to arise.

The logic of prophetic works of Lao literature

In our analysis of the 'logic' of prophetic works of literature as a response to the threat of modernization on traditional culture, this essay will investigate prophetic literature in comparison with traditional literature through a discussion of a) the construction of a religious identity, b) claims of sacred origin, c) types of religious teachings and karmic enforcement, d) the prescribed handling of the texts, and finally, e) their social and political commentary.

The construction of religious identity in literature

Similar to traditional literature, the legitimacy of an author's message in a work of prophetic literature is dependent upon claims to the sacred nature of its origins. In order to understand how such claims are justified, we must first consider the construction of religious identity in traditional works of literature.[6] Regardless of its patronage by the temple, the majority of traditional literature is not scriptural in origin. Individual stories frequently bear close similarities to tales within the oral story-telling tradition, and it is not uncommon to find that the element of religious teaching within a given work is relatively minimal, and even subservient to the role of the story as romance and entertainment. However, regardless of either the origins and/or content of individual tales, written literature is perceived by its audience as a source of religious authority. The religious identity of literature is established both through conventions in the composition of individual works, and the existence of that individual work within the larger tradition. The religious quality that is attached to literature, much of which was inherent in the tradition in Lan Na prior to its introduction into Lan Sang, is a product of both the social context of its usage and the nature of the literary medium itself. As a result of the central role of the temple in the patronage of the literature, there are a number of factors in the recording, storage, and performance of traditional literature that serve to establish its religious credentials, including:

- The script in which literature is recorded; There are two types of scripts, the Tham (literally, *dhamma*) script, which is intended for the recording of religious works, and the Lao script, which is made use of for topic matter that is more worldly in nature. In actuality, however, in many cases the use of a given script denotes less the content of a given text than its social use. Works in Tham are typically stored and performed inside the temple, whereas writings recorded in Lao are kept and performed in private homes. In the case of poetry, on the other hand, identical works can be recorded in both scripts and made use of either in the context of religious sermons or entertainment. The re-recording of a poem from Lao into Tham can be referred to as 'ordaining a book'. In prose works, however, which are generally composed in a form known as *Nitsay* (which shall be discussed in greater detail later in this section), the restrictions are greater, and they can only be recorded in Tham and are usually stored inside of the temple.

- Performers and performance; works recorded in the Tham script are typically performed within the temple by monks and novices. They are performed as a part of religious sermons, and events within the annual cycle known as *Hit Sip Saung*, which often have their own specific religious significance.
- Place of storage; literary works in Tham are generally stored in the temple inside of a library known as *Hau Trai* ('Room of the *Tripiṭaka* Scriptures'), in which writings are not differentiated as being of scriptural or non-scriptural origin. (When works in Tham are occasionally found in private homes, they tend to be placed upon altars where sacred objects, such as Buddha images, are stored.)
- Skills prerequisite to the creation, preservation, and consumption of literature; the major skills involved in the literary process are learned at the temple, including, for example, literacy, methods of transcription, chanting styles, etc.
- The central role of *kamma* in the literary process; both the promise of positive *kamma* and the threat of negative *kamma* serve as major motivational factors behind the creation of literature, the donation of materials required for its creation, its performance, and participation as a part of its audience.

As can be seen in many of the above points, the religious perception of the literature is based upon the patronage of the Buddhist temple, and the opportunities that the written medium allows for its control of literary production and consumption. In addition, the religious perception of literature is also a result of the limitations of the same medium, and obstacles in the distribution of literature that effectively prevent an individual from gaining a broad or thorough understanding of the tradition. Obstacles in gaining a thorough knowledge of literature include, for example, a) the time-intensive method of its circulation, in which the transcription of even a single manuscript can take months to complete, b) the impossibility of establishing the authorship of individual works and the date of their composition, c) difficulties in communications, which renders impossible any overview of the literary tradition as a whole, etc.[7] These types of limitations have contributed to the Lao perception that literature was of mythical proportions and beyond the mastery of a single individual. It is perhaps not surprising that the religious identity of literature and the mythical proportions of the tradition came to be exploited for the benefit of those who were knowledgeable (or perceived to be knowledgeable) in that tradition, and invested the works with an authority that was directly translatable into power. For this reason, access to literary works was not only limited by the nature of its medium and poor communications, but also intentionally restricted by both the temple, where the majority of the works were stored, and private owners of individual manuscripts.

An understanding of the religious identity of traditional literature provides an important foundation from which to approach the study of prophetic works of literature. As predictions of the future, a crucial concern of such writing (to which composers devoted much of their text) was the establishment of its authority as religious discourse. We can observe that they made use of many of the identical conventions as conventional literature in their achievement of that objective. It is important to note the degree of flexibility in the construction of literary works as religious texts, as clearly illustrated in the use of the Tham script in the 'ordination' of a work of literature based upon intended social usage rather than actual content. This type of flexibility was instrumental in the legitimization of prophetic works. Based upon available evidence, prophetic works of literature were primarily stored in private homes rather than the temple.[8] Whereas it would not perhaps have strictly been forbidden to keep such works in a temple, the type of social commentary contained in their content, and particularly the direct criticism of the state of the monkhood, meant that it would have been highly unfeasible for them to have been performed by monks or even during the type of communal occasions when literary works were customarily read. Regardless of such restrictions, however, it is significant that their authors insisted on composing the great majority of prophetic literature in the form of *Nitsay* prose, which can only be recorded in the religious Tham script that is generally intended to be performed by monks in a temple.

Claims of unique origins

In general, individual works of traditional literature do not devote a lot of space or effort to the repetition of specific claims of sacred origin, which are pretty well established through the conventions described in the previous sections. In addition, claims to unique origins of individual works are not attempted, as they would contradict the very foundation from which such works claim their authority – as part of a larger tradition.

In contrast, a primary characteristic of prophetic works of literature is the great emphasis on the sacred origins of a work, and the uniqueness of those origins, which is repeatedly stated throughout the text. Prophetic works are attributed to either the Buddha (in one example the Buddha together with the Future Buddha, Phra Maitreya), Indra, or a combination of both.

In *Pheun Meuang Krung*, for example, the Buddha journeys to Southeast Asia and makes a prophecy to his disciple Ānanda, which is put into writing by Lord Indra, whereas in *Kala Nap Meu Suay*, the Buddha prophesies in answer to a deity who asks him about the state of Buddhism after the Buddha's own enlightenment. In *Tamnan Hin Taek* (Chronicle of the Broken Rock), the Buddha preaches to Phra Maitreya in response to the concerns of a sacred hermit, and the text is subsequently attributed to both the present and future Buddha. In *Kham Saun Phraya In* (The Teachings of Lord Indra), *Fa Samang Kham*, and *Nangseu Tok Jak Meuang In* (Writing That Has Fallen From the Land of Indra), the words are held to be specifically composed by Indra.

In traditional Lao literature, we have already observed the use of the written medium as a means through which to establish the sacred quality of the content. This characteristic is especially developed in works of prophetic literature in order to establish their unique origins. In *Tamnan Hin Taek*, for example, the work is uncovered by a farmer when he goes to his fields and discovers that a bolt of lightening has struck a great boulder, revealing writing that is miraculously inscribed on its inside. He is unable to make sense of the writing, which is later interpreted by a noble of high-ranking position, who states: 'The content is truly profound. . . . The writing on that stone is not composed by ordinary human beings. . . . It is likely that it has been inscribed and brought down by deities, and encountered by us as a result of our great merit' (Niyom Suphawit 1989: 4). In *Pheun Meuang Krung* and *Fa Samang Kham*, the manuscript is described as being brought down by Indra in a golden container. The significance of the medium in the establishment of the miraculous nature of the texts can be seen in the fact that it serves as the title of some of the works, such as *Tamnan Hin Taek* ('Chronicle of the Broken Rock' i.e. where the writing is inscribed), and *Nangseu Tok Jak Meuang In* ('Writing That Has Fallen From the Land of Indra'). Note that the word '*nangseu*' ('writing' or 'book') is not commonly used in the title of literary works. Whereas composers of prophetic literature make use of traditional conventions in the construction of their sacred identity, the extent to which they attempt to establish their unique and powerful origin indicates that in comparison to traditional literature there is a greater sense of insecurity concerning the level of acceptability of such works among their intended audience. Whereas the reasons behind this insecurity will be discussed at greater length later in this essay, it is sufficient to say that in the construction of what are essentially 'underground' religious works that are largely performed exclusively outside of the temple, there is a need to authenticate the content in a manner that would not be necessary for works composed directly under religious patronage.

Types of specific teachings and karmic enforcement

In terms of instructions as to how an audience is specifically told to act, traditional and prophetic works of literature are in many ways remarkably similar, reflective of the popular practice of Buddhism in Southeast Asia. Audiences are repeatedly exhorted to a) follow the Five Precepts, b) pay respect to the Triple Gems, c) give support to the monkhood, etc. At the same time, people are taught established codes of behaviour in the interaction between different individuals and groups of people in society (such as relationships between children/parents, students/teachers, subjects/rulers, etc.), which are all placed within the context of Buddhism.

Whereas there is great similarity in the nature of their basic teaching, there is also a major difference between traditional and prophetic works of literature in the way in which such teaching is taught. On a fundamental level, both forms of literature place their teaching within the larger framework of *kamma*, through which the audience will be rewarded and/or punished in terms of the level of their conformance to the wishes of their authors. The exact use of *kamma*, however, differs considerably between the two groups of works. In traditional literature, proper patterns of behaviour are largely taught indirectly through the stories that are told. It is also not uncommon for an author to insert an occasional remark directly aimed at the audience in which they are told to observe the Five Precepts, support the temple, etc., for which they will reap the positive consequences of their *kamma*. In prophetic works, the use of *kamma* differs in a) the great frequency of direct demands upon the behaviour of the audience, and b) the consistently intimidating nature of the threat of karmic punishment by which it is enforced. In prophetic works, large portions of the texts are devoted to the depiction of various types of human suffering in the immediate and not so immediate future, such as war, starvation, separation of families, the abandonment of entire villages, etc., which doubtlessly reflect the social circumstances of the time of their composition. In addition, however, the author appears to dwell on the morbid details of the punishments, as in 'if you sit you will die, if you lay down you will die, you will cough up blood and die, you will die from a variety of diseases, you will have head aches, blurry eyes, animals will kill, eat, and bite you',[9] 'you will die by scorpion bites, tiger bites, centipede bites, snake bites',[10] etc. The authors state consistently that the only way in which such suffering can be avoided is to act in conformance with the morality set forth in the text. On one level, there is a definite connection between the claims of the unique, and uniquely powerful, origin of the texts, and the power that is made use of to coerce the audience into acquiescence to their demands.

The increased role of coercive power in prophetic literature is illustrated in a shift in emphasis from the Buddha to the Lord Indra. In traditional Lao literature, the Lord Indra is primarily made use of as a deity of great power who intervenes in our world on behalf of the Buddha and the Buddhist religion. Whereas he is clearly subservient to the Buddha, he is also seen as a representation of sheer power in a manner that would be impossible to be attributed to the Buddha, a characteristic that is evident in traditional literature, and particularly comes to the foreground in prophetic works.[11] Whereas a composer would hesitate to present a picture of the Buddha as a great destructive force wreaking havoc on mankind, Indra – as a symbol of power in the service of the greater good – is portrayed in works of prophetic literature as committing (or ordering) deadly attacks on thousands or millions of humans who are labelled as sinners. It is in this role as an enforcer and powerful agent of righteous anger that Indra becomes such an important figure in (and frequently the attributed author of) prophetic literature, in which he is the central actor, and the Buddha is relegated to the background as the necessary justification behind his violent actions. Indra, for example, as the author of the widespread prophetic work *Kham Saun Phraya In*, warns his audience: 'If you do not follow the customary conventions, I personally will smash your head into seven pieces with a heavy piece of metal', a statement that would be difficult to place into the mouth of an enlightened being. In *Tamnan Hin Taek* the Lord Indra recognizes that human beings have grown immoral, and no longer act in accordance with the Buddha's teachings. He therefore devises a strategy to resolve the situation, which involves ordering his subordinates to kill sinners, consisting of the majority of mankind. Similar to the relationship between the Buddha and the Lord Indra is the relationship between the Man of Merit (sometimes stated to be Phra Maitreya), and the various non-human entities such as guardian deities (*rakkha*) and local spirits (*phi*). In *Pheun Meuang Krung* for example, the arrival of the Meritorious One and the dawning of a new age on earth is preceded by the arrival of vast numbers of these creatures, who appear on earth in order to destroy the multitudes of immoral humans who are not fit to take part in such an age. Despite the emphasis on righteous and extreme violence, however, on certain occasions, the authors feel the need to legitimize it in the context of Buddhist teaching. In *Tamnan Hin Taek*, Chatulok is sent down to earth by the Lord Indra for the express purpose of 'taking all sinners'. When he is asked by the very same Lord Indra why so many people have died, his answer is: "No one caused their deaths. It is the result of their own *kamma*' (Niyom Suphawit 1989: 8). In a similar fashion, when, in *Pheun Meuang Krung*, the Buddha is asked by a disciple why enlightened beings do not save mankind from the disasters that befall them, his answer is that it is impossible as a result of the immorality of the humans, who cannot escape their *kamma*.

For all the horrendous display of power by the authors of prophetic works of literature, the precarious nature of that power is clearly illustrated by the extent of the effort they find it necessary to exert merely in order to compel their audience to believe in their words, a belief that the authors of traditional literature would have simply taken for granted. If the audience accepts the contents of prophetic works as the truth, they will escape a variety of dangers described in the authors' prophecies, they will see the Future Buddha or Man of Merit, etc. To the contrary, if they do not, they will cough up blood and die, all members of the household will die, they will never see the Man of Merit, etc. In *Tamnan Hin Taek*, for example, the author writes: 'There once was a person who did not believe in these sacred teachings . . . He said: "I do not believe . . ." Not long after he said this all three members of his household died. None were left. For that reason, everyone should believe' (*ibid.*: 9). In addition to coercing an audience into accepting the truth of their writings, the authors of prophetic works of literature also provide an equal amount of incentive in order to ensure their writings' wide distribution. The audience is instructed both to keep prophetic works of literature in their homes and distribute them to others. They are warned that *phi* will travel to each house to destroy sinners, sparing only those households that have prophetic works in their possession. If, however, one is to keep prophetic literature to oneself and make no attempt to circulate its content, the inevitable result will be 'great trouble' and ultimately 'death'. This type of negative reinforcement is not commonly found in traditional works of literature.

The prescribed handling of the text

We have observed that *kamma* provides a fundamental motivational factor in the promotion of all aspects of the literary cycle, including the creation. preservation, performance, and consumption of literary works. The transcription, donation of materials necessary to the transcription, performance, participation as an audience, etc. all have very specific amounts of *kamma* (and specified rewards) to serve as incentive towards the continuation of the tradition. In addition, manuscripts not uncommonly describe the respectful manner in which they must be treated as a result of their sacred origins. In certain stories, for example, the audience is told that the texts must be coated with gold, held at a proper height, formally shown respect with an offering of flowers and incense, not performed on certain occasions, etc.[12] Specific instructions regarding the treatment of prophetic manuscripts do not substantially differ from those of other types of literature. However, there is a greater emphasis that is placed on the importance of the respectful treatment of manuscripts as a whole, which fits in with the general thesis that their authors are more insecure concerning the acceptance of their writings among their intended audience. Whereas in traditional literature instruction concerning the treatment of manuscripts generally occurs exclusively at the end (or at times beginning) of a text, in prophetic writings similar instructions occur consistently throughout. In addition, there is also a greater extent to which the threat of bad *kamma* is stated in relationship to the improper treatment of the manuscript, which is equal to, if not exceeding, threats for failure to follow the Five Precepts, the Triple Gems, etc.[13]

Social and political commentary contained in literary works

In our examination of social and political commentary in prophetic works of literature, we first need to address a question that becomes apparent from the previous sections: if the major objective of their composers is simply to ask an audience to follow patterns of behaviour that have commonly been taught in works of literature and religious sermons for centuries, why do they feel the need to make so much effort both to a) establish the unique and powerful origins of their works as a source of religious authority, and b) intimidate through such a persistent threat of such extreme forms of punishment? In answering this question, we must take into account a distinction between the context in which such teaching is presented in traditional and prophetic works of literature, and the extra meaning that it thereby comes to take on in the latter type. In traditional literature, the basic teachings (such as the following of the precepts, etc.) are presented as if normal practice that is logically followed by people in the 'world', a 'world' that literature is made use of to preserve. People who fail to follow such practices are exceptions rather than the norm, and their behaviour is eventually corrected (through their death or otherwise), and the norm preserved. The 'world' of prophetic literature, however, is a 'world' that has very much changed, in which failure to act in accordance with traditional conventions has become the norm. As a result, exhortations for people to follow basic teachings, such as the observance of the Five Precepts, etc., take on a social significance as a condemnation not only of individuals but also an abnormal world, in which 'normal' and 'logical' practices are no longer observed.[14] This extra meaning can be seen in the fact that such teachings are by and large expressed a) negatively as threats and admonishments rather than more neutrally, as is generally the case in traditional literature, and b) within the larger context of social and/or political statements concerning society as a whole. Commentary of this nature in prophetic works is expressed as very specific criticism directed at the actions of three different groups of people: a) political authorities (including kings, nobles, and government officials), b) the Buddhist temple, and c) the general population.

Social and political commentary is not unique to prophetic works, but also exists within the content of traditional literary works. It is common, for example, to find stories that depict an evil king, who as a result of his misdeeds is eventually driven from his throne. In this type of story (as illustrated, for example, by *Thao Kamphra Kai Kiaew, Suphrom Mokkha,* etc.), however, the conclusion ultimately serves to reaffirm the legitimacy of the institution, which through the law of *kamma* possesses a self-correcting mechanism to protect it from abuse. It is far less common to find criticism of the monkhood (which as far as I know consists of nothing more than humorous depictions of mischievous novices).[15] This should not be surprising considering the central role that the temple plays in literary production.

In contrast to traditional literature, both the specific types of criticism that are contained in prophetic literature and their objectives are considerably different in nature. Rather than providing an example of the corruption of an individual within an institution and its ultimate 'correction', prophetic works portray the state of the institutions themselves as being corrupt, and lacking a self-correcting mechanism (at least in the foreseeable future), in which such corruption can properly be addressed. Indeed, as repeatedly stated throughout the works, the decline of the institutions is a normal (if regrettable) state of affairs, as a result of the late stage of the Buddhist era, as affirmed by none other than the Buddha himself.

In order to understand the logic of social and political commentary that is the subject of prophetic works of literature, let us briefly consider the criticism of political authorities and the Buddhist temple that is contained in their content. A commonly found criticism of political authorities is that the monarchy, nobles, and government officials have no legitimacy in their rule as a result of the fact that the government of Siam has appointed commoners to administrative positions that customarily should be filled by those of noble blood. In *Pheun Meuang Krung*, for example, the suffering of the Lao and other groups under Siamese domination is declared inevitable, as the Siamese royalty have been descended from common stock since the fall of Ayutthaya. Prophetic works also condemn specific actions of kings and government officials, the barbarity of which is often blamed on their low birth. Examples include corruption, favouring rich people in legal cases, excessive taxation, and extortion of money from poor villagers. Criticism of the low birth of high officials is also typically expressed through the use of symbolism, including, for example, 'wolves becoming royal lions', 'evil people riding beautiful elephants', 'golden swans bowing down to black crows', etc.[16] In its criticism of religious institutions, prophetic literature frequently portrays monks as being lazy, having no interest in Buddhist studies, and failing to observe rules of monastic discipline. In addition, they are condemned for greed, and their desire to engage in commercial pursuits. In *Kham Saun Phanya In*, the author declares that monks nowadays are similar to 'rotten fish wrapped up in banana leaves'.

In the context of this type of social commentary, it may be tempting to approach prophetic literature from a modern perspective as a form of secular writing in which the primary significance of religious expression is in the legitimacy that it confers on political incitement aimed at contesting the powers that be. To the contrary, however, in the context of the society in which the works were originally composed, it is less appropriate to consider the use of religious commentary as a means through which to express a political message than to understand the use of political commentary as part of a larger message that is essentially religious in nature. Whereas the criticism of worldly institutions is in one sense political, its cause, meaning, and ultimate solution is envisioned entirely within the religious context of a traditional Lao world-view.

In analysing the religious dimension of social commentary in prophetic works of literature, let us return again to our previous observation that in works devoted to the future, it is significant to find such a preoccupation with the past. A primary objective of prophetic works is an aggressive insistence in the continued authority of that past, the relevance of which is not in spite of the changes of the present but precisely because of them. One major importance of the past is its role as a vehicle through which meaning is given to the seemingly meaningless turmoil that engulfed Laos and Northeastern Thailand in the nineteenth and early twentieth centuries. As such, psychologically, it provides an important source of reassurance to people who are uprooted, whether physically through war and political instability, or mentally as a result of the insecurity of the times. Buddhist prophecy has a lot to say about the abnormal state of the present; it was not necessary to go outside the framework of Lao traditional culture to be given sense and meaning. As the nature of the changes were clearly against the interests of the people who produced the literature, it is not surprising that there is no ambiguity in the meaning of the change according Buddhist prophecy. It is 'immoral', 'abnormal', and 'evil', and yet at the same time part of the natural course of events, which will in the end (if in a time frame that may well be beyond the life of the composers and their audience) only serve to reaffirm the authority of the past. After all, whereas on a superficial level it may appear that the Lao are powerless against the Siamese and/or French authorities, ultimately these foreigners have been created by – and are forced to act in accordance to – Lao traditional culture, a culture that dictates their present appearance, judges their actions as immoral, and eventually will see them destroyed, together with the Lao people who are foolish and ill-advised enough to support them.

A second important role of the past in prophetic literature is as a compass that dictates the way in which people must navigate through the uncertainty of the present. The present and future depicted in prophetic texts is a world of great danger, filled with suffering and death. It is only through the conformance to the traditional cultural practices of the past (as represented by the observance of the Five Precepts, respect of one's elders, etc.) that one can circumvent the types of dangers that are so heavily advertised in the texts. Never is there a suggestion that the suffering that is brought about by the social change of the period (inclusive of government oppression, war, etc.)

can be overcome through a solution that is either political or military in nature. Rather, the only solution is moral, which requires a restoration of the moral and orderly 'world' of the past. Whereas one cannot deny the pessimist perspective of such writings (which is reflective both of the times in which they were written and the conventions of Buddhist prophecy), it is noteworthy that many of the prophecies do in fact end with a restoration of order either a) with the arrival of Phra Maitreya in the distant future, or b) a Man of Great Merit (occasionally also referred to as Phra Maitreya), who will appear within the lifetime of the audience. An individual's ability to escape the turmoil of the present is largely determined by his or her ability to come into contact with the Man of Merit in this lifetime or Phra Maitreya in a future one, which can only be achieved through the conformance of one's behaviour to traditional convention, through which positive *kamma* will be generated to spare one from punishment.

In addition to its preoccupation with the past, a further illustration of the religious dimension of social commentary in prophetic works can be seen by the fact that the majority of criticism is directed neither at political nor religious authorities, but rather the general public. Whereas the improper deeds of the government and the temple result in the suffering of the common people, it is ultimately their own weak morality that is the cause of their punishment. As stated consistently by the composers of such works, human suffering in the late stage of the Buddhist era is the result of the failure of the public to act in accordance with the 'compass' of tradition, whether that suffering is to be inflicted by non-human entities or government agencies.

In many ways, prophetic writing can be interpreted as a tradition of underground religious literature in Lao society, rooted in two seeming contradictions: a) the essence through which it makes sense of the world and legitimizes that sense is religious in nature, and yet it appears to have been excluded from public performance inside of the temple, and b) a major motivation in its composition is the preservation of the major institutions of society, and yet according to its authors, such a conservative goal can only be achieved through radical change. Such contradictions, however, do not represent a major shift in the world-view of its composers or their concept of literature and what it was intended to accomplish in society, but rather the state of the times, in which the preservation of the traditional world was no longer synonymous with the upholding of the status quo.[17]

Part Two: Lao prophetic works of literature from the mid-twentieth century onwards

By the mid-twentieth century, the Lao culture of Northeast Thailand, and to a lesser extent Laos, had changed radically from a half a century earlier. This type of change is aptly illustrated in the interpretation of the Lao and

Northeast Thai of their own literary tradition from this period onwards. Typically, in the transformation in the social use of traditional Lao literature, one initially finds an attempt to maintain the relevance of literature through the use of older literary forms in the communication of modern concerns, and subsequently the use of older works of literature as cultural artefacts that are used to represent the past in a way that is meaningful to the present.[18] One finds a similar pattern in the twentieth century use of prophetic literature. In this section, we will consider three examples of the modern use of prophetic literature, including a) the composition of *Panha Tamnai Lok* (Riddles of Buddhist Prophecy), in Northeast Thailand in the mid-twentieth century, b) interpretations of *Kala Nap Meu Suay*, a prophetic work of literature from the nineteenth or early twentieth century, and c) the interpretation of *Kala Nap Meu Suay* and its adaptation in the song-writing of a political band of the 1970s from Northeast Thailand known as Caravan.

Panha Thamnai Lok *(Riddles of Buddhist Prophecy)*

Ironically, the very centres of modernization that were so rapidly to destroy traditional literature were also to play an important role in its preservation. However, the circumstances of that preservation were inevitably to have a profound effect on how literature was to be preserved – and changed in the process. By the mid-twentieth century, the continued survival of traditional literature in Northeast Thailand was dependent to a large degree not upon the Buddhist temple in rural communities, but rather printing houses, mostly run by Chinese in the larger towns. These presses helped to maintain the relevance of literature through a) cheap mass production made possible by the introduction and spread of printing technology, and b) their transcription in the Thai script (but not language), as newer generations of Lao speakers were no longer educated in the scripts in which traditional literature had been recorded. Whereas these printed works could be made use of in temples, by and large they served as entertainment to be read individually or performed together with music. *Panha Tamnai Lok* (Riddles of World Prophecy), by A. Kawiwong, is a work of prophecy that was published in 1959 by a small publishing house in Khon Khaen, Northeast Thailand.[19]

Panha Tamnai Lok is written in the form of Buddhist prophecy. It is composed as a series of inter-related riddles, ambiguous in nature, each of which is answered at length to explain the state of our world in the future. The style of the work is reminiscent of the well-known prophetic work *Khwam Fan Phanya Patsen* (The Dreams of Phanya Patsen), upon which the work is likely to have been based.[20] In addition to its style, there are a number of basic aspects of the work that show the influence of traditional Buddhist prophecy, including, for example: a) the claims to the sacred origin of the riddles that comprise its context, which are stated to have been formulated by

Shiva, b) the negative assessment of the future, which includes both criticism of the general population (in a similar manner to the prophetic works of at least half a century earlier) and political institutions, and c) statements concerning the role of Phra Maitreya in the alleviation of the abnormal state of the world. At the same time, however, there are also a number of important aspects to this work that indicate that the intention of the author is not to make sense of social change through a traditional Buddhist world-view, but rather simply to make use of that world-view as a conventional means with which to construct a statement that is essentially political in nature. As a result, one can observe serious tensions, and ultimately contradictions, between the political message that the author intends to convey to his audience and the religious framework that is made use of in its presentation.

The shift in the use of prophetic literature from the past can be seen in a number of statements that clearly illustrate that the author does not share the traditional religious view of the world from which early works of prophecy were generated and given meaning. As a major objective of earlier prophetic works was to find meaning in social change, *Panha Tamnai Lok*, in its introduction is somewhat similarly claimed by its author to be of interest to its audience as an explanation of why revolutions are a common occurrence throughout the world. However, whereas works of prophecy through the early twentieth century legitimize their prophecy through the sanctity of their religious origins, the primary means through which the author of *Panha Tamnai Lok* provides justification for his composition to a new generation that has been educated in secular government schooling is with the writings of H. G. Wells, as explained in its introduction. As the Thai increasingly turned to the west rather than the temple for guidance, the foreboding state of the world depicted in works of western fiction rather than scriptural sources provided important evidence that the destructive state of the world and its future should be accepted as a universal and universally recognized phenomenon.

The shift in the world-view of the author is illustrated rather dramatically in his refutation of two of the fundamental principles of prophetic literature: a) the assertion that the abnormal state of the world is the result of the late stage of the Buddhist era, and b) the belief in the coming of Phra Maitreya, and the hope for salvation. First, the author declares that the world has always been in the same miserable state and always will be up until the time of its final destruction. Second, in a manner somewhat surprising for a work of Buddhist prophecy, in the beginning of the work, in the interpretation of the first riddle, the author appears to make fun of people's belief in the coming of the Future Buddha, as follows:

> Riddle Number One: "Oh Stork, Why do you not make noise?"
> Reply of the Stork: "Because the fish do not come out"

In the author's explanation, he writes: '. . . the reason that the stork does not make noise, people are waiting for Phra Maitreya, the Man of Great Merit, to come down. Everybody is waiting for the Man of Merit to come to help. They can wait forever and they will never see him.' The above two statements are noteworthy not only in their disagreement with the very principles which form the foundations of prophetic literature, but also the fact that each is contradicted in the passage by which it is immediately followed. After stating that the world will always be in the same degraded state until the final day of its destruction, the author briefly describes the dawning of a new and better age heralded in by the arrival of Phra Maitreya. In a similar fashion, after he warns people that they will never see Phra Maitreya, no matter how long they wait, he once again describes the future arrival of Phra Maitreya on earth. In each of these two instances (which are the only references to Phra Maitreya in the entire text), we can observe that the author has no desire either to convey the message that the suffering of mankind is the result of the late stage of the Buddhist era, or that it is redeemable through a religious solution. He appears obliged to make his prophetic work conclude in the way that prophetic works are supposed to conclude, but at the same time is not willing to have his work retain the meaning that is ultimately inherent in that conclusion. Perhaps not surprisingly for a composition that is stated to explain the reason behind 'revolutions throughout the world', it appears to be the opinion of the author that only a fool would believe in a mystical solution to a problem that is essentially political in nature.

The political orientation of the author is clearly observable in the interpretation of individual riddles, of which eight out of a total of twelve are explained as an indictment of political institutions, whereas the other four serve as descriptions of the general immorality of the population. The political criticism that is contained in the work is essentially no different than that addressed by social critics in Bangkok during this period (many of whom at this point of history would have been in Lat Yao prison), other than in the style of its presentation. The government is accused of being corrupt, outwardly speaking of its desire to develop the country but in actual fact using its resources to enrich itself. Through excessive taxation and other means, it is said to extort money out of a public that is already desperately poor. The soldiers are declared to have too much power, and yet the public, fearful of punishment, is afraid to speak. Two further examples illustrate the use of prophetic imagery in the expression of a modern political message:

1. Riddle Number Five: "Oh Owner of the Cows, why do you not free your animals (to graze)?"
Reply of the Owner of the Cows: "I have an upset stomach"

According to the interpretation, the owner of the cow, representative of the government of Thailand, does not allow its people to have freedom. The government claims that

> it is ruling over the entire country in a new and civilized fashion known as democracy. In a democracy, when the public agrees (with a specific policy) they give their opinion and act in accordance with that opinion. This is what they have announced to the public. But afterwards their declarations did not turn out to be true. We, the Thai public, are truly fed up, and yet if anyone makes a brave and frank statement concerning our frustration, death will be the only result. The officials carefully observe those who are brave enough to speak. They are then able to tie them up and kill them.
>
> (*Panha Tamnai Lok*: 10–11)

2. Riddle Number Eleven: "Oh Frogs, Why do you cry so?"
Reply of the Frogs: "We cry because we are being chased by a snake"

According to the interpretation, the frogs, symbolizing the people of Thailand, are in great turmoil, because the 'snake' (i.e. the Thai government) suppresses and extorts money from them. According to the author,

> Each administration is the same. We, the public, are the ones that put them in power because we wish to be able to rely upon them to help us when we are destitute . . . However, the moment they are in power they forget all about the public. They do not turn to look at our tears. We cannot depend upon them. The new administration is absolutely no different.
>
> (*Panha Tamnai Lok*: 16)

What is remarkable about the political criticism that is contained in *Panha Tamnai Lok* is less the style of the criticism (which is after all based upon traditional conventions in the expression of worldly affairs) or its content (which arguably is a fairly straightforward assessment of Thai political dictatorships of the 1950s) than the very fact that it was published and circulated in such a climate. Were similar sentiment to be expressed in other forms, such as political commentary in the columns of a newspaper, or even short stories or novels, they would not have seen the light of print, and it is not improbable that their authors would serve some time in prison. However, as a result of its publication in small regional publishing houses in the Lao language in the form of Buddhist prophecy composed in poetry, it was easier for such writing to escape detection. Ironically, however, the very form that served to hide the literature from hostile authorities was also of use in providing it with a wide circulation. First, whereas a small minority of Northeastern

Thai would have been receptive to modern styles of writing composed in the Thai language, there was a large audience of works composed in traditional forms in the Lao language, as testified by the success of regional publishing houses during this period. Second, in contrast to modern prose, traditional poetry such as prophetic works was not read silently by individuals, but rather the subject of public performance.

Kala Nap Meu Suay

One of the few works of prophetic literature that is composed in poetic form, this has been the subject of a variety of interpretations in Northeast Thailand and Laos. Among works of prophetic literature, it is one of the most open to creative interpretation, as it consists of a sequence of ambiguous imagery depicting the world in disarray, with little in the way of specific commentary.[21]

In one interpretation, imagery of the poem serves as propaganda in support of the communist revolution in Laos. The imagery is analysed as a depiction of the corrupt state of Laos under the Royal Lao Government. and its rectification through revolution. Interestingly, the version of this interpretation that I have access to is in *Phaya*, a publication by Bunkeut Phimawonmethakun, the Chair of the Cultural Council of the province of Khon Kaen in Thailand, published by a small press in the province in 1996. The pro-communist sentiments of the interpretation (not to mention the communist terminology used in its expression) is probably explainable less in terms of the subversive tendencies of the Chair of the Khon Kaen Cultural Council than his predilection for plagiarism.[22] Here imagery that was originally composed as a symbolic description of the chaotic state of Lao and Northeast Thai society in the nineteenth century is converted into a condemnation of the state of Laos under the Royal Lao Government. For example, the poem reads:

> Frogs cried out, intending to read verse
> Poisonous snakes and sea serpents grow fearful

According to the interpretation, in the 'rotten' society of pre-communist Laos, immoral people have great power, and people of morality grow fearful.[23] In this type of society, the obstacles to revolution are considerable, as can be seen in the interpretation of the following image:

> The jackals howl at the elephant; How funny!

According to the interpreters, the capitalists and imperialists, who are a small minority of the nation's population, will threaten and throw up obstacles in the face of the masses in order to prevent any substantial change in society.[24]

The success of the revolution is assured, however, as can be seen in the following lines:

> The earthworm will know how to fly in the sky;
> Great boulders will rise above the water and float

According to the interpreters, 'the great masses, which consist of laborers, farmers, and the poor, who have been oppressed by the capitalists and imperialists, will be freed from their oppression, and rise up to build a new scientific society in which everyone will have equal dignity as human beings'.[25]

A second interpretation is presented in the work *Kala Nap Meu Suay* by Sawing Bunjeum, published in a small printing house in Ubon province, Northeast Thailand, that is owned by the author. Sawing's book is a transcription of several related poems, the content of which are explained in an extensive series of footnotes. It is worthy of note that the footnotes to *Kala Nap Meu Suay* frequently occupy more space within a given page than the text of the poem itself. Similar to the previous interpretation of the verse, Sawing's commentary appears to be more the expression of the author's dissatisfaction with the state of contemporary society than a key to an understanding of the verse. The creative interpretative style can be seen in the following examples:

> 1. Wise men fill up the great rivers, until (their water) is lacking and dried

According to the interpreter, 'There are people with doctorate degrees all over. But the public gets no knowledge out of them at all' (Sawing Bunjeum n.d.: 128).

> 2. The mortar will distance itself from the paddy, with which it has become bored
> The bamboo basket filled with weaving shuttles will grow bored of women's dresses and the spinning wheel

According to the interpretation, 'people will turn their back on their own culture' (*ibid.*, 130)

> 3. Small chickens cry, asking to drink the milk of the crow
> Puppies will cry, asking to drink the milk of the tiger

The interpreter writes: 'Villagers will ask for money from people who are campaigning for positions as government representatives, who will swallow them whole as chickens are eaten by crows and puppies are devoured by tigers' (*ibid.* 131).

The specific interpretation of imagery within *Kala Nap Meu Suay* by Sawing Bunjeum and his understanding of the world is the product of a cultural and political environment that is quite far removed from the period of time in which prophetic works originated. At the same time, however, it would be difficult to deny that there is a similarity between Sawing and the authors and audiences of the works that he interprets in the way that they both manipulate ambiguous imagery in the presentation of a critical assessment of the status quo. Similar to the people who are likely to have authored Buddhist prophecy in earlier times, Sawing is a man who spent many years in the monkhood and received a high level of religious education. On one level, considering the type of criticism that the author is fond of expressing concerning both the government and the state of the monkhood, is it not a little ironic that: (a) funding for the book was made possible through the help of an abbot of the Thammayut sect who is the administrative head of the tenth religious district in Northeast Thailand; and (b) an introduction to the work, praising the author, was written by a civil servant of high rank who in the past had arranged for the author to further his religious studies in India? As in earlier times, therefore, the social commentary of Sawing Bunjeum is given a certain degree of legitimacy and authority through the religious context of its expression and the religious credentials of its author.

Caravan

The band Caravan was formed in the early 1970s by a group of people from Northeast Thailand to create left-wing political music, and was influential as part of the student movement that led to the overthrow of the dictatorial government of Thailand in 1973, and later as members of the underground Communist Party of Thailand. As the poorest region of the country, Northeast Thailand came to be emblematic of political and economic injustice in Thailand. The political message of the music of Caravan, therefore, was not only in the words that they wrote, but also their self-conscious identification with the region from which they originated. In the construction of their identity, Caravan made use of regional language (Lao and Khmer), composed songs in regional musical forms as performed on regional instruments, and adapted passages from regional literature, including the prophetic work *Kala Nap Meu Suay*. A small passage from the poem is included as part of their song *Pla Nauy Kin Pla Yai* (Little Fish Eats Big Fish), as follows:

> The amazing shrimp join together and eat the giant catfish
> The small '*siw*' fish swallow the crocodiles, that flee to hide in rock fissures

According to an explanation of the song's content in a book of music produced by the band, the above verse was originally composed by a Northeastern

Thai poet during the time of the millenarian uprisings.[26] 'The revolt of the masses (against their oppressors)', write the authors of the book, 'is comparable to the small fish (in this poem, which must necessarily rise up in rebellion) as long as the fearful giant catfish and crocodiles are to act in a wild manner, comparable to the criminals who govern our country.'[27] In the context of the actual poem, however (together with similar imagery by which it is both preceded and followed), the above imagery is more likely an expression of criticism of the topsy-turvy state of the world in which people lacking in noble descent are allowed to take part in the governing of their country, which goes against all established tradition.[28]

In conclusion, a comparative study of modern and pre-modern works of Lao prophetic literature illustrates the historical, cultural, and literary dimensions of the 'meaning' of the future as prophesied in the past. On one level, this article is intended to show the richness of the body of Lao prophetic literature (which in itself is a part of a greater inter-related mainland Southeast Asian tradition) as a source that is highly valuable in its potential to deepen our understanding of the region. On a larger level, Lao prophetic literature is only one piece in a much larger puzzle, and it is hoped that one day the great wealth of literary documents in existence will be collected and play their proper role in the construction of a broader cultural history of Laos and Northeast Thailand.

Notes

1 A comparative study of these traditions (and particularly that of Lanna) would shed valuable light on the Lao tradition. One important work of prophetic literature found in Laos, *Kham Saun Phraya In*, makes several references to geographical locations and historical (or mythical?) figures of Lan Na, and is likely to be of Tai Yuan origin.

2 The brief description of Lao religious literature in the context of the history of the kingdom of Lan Sang and its aftermath that follows is summarized from Koret (1994).

3 See the appendix to Koret (1994).

4 We can observe this type of sentiment also in the related work *Leup Phasun* – 'The extinguishing of the sun (light)' (a poem probably composed in the mid-nineteenth century which has much in common with prophetic works), in which the author deliberately writes in a unique style that is disorienting to its audience. He presents himself (seemingly self-depreciatingly) as a religious teacher who has strayed from the proper *Vinaya* discipline in his conduct, while at the same time saying that he has a 'reason' for doing so.

5 Note that among the Lao, Buddhist prophecy is not unique to the nineteenth and twentieth centuries, but has also been a topic addressed in literary works that are probably far earlier in their date of origin. Works of Lao prophetic literature of the nineteenth and twentieth centuries can be considered to belong to one specific category, however, because they each share a number of similar characteristics that are not commonly found in other works, including, for example, the use of

Buddhist prophecy as a) the primary subject matter of the texts, and b) a means towards a similar objective, i.e. as a type of expression through which to come to terms with the social and political turmoil of the time of their composition. In addition, writings within this category make use of a variety of similar conventions ranging from the type of origins that are claimed by their authors to the use of a specific set of imagery and phrasing. The extent of such similarity indicates that in many cases individual texts were composed by people who were familiar with other works within the same tradition.

6 For more detailed discussion, see Peter Koret '*Why Love Poetry is Sold in Shops Selling Religious Paraphernalia: Religion and Romance in the Literary Traditions of the Lao*' – unpublished paper delivered at National University of Singapore Conference on Laos, January 2004.

7 A more complete discussion of this type of limitation in the understanding of literature can be found in Koret (1999).

8 Based upon personal research.

9 *Kham Saun Phanya In*, p: 7.

10 *Tamnan Hin Taek*.

11 In the context of traditional literature, this can also be seen in comparisons of the Lan Na and Lan Sang versions of *Thao Khatthanam*. In the Lan Na versions, the hero, who is a model of righteous behaviour, is described as the *bodhisattva*, and his father is the father of the Buddha, whereas in Lao versions, in which his power and romantic appeal takes precedence over his position as a religious role model, his father is the Lord Indra.

12 The latter prohibition frequently refers to the performance of literature after childbirth, which, although popular, can be considered improper.

13 Often there is a connection made between the two, and lack of respect given to the manuscript is specifically stated to be the result of its offence to Buddhism.

14 This does not mean to imply that on a day-to-day basis people were any less observant of Buddhist teachings than they had been in the past. However, this type of religious admonition was central to the framework in which the chaotic state of the world and the era was given meaning.

15 Note that oral literature goes much further in this regard.

16 Quoted from Phon Phanao Temple Research Center (1968) *Kala Nap Meu Suay* (Vientiane: Phon Phanao Temple); Phon Phanao Temple Research Center (1968) *Kap Kham Saun Phra Muni* (Vientiane: Phon Phanao Temple [also published as Ariyanuwat, Dr Phra]) *Kap Phra Muni* (1990) (Maha Sarakham: Apichat Publishing House); and *Kap Vithun Bantit* (Versified Teachings of the Wise Man, Vithun) in Phra Ariyanuwat (1990) *Kap Phra Muni* (Maha Sarakham: Mahachai Temple).

17 To the contrary, the aim was to return to the *status quo* of the past. Note that limitations in the performance of prophetic works of literature do not in any way mean to imply that the temple was not actively involved in their production. Similar to what we know about influential figures in the millenarian movements during this period, the composers of prophetic works of literature were likely to have either been monks, or men who had achieved a religious education at the temple, as is evident by the type of knowledge that is displayed in their composition.

18 This topic is described in greater detail in Koret (1999).

19 Note that the date is that of the specific publication of the work, and its original composition could be years or even decades earlier.

20 Typical of literature, there is no statement by A. Kawiwong to indicate that he either wrote the work or copied it from a manuscript. In any case, whether or not

the riddles are of older origin, their interpretation is clearly the work of A. Kawiwong.

21 A study of this poem – and specifically why it is composed in poetry rather than prose – would be the profitable subject of a paper in and of itself.

22 The author does include a number of Lao books in his bibliography. The most likely candidate to be the source of origin is *Kham Phanya Phasit Lae Kham Tong Toey* by Duangchan Vannabuppha, published in Luang Prabang in 1991.

23 p. 234.

24 p. 243.

25 p. 244.

26 When I asked the author of the song about the historical circumstances of its original creator, he informed me that he was uncertain of any specific details.

27 *Tamnan Kharawan* (Chronicle of Caravan) by Khana Phu Jat Ngan Sip Saung Phi (Kharawan: 308–309).

28 In addition, the same band also composed a song, *Seung Isan*, in criticism of the American military presence in Northeast Thailand during the Vietnam War in imitation of a major prophetic work of literature, *Kap Phra Muni*. The song was written in the same poetic form as the prophetic work, with a similar use of phrasing, in which original criticism of Siamese administrators in the nineteenth and early twentieth centuries was rehashed in attacks on the Thai Government of the 1970s.

9

IN DEFENCE OF THE NATION

The cult of Nang Thoranee in northeast Thailand

Elizabeth Guthrie

This essay stems from my research into the cult and history of the Buddhist earth deity, known in Thailand as Mae or Nang Thoranee, "mother" or "lady earth". This deity is a minor character in the story of the Enlightenment. The story of how she witnesses for the Bodhisattva against Māra the Evil One by wringing a deluge of water from her long hair can be found in a life of the Buddha called the *Paṭhamasambodhi* known throughout mainland Southeast Asia (Cambodia, Thailand, Laos, Burma and Sipsong Panna).[1]

In general, earth deities are symbols of fertility, and their cults are concerned with the production of bountiful crops, rain, wealth and childbirth. However, while the Buddhist earth deity is associated with the life-giving elements of the soil and the water, she is also an aggressive deity, able to protect the *bodhisattva* and the site of enlightenment from evil forces. This essay will explore her contemporary cult in northeastern Thailand, where she is believed to have the power to defend the Thai nation and its inhabitants, as well as Buddhism, from external threats and invaders.

Over the past few decades there has been a proliferation of "nationalist" religious cults in South and Southeast Asia that seem to come into being in response to political and social change. Some of these cults are addressed to new deities such as the pan-Indian cult to the goddess Santoṣī Mā that first appeared when a movie about the goddess was released in 1975.[2] The Thai cult to Rāma V (also known as Chulalongkorn, r. 1868–1910), expressed by the worship of photographs, amulets and statues of this popular monarch, has flourished among urbanized middle-class Thais since the 1997–8 collapse of the Thai economy.[3] The monkey god Hanumān has a venerable lineage that can be traced back many centuries, but his cult took on new life after the *Rāmāyaṇa* appeared in serialized form on Indian television in 1987–8.[4]

Babb (Babb and Wadley 1995) and others have argued that the media (print, movies, television) have standardized and disseminated a limited number of key religious symbols and images throughout South Asia, creating a shared national identity that transcends traditional cultural and social boundaries[5] and fostering a "democratic devotionalism, a populist piety, of extraordinary proportions in the present age". This media-nourished piety is not dependent upon particular temples, geographical location, or religious specialists; busy devotees are able to devise their own rituals and calendars of worship, and their temples are "non-sectarian, one-stop, full-service".

If new deities such as Santoṣī Mā or Rāma V have emerged in response to the changing needs of Asia's urbanized societies, how do we understand the modern cults to ancient deities, such as those addressed to Hanumān and Nang Thoranee? In a provocative article on the political use of the *Rāmāyaṇa* in India, Pollock described how the character of the cult to Rāma changed over the centuries, and has been used to express a "theology of politics and a symbology of otherness". Pollock noted that, although the story of Rāma is ancient, the cults to Rāma did not flourish until the twelfth to fourteenth centuries, when much of India was under the control of the Sultanate and Hinduism was under threat. Pollock argued that the *Rāmāyaṇa* was promoted by the Hindu elites as a "privileged instrument for encoding or interpreting the political realities of the twelfth to fourteenth centuries". The *Rāmāyaṇa* was chosen over the many other martial epics available because of its "demonization of the Other . . . those who stand outside this theologically sanctioned polity" (Pollock 1993: 281). Pollock concluded his article by positing a relationship between the political semiotics expressed in the *Rāmāyaṇa* in medieval India and the contemporary cults to Rāma that encourage sectarian violence against Indian Muslims (ibid., 261).[6]

Like the *Rāmāyaṇa*, the episode in the story of the Buddha's Enlightenment when Māra is defeated, the *māravijaya*, has served as a political vehicle for the Buddhist nations of mainland Southeast Asia for centuries. In a Thai chronicle describing King Naresuan's famous victory over the Burmese Uparājā in 1593, for example, the Burmese ruler is represented as Māra and Naresuan as the Bodhisattva (Chutintaranond 1992: 92). A memoir written in the early nineteenth century by Princess Narintharathewi compared the victory of Rāma I over the then-reigning King Taksin to the Bodhisattva's defeat of Māra.[7] Murals of the *māravijaya* from the Ayutthayan Period often depict the hordes of Māra as the rapacious Europeans who were vying with each other to colonize Thailand along with neighbouring Vietnam, Cambodia and Lao.[8] More recently, artist Panya Vijinithanasarn painted a *māravijaya* in Wat Buddhapadipa in Wimbledon that includes Margaret Thatcher and Ronald Reagan in Māra's army, and arms the Evil One with nuclear warheads. Nang Thoranee's role in the *māravijaya* as the aggressive deity who puts the army of *māra*-s to flight with a deluge of water from her long hair, in combination with her association with the soil, and the site of enlightenment, qualify her to express a "theology of politics and a symbology of otherness" in Theravada Buddhist Thailand.

The northeast – Isaan – is one of Thailand's poorest and least developed regions; its people are known for their independence and determination in the face of hardship caused by poor soil and inadequate water supplies. Bangkok's political control has often been precarious in the region. Since the time of General Sarit Thanarat, who held power in Thailand from September 1957 until his death December 1963, Thailand's leaders have tried to stabilize the region through development, instituting national projects such as dams to improve agriculture, the establishment of Khon Kaen University, and a teaching hospital. Private businessmen have been encouraged to locate industrial plants in the province to counteract the region's chronic unemployment. Khon Kaen City, the capital of the province, was built in 1965 at the instigation of General Sarit Thanarat. This large city was carefully designed by city planners and has a modern water treatment plant, an adequate electrical supply, and, as its proud residents point out, few traffic jams as the streets are wide, and laid out on a grid. Like all Thai cities, the centre of Khon Kaen City (and by extension, the province of Khon Kaen) is marked by a *lak muang*, the traditional Thai City Pillar.[9] The *lak muang* is located on top of a small hill at what is essentially the crossroads of the city on the main road into Khon Kaen City, Klang Muang Road. The *lak muang* has the usual shrine built around it, and has an attendant who maintains the site and assists devotees who come to make offerings.

Nang Thoranee's shrine is adjacent to the *lak muang*. It is located on a site where a natural spring emerged from the ground at the foot of the hill where the *lak muang* is situated. A statue-fountain of the beautiful earth deity kneeling and wringing water from her long hair is the focal point of the shrine. This statue-fountain was commissioned by the former Governor of Khon Kaen, Chamnan Pocchana, and designed by a well-known local artist named Mahā Surakhom. The statue was built from cast cement on a metal armature at a site at the back of the nearby Town Hall. The cost of construction, 150,000 *baht*, was met by donations rather than civic funds. On 4 September 1981 the completed statue was inaugurated at a ceremony held at the Town Hall, and then transported by truck to its present location adjacent to the *lak muang*. After the statue was positioned, water from the natural spring was piped to her hair to spill into a basin in front of the shrine. The official installation ceremony of the statue on the site took place on 5 September 1981.

The Mae Thoranee shrine has been renovated by her devotees many times since it was first consecrated. It is presently surrounded by a high fence, and entrance to the shrine is through a big gate decorated with Taoist symbols and the names of donors. The enclosure also contains shrines to the *phi* (local spirits), the seven stations of the Buddha,[10] and various other items of statuary, including a Chinese dragon and an oven for burning paper offerings. The statue-fountain of the earth deity is painted gold and red, an effect that is "Chinese" rather than "Thai". In addition to the statue-fountain, there is also a subsidiary statue of Nang Thoranee. Both the statue-fountain and the smaller statue receive a cult. Devotees may bring their own offerings with them, but a complete range of offerings is available for sale at a stall on the site: garlands of marigolds, candles, betel leaves, areca nuts and incense. The subsidiary image is regularly "made up" with cosmetics, and both images are "dressed" in lengths of fabric and adorned with costume jewellery. There are several dedicatory inscriptions at the site, commemorating the original construction of the fountain in 1981, and subsequent renovations and improvements to the site (such as the electrification of the shrine in 1987). A red plastic plaque set in front of the main image has been inscribed in gold with the *Thoranee Gāthā*.[11]

The Thoranee shrine in Khon Kaen bears a strong resemblance to similar shrines elsewhere in Thailand. This similarity is intentional: when Governor Chamnan commissioned the statue, he asked the artist to use a Thoranee shrine located in Bangkok on the northeast corner of the Sanam Luang, at the intersection of Rajadamnouern and Rajini Roads at the foot of the Phipoplila Bridge as a model. In addition to being located in the heart of Ratanakosin Island, near the Royal Palace, the site of this shrine is adjacent to Bangkok's City Pillar shrine. Devotees purchase the traditional offerings of candles, incense, marigolds and scarves from a nearby stall for Thoranee, and they pray to her for good fortune or recite the *Thoranee Gāthā* inscribed on a plaque on the base of the statue.[12] They drink the water that streams from the statue's hair into a basin in front of the statue and catch the water in bottles to take away. In addition to preventing sickness, the water from Thoranee's hair is believed to prevent traffic accidents when sprinkled on cars.

The Bangkok Thoranee statue-fountain was commissioned in 1913 by the Queen Mother Samdech Phra Sri Patcharindhara Boromarajinatha, also known as Saovapha, to commemorate the occasion of her fiftieth birthday. The queen, who was born in 1863, and died in 1919, was the favourite wife of King Rāma V, and the mother of Rāma VI and Rāma VII.[13] Saovapha enlisted her sons and brothers-in-law to design and construct the statue-fountain, and donated 16,437 *baht* from her personal funds to pay for the cost of construction. Archives preserve a letter from the Queen to the Minister of Defence of Bangkok, General Phraya Yamarājā, containing her instructions for the consecration ceremonies on the twenty-seventh day of the ninth month of December (1917):

> Tomorrow I will make merit on my birthday by voluntarily performing a meritorious act. I have donated my own wealth to have the statue of Nang Phra Thoranee, who is the remedy for disease, cast and established at the foot of the Phan Phipoplila. The statue is now ready to be consecrated, and I ask that the merit for the fountain be reassigned for

> the sake of all sentient beings, to be a gift for the public good, to assuage thirst, to heal sickness, to alleviate heat and to increase health according to the great solicitude of the triple gems . . . .
>
> – signed Saovapha[14]

Saovapha's concern for the health of the public, and their access to pure drinking water, refers to the fact that at up until that time most Bangkok residents took their water directly from the Chao Phaya River, resulting in illness and death from water-borne diseases, especially in plague years.[15] In 1909, a year before his death, King Chulalongkorn had ordered the construction of Bangkok's first water treatment plant, which was completed on 4 November 1914 (Van Beek 1995: 164). The plant provided the pure drinking water that flowed from the pipe in Thoranee's hair. In this region, where one of the ancient epithets of the earth deity in both Thailand and Cambodia is *mcās' tik dī*, "lord of earth and water",[16] oaths of fealty are consecrated by the pouring and drinking of sacred water, and the control and provision of water is a primary responsibility of the ruler of the land. This confluence of earth, water and government in Saovapha's Thoranee shrine is further reflected in the use of the earth goddess's image for the logos of the water departments of the municipalities of Bangkok.

A similar logo of Thoranee was adopted by the Thai Democratic Party (Thai *Pak Prachatipat*) for the Party's seal when it was established on 6 April 1946. This logo has symbolized the Party through many election campaigns, and is recognized throughout Thailand. A special programme commemorating the fiftieth anniversary of the Thai Democratic Party broadcast on national television in the late 1990s explained why the image of the earth deity was chosen. When Seni and Kukrit Pramoj and the other founding members of the Party were drafting the Party's constitution in Pramoj's law office on Rajadamnoeurn St, they realized they needed a logo for the new party. They looked out the window for inspiration and saw Saovapha's Thoranee fountain on the Sanam Luang. It was decided that this image, which emphasized the importance of earth and water for Thailand, together with the Pali motto *saccam eva amatavaca*, "truth is indeed the undying word" symbolized the values of the Party.[17] As the Secretary of the Democratic Party wrote in his autobiography:

> It was agreed that the symbol for the Thai Democratic Party would be the figure of Nang Thoranee squeezing out her hair, a figure that has the meaning of cool shade, abundance and the happiness that emanates from the earth.
>
> (Sotthisankrām 1984: 94)

These ideas about a benevolent earth deity, the restorative powers of water and the centrality of truth expressed by the founders of the Thai Democratic

Party and in Queen Saovapha's dedication were important symbols for Thai politics during the first decades of the twentieth century. During the second half of the twentieth century, as Thailand became embroiled in the Second World War, and then the war in Vietnam, Laos and Cambodia, the earth deity's wrathful nature became more important for Thailand's political symbology.

Although Thailand was never colonized, during the Second World War the power of the Thai monarchy was at a low ebb, the country was occupied by foreign invaders, and Bangkok was bombed. During this period, the Thoranee shrine was not maintained, and it became dilapidated and spoiled. Thieves vandalized the statue and stole the water pipes, and the water in the fountain dried up. In 1957, when General Sarit Thanarat took over leadership of the country, he ordered that the Thoranee statue be renovated. The worn paint was scraped off the statue and it was re-gilded; water pipes were reconnected to the water supply and the fountain flowed like before. Electricity was installed in the statue to illuminate and beautify the interior of the shrine at night. The surrounding area was landscaped, trees and a decorative hedge were planted, footpaths and fountains of gushing water were built in a circle surrounding the statue.[18]

Since Sarit Thanarat renovated the fountain on the Sanam Luang, there has been a close relationship between Thoranee and the Thai political right: the concern for national security as the conflict in the Vietnam War escalated and spread throughout Southeast Asia. Alarmed by the destruction of the *sangha* in Cambodia by the Khmer Rouge, the Thai *Sangha* formed an alliance with the Thai Military, and left-wing political groups (including the Thai Democratic Party) were accused of being communists. The politics of this period are too complex to discuss in detail here, but because of its strategic location between the Royal Palace, Thammasat University, Wat Mahāthāt (the headquarters of the right-wing monk Bhikkhu Kitthiwuttho) and the Democracy Monument, Nang Thoranee witnessed many scenes of political protest. In 1973, 1976, and again during the military coup in 1991, fierce battles between right-wing activists, the military, and student protesters were fought in front of the statue fountain on the Sanam Luang. In the political discourse of this era, Nang Thoranee was depicted as the ferocious defender of Thai Buddhist nationalism, and communists and student activists were condemned as *tmiḷ*, the forces of Māra (Kitthiwuttho 1976; see also Morrell and Samudavanija 1981).

There are other Thoranee statue-fountains in Thailand (and in Laos and Cambodia, but that is another story) (Guthrie 2004). These images do not exist in a vacuum; like the Thoranee shrine on the Sanam Luang, they were commissioned and maintained by devotees who hold specific beliefs about their meaning. One of the links between Thailand's Thoranee statue-fountains is the political discourse that they enabled, particularly throughout the 1960s and 1970s.

During this time, mainland Southeast Asia was a battleground of conflicting ideologies of western-style democracy and communism. Thailand was a country under siege, from the outside and within, and Thailand's continued existence as an independent nation seemed to be at risk. Despite the Thai military's long-standing commitment to the United States' war in Southeast Asia, many Thai people disapproved of American policies and resented the presence of US military bases on Thai soil. Thai society was torn by a series of coups and student uprisings, culminating in the failed student uprising of 1976. When the Thai military returned to political power in 1976, students and intellectuals fled Bangkok, some to continue their struggle for democracy in the *maquis*, while others joined forces with the Thai Communist Party. The refugees from Cambodia, Laos and Vietnam who poured over Thailand's borders further threatened Bangkok's control over its border regions. After 1979, when the Khmer Rouge had been ousted from Phnom Penh by invading Vietnamese troops, they waged guerrilla warfare against the Vietnamese invaders from inside Thai territory. Thai villagers were caught up in the conflict, their fields and property damaged, and civilians killed, and thousands of Thai soldiers were mobilized to secure Thailand's borders.

Khon Kaen province grew increasingly unstable during this period, and by 1979, villages in the province were known to be *sii chomphuu*: "communist". In addition to sending soldiers to maintain political control, the military government appointed Chamnan Pocchana, a conservative and capable administrator and protégé of General Sarit Thanarat, to be governor of Khon Kaen province; he held this post until 1983. Chamnan's task was to quell the insurgency and maintain stability by reasserting Bangkok's control over the region. During his first year as governor of Khon Kaen, Chamnan commissioned two public monuments: one was a cast-bronze statue of General Sarit Thanarat, "the father of the people during disturbed times", erected in Khon Kaen City's new bus station; and the second was the statue-fountain of Thoranee. In an interview, the former governor, now retired in Bangkok, stated that he commissioned the statue-fountain in order to create a peaceful landscape in the middle of Khon Kaen, to provide water to the people, and alleviate heat. While the shrine is certainly a beautiful spot in the centre of town, with its bright colours, landscaping and fountain of water, many people in Khon Kaen have explained that Nang Thoranee has the power to defend the province of Khon Kaen from invaders as well as protecting her devotees from misfortune. In fact, she is so powerful that shortly after the installation of the statue-fountain in 1980, the communists and their sympathizers disappeared from the northeast without any fighting.

The first time I visited Khon Kaen's Thoranee shrine was during Thai New Year, 14 April 1998. I remember that day well: it was about 40 degrees centigrade, the shrine's atmosphere was thick with incense and vibrant with the sound of prayers as a procession of devotees arrived to lay their offerings of candles, incense, and wreaths of yellow marigolds in front of the main image and at the subsidiary shrines on the site. The interest in Thoranee was in part due to the fact that it was Thai New Year, Songkran, a time when people visit such religious sites, but also because of a new threat to the Thai nation: the colonization of the Thai economy by foreign investors and the International Monetary Fund (IMF). On 2 July 1997, Thailand's booming overheated economy had collapsed, and on 20 August 1997 the government had been forced to accept a "rescue package" of US $17.2 billion from the IMF. This loan stemmed the free-fall of the Thai *baht* and restored financial stability to the country, but also committed Thailand to harsh economic reforms imposed by the IMF. By New Year 1998, many Thai people in Khon Kaen were suffering severe hardship as jobs and homes disappeared and businesses collapsed; once again, they turned to Nang Thoranee to protect them from an uncertain future at the hands of the IMF.

A series of articles in the newspaper *Siam Rath* reported that, although Thailand was bankrupt and foreign countries were trying to take over its economy, there was gold in the ground in Lopburi. This gold is usually hidden, can only be used in times of great need, and can only be used for the whole nation, not for individual wealth. Soon, Thoranee will open up the gold mine, pay the country's debts and make Thailand rich again so the country will not be a slave to foreigners.

During the height of Thailand's financial crisis, a Thai-Chinese millionaire named Sia Chaleurn whose sausage factory was based in Khon Kaen established a company named The Thoranee Asset Mining Company to search for Thoranee's gold mine in Lopburi, located on land owned by the military.[19] Sia Chaleurn had heard about the gold mine when Thoranee spoke to him through a medium named Ratana Maruphikat. The medium Ratana, who began being possessed by Thoranee when the economic crisis began, wrote a popular book called *A Message from the Spoiled Earth*. In this book, she explained that she had been asked to broadcast the news to the Thai nation that

> Phra Mae Thoranee will come back to get rid of bad people and clean and renew the country and to invite Phra Sri Ariya [Maitreya] to become the fifth Buddha. Now the world will be a happy and peaceful and plentiful place with good relationships, kindness, human rights, harmony and equality.
>
> (Marutphitakasa 1999)

On 15 November 1997 the Thai Democratic Party headed by Chuan Leekpai, was elected to bring the country out of the financial crisis (Sharma 2002). During Chuan Leekpai's term of office (1997–2001) the symbol of Thoranee was again thrust into the public consciousness. The Thai Democrat

Party Headquarters located on 67 Set Siri Road, near the Railway Station in Bangkok, was renovated and a new shrine to Thoranee was built. The Party's web page (www.democrat.or.th) was illustrated with a pulsating blue graphic representation of Thoranee, and during the election campaign Party members wore caps and jackets decorated with badges of Thoranee wringing out her hair.

Despite the Democratic Party's reputation for honesty and financial prudence, the government quickly became unpopular as the stringent economy measures imposed by the IMF caused unemployment to rise and wages to fall. There was much social distress as people lost their homes and livelihoods, businesses failed, and Thai banks were sold to foreign financial institutions. The press was full of criticisms of Chuan Leekpai and his Party for failing to protect Thailand from foreign investors, and for allowing the IMF free reign in the Thai economy. Thoranee appeared on the cover of the current affairs periodical *Madichon*.[20] Like all political cartoons, there are many subtexts; relevant for this paragraph is the suggestion that Chuan Leekpai, depicted here dressed up like Thoranee, has prostituted himself and Thailand to the IMF.[21] Other articles in the press complained that the government was betraying both Thoranee and the motto of the Party: *saccam eva amatavaca*:

> Unfortunately this party doesn't seem to react or even keep their motto. They have her only for the badge on people's shirt or jacket- so where is the meaning?

and

> Every single inch of the land belongs to Phra Mae Thoranee, the one who this party respects. So Chuan Leekpai, don't keep quitting, don't just sit and watch. Whether Phra Mae Thoranee assists or not depends on your decisions, Chuan Leekpai: Phra Mae Thoranee must be encouraged to rescue the nation.[22]

On 15 December 2002, I visited the shrine again. The shrine seemed rundown and the atmosphere was depressing, with only a few devotees in evidence. Thoranee's red and gold paint had become shabby, the grounds were unkempt, the water in the fountain's basin was stagnant, and the shrines to the *phi* had disappeared. I spoke with three women who came to worship Thoranee, lighting candles and incense and arranging flowers on her statue. The first woman told me she was a second-hand dealer from out of town. She had heard that Thoranee can give good luck and had dropped by to see the shrine and ask Thoranee for help with her business. Next, I asked an elderly woman and her middle-aged daughter why they had come to the shrine. The daughter told me she and her mother had come from the neighbouring province of Korat to sponsor a traditional dance ceremony in front of the City Pillar, which is adjacent to the Thoranee shrine, for her mother's health. While the primary focus of their visit was the City Pillar, they decided to also pay their respects to Thoranee and ask for her blessings.

The fact that the few devotees at the shrine were from out of town and the run-down state of the grounds suggested that all was not well with the cult to Thoranee in Khon Kaen City. Further research revealed that for several years the medium in charge of the shrine, Manop, had been embroiled in a legal battle with the municipality of Khon Kaen. I was fortunate to be able to hear both sides of the controversy, from Manop, and from an informant familiar with the city's court case.

The medium Manop lives in a comfortable, modern house in a quiet neighbourhood on the outskirts of Khon Kaen city. Signs on the exterior of his house advertise Manop's name, telephone number and profession ("Medium to Phra Mae Thoranee"). Manop is middle-aged and has a young wife (the caretaker I saw working at the shrine in 1998) and a child. He told me that before he became a medium for Nang Thoranee, his name was Naran Ning, and he worked as a reporter. One large room in his house is set up as a shrine. It is a hodge-podge of images and statues of various deities, including (but not exclusively) Thoranee, and ritual paraphernalia (conches, drums, bells, tridents, etc.). Much of his paraphernalia was donated by grateful clients. Manop also displays photographs of himself in the company of politicians.

My interview with Manop confirmed much of the information about the Thoranee shrine, but from a different perspective. For example, he told me that in 1980, the governor's wife, Chanda, visited and asked him how to make Khon Kaen peaceful again. Manop suggested that she tell the governor to build a shrine to Thoranee in the middle of the city, so Thoranee could drive away the communists and bring peace to the province. Soon after the statue was installed, the communists disappeared from the region without any fighting. After this proof of Manop's abilities, the governor's wife invited Manop to come and take care of the shrine as its official medium, but at first he refused. After several requests he accepted the job, and has been the official medium for Thoranee since 1981. He has a legal contract with the city that gives him the right to rent the site of the shrine. He paid 10,000 *baht* for the contract, and pays a monthly rent of 1,500 *baht* for the shrine, and an annual payment of 1,700 *baht* for insurance. Manop was keen to emphasize that he does not misuse any of the donations given to the shrine. He explained that he has many enemies, people jealous of his financial and professional success as Nang Thoranee's medium. As a result of their criticisms, the city now wants to break his lease. For several years, Manop has been embroiled in a legal battle with the city to retain his hold on the contract.

I was able to hear the other side of the story from an informant close to City Hall. My informant explained that over the past few years, the Thoranee shrine had become spoiled, and the pool of water flowing from her hair had become stagnant. The main reason for the changes was the construction of the new Mittaphap highway into Khon Kaen City. Ever since the new highway was built, and the City Pillar displaced from its position as the centre of the city, the natural spring that supplied the water to Thoranee's hair has dried up, indicating that she is no longer present at the site. Another reason is that Nang Thoranee has abandoned the site. This happened during the financial crisis, a time when much money flowed into the shrine. During this time, the medium Manop was believed to have misused some of the donations for his personal enrichment. At the same time, the medium became involved with a young woman and now has a young child (while mediums can be married, and have children, their relationships with the deities who possess them are based on their ability to keep the precepts while they are acting as mediums). In an attempt to resolve this problem, the mayor of the city has proposed a plan to move the City Pillar to a new site at the new centre of the city. Thoranee's shrine will also be moved so it is once again adjacent to the City Pillar. The plans for the new shrines have been drawn up. but there is popular opposition to the move.

In conclusion, the ancient Buddhist earth deity is a multivalent and flexible political symbol, able to readjust to the left or right as circumstances dictate. When she is needed to chase away communists, she obliges; when she is needed to save Thailand from takeover by foreign financial interests, she is called into action. In addition to this "theology of politics", Thoranee's cult has a special significance for Thailand's northeast. Since the time of its establishment in 1980, the Thoranee shrine in Khon Kaen City has been used to express a "symbology of otherness", identifying this isolated and underdeveloped region with the rest of the nation, and helping its governors to forge a united Thai Buddhist front against all invaders, be they communist or foreign multinationals. And finally, the cult of Thoranee reflects the political and economic realities of Thailand's changing society. As the old crossroads are shifted, and Thai Isaan transforms itself into a modern industrial and educational centre, the earth deity provides an essential and stabilizing link between the rapidly changing boundaries of the present and a timeless Buddhist past.

Notes

1 A transliteration and a translation of the relevant stanzas of the *māravijaya* from the critical edition of the *Paṭhamasambodhi* (Cœdès and Filliozat 2001: 150) follow. Translations are mine unless otherwise noted.

> *Tadā Vasundharā vanitā bodhisattassa sambhārānubhāvena aṭṭānaṃ sandhāretum asakkontī paṭhavitalato uṭṭhahitvā itthisāmaññatāya bodhisattassa pūrato*

ṭthatvā "tāta mahāpurisa ahaṃ tava sambhāraṃ jānāmi tava dakkhiṇodakena mama kesā alliyanti idāni parivattayissāmi" ti vadantī viya tāvad eva attano kese parivattitvā visajjesi. Tassā kesato yathā gaṅgodakaṃ sotam pavattati. Yathāha pasāretvā mahāvīro cakkalakkhaṇarañjitaṃ. Erāvaṇasadisoṇḍaṃ pavāḷaṇkurasadisa Vasundharāvanitaṃ taṃ dassesi sākyapuṇgavo sandhāretuṃ asakkontī palāyiṃsu. Girimekhalapādā pana pakkhalitvā yāva sāgarantaṃ pavisanti chattadhajacāmāradīni obhaggavibhaggāni pātāni ahesuṃ. Acchariyaṃ disvā māro savimhayabahulo. Yathāha pāramītānubhāvena mārasenā parājitā. Nikkhantudakadhārāhi sakkhikese hi tāvade disodisaṃ palāyanti vidhaṃsetvā asesato ti

Then the Earth, unable to withstand the accumulation (of perfections) of the *bodhisatta* emerged from the earth's surface in the likeness of a woman and stood in front of the *bodhisatta*. "Dear Great Man, I know that you have fulfilled your obligations, my hair is overflowing with your donative libations and I will wring it out." Speaking as if she were animate, she grasped her hair and twisted. The water collected in her hair fell down flowing like the Ganges River.

Thus he said: Having extended my hand marked with the signs of the wheel, resembling the horn of Erāvana, like a ram made of coral the Great Man, the Bull of the Śakyas touched the Earth. Unable to resist his appeal, she rose up before him in the form of a woman, and twisted her hair, from which flowed a flood like the Ganges River. The army of Māra was not able to withstand the flood, and was routed. The feet of Girimekhalā slipped and he fell into the ocean. The parasols, standards and fly-whisks broke and fell. Seeing this disaster, Māra was filled with astonishment. Thus he spoke: 'The power of the perfections of the *bodhisatta* prevailed over the army of Māra, and the torrents of water pouring from the hair of his witness have completely dispersed them and sent them flying in all directions.'

2 McKean (1996: 250–280) and Hawley and Wulff (1996: 1–28). Bhārat Mātā and Santoṣī Mā, like all Indian goddesses, can be understood as a manifestation of the Great Goddess, however before the movie's release, few Indians had ever heard of Santoṣī Mā; the cult to the deity Santoṣī Mā was created in the 1980s as a political vehicle by militant Hindu nationalist parties.

3 Rāma V is associated with ensuring Thailand's independence from European colonialism during the nineteenth century; today his devotees (mainly urban, middle-class Thais) ask for good fortune, prosperity and for the protection of Thailand's national and economic sovereignty. In Bangkok on Tuesdays and public holidays, thousands of devotees come to make offerings in front of an equestrian statue of the king opposite Abhisek Dusit Throne Hall; by early evening the surroundings are carpeted with masses of pink blossoms and candles.

4 Babb (1995: 14) writes that Ramanand Sagar's serialization of the *Rāmāyaṇa* for Indian television was a "watershed" in the history of the epic.

5 Babb and Wadley (1995: 16–17 and 37); Lutgendorf (1994: 244).

6 In this article Pollock refers specifically to events such as the pilgrimage by the leader of the Bharatiya Janata Party to Ayodhyā in 1990 and the destruction of the mosque built at Rāma's birthplace by Hindu militants in 1992, events accompanied by bloody sectarian riots across India.

7 Passage cited and translated by Jory (1996: 97).

8 See, for example, Ringis (1990: plates 15–16).

9 Quaritch Wales (1931: 302–3). The City Pillars, or *lak muang*, are also called

inthakila \inthakin\. These pillars are located in the centre of the city or *muang*, and receive a cult: the usual offerings of candles, incense and flowers but also traditional dance performances accompanied by live music.

10 The Buddha's activities around Bodhgaya for seven weeks following the Enlightenment – (1) defeating Māra whilst meditating under the *bodhi* tree; (2) steadfast gazing; (3) meditating on the jewelled walkway; (4) meditating in the jewelled house; (5) meditating under the goatherd's tree and rejecting the daughters of Māra; (6) meditating in the coils of the snake king Mucalinda; and (7) the encounter with the merchants whilst meditating under the *rājāyatana* tree – are described in the Life of the Buddha called the *Nidānakāthā*. Buddhist iconography popular in Burma and Thailand commemorates the seven weeks with the "seven stations", a set of seven images or shrines (Stadtner 1991).

11 The *gāthā* reads:

> *Tassā kesato yathā gaḍgodakaṃ sotaṃ pavattati.*
> *Yathāha pasāretvā mahāvṭro cakkalakkhaṇarañjitaṃ.*
> *Erāvaṇasadiso ṇḍaṃ pavāḷaḍkurasadisaṃ.*
> *Vasundharāvanitaṃ taṃ dassesi sākyapuḍgavo*
> *Sandhāretuṃ asakkontṭ palāyiṃsu.*
> *Girimekhalapādā pana pakkhalitvā yāva sāgarantaṃ pavisanti chattadhajacāmāradṭni obhaggavibhaggāni pātāni ahesuṃ. Acchariyaṃ disvā māro savimhayabahulo.*
> *Yathāha pāramṭtānubhāvena mārasenā parājitā*
> *Nikkhantudakadhārāhi sakkhikese hi tāvad*
> *Disodisaṃ palāyanti vidhaṃsetvā asesato ti.*

12 This *gāthā* reads:

> *tassā bhassito yakā gangā*
> *sotaṃ pavattanti*
> *mārasenā patithathantu*
> *osaka gomato palayiṃsu*
> *parimanubhāvena mārasenā*
> *parajita disodisaṃ*
> *palāyanti vidaṃseti*
> *assato – la la – sādhu*

These *Thoranee Gāthā*-s are "spells" or prayers recited by devotees. They are abbreviated and contain many misspellings and grammatical errors (for example, *yakā* for *yathā* above), but they have a close relationship to the text of the *māravijaya* of the *Paṭhamasambodhi*.

13 Smith (1947). Smith became the Queen's personal physician after the death of the King until her death, and his book is in part a biography of Saovapha from his perspective.

14 Oudumaphra (1984: 454–455). In this dedication Saovapha documents her meritorious deeds, asks for the merit to be shared among all sentient beings, and refers to the pouring of water as a "truth act" or "truth vow". For the latter, see Burlingame (1917).

15 Smith (1947) described the devastation wrought in Bangkok by water-borne disease.

16 Bauer (1992). The Khmer *cās, mcās', amcās'* and Thai *cau*, meaning "master", "elder", "old one", appear to have been borrowed from old Mon.

17 *Saṃyutta Nikāya* 452- 5.1.189.

18 *Phak Kruang*, 21 August 1999.

19 Sia Chaloeurn's main business is a sausage manufacturing company based in Khon Kaen that exports food all over Asia.
20 *Madichon*, 31 August 1999.
21 Many thanks to Louis Gabaude, EFEO Chiang Mai, for explaining this cartoon to me.
22 *Madichon*, 27 September 1999, translation K. Aphaivong.

10

KING, *SANGHA* AND BRAHMANS

Ideology, ritual and power in pre-modern Siam

Peter Skilling[*]

I Ritual: hybridity and complexity

This essay explores inscriptions, the *Three Seals Law Code*, chronicles, royal eulogies,[1] and other primary sources in an attempt to understand some of the conceptions and idealizations of kingship and religion and the intricacies of ritual relations from the Ayutthaya to the early Ratanakosin period. I include brahmans because I do not believe that the Buddhism of Siam (or that of the region) can be studied in isolation, without taking into account the social and ideological ecologies within which it and other knowledge and ritual systems have functioned. If Buddhism was the dominant discourse in the ideological hierarchy, it was not the only one, and the brahmanical discourse should not be ignored. Brahmans played, and to a degree still play, a significant role in the state rituals of successive Siamese kingdoms. They presided over their own brahmanical rites and participated in ceremonies with Buddhist monks. In both cases they received offerings, and otherwise they – or the deities they cared for – received land grants with attendant privileges.

The importance of ritual and ritual status to the social and political orders is self-evident, even if it is not fully understood. Ritual was essential to the political functioning of the states that evolved within and beyond the boundaries of modern Thailand. We might describe these polities as 'ritual states' rather than as 'theatre states'. Ritual in the sense of spectacle, of public performance, shares many features with theatre – stage, props, costume, rehearsed actions and speech – but the resemblance does not go far beyond that.

Is it adequate to conceive of politics simply in terms of explicit exercise of power, of trade or market forces? Ritual itself is a product and an expression of power, and most if not all political entities (and perhaps most if not all human organizations) indulge in ritual performance – the ritual state is not, after all, a Siamese, South-East Asian, or even South Asian invention. And given the significant role of ritual in state economies and regional and trans-regional diplomacy, it cannot be dismissed as pre-modern extravagance or despotic caprice. The annual outlay on royal finances was enormous. Classes of artisans and functionaries depended for their livelihood on ritual. Ritual needs influenced trade, since certain ritual paraphernalia – for example the *cāmara*, the whisk fashioned from the tail of the yak – had to be imported over long distances.

Religieux were enlisted to protect the state and promote prosperity and well-being. A distinctive feature of Siamese religion is the hybridism of its rituals.[2] The complexities of ritual life demonstrate the inadequacy of describing pre-modern Siam as 'Theravadin', or, even more so, of conceiving of Theravada as a 'state religion'. As far as I know, the term 'Theravāda' does not occur in chronicles or inscriptions from the early Ayutthaya period on, and the idea of 'state religion' is alien to the region of the period. In this chapter I reserve the term 'Theravada' for the monastic lineage – the aggregate or series of lineages, changing with time and place, that emanate or claim to emanate from the Mahāvihāra tradition of Ceylon.

These monastic lineages did not, in fact, generally choose to identify themselves as 'Theravadin' or even, much of the time, 'Mahāvihārin'. Rather, they used specific terms that changed as new lineages were introduced over the centuries. They described themselves as belonging to the Sīhala-vaṃsa (the lineage from Ceylon), to the Laṅkā-vaṃsa (the lineage from Lanka), or to the Rāmañña-vaṃsa (the lineage of the Mon country), and so on. 'Sīhala-bhikkhu' did not necessarily refer to a monk from Ceylon – in texts like the Pali chronicle *Jinakālamālī* it means 'monastic [ordained within] the Ceylonese lineage'. Monks might belong to the 'town-dwellers' (*gāma-vāsī*) or 'forest-dwellers' (*araññavāsī*). Medhaṃkara Mahāthera, who in the fourteenth century composed the learned cosmological text *Lokadīpakasāra* at Muttima-nagara (modern Martaban) in the Mon country, is described in the colophon as 'an ornament of the lineage of renowned great elders belonging to the forest-dwellers of the Island of Ceylon'.[3] In the late 1680s at Ayutthaya, Simon de La Loubère (1642–1729), 'Envoy Extraordinary' to the court of King Narai (r. 1656–1688), observed that 'There are two sorts of *talapoins* at Siam, as in all the rest of the Indies. Some do live in the woods, and others in the cities.'[4] In northern Siam monks might belong to the lineage of Wat Suan Dok or Wat Pa Daeng. At the time the *Jinakālamālinī* was compiled, that is, in the first three decades of the sixteenth century, there were three lineages in the northern Siam: the Nagaravāsī, the Pupphavāsī, and the Sīhaḷabhikkhus, i.e. the city-dwellers, the Suan Dok monks, and the Wat Pā Daeng monks.[5]

In the South, in the central Malay peninsula, there were four ordination lineages called the 'four *kā*'. '*Kā*' being an abbreviation of 'Laṅkā', we may describe them as the 'four Laṅkā lineages':[6]

Kā kaew	Pā Kaew (Vanaratana) lineage
Kā rām	Rāmañña lineage
Kā jāta	Pā Daeng lineage (?)
Kā doem	Former lineage

This classification of lineages evolved at an uncertain date, certainly in the Ayutthaya period. It was centred in Nakhon Si Thammarat, and spread to neighbouring states like Chaiya and Phatthalung. The 'Register of Royal Officers in Muang Nakhon Si Thammarat', a document issued in Lesser Śaka Era 1172 (CE 1811), during the Second Reign,[7] lists four officials with a rank of 200 *sakdinā* who supervised the corvée labourers who bore the palanquins for the royally ranked monks (*rājagaṇa*) belonging to the 'four *kā*'.[8]

If Theravada monasticism is to have a history, we must pay attention to the development and self-conception of these lineages. The fact that the lineages have evolved from the Theravada of Sri Lanka – or more distantly from the Thera lineage at the time of the Thera/Mahāsāṃghika split that took place in Northern India in the third century BCE – should not prevent us from studying their individual and regional evolutions. Further, we should ask to what degree it is appropriate to indiscriminately apply the term 'Theravada' – the name of a monastic lineage with a trans-regional history of over two thousand years – to religion, art, or architecture. Does the use of the term level differences, and confound the singularities of history? Does it set up an ideal and ahistorical 'religion', against which the actual becomes a deviant, and even degenerate, 'other'? Does it evoke the trope of decline? Does it lull us into the complacency of thinking that we understand something when we do not? These questions need to be addressed, and for the present I prefer to use the term sparingly and cautiously.

Complex hybridity and **samana-chi-phrām**

The complex and hybrid nature of Siamese religion is reflected in the Thai phrase *samana-chi-phrām* (*samaṇa-jī-brāhmaṇa*), which may be analysed into 'mendicants, renunciants, and brahmans'. We may compare it with the phrase ubiquitous in the Pali canon, *samaṇā vā brāhmaṇā vā*, 'religieux or brahmans' – in both cases the compounds have a comprehensive sense of 'religieux of all stripes'.[9] And this is important: for the most part there is no abstraction in terms of 'religion', 'creed', or 'faith' – distinctions are recognized, rather, in terms of ritual and function. Insofar as I make such distinctions in this chapter, they are provisional shorthands, and not discrete or exclusive systems.

A ruler has relations with specific deities, and supports the *samana-chi-phrām* as appropriate throughout the ritual year. King Rāma I, founder of the Chakri dynasty, consciously forged an ideology that drew on the past – Ayutthaya and Thonburi – and suited current circumstances. He was not only devoted to the Śāsanā, but was also well versed in the scriptures. He expressed his ideals in a celebrated verse:[10]

> I will devote heart and mind
> To exalt and elevate the holy Buddha Śāsanā.
> I will ensure the safety of the entire realm
> And protect the people and the nobles.

In the preamble to his version of the *Rāmakian*, Rāma I expresses his ideals at length in *rāy* verse.[11] Rāma I's first 'Edict on the Saṅgha' states that the King:[12]

> . . . compassionately sought out means to enable monks (*samaṇa*), brahmans, ministers (*senāpatī*), and populace (*prajā-rāṣṭra*), all of them, to realize the three felicities (*sampatti*) [those of the human world, of the heavens, and of *nirvāṇa*], and to escape from the sufferings of the four realms of loss and from the terrors of cyclic existence (*caturāpāyadukkha lae saṅsārabhaiya*).

This is the duty of the king in Thai documents: to care for *samana-chī-phrām*, or religious specialists as a whole, for the ministers and nobles, for the populace, and to support and defend Buddhism. The monarch – the supreme supporter (*upathambhaka*) of the Buddha Śāsanā[13] – must ensure that the populace lives at ease and in peace (*yū yen pen suk*).

The hybridity of religious personnel and objects of worship in Sukhothai is evident from Inscription 4 from Wat Pa Mamuang, in Khmer, composed in Greater Śaka Era 1269 (CE 1349), during the reign of King Lithai (Mahādharmarāja I).[14] The epigraph records, *inter alia*, the setting up of an image of Īśvara,[15] as well as of Viṣṇu, in a temple.[16] It refers to 'ascetics, brahmans, penitents, and religieux',[17] and perpetual offerings to all *tapasvi* and brahmans.[18]

The juxtaposition of brahmanical and Buddhist signifiers and the joint participation in rituals is common. Perhaps the earliest record of this is in the Wat Maheyong inscription from Nakhon Si Thammarat.[19] The fragmentary Sanskrit text, in characters dating between the seventh and the ninth centuries, records donations of buildings and materials to Buddhist monks (both as a community and individually), and of food to the community of the twice-born, the brahmans (*dvija-gaṇa*).

The court used Buddhist and brahmanical cosmological, mythological, calendrical systems, as appropriate to circumstances. The perennially popular story of Rāma, called Thai the 'Glory of Rāma' (*Rāmakīrti*), was expressed in poetry and performance – in court and local versions, in dance and in several varieties of shadow puppetry. The epic was depicted in mural painting, for example in the galleries of the 'Emerald Buddha' temple, and in stone relief carvings, set in the perimeter wall of the *uposatha* hall of Wat Pho (Wat Phra Chetuphon) in Bangkok.[20]

Rites invoke a pantheon of deities, Buddhist, brahmanical, ancestral, and local. Inscription 45 – a pact between Sukhothai and Nan dated 1393 – invokes the powers of local and ancestral spirits, and of deities according to both brahmanical and Pali systems of classification.[21] Oaths like the Ayutthaya-period *Lilit ongkān chaeng nam* invoke cosmopolitan hosts of deities. In the Ratanakosin period, in 2530 (1807), in a royal ritual the *saṅgha* offered water charged by Buddhist chanting (*nam phra phutthamon*); then the brahmans offered blessing water from conch shells (*nam sang asiarawat phak*) after which they blew conches in celebration (*jayamaṅgala*).[22]

The hybrid nature of Siamese ritual is seen in language, ceremonial materials, rites, and participants.[23] Pali is paramount if not predominant. Not only do the monks recite *Paritta* and other texts in Pali, as to be expected, but the brahmans also recite formulas in Pali – or a thoroughly hybrid Pali-Sanskrit-Thai.[24] The shared ritual language is a hybrid of Thai, Pali, Sanskrit, and Khmer. Even when a text may appear to be in Pali, it may be written in Thai syntax and verse (see Prapod op. cit.). In written documents different scripts are used for different purposes. Thai-language text is written in Khom-Thai or Thai script, or, for example in a paper accordion manuscript of the *Ongkān chaeng nam*, in a South Indian Grantha script adapted for Thai.[25] Pali is written in the Khom script, as are the formulae inscribed on talismans and magic diagrams. Manuals may be written in Thai script, but with the embedded Pali in Khom script.[26]

I prefer to avoid the term 'syncretism', with its implications of adulteration of an imagined 'pure' religion. Even if 'syncretism' is acceptable as a descriptive term, it is not an accurate model or teleology. 'Hybridism' is a creative and selective use of diverse forms, an expression of ideologies in which the boundaries are fluid, if they exist at all. How did this hybridism develop, how does it function, how and why does it change? How different is it in different regions and societies – the North, the Centre, the South, or among the Mon, the Lao, the Khmer? At present we understand this very little at all, and much more research into original sources is needed, accompanied by constant assessment of our assumptions and categories.

An intriguing document for the study of 'religion' is an inscription from Kamphaeng Phet dated Greater Śaka Era 1432 (BE 2053 = CE 1510).[27] The epigraph, inscribed on the base of a large bronze image of a standing Īśvara, records the meritorious deeds of Chao Phraya Dharmāśokarāja, ruler of Kamphaeng Phet and descendant of Sukhothai royalty. The inscription states in part that:

> Chao Phraya Dharmāśokarāja set up this Lord Īśvara to protect four-footed and two-footed creatures in Muang Kamphaeng Phet and to help exalt the religions (*sāṣaṇā*) – the Buddha-sāṣana, the Saiyasāṣana, and the Debakarrma – to not let them lose their lustre and to make them as one.

Here three categories are explicitly mentioned – but, apparently, given equal weight – Buddhasāṣanā, Saiyaśāṣana, and Debakarrma. Cœdès explained 'Saiyaśāṣana' as Pali Seyyasāsana, 'littéralement "la religion excellente", . . . une désignation courante de la religion brāhmanique',[28] and translated 'Debakarrma' as 'le culte des divinités'.[29] Although the precise meanings may not be clear, it seems safe to say that the categories were functional and non-exclusive, and did not refer to 'religions' in the modern sense.[30]

II Figures of the king

> All beings rely on the *kṣatriya*, who builds *pāramī* and by nature has compassion and leads *samaṇa* and *brāhmaṇa*, the citizens, to be established in virtue.
>
> King Rāma I[31]

State ideologies centred in the person of the king. The king was a Mahādhammika-rājādhirāja – a 'Great, Righteous, Superior King of Kings'. In Inscription 3, dated 1357, King Lithai of Sukhothai is consecrated as Śrī Suriyavaṃsa Mahādharmarājādhirāja.[32] In Inscription 5, he is described as Śrī Suriyavaṃsa Rāma Mahādharmarājādhirāja.[33] In Inscription 4, the Khmer version of the preceding, he receives the same title, prefixed by the Khmer title 'Phra bāt kamrateng añ'.[34] In addition, the king could be a *bodhisattva*, a Buddha, a *cakravartin*, or a deity.

Royal titles reveal the intricate conceptions of kingship:[35]

> *Somdet phra chao rāmādhipatīndra śrī surindra paramacakrabartisara pavaradhammika-mahārājādhirāja-jāti-hariharin-indra-tejo-jaiyamahaisuriya-savarryādebādideba-tribhūvanārtha-paramapāda-pabitra phra buddhi chao yu hua.*[36]

> *Phra pāda somdet phra chao ekādadharaṭha-iśara*[37]*-paramanārtha-paramapabitra phra buddhi chao yu hua phu song daśabidharājad-harrma-anantasambhārātireka-eka-aṅga-suriyavaṅṣaviśuddhi-paramabuddhāṅkūra-paramapabitra.*[38]

> *Phra śrī sarrbejña somdet phra rāmādhipatī sindara-parama-mahācakrabartiśvara-rājādhirāja-rāmeśvara-dharmikarāja-tejo-jaya-parama-debādideba-trībhūvanādhipeśra-lokajeṣṭha-viśuddhi-*

makuṭa-buddhāṅkūra paramacakrabartiśvara-dharmikarājādhirāja an prasert.[39]

The long titles – often in *rāy* metre – invoke idealized images of the ruler, as warrior and powerful spiritual and temporal leader, using Thai, brahmanical and Buddhist figures. They rarely include other qualities – kings as poets, dramatists, or merchants.[40] Given the orality of contemporary culture and the belief in the power of language, the titles were potent condensations of the royal person.

King as **bodhisattva**

King Rāma I referred to people making merit as a support for attainment of the level of a Buddha (*phra buddha-bhūma*), the level of a Paccekabuddha (*pacceka-bhūma*), or the level of an Arhat (*arahata-bhūma*).[41] These, in hierarchically descending order, are the three goals open to one who wishes to practise Buddhism.[42] The king perfects the *bodhisambhāra*, often used in expressions of taking refuge in the compassion of the king. Literally, the term means 'requisites of awakening', and refers to two requisites, merit (*puñña*) and wisdom (*ñāṇa*).

King Lithai of Sukhothai announced his aspiration to Buddhahood publicly in inscriptions. In Inscription 4, he 'aspires to become a Buddha in order to lead all beings out of the Three worlds' (*traibhava*). In Inscription 5, he aspires to lead all beings out of the suffering of cyclic existence (*saṅsāra-dukkha*). Inscription 6 – stanzas composed in Pali by Mahāsāmi Saṅgharāja in praise of Lithai – compares the king's perfection of giving (*dānapāramī*) to that of Vessantara, his perfection of wisdom (*paññāpāramī*) to that of Mahosatha, and his perfection of moral conduct (*sīlapāramī*) to that of Sīlavarāja.[43] Here *jātaka* literature and ideology intersect – the *jātaka* stories are presented as ideals, as role-models for kings, and kings incorporate *jātaka*s into their public image. Widely disseminated through the media of the sermon and the painted image, the *jātaka*s had a deep and enduring social role.

Kings of Ayutthaya also adhered to the *bodhisattva* ideal. The preamble to a law dated CE 1433 (BE 1976) states that 'His Highness has set his heart on the performance of the perfection of giving (*dānapāramī*) with the aspiration (*prāṭhanā*) for realization of awakening (*bodhiñāṇa*), to lead all beings to freedom from the fears of cyclic existence and the suffering of the woeful realms'.[44] In the 'Palatine Laws' (*kot monthianbān*) princes of the highest rank – those whose mother is an Agramahesī – are called '*no phutthāngkun*', 'sprouts (Thai *no*) of the sprout (Pāli *aṅkura*) of the Buddha', that is, children of a *bodhisattva*.[45] Boromarāja IV (r. 1529–1533) was also known as No Buddhāṅkura.

The 'Eulogy of the Glory of King Prāsāt Thong' identifies Prāsāt Thong

(r. 1629–1656) not only *as* a *bodhisattva*, but with a specific *bodhisattva* among the ten future Buddhas starting with Metteyya of the Mahāvihāra tradition.[46] It states that in a former life Prāsāt Thong was the elephant of the Pārileyyaka forest (*kuñjara pā lī laiyak*). This elephant devotedly looked after the Blessed One for three months, when, in the tenth year after his awakening, he sought out the solitude of the jungle rather than endure the quarrelling of the monks of Kosambi (see Malalasekera 1983, vol. II: 191–192). The elephant is destined to be the tenth future Buddha named Sumaṅgala.[47]

The *Royal Chronicle of Thonburi*, 'Phan Chanthanumāt edition' (composed during the First Reign, that is, during the time of Rāma I), opens with the statement that in BE 2309, before the fall of Ayutthaya,[48]

> The miraculous King [Taksin] who counted among the sprouts of a Buddha (*no buddhāṅkūra chao*) realized in his wisdom that Krung Śrī Ayutthaya was in danger because the ruler of the country and the people were unrighteous. He therefore exerted with the strength of compassion (*kamlang karuṇā*) towards monks, brahmans, and teachers (*samaṇabrāhmaṇācārya*), [fearing that] the excellent Buddha Śāsanā would decline and disappear. He therefore assembled his followers and troops of soldiers, Thai and Chinese, about one thousand in number, well-armed with all types of weapons, accompanied by high officers . . . and went to camp at Wat Phichai which was an auspicious and powerful site (*maṅgala-mahāsthāna*). By force of the radiance (*tejas*) of his paramount requisites of awakening (*paramabodhisambhāra*), the deities who guard and protect the Holy Buddha Śāsanā shouted out in approval (*sādhukāra*) and caused rain to fall as an auspicious indication of great victory (*mahābijaya-ṛkṣa*) as the army set forth from Wat Phichai . . . the Burmese were unable to withstand his perfections (*pāramī*) and retreated.

Before he came to the throne, the future King Taksin had already aspired to Buddhahood. The *Royal Chronicle of Thonburi* relates the story as follows:[49]

> Wednesday, eighth of the waxing moon of the third month. [King Taksin] went to pay homage (*namaskāra*) to the Buddha image (*phra paṭimākara*) at Wat Klang Wat Doi Khao Kaew. He asked the resident monks, 'Do you lords remember: when this layman still lived at Ban Rahaeng, he lifted a glass bell above his head, and made a resolution of truth (*satyādhiṣṭhāna*) to test his perfection (*phra pāramī*): 'If in future I will really succeed in realizing the holy, paramount consecration of the wisdom of full awakening (*phra paramābhiṣeka-sambodhiñāṇa*), when I strike this bell may it break only at the knob, that I may make from it a glass *cetiyaṭhāna* to hold

> paramount physical relics (*phra parama-sārīrikadhātu*).' After making the vow, I struck the bell, and it broke only at the knob. This was seen firsthand as a marvel. The monks responded that this was true in accordance with the royal statement.

After he took the throne to reign in Thonburi (r. 1767–1782), Taksin is described as a *bodhisattva* in the 'Praises offered by the Saṅgha to Somdet Phra Chao Krung Thonburi', dated Lesser Śaka Era 1141 (1779):[50]

> The King (*phra mahākraḥṣatra*) is the mainstay of the lineage of sprouts of Buddhahood. His Majesty will have Ayodyānagara [i.e. Thonburi] made as delightful as the Tāvatiṃsa heaven. His majesty is Phya Tham Lert Lok . . . He will gain omniscience (*phra sabbaññutañāṇa*) . . . His Majesty accomplishes the ten perfections . . . [these are listed] . . . Without fail he constantly offers the four requisites to the *bhikkhu-saṅgha* who possess the virtues of ethical conduct.[51]

Two of the decrees (*phra rājakamnot*) issued by King Rāma I of Ratanakosin in Lesser Śaka Era 1144 (CE 1782), the first year of his reign, show that he aspired to Buddhahood as soon as he took the throne. The preamble to Decree No. 36 states that the king has the royal aspiration to seek the realization of awakening at the level of a Buddha (*rājapranidhānaprāthanā phra buddhabhūma-bodhiñāṇa*)'.[52] Decree No. 35 states that the king 'practices the *pāramī* in order to realize the supreme consecration of the realization of perfect awakening' (*paramābhiṣeka-sambodhiñāṇa*).[53]

The opening of King Rāma I's *Rāmakian* elaborates the author's aspirations:[54]

> The Somdet Paramount Righteous King (*paramadharmikarāja*)
> Has taken birth below [in the human world], just like Phra Nārāyaṇa.
> He has greatly expanded [the kingdom's] boundaries
> And built glorious things, bright, bejeweled, and beautiful.
> He treasures the lofty aspiration
> In his heart imbued with profound wisdom
> As he cultivates [the path of a *bodhisattva*] predominant in faith (*śraddhādhaik*)
> With omniscience (*sarvajña*) as his goal.
> He cuts off miserliness (*macchariya*) completely
> And breaks the wheel of cyclic existence
> He leads the way across the flood to the security of peace (*yogakṣema*, i.e. Nirvāṇa)
> Lovingly favouring and rescuing people bound by fetters (*saṃyojana*).

To the poverty-stricken
He freely dispenses his wealth
Never tiring of spending, of exchanging money for merit (*puṇya*).

Here King Rāma I is described as a *bodhisattva* 'predominant in faith',[55] one of the three types of *bodhisattva* postulated in Mahāvihāra tradition – *saddhādika, paññādhika,* and *viriyādhika* (see Skilling 2002). In his *Saṅgītiyavaṅśa*, a Pali chronicle composed in the First Reign, Somdet Phra Phonnarat describes both King Rāma I and his younger brother, the Wang Nā or Uparāja (1743–1803), as *bodhisattva*s, the elder as *saddhādhika*, the younger as *paññādhika*:[56]

> *tadā ayojjhanagarapubbe dve rājāno buddhāṅkūrā bodhisattā mahāpuññāpāramisannicitā bhātaro saddhādhikā paññādhikā sabbaññutañāṇabhipatthitā vasantā. . . .*
>
> Previously, at that time there dwelled in the city of Ayojjha two kings, sprouts of future Buddhas, *bodhisattvas*, who had accumulated great merit and perfections (*pāramī*), predominant in faith, predominant in wisdom, aspiring to the wisdom of omniscience. . . .
>
> *atha tesaṃ dvinnaṃ saddhādhiko hiri-ottappasampanno brahmavihārajutindharo sīlādiguṇādhiko jeṭhādhirājā divase divase macchasakuṇādike satte mocetvā atidukkaraṃ sudhābhojanāhāraṃ attano adhivāsetvā bhikkhusaṅghassa saṅgītikāle tampi adāsi atidukkaraṃ*
>
> Of the two, the elder king, predominant in faith, endowed with a sense of shame and with conscience, resplendent in the [four] *brahmavihāra*, exceptionally endowed with the virtues of morality, etc., every day having set free fish, birds, and other living creatures, having himself respectfully presented pure food to the community of monks, he presented it at the time of the *saṅgīti*.
>
> *kaṭṭhapaṇṇāhārikañ ca dhaññataṇḍulakoṭanañ ca katvā sayaṃ paccāpetvā kāyabalena kusalacetanāvisesena paññādhiko atikusalo mahiddhiko mahāpuñño tathāvidho sīlādiguṇasampanno buddhāṅkūro sabbaññutañāṇābhipaṭṭhano anujādhirājā ca tesaṃ tañ ca aññaṃ mahādānaṃ adāsi.*
>
> Having brought firewood and leaves, and having pounded the grains to husk the rice, having cooked it himself with his own physical strength and with a rare determination, the younger king, predominant in wisdom, exceptionally talented, extremely meritorious, a sprout of the Buddha endowed with virtues of morality, etc. like

those [of his elder brother], aspiring for the wisdom of omniscience, gave to them and others great offerings.

King Rāma II is described as a *bodhisattva* in a *khlong dan* poem, a eulogy composed by Phrayā Trang, who compares the king to Iśvara, Indra, and Brahmā, to a *bodhisattva*, and to Maitreya.[57]

An elaborate description of the qualities of King Rāma III (r. 1824–1851) is given in a royal order dated Lesser Śaka Era 1186 (CE 1824), the first year of his reign:[58]

> He is a lord paramount righteous king of kings (*somdet paramadharrmika-rājādhirāja chao*), an upholder of the ten royal virtues, devoted with endless energy to great awakening (*anantaviriyayāmahābodhābhirata*), endowed with ultimate great perfections (*paramartha-mahāpāramī*), endowed with the pure royal patience and wisdom (*phra rājakhantī-prījāñāṇavisuddhi*) . . . He maintains the four *saṅghahavatthu* according to ancient royal custom. His royal heart firmly delights in the accumulation of merit (*kuśala*) to foster, support, and protect the excellent Buddha Śāsanā (*pavara-buddha-śāsanā*), to cause it to endure, flourish, and shine for a full five thousand years. He possesses excellent royal love and compassion (*pavara-rāja-mettā-karuṇā*) for the world of sentient beings (*sattvaloka*), and intends to foster and protect the land (*phaen din*), to allow all monks, religieux, and brahmans (*samaṇa-chiy-brāhamaṇa*), commoners, citizens, and servitors of the dust of his holy feet (*phrai fā anāprajārāṣṭra lae khā tūn la-ong thulī phra bāt*) to live at ease and in happiness in every place within the boundaries of the realm (*khet-khop-khandha-semā*).

King as Buddha

Epithets of the Buddha were regularly used in titles given to kings. These include 'Phra Sisanphet', which is from Sarvajña, 'Omniscient' and 'Somdet Phra Buddha Chao Yu Hua', 'Mighty Holy Buddha Lord above [my] head'.[59] The latter is frequent in reference to a reigning monarch, or in direct address. Phra Boromatrailokanath (r. 1448–1488) is Paramatrailokanātha, 'Paramount Saviour of the Triple World'. Kings were posthumously called Phra Phuttha Chao Luang. Their death was described as a 'nirvāṇa'. There do not seem to be any ancient tracts that attempt to explain the concept, or modern investigations of, how, when, or where it arose.

The victorious king mirrors the Buddha; the victorious Buddha mirrors the king. Images of the 'adorned' or 'crowned' Buddha (*phra phuttharūp song khruang*) were produced in large numbers in Ayutthaya and Bangkok. In some cases they were explicitly identified with kings, as for example the images of King Rāma I and King Rāma II set up by King Rāma III, which today grace the main altar complex of the 'Emerald Buddha' in Wat Phra Kaew in Bangkok.[60] These are standing crowned Buddhas in ornate and delicate royal attire, all gilded. The names assigned to the two Buddha images by King Rāma III are also the posthumous names of the kings used to this day (with a slight modification to the name of King Rāma II instituted by King Rāma IV):

Phra bāt somdet phra buddha yot fā cuḷālok (Rāma I)
Phra bāt somdet phra buddha loet lā nabhālaya (Rāma II).[61]

The conception of the Buddha in Siam is bound up with ideas of victory (*jaya*), glory (*śrī*), radiance (*tejas*), and of merit (*puñña*), wisdom (*paññā*), and perfection (*pāramī*). Impartial, universally compassionate, the Buddha is the source of blessings and protection. A popular verse expresses this conception of the Buddha:

mahākāruṇiko nātho atthāya (hitāya, sukhāya) sabbapāṇinaṃ
pūretvā pāramī sabbā patto sambodhiṃ uttamaṃ.

The greatly compassionate saviour
For the sake (benefit, and happiness) of all breathing things
Fulfilled all the perfections and realized ultimate full awakening.

The *Jinapañjara-gāthā* opens by invoking the fact that Buddhas have vanquished Māra: *jayāsanāgatā buddhā jetvā māraṃ savāhanaṃ*, 'seated on the victory throne, the Buddhas, having defeated Māra and his [elephant-] mount'. The *Jayamaṅgala-gāthā* invokes eight victories of the Buddha to bring victory, success, and good things. Each stanza ends with the refrain *taṃ tejasā bhavantu te jayamaṅgalāni, sadā sotthī bhavantu te* – 'by that radiance may there be for you victory and blessings, may there always be well-being for you'.

These qualities parallel the qualities of kingship, as is stressed in texts such as the *Vidita-jātaka*. The king as *bodhisattva* accumulates merit and wisdom, the requisites of awakening (*bodhisambhāra*). He cultivates the perfections, and at the same time he is fit to rule owing to the merit and perfection that he has already accumulated.

King as cakravartin

The ideal *cakravartin* with his seven treasures is described at length in the *Traibhūmikathā*, a cosmological treatise composed by King Lithai (r. 1346/7–1368/74?) when he was Uparāja at Si Sajjanālaya, an important city in the Sukhothai complex.[62] The term occurs once in Sukhothai epigraphy, but not as a title.[63] In contrast, it is frequent in Ayutthaya documents, including law books, literature, and inscriptions, in which kings are described as 'Paramamahācakravartin' or 'Culacakravartin'. One king bore the name Mahāchakkapat, that is, Mahācakravarti (r. 1548–1569). One of the common royal titles is Somdet 'Phra Paramarājādhirāja'. This and titles like Jaiyarājādhirāja (r. 1534–1537) or Mahindrādhirāja (brief reign in 1569) express sovereignty and victory.

Sukhothai, Ayutthaya, and Ratanakosin kings belong to the Sūryavaṃsa, the 'Solar Lineage'. The king is a hero, his virility demonstrated by his large harem and many children. His exploits are praised in poems, and he is identified with Rāma, the great *kṣatriya* warrior of the *Rāmakīrti*. A king should possess the five types of regalia – the *kakudharājabhaṇḍa*.[64] The regalia includes the 'glorious victory sword' (*khan jayaśrī*), or the *phra saeng*. Phokhun Phā Muang of Sukhothai (circa mid-thirteenth century) was given a *khan jayaśrī* by the king of Muang Śrī Sodharapura, that is Angkor Thom.[65] King Lithai received regalia (the crown and the white sunshade) and victory sword, as mentioned in Inscriptions 4 and 5 from Sukhothai.[66] The discovery of white elephants during a king's reign are important signifiers of his power, since it is his merit that attracts them.[67]

In the late nineteenth century, King Rāma V (Chulalongkorn, r. 1868–1910) instituted the practice of presenting a royal sword, the *phra saeng rājasastrā*, to the then administrative units, the *monthon*. When the administrative system changed, the swords were presented to the provinces (*changwat*). Exquisitely fashioned, with bejewelled gold handles and sheaths, the swords were kept in the *monthon* or provincial treasuries. When the king visited a province to remain for at least one night, the sword would be taken out and presented to him by the governor in a public ceremony conducted upon his arrival.[68] The custom is followed today. King Bhumibol Adulyadej initiated a new custom, that of bestowing a Buddha image named Phra Buddhanavarājapabitra to each province. These were presented by the king himself to twenty-one provinces between 2510 and 2528 (CE 1967–1985),[69] and by his appointed representative Crown Prince Mahā Vajiralongkorn to thirty-one provinces between 2532 and 2533 (CE 1989–1990). At present all seventy-six provinces have received a Phra Buddhanavarājapabitra image.

King as a deity

The king is Rāma, his capital Ayodhyā. The first king of Ayutthaya was 'Rāma the Lord' (Rāmādhipati, r. 1351–1369), and Rāmādhipati remained an epithet of kings throughout the Ayutthaya and early Bangkok periods. The second king was Rāmesuan (Rāmeśvara, r. 1369–1395, with a brief interruption in 1388); his successor was Rāmarājā (r. 1395–1409). The king is Indra, as in the name Indrarājā (Indrarājā I, r. 1409–1424; Indrarājā II,

r. 1488–1491). The king is Nārāyaṇa, as seen in the name Somdet Phra Narai (r. 1656–1688).

The special vocabulary used for referring to royalty (*rājaśabda*) expresses the divinity of kings. The birth of a king is a descent or entry into the world (*phān phibhob*). The death is a return to heaven (*suwannakhot* = *svarggata*). The buildings, pavilions, gates, and gardens in the palace bear names that evoke the pleasures of the paradises of Indian and Buddhist mythology and the powers of the *cakravartin*.

Royal policy

The ideals of royal policy are prescribed in a variety of texts. The classical sources were the *Tripiṭaka* and the commentarial and ancillary Pali literature of Sri Lankan Mahāvihāra Theravada. Especially important was the *Jātaka*, with its ideologies of *bodhisattva* and *pāramī*. The ideal code of conduct was the 'ten duties of a king', the *dasabidha-rājadhamma*. When a king was seen as a *bodhisattva*, his conduct was interpreted in the light of the requisites (*sambhāra*) and the ten perfections (*dasa-pāramī*).

Normative texts included *nīti* literature such as *Rājanīti*, one version of which was translated into Thai in 1805 (BE 2348), that is, during the First Reign, from a 'Pāli version from Pagan'.[70] Texts on strategy such as *Pichai sonkhrām* (*Bijaiya-saṃgrāma*, '[Manual for achieving victory] in war') and the *Pūm rājadharma* attribute the various troop formations to the sage Kāmandakī, author of the *Nītisāra*. The *Mahādibbamanta* and other hybrid chants were recited when the troops set out for the battlefield.

Diplomacy was governed by strategy and by a desire to promote the *Śāsanā*. Images of the Buddha might be sent to tributary states (*padeśarāja*), and images and palladia might be brought back to the capital from defeated neighbours, as in the case of the Emerald Buddha. In certain periods, such as the eighteenth and nineteenth centuries, the court saw itself as the centre of the *Śāsanā*, with a duty to spread and foster it in other countries. Thus monks were sent to Sri Lanka to revive the higher ordination, as were scriptures and other items.

The ten royal virtues

The ten royal virtues (*dasabidha-rājadhamma*) do not seem to be known in the Buddhist literature of India. Indian Buddhist texts use another, older list, the ten wholesome paths of action (*kuśalakarmapatha*) as their norm. The ten *karmapatha* – also known in Pali – are, however, ethical guidelines for all, not only for kings. The history of the ten royal virtues remains to be investigated. Where was the list drawn up – in South India, in Sri Lanka, or in South-East Asia? The ten are mentioned in the *Jātaka*,[71] usually in the phrase *dasa rājadhamme akopetvā dhammena rajjan kāresi*, where they are also listed.[72] The ten *rājadhamma* are mentioned in a Polonnaruwa inscription of King Vijayabāhu I near the end of his reign, that is in the early twelfth century.[73]

Reference is made to the ten royal virtues in inscriptions from Sukhothai, such as the Nakhon Chum inscription from Kamphaeng Phet, which attributes the ten virtues to King Lithai,[74] or Inscription 5 from Sukhothai.[75] The *Traibhūmi phra ruang* also discusses the ten. The Ayutthaya poem *Lilit yuan pai* states that King Boromatrailokanāth (Paramatrailokanātha, r. 1448–1488) possessed the ten qualities. In his poem *Lilit taleng pai*, Somdet Phra Mahāsamaṇa Chao Krom Phra Paramānujita Jinavarorasa (1790–1853) praises King Naresuan (Nareśvara, r. 1590–1605) for the same reason.[76] In eulogies of kings the possession of the ten becomes a standard trope.

III The institution of the saṅgha

The institution of the monastic order, the *saṅgha*, was open to most, if not all, males, at least in theory. Entry into the *saṅgha* opened the opportunity to climb the social ladder. Monks who succeeded in the educational system could be appointed to royal monastic rank (*phra rajagaṅa*) and rise – according to ability and ambition – through the hierarchy (Wyatt 1994). In Ayutthaya and Ratanakosin, some high-ranking monks came from humble backgrounds. In Ratanakosin the position of Saṅgharāja – 'King of the Saṅgha', head of the monastic order – was occupied by commoners in some cases, in others by members of the royal family.[77]

Monastics were included in the *sakdinā* system.[78] The *Three Seals Law Code* lists the social rank (*sakdinā*) of religieux:[79]

A *sāmaṇera* who knows the Dharma is equal to 300 *nā*;
A *sāmaṇera* who does not know the Dharma is equal to 200 *nā*;
A *bhikṣu* who knows the Dharma is equal to 600 *nā*;
A *bhikṣu* who does not know the Dharma is equal to 400 *nā*;
A *phra khru* who knows the Dharma is equal to 2400 *nā*;
A *phra khru* who does not know the Dharma is equal to 1000 *nā*;
A *brahman* who knows the arts and crafts (*śilpaśāstra*) is equal to 400 *nā*;
A *tayom brahman* is equal to 200 *nā*;
A white-robed ascetic (*ta pa khao*) who knows the Dharma is equal to 200 *nā*;
A white-robed ascetic who does not know the Dharma is equal to 100 *nā*.

Monks received offerings from the king, such as monastic requisites, ceremonial fans, and palanquins, in accordance with their rank or scholastic attainments. Monks of a certain rank received a regular royal stipend (*nityabhat*). Every year after the completion of the rains-retreat, the king visited royal monasteries to offer robes to the monks. A royal *kaṭhina*, whether by land or by water, was an opulent display of royal munificence, occupying much of the state apparatus, a grand affair which inspired poems like the 'Lilit on the Royal Kathin Procession' (*Lilit krabuan hae phra kathin byūhayātrā*), composed by Prince Paramānujitajinorasa (1790–1853) in praise of a procession in the reign of King Rāma III.[80] Equally grand was the annual (at least in theory) pilgrimage to Phra Phutthabat (Buddhapāda), the shrine of the footprint of the Buddha in Saraburi province (see Skilling 2005).

Powerful kings were able to keep the *saṅgha* in check – the model of Aśoka was always to hand. La Loubère noted that just before he arrived in Siam the king had diminished the ranks of the *saṅgha* – 'these privileged persons' – by holding examinations to test their knowledge of the Pali language and scriptures. As a result, he had 'reduced several thousands to the secular condition, because they had not been found learned enough' (Loubère 1986: 115). In Lesser Śaka Era 1135 (CE 1773) King Taksin of Thonburi issued a 'Decree on the Training in Ethics (*sīlasikkhā*)', which gave the text of the monastic code (*Pātimokkha*) in Thai. Each of the 227 rules was followed by a brief statement of the result of breaking it. For example, the first four rules, the *pārājika*, which entail expulsion from the order, are followed by 'one who breaks [the rule] falls to the Hell of Unremitting Torment (*Avīcinaraka*)'. The decree concludes with the statement:

> These are the 227 training rules (*sikkhāpada*): let a monk of good family (*samaṇa-kulaputra*) who does not know the commentaries (*aṭṭhakathā*) or the canon (*pālī*) study them until they are bright and clear in his mind (*khandha-santāna*), and then ordain and practice according to this order in every respect.

Not long afterwards, King Rāma I was dissatisfied with the state of the monastic order. Starting in the first year of his reign (1782) he issued a series of ten edicts, the *Kot phra song*, to reform the conduct of the monks.[81]

According to the *Three Seals Law Code*, monks of rank could act as witnesses in legal cases. In several instances we have contemporary records showing that high-ranking monks were witnesses and guarantors of treaties, such as the pact of mutual assistance between Sukhothai and Nan dated 27 February, 1393.[82] The titles of two out of the (probably) four monks who participated are preserved:

> Somdet Phra Mahāthera Saṅgharāja Rattaṇavaṅśācārya
> Phra Mahāthera Dharrmasenāpati.

Monks also acted as witness in the treaty of 1560 between King Jayajeṭṭh-ādhirāja (1548–1571) of Candapurī (Laos) and King Mahācakrabarti (1548–1569) of Ayodhyā, recorded in a bilingual (Lao/Tham: Thai/Khom) inscription dated 1563.[83] A *cetiya* called Phra Dhātu Śrī Song Rak was erected at Muang Dan Sai (Loei) to commemorate the alliance. This is worthy of note: *cetiya* were not only built to enshrine relics. They were also built to commemorate events such as an alliance or a military victory.

The Jesuit Marcel Le Blanc (1653–1693), who visited Siam in the 1680s, wrote that during the reign of King Narai (1656–1688) 'the Talapoins or priests of the idols constitute a third estate in the kingdom' (Le Blanc 2003: 10). He observed that the members of the *saṅgha* 'always take the place of honour, and the great mandarins bow before them, and when they go to the palace, the princesses and ladies of the seraglio spread, out of respect, under the feet of these Talapoins the cloth they wrap around their neck. By their solidarity and the credit they command, they are the most formidable faction in the kingdom' (ibid.: 11). Le Blanc describes the explicit role of monks in Petchrāja's coup.[84]

IV Brahmans

> The Kṣatriya does not flourish without the Brahmin, and the Brahmin does not prosper without the Kṣatriya; but when Brahmin and Kṣatriya are united, they prosper here and in the hereafter.
>
> *Manu*[85]

Early evidence – Chinese reports, inscriptions, icons, and structural remains – attest to the presence of brahmans and Brahmanism in South-East Asia, including Siam – above all in the old centres of power and trade in the Malay peninsula, but also in central states like Dvāravatī, Sri Thep, and Muang Phra Rot. Ayutthaya Brahmanism is often traced to Cambodia, to the Khmer court of Angkor, but this strikes me as an oversimplification of a long historical process.[86] Evidence of brahmanical practice is plentiful in the Chao Phraya valley, and brahmans must have been important agents in the societies of the region from the earliest period. There are numerous *liṅga*, images of Viṣṇu, images of Sūrya, and brick towers (*prāng*) and stone and brick foundations. It is plausible to suggest that the brahmanism of early Ayutthaya developed from that of the earlier states of the Chao Phraya valley, bearing in mind that social groups are never static, and that the brahman community and court practices would have undergone regular replenishment, from India, Angkor, or elsewhere, and would have been regularly reinvented and adapted.

We have seen above that rulers at Sukhothai and Kamphaeng Phet set up costly images of brahmanical deities, and that at Sukhothai there was a *devālaya*, a building to house the images. The Khmer-language inscription from Wat Pa Mamuang (Inscription 4) referred to above records royal endowments to the *devālaya*.

Other centres of power – Ayutthaya, Phetchburi, Phatthalung, and Nakhon Si Thammarat – had brahmanical shrines, which came to be called *bot phrām*.[87] Phetchburi, Nakhon Si Thammarat, and Bangkok had 'giant swings' for the performance of the annual Triyampawāy ritual, when Īśvara descended to earth for a week at the beginning of the new year.[88] During the festival, with the ensuing Tripawāy festival in which Nārāyaṇa descended to earth, there were elaborate rites, with music and dance, including *ram saneng*, arts that are now, unfortunately, lost. Brahman families (*trakūl*) lived in Nakhon Si Thammarat,[89] Phatthalung,[90] and Chaiya[91] in the South, and in at least Phetchburi and Ayutthaya (and later Ratanakosin) in the Centre. Their religious and social role was determined by birth – in that sense, they were a caste, though references to the system of four *varṇa* in Siamese records seem to be the imposition of an abstraction rather than a social reality. The ritual position was transmitted patrilineally: only male brahmans had ritual functions, but only chosen sons were trained or ordained to become brahmans. That is, every male born into a Brahman family did not become a ritual specialist.

That brahmans were essential to the functioning of the state is seen from the fact that when King Rāma I established Bangkok he established a brahmanical shrine complex in the heart of the capital, in imitation of the *bot phrām* at the former capital. This, the 'Devasthāna', remains a functioning institution to this day. Griswold and Prasert note that the courts of South-East Asian rulers had brahmans 'to advise on statecraft, law and technical matters; to regulate the calendar and cast horoscopes; to manage the Swinging Festival, the First Ploughing, and rites for the control of wind and rain; to perform ceremonies; and to discharge a host of other tasks.'[92] Brahmans are essential to the coronation – at which, for example, they present the regalia to the king – and to many of the 'royal ceremonies of the twelve months'. Some of the duties and privileges of the brahmans are stipulated in the collection of documents published under the title 'History of the Brahmans of Nakhon Si Thammarat'.[93] The first document lists twenty 'auspicious ceremonies' (*maṅgalabidhī*) to be performed by brahmans alone, followed by five ceremonies to be performed together with the monks.[94]

In Ayutthaya and in early Ratanakosin, important roles of the brahmans included the performance of ritual (*bidhīkarma*/*phithikam*) – which they shared with the *saṅgha* and with members of the court such as the *Krom ālak* – and the judging of legal cases (*tat sin khadī*). 'Khun Chai Aya' (Khun jaiya-āñā mahāvisuddhi prīchā-ācārya) was an important position in the legal system until the Fifth Reign, when the position itself was retained but no longer occupied by a brahman. The code on civil hierarchy lists the *sakdinā* for the brahmans, starting with Mahārājaguru with 10,000.[95]

The personnel devoted to rites are listed with their ranks in the 'Register of Royal Officers in Muang Nakhon Si Thammarat', a document issued in

Lesser Śaka Era 1172 (CE 1811), during the Second Reign. One section gives the titles of the officials in charge of brahmanical ceremonies and institutions. The institutional functions included supervision of the ritual swing (*ching chā*), of brahmanical temples (*devasthāna*) and of the *ho phra*, along with their servants or *khā phra*.[96] Most of the officials had a rank of two hundred *sakdinā*. Separate officials were in charge of the rituals and images of Phra Isuan (Īśvara, also called Phra Sayumbhūvanāth) and Phra Narai (Nārāyaṇa), each of whom had his own shrine.

The 'History of the Brahmans of Nakhon Si Thammarat' describes royal land-grants made to maintain the images of deities (*devārūp*). Grants of households and land were made to images of Phra Nārāyaṇa and Phra Iśvara. The land and produce was administered by appointed brahmans of rank, and the inhabitants – the brahman families – enjoyed privileges like freedom from taxation and from interference by government officials.[97] High-ranking brahmans had special funeral rites, detailed in the 'History'. After cremation, the relics (*dhātu*) of a brahman of the first rank were to be placed in a pot and carried in procession – to the music of wind instruments, drums, gongs, singing, hand-bells, horns, and conch-shells – to a body of flowing water. The leader of the procession should raise the relics above his head, stand in the middle of the water, and send them to the place of god.[98]

The practice of granting land, including villages with their inhabitants and products, to brahmans and monasteries began in India, and was introduced to South-East Asia at an early date.[99] Early inscriptions in the region concern such grants, and it is likely that grants made to brahmans in Ayutthaya represented a continuity of pre-Ayutthaya practice. No Sukhothai grants to brahmans are preserved, but we have seen that there were brahmanical temples. The practice of granting land to religious institutions, such as monasteries, temples, *cetiya*, or images, Buddhist and brahmanical – the *kalpanā* system – had an enormous effect on the economy, since the grants removed both land and people from the obligations of tax and corvée service.

The legal – and hence social – status of brahmans may be gauged from the *Three Seals Law Code*, in which they figure prominently, in terms of crimes they might themselves commit, of crimes committed towards them, and of their duties and privileges in state ritual. For example, the 'Law on Disputes' lays down severe punishments for those who physically abuse religious figures and teachers:[100]

> If someone gets into an argument with and beats, curses, slashes, or stabs a *samana, brahmana*, or *buḍḍhācāriya*, or his or her own father, mother, or grandfathers and grandmothers, wounding them heavily with iron bars: have him flogged thirty times (3 *yok*), paraded on land for three days and in a boat for three days, have the fingers of both hands amputated and have him floated on a raft for the public to see.

> If he beats any of them heavily with a club and wounds them, have him flogged thirty times, paraded on land for three days and in a boat for three days, have the fingers of the right hand amputated and have him floated on a raft.
>
> If he beats any of them heavily with his hands, have his ten fingernails pulled out, have him imprisoned for six months, raised on a tripod for three days, and flogged with a leather lash thirty times. His chest should be tattooed with the statement 'I beat my father, I beat my mother'.
>
> If he beats them with a stick but not heavily, have his ten fingernails pulled out, have him imprisoned for six months, raised on a tripod for three days, and flogged with a leather lash thirty times.
>
> If he beats them with his hands but not heavily, have the five nails of one hand pulled out, have him jailed for three months, and flogged with a leather lash twenty-five times.
>
> If they die he should be executed.

Literary roles

The role of brahmans in literature gives them a permanent place in the Buddhist imagination, which cannot do without them. According to Mahāvihāra texts, in their final human lives Buddhas-to-be are born only in brahman or *kṣatriya* families.

Brahmans inhabit the *jātakas* in general, including those composed in Siam. The most famous – or infamous – literary brahman is Jūjaka, whose immortality is assured not by his good deeds, but by his role in the *Mahājāti* or *Vessantara-jātaka*, a tale told and retold in sermon, enacted in ritual, and depicted in mural and cloth painting. Jūjaka has a life of his own, and may be supplicated for wealth or success through images or *yantra*. A bronze image consecrated in 2001 (BE 2544) at Wat Thalung Thong has on the base the mantra '*oṃ siddhi siddhi jūjako svāhāḥ*'. Another well-known brahman is Doṇa, who was appointed to distribute the relics of the Buddha after the Mahāparinirvāṇa and the cremation. Doṇa's distribution of the relics is depicted in mural paintings of the life of the Buddha.

It is traditionally believed that Ayutthaya brahmans composed several classics of Thai literature, for example *Cintāmaṇi*, the manual of Thai writing, language, and prosody, composed, according to a colophon, by Phra Mahārājakhrū Horādhipati.[101] He also is held to have composed 'Sua Kho', based on a *jātaka*, and the 'Eulogy of the Glory of King Prāsāt Thong'.[102] But these attributions of authorship have been contested, and unless further evidence comes to light, the question must be left open. The role of brahmans in education included acting as tutors for princes. Experts in astronomy and astrology (*horaśāstra*), brahmans controlled the calendar.[103]

V Conclusions

In this chapter, I have examined the ideals of kingship and of two powerful social institutions, the monastic order (*saṅgha*) and the brahmans.[104] The ideals are hybrid, distinctively Thai, set in a complex cosmology.[105] The texts that support this hybridism include *jātaka*s, *nīti*, law books, and ritual manuals. Ritual languages have included Thai, Khmer, Sanskrit, and Pali, and in some cases Tamil and Mon. South-East Asian law books (*dharmaśāstra*) and chants for Brahmanical ceremonies cite verses or passages in Pali: that is, Pali becomes the classical legal and ceremonial language of the region. Traditions overlap, and replenish each other. Our sources are multivocal. I have not expected to find, let alone construct, a single definition of kingship, or of the relations between ruler, *saṅgha*, and brahmans.

The relation between kingship and religion is too often portrayed in terms of 'legitimation'. I find the concept of legitimation to be unsatisfactory – it simplifies a complex of social and conceptual forces, and in the end explains little. King, *saṅgha*, and brahmans were partners in a complex organism of state protection and state welfare Buddhism. *Nirāt Nong Khai*, a poem composed by Luang Phatphongphakdī (Tim Sukhayāng, 1847–1915, written when he was Khun Phipit Phakdee), paints a vivid picture of the rites conducted before the troops set out to fight the 'Chinese Ho' in Laos in 1875, during the Fifth Reign:[106]

> At three in the afternoon, as the auspicious moment nears,
> Hubbub erupts as commoners and nobles get ready to leave.
> When Somdet Chao Phrayā hurries up
> The Chao Khun comes out to greet him with a bow.[107]
> All together the monk and brahman astrologers
> Sat scattered in groups and rows in great numbers.
> Officials set up a line of bench-seats
> For the aspersing of the water, a beautiful dais.
> The commander of the troops pays respect to the
> Somdet
> And then goes to the dais at the head of the field.
> He asperses water charged with Buddhamantra to bring success
> in war
> Then stands and tramples a wooden effigy of the enemy.
> The monks, representatives of the Buddha's lineage
> Chant '*jayanto*'[108] together in chorus
> Victory gongs resound and reverberate
> Brahman astrologers rattle two-faced drums
> Phra Khru Hora gives victory blessings to empower the troops
> Senior brahmans blow conch-shells
> The Chao Phrayā-s advance together

And the nobles sit together in numbers
Uttering blessings to bring success.

Monks and brahmans received royal titles and ranks in the *sakdinā* system. In times of war, brahmans and monks both blessed the armies. Before the troops went to war, a '*khlōn tawān*' or ceremonial 'gateway to the jungle' was erected.[109] Two brahmans sat on it and aspersed the troops with holy water.[110] According to the 'Register of Royal Officers in Muang Nakhon Si Thammarāt' (CE 1811), the brahmans in this position in Nakhon Si Thammarāt, each with two hundred *sakdinā*, bore the titles Khun Ñāṇasambhūv and Khun Veśanubhaktra.[111] A brahman with the title Khun Jaiyabārmī, with the same rank, was in charge of erecting the *khlōng thawān*. Monks blessed the armies by reciting the *Mahādibbamanta*, itself a hybrid text *par excellence*, that evokes all possible deities without any discrimination.[112] Strategists consulted *Phichai Songkhrām* manuals to prepare troop formations.

Nobles participated in the ideology of merit and status, extending their patronage to the repair and building of temples, and then offering the temple to the king, who would grant it 'royal temple' status (*thawāy pen phra ārāma luang*). Did brahmans also endow temples? This is not clear, although there are traditions that they did so, which need to be investigated further. Elite patronage extended into tributary or subject states: Chao Phrayā Bodin Dechā, for example, left a record of his renovations of temples in Phnom Penh, Cambodia (Bernon 2003). Chao Phrayā Bodin Dechā (Sing Singhaseni, 1777–1849) was the leading general in the wars of King Rāma III's reign. In the inscription, which dates to Lesser Śaka Era 1201 (CE 1840), he relates that after the seizure of Phnom Penh the religious foundations were damaged and ruined, and he used his private funds to repair '*vihāra, uposatha* halls, Buddha images, *stūpa*s, and *cetiya*s'. Furthermore, when he did this he aspired to become a Buddha, and nothing less.

The economic role of ritual was great. Inscriptions, royal chronicles, and royal orders often give detailed inventories of the expenses, and it should be possible for an economic historian to estimate, at least roughly, the amount of exchequer dedicated to state ritual. An early itemization of royal expenditures is seen in the Khmer-language inscription from Wat Pa Mamuang in Sukhothai. King Rāma I transported Buddha images from Sukhothai and from the old capital in large numbers, and had them restored and gilded. Some were huge, such as Śrī Śākyamuni, the image which he enshrined in Wat Suthat. During the reign of King Rāma III, Ratanakosin was a flourishing power; new trading relations were formed, and economic and social change was rapid. Rāma III built three new temples, restored fifty temples, and sponsored Buddha images and *Tipiṭaka*s. He built gates and fortifications, boats and cannon.[113]

The aspiration to Buddhahood of the kings of Sukhothai, Ayutthaya,

Thonburi, and Ratanakosin was publicly proclaimed, in inscriptions, edicts, decrees, chronicles, and poems, and in their very names, titles, and epithets. That they were *bodhisattvas* was part of their image. There does not seem to be any treatise that attempts to explain the practice. Was there any explicit ritual, or was the aspiration simply made on the occasion of issuing edicts or dedicating merits? It is interesting that the *bodhisattva* kings are identified with one or other of the three types of *bodhisattva* described in Mahāvihāra tradition, as in King Rāma I's preamble to his *Rāmakian*, or in Somdet Phra Phonnarat's *Saṅgītiyavaṅśa*, both composed in the First Reign. Not only kings, but also other members of the royal family, were *bodhisattvas* by birth, as 'sprouts of the Buddha'. This concept, 'bodhisattvahood by birth', merits study. It strikes me as unique to South-East Asia. Are there parallels in Sri Lanka, or elsewhere? In the First Reign, the Uparāja, the king's brother, was publicly described as a *bodhisattva*, and in the Third Reign one of the leading nobles, the commander of the Thai armies Chao Phrayā Bodin Dechā, describes himself emphatically as a *bodhisattva* in an inscription set up in the conquered city of Phnom Penh. The *bodhisattva* ideal had a strong following, not only among the nobility: high-ranking and ordinary monastics also recorded the aspiration, for example in colophons and inscriptions.[114]

Much more research on the role of brahmans is needed. The *Three Seals Law Code* suggests that in early to mid-Ayutthaya they were powerful and privileged, a unique group whose status came with birth. What happened to brahmans with the fall of Ayutthaya is not clear, and I have not found any evidence for their status in the Thonburi period – a period, after all, of turbulent reconstruction and ideological confusion. Were there brahmanical shrines in Thonburi? Were brahmanical rites performed? Did King Taksin support the brahmans? Such questions await answers.

The brahmanical texts and rites we know today are for the most part subordinated to Buddhism. This raises the question: when did the brahmans become Buddhist, or begin to situate their rituals within a Buddhist frame? Did this process begin in Ayutthaya? Or did it start during the reign of King Rāma I?[115]

The Ratanakosin reconstruction of King Rāma I was a reinvention of Ayutthaya society and reformulation of state ideals. King Rāma I was deeply committed to Buddhism, and his edicts show clearly that he wanted to ensure that in rites and ceremonies Buddhism came first. This trend was continued, to a greater degree, by King Rāma IV, who refashioned rituals and introduced Buddhist rites to supplement or replace brahmanical ceremonies. But this period is beyond the range of this essay.

A note on sources

This essay presents, for the most part, original Thai sources in my own translations.

The Three Seals Law Code

For the *Three Seals Law Code*, I have used the five-volume Khurusapha edition, cited by section title, volume, and page: *Kotmāy trā sām duang*, Bangkok: Ongkān khā khong khurusaphā, 2537 [1994]. (The long title, from the original edition by Robert Lingat, is *Pramuan kotmāy rajakān tī 1 chulasakarāj 1166 phim tām chabap luang trā 3 duang*). A useful aide is Ishii Yoneo *et al.*, *The Computer Concordance to the Law of the Three Seals* (5 vols, Bangkok: Amarin Publications, 1990).

Inscriptions

The first two volumes of the corpus of Siamese inscriptions were bilingual, in Thai and in French, compiled by George Cœdès: *Recueil des inscriptions du Siam I, Inscriptions de Sukhodaya* (Bangkok: Bangok Times Press/Bibliothèque Nationale Vajirañāṇa, Service Archéologique, 1924). The volume contains an introduction on the epigraphy of Siam, the inscriptions of Sukhothai, and a list of the inscriptions of Siam, and romanized texts with translation of inscriptions I to XV. *Recueil des inscriptions du Siam II, Inscriptions de Dvāravatī, de Çrīvijaya et de Lăvo* (Bangkok: Bangok Times Press/Institut Royal, Service Archéologique, BE 2472 (1929 AD)). The volume contains an introduction on Dvāravatī, Grahi, Tāmbraliṅga, and Lăvo, and romanized texts with translations of Inscriptions XVI to XXIX. A revised second edition was reprinted, in reduced format, by the Fine Arts Department in 2504 [1961].

The most valuable source in English remains Prasert Na Nagara and A. B. Griswold, *Epigraphic and Historical Studies* (Bangkok: The Historical Society, 1992), referred to herein as *EHS*. This is a collection of studies originally published in the *Journal of the Siam Society* between July 1968 and July 1979. Reference is made to the study number (*EHS* 1, *EHS* 2, etc.) followed by page number of the text with location in the inscription by face and line, then page number of the translation. For concordances of the study numbers with the original publication in the *Journal of the Siam Society*, see J. C. Eade, *The Thai Historical Record: A Computer Analysis* (Tokyo: The Centre for East Asian Cultural Studies for UNESCO, the Toyo Bunko, 1996), p. xv, or Piriya Krairiksh, *Charuk pho khun rām khamhaeng: wannakhadī prawatisāt kān muang haeng krung syām* (Bangkok: Matichon 2547 [2004]), pp. 293–296. For a bibliography of Sukhothai inscriptions (in Thai), see ibid., pp. 298–303; for summaries with bibliographical references (in Thai) see ibid., pp. 315–360. *EHS* and Piriya's *Charuk* are reprints: it is regrettable that little work on the inscriptions of Sukhothai, Ayutthaya, or Bangkok has appeared since in European languages.

Useful for the study of Sukhothai inscriptions is Ishii Yoneo *et al.*, *A*

Glossarial Index of the Sukhothai Inscriptions (Bangkok: Amarin Publications, 1989).

Chronicles

A new edition of the 'Corpus of Chronicles' (*Prachum phongsāwadān*) has been undertaken in celebration of the fiftieth anniversary, or golden jubilee, of His Majesty King Bhumibol Adulyadej's accession to the throne in 1996 (BE 2539): *Prachum phongsāwadān chabap kāñcanābhiṣeka* (Bangkok: The Fine Arts Department, 2542 [1999]–), vols 1–10 plus one index volume (2544 [2001], for vols 1–5) published as of 2548 (2005).

For the most part, the chronicles have been edited anew, and some new texts have been added.

Foreign language access to the rich chronicle materials is limited. For a synoptic translation of the chronicles of Ayutthaya, see Richard D. Cushman (tr.), David K. Wyatt (ed.), *The Royal Chronicles of Ayutthaya* (Bangkok: The Siam Society, 2000), a stupendous accomplishment. For Chao Phrayā Thiphakorawong's chronicles of the First and Fourth Reigns, see the well-annotated and thoroughly indexed translations published by the Centre for East Asian Cultural Studies, Tokyo: Thadeus and Chadin Flood (tr.), *The Dynastic Chronicles, Bangkok Era, the First Reign* (vol. 1, 1978); Chadin Flood, *The Dynastic Chronicles, Bangkok Era, the First Reign* (vol. 2, 1990); Thadeus and Chadin (Kanjanavanit) Flood, *The Dynastic Chronicles, Bangkok Era, the Fourth Reign* (5 vols, 1965–1974).[116]

I have benefited from the well-researched and thoroughly annotated work by Saichon Satyānurak, 'Buddhism and Political Thought during the Reign of King Rāma I' (*Phutthasāsanā kap naew khit tāng kān muang nai rājasamai phra bāt somdet phra phuttha yot fā chulāloka (po. so. 2325–2352)*, Bangkok: Matichon, 2546 [2003]). Saichon's exemplary study cites not only published works like the *Three Seals Law Code*, but also unpublished archival sources. Another useful work is Preecha Changkhwanyun, *Thammarat–Thammarājā* (Bangkok: Chulalongkorn University Press, 2542 [1999]).

One of the most important sources to appear is the 'Encyclopædia of Thai Culture', published in Bangkok in 1999 (BE 2542) in four sets, one for each region: *Sārānukrom wathanatham thai phāk tai*: The South: 18 volumes; *Sārānukrom wathanatham thai phāk klāng*: The Centre, 15 volumes; *Sārānukrom wathanatham thai phāk nua*: The North, 15 volumes; *Sārānukrom wathanatham thai phāk isān*: The North-East, 15 volumes.

Another important publication is *Tamra 12 duan khat tae samut khun thipmontian chao wang wai* (Bangkok: 2545).

European-language literature

I do not generally refer to European-language secondary literature, which in any case is limited. Mention may be made of the pioneering works of H. G. Quaritch Wales, especially: *Siamese State Ceremonies: Their History and Function with Supplementary Notes* (Richmond, Surrey: Curzon Press, 1992: reprint of *Siamese State Ceremonies*, first published in 1931, and *Supplementary Notes on Siamese State Ceremonies*, first published in 1971); *Ancient South-East Asian Warfare* (London: Bernard Quaritch Ltd, 1952); *Ancient Siamese Government and Administration* (London: Bernard Quaritch Ltd, 1934, repr. New York: Paragon Book Reprint Corp., 1965).

Wales' pioneering work must be used with caution as there are numerous mistakes, misunderstandings, and mistranslations. Classical studies include: Yoneo Ishii, translated by Peter Hawkes, *Sangha, State, and Society: Thai Buddhism in History* (Honolulu: The University of Hawaii Press, 1986: Monographs of the Center for Southeast Asian Studies, Kyoto University, English-language Series, No. 15); Craig James Reynolds, *The Buddhist Monkhood in Nineteenth Century Thailand*, a thesis presented to the Faculty of the Graduate School of Cornell University for the Degree of Doctor of Philosophy, December 1972; Trevor Ling, *Buddhism, Imperialism and War: Burma and Thailand in Modern History* (London: George Allen and Unwin, 1979).

A note on dates and transliteration

Dates are given in Śakarāja and Buddhist Era, as appropriate. The Christian Era (CE) is added in square brackets to bibliographical references. Regnal dates are from David K. Wyatt, *Thailand: A Short History* (2nd edn, Chiang Mai: Silkworm Books: 2003, pp. 309–313). For a newly annotated version of 'Athibāy rajakān khrang krung kao', Prince Damrong Rajanubhab's list of the kings of Ayutthaya first published in *Prachum phonsāwadān* Part 5, 2460 [1917], see *Prachum phongsāwadān chabap kāñcanābhiṣeka* (Bangkok: The Fine Arts Department, 2542 [1999]), vol. 1, pp. 355–366.

Transliteration follows the simplified Royal Institute system (*Romanization Guide for Thai Script*, Bangkok [1968] 1982), with the modification that for long vowels I use the standard Indic diacritics (*ā, ī, ū*). Pāli or Sanskrit words are given as cited in the source, without standardization, for example *saṅghaha-vatthu* instead of *saṅgaha-vatthu*. In citations I retain the transliteration of the work quoted, for example 'Sukhodaya' for 'Sukhothai', 'Iśvara' for 'Īśvara', *niti* for *nīti*, and so on. For modern place names I follow *Prakāt samnak nāyok rathamontri lae prakāt rājabanditayasathān ruang kamnot chu thawīp prathet muang luang mahāsamut thale lae ko lae ruang kān khian chu changwat khet amphoe lae king amphoe* (Second Impression, Bangkok: The Royal Institute, 2524 [1981]).

Notes

* I am grateful to Santi Pakdeekham for his many suggestions regarding sources for the ideas presented in this essay. The texts translated here are not easy, often employing old words not found in the lexicons (and, if poetry in general defies translation, Thai poetry with its complex rhymes and its emphasis on sonance and alliteration, is especially defiant). My translations are provisional attempts to convey certain meanings. This is not the place to grapple with the semantic subtleties, which I have had to gloss over.

1 The genre of royal eulogies is attested in the inscriptions of Sukhothai, and continues to the present day. See Yuphorn Saengtaksin, *Wannakhadī yo phra kiat* (Bangkok: Onkān khā khong khurusaphā, 2537 [1994]).

2 I use the trope of hybridity in a linguistic rather than a genetic sense. See e.g. Crystal (1999: 151), 'hybrid: a word composed of elements from different languages'. Hybrid rituals draw on different languages and practices.

3 *sīhaladīpe araññavāsinanaṃ pasattha-mahātherānaṃ vaṃsālaṃkārabhūta*, cited in Prasert and Griswold (1992: 535). Prasert and Griswold's work is henceforth referred to as *EHS*.

4 La Loubère (1986: 114). 'Talapoin', derived from Mon, entered European languages from Pegu, and from the sixteenth century onwards was a common term for 'Buddhist monk'. See Yule and Burnell (1903, repr. 1984: 890–891), Lewis (1991: 230b). For the Mon forms see Shorto (1971: 172), s.v. *trala'*, *trila'*, etc.

5 Penth (1994: 171). See also Saeng Manavidura (1978: xliv–xlv). Both Penth and Saeng use the term 'sect', which is, however, inappropriate. These were monastic ordination lineages within the greater lineage of Mahāvihāra Theriya. They did not have lay members, and did not disagree on doctrine – only on monastic procedures.

6 Prince Damrong Rajanubhab, *Tamnān gaṇa saṅgha* (Bangkok, 2466 [1923]), pp. 39–41; Sutthiwong Phongphaibūn, 'Kā 4 fāy: khana song', in *Sārānukrom wathanatham thai phāk tai* (Bangkok, 2542 [1999]), vol. 1, pp. 286–288. See also Chaiwut Piyakun, 'Kalapanā Wat Khian Bāng Kaew', *Sārānukrom wathanatham thai phāk tai* (Bangkok, 2542 [1999]), vol. 1, pp. 283–285; Gesick (1995). The identity of *Kā jāta* is not certain. Prince Damrong interpreted it as a lineage of monks from Lanka itself (taking *jāta* as *jāti*). If we take *jāta* in the sense of 'red', the name suggests the Pā Daeng lineage – which would place Vanaratta (Pā Daeng) and Vanaratana (Pā Kaew) side by side in Ayutthaya-period Nakhon.

7 *Tamniap khā rājakān muang nakhon si thammarāj* in *Prachum phongsāwadān chabap kāñcanābhiṣeka*, vol. 5 (Bangkok: The Fine Arts Department, 2542 [1999]), p. 163.

8 For *sakdinā*, see below.

9 Cp. the inclusive phrase *satva tanglāy muan ying chāy śramaṇa brāhmaṇā* (here the text is broken) in an inscription 'in which King Rāmarāja of Ayudhyā promulgates a law in the vassal kingdom of Sukhodaya in 1397': *EHS* 4 (text) p. 116, Face I, line 11, (tr.) p. 126.

10 *Prachum phleng yāo chabap ho samut haeng chāt* (Bangkok: Khlang Witthayā, 2507 [1964]), p. 15.

11 Phra bāt somdet phra phuttha yot fā chulālok mahārāj, *Bot lakhon ruang rāmakian* (Bangkok: The Fine Arts Department, 2540 [1997]: *Wannakam samai ratanakosin, muat banterngkhadī*), vol. 1, pp. 1–2. An excerpt is translated below.

12 *Kot phra song 1*, in *Three Seals Law Code* 4: 166.

13 *agra-mahā-sāsanūpathambhaka phra buddhasāsanā*: Saichon Satyānurak, *Phutthasāsanā kap naew khit tāng kān muang nai rājasamai phra bāt somdet phra phuttha yot fā chulālok (po so 2325–2352)* (Bangkok: Matichon, 2546 [2003]), p. 230, citing the *Three Seals Law Code*.

14 Cœdès (1924: 93) (henceforth referred to as Cœdès, *Recueil I*); *EHS* 11 Part I, Section 5, (text): 486, Face I, lines 52–53 (tr.): 491.

15 *rūp phra iśvara*: line 50.

16 *pratiṣṭhā phra maheśvararūp viṣṇurūp . . . devālayamahākṣetra*: lines 52–54.

17 *śramaṇa brāhmaṇa tapasvi yati*: line 42.

18 *tapasvi brāhmaṇa phong pūjā nitya*: line 54. The translation of *tapasvi* as 'penitent' is not satisfactory. The term occurs with some frequency in the epigraphy of the region – for example in Inscription 19 – and requires further study. For a stylistic study of brahmanical images from Sukhothai, see Subhadradis Diskul (1990).

19 Cœdès (1929: 34–36). Henceforth referred to as Cœdès, *Recueil II*.

20 See Niyada Laosoonthorn, *Silāchamlak ruang rāmakian wat phra chetuphon mangkhalārām/The Ramakien Bas-reliefs at Wat Phra Chetuphon* (Bangkok: Mūlanithi Thun Phra Phuttha Yot Fā nai Phra Boromarājūpathamb, 2539 [1996]).

21 See also Inscription 64, the Nan version of the pact. The two versions are edited, translated, and discussed in *EHS* 3, pp. 67–107.

22 Saichon, *Putthasāsanā*, p. 103.

23 See Prapod Assavavirulhakarn (2003). For an earlier study of a text belonging to the same family, see Jaini (1965). Note that Jaini's title is misleading, since the text is more probably from Siam.

24 For some hybrid texts from Phatthalung, see Chaiwut Phiyakūn, *Kān pariwat wannakam thong thin phāk tai praphet nangsu but ruang tamrā phrām muang phathalung* (Songkhla: Sathāban thaksinkhadī suksā Mahāwithayālai Thaksin, 2543 [2000]).

25 See the manuscript illustrated in *Phochanānukrom sap wannakhadī thai samai ayutthayā lilit ongkān chaeng nam chabap rājabandithayasathān* (Bangkok: The Royal Institute, 2540 [1997]), pp. 10–11. 'Khom' is a script that evolved from the Khmer script to be used for writing Pāli and Thai in Siam.

26 Hybrid language is also used in Khmer religion. Saveros Pou has called this 'Khmero-Pāli' (Pou 1991: 13–28).

27 Inscription 13, in *EHS* 14, pp. 625–640, with four figures.

28 *Recueil I*, p. 159, n. 1. That is, Cœdès derives the term from Sanskrit *śreyas*, 'excellent', 'superior'. As far as I know, the term *śreya-śāsanā* does not exist in Indian literature – to begin with, *śāsanā* is not usually used in the sense of religion – and the term *seyya-sāsanā* is not known in Pali literature, at least that of Sri Lanka. The Khamphaeng Phet inscription – one of the earliest, if not the earliest, surviving occurrence of the term – uses *sāṣana* as the final member of the compounds. It also uses *śāṣanā*, spelled *sāṣaṇā*, as an independent word. In the compounds 'Buddha-sāṣana' and 'Saiya-sāṣana', *-sāṣana* would, however, be pronounced *sāt*, and thus be a homophon, in Thai pronunciation, of *śāstra*. In later cases, *śāstra*, often spelled *sātra*, is commonly used.

It has been suggested that the term *śreya-śāstra* may derive from *Śaiva-śāstra*, or that it derives from *seyya* in the sense of lying down, horizontal, perhaps with reference to *tiracchāna-vijjā*. I am not convinced by either explanation. Further research into the early occurrences and evolution of the term is needed. The 'History of the Brahmans of Nakhon Si Thammarat', in the last section, apparently written in Lesser Śaka Era 1096 (CE 1734–35), uses the term '*saiyaśātra*' twice for brahmanical rites: *Tamnān phrām muang nakhon si thammarāj* ([Bangkok]: Rong phim Sophon Phiphatanakorn, 2473[1930]), p. 45. At the end of his *Rāmakian*, Rāma I states that 'this royal composition, *Rāmakian*, has been written following brahmanical legend (*niyāy saiy*): it does not have any profound substance (*kaen sān*) – I have [written it] with the aim to celebrate and worship [the Buddha]': Phra bāt somdet phra phuttha yot fā chulālok mahārāj, *Bot lakhon ruang rāmakian* (Bangkok: The Fine Arts Department, 2540 [1997]): *Wannakam samai ratanakosin, muat banterngkhadī*, vol. 4, p. 582. The passage shows that by Lesser Śaka Era 1159 (CE 1797), when the work was concluded, the short form '*saiy*' was in use. One should not take Rāma I's statement as a devaluation of Brahmanism: at the end of *Unarut* he makes a parallel remark, this time calling his source an 'ancient tale': 'the royal composition *Unarut* does not have any profound substance (*kaen sān*); I have composed it after an ancient tale (*ruang borān*), to celebrate the city': *Bot lakhon ruang unarut: phra rājaniphon nai phra bāt somdet phra phuttha yot fā chulālok mahārāj* (Bangkok: The Fine Arts Department, 2545 [2002]), p. 449. Two of the sketchbooks of brahmanical deities use *saiyasātra* or *śaiyāśāstra* in their titles: *Phra samut rūp phra saiyasātr* and *Tamrā phāp thevarūp saiyāśāstra* (*Tamrā phāp thevarūp*, pp. 95, 179).

Another sense of the term is magic or sorcery. The study of this term, and of other indigenous terms for Brahmanism and Buddhism, not only in South-East Asia but in general, is a desideratum. For Sri Lanka, see Carter (1993: 9–25).

29 'Debakarma' (*devakarma*) seems to be connected with elephant training: see *Tamrā phāp thevarūp*, pp. 28, 53, 101, 102, 191, 192, where Gaṇeśa is represented in two forms – standing and seated – as 'Phra Devakarrma'.

30 In early modern usage, Śreyaśāsana came to be used in contrast with Buddhaśāsanā, for example in Prince Damrong Rajanubhap, 'Tamnān kān ken tahān thai', originally published in 2464 [1914], reprinted in *Prachum phongsāwadān chabap kāñcanābhiṣeka*, vol. 5 (Bangkok: The Fine Arts Department, 2542 [1999]), pp. 211, 233. The term is used in modern polemics, as in an article by Sulak Sivarak, 'Phut kap saiy nai sangkhom thai' [Buddhism and ritual in Thai society] (*Silpawatthanatham/Art and Culture*, vol. 15, no. 7, May 1994, pp. 76–91) or an ensuing book by the same, *Phut kap saiy nai sangkhom thai* (Bangkok: Khana Kammakān Sāsanā Puea Kān Phathanā/Sathāban Santiprachātham, 2538 [1995]).

31 From the *Three Seals Law Code, Phra rājakamnot mai*, Section 36, cited in Saichon, *Phutthaśāsanā*, p. 230.

32 *EHS* 11 Part I, Section 2 (text), p. 441, Face I, line 7 (tr.), p. 449.

33 *EHS* 11 Part I, Section 6 (text), p. 502, Face I, lines 13–14 (tr.), p. 508.

34 *EHS* 11 Part I, Section 5 (text), p. 486, Face I, lines 12–13 (tr.), p. 490.

35 For a newly annotated version of 'Athibāy rajakān khrang krung kao', Prince Damrong Rajanubhab's list of the kings of Ayutthaya first published in *Prachum phonsāwadān* Part 5, 2460 [1917], see *Prachum phonsāwadān chabap kāñcanābhiṣeka* (Bangkok: The Fine Arts Department, 2542 [1999]), vol. 1, pp. 355–366. Titles of kings used in the *Three Seals Law Code* are analysed in Vickery (1984).

36 *Phra aiyakāra ājñā luang*, BE 1895 [CE 1352], in *Three Seals Law Code*, 4: 2–3.

37 Read *-ekādāsaratha-īśvara-*.

38 *Phra aiyakāra luang*, BE 1976 [CE 1433], Section 13, in *Three Seals Law Code*, 4: 17.

39 Wat Cuḷāmaṇī Inscription of Phra Paramatrailokanātha, BE 2223 (CE 1680).

40 'The kings of Ayutthaya . . . were considered in ritual to be *avatars* of Hindu deities such as Vishnu or Indra. But to the Europeans who came to Siam in the

seventeenth and eighteenth centuries, the ruler of Ayutthaya was the principal trader in the Kingdom, and thus a formidable competitor as well as trading partner': Dhiravat na Pombejra (1998: 67). John Crawfurd, sent as British envoy to Bangkok in 1822, noted this for Ratanakosin: 'The King of Siam is both a monopolist and a trader' – see Crawfurd (1987: 380).

41 *Three Seals Law Code, Phra rajakamnot mai*, Section 13, 5: 243. The spelling '*bhūma*' for Pāli-Sanskrit '*bhūmi*' is a Thai hybrid form.

42 These goals were common to all Buddhist schools in ancient India, and reference to them should not be construed, as is too often the case, as 'Mahāyāna influence'. Mahāyāna ideology evolved from the reinterpretation of the three goals, and not *vice versa*. For the *bodhisattva* in Mahāvihāra tradition see, e.g., Bhikkhu Bodhi (1978), or Rahula's classical essay, 'The Bodhisattva Ideal in Theravāda and Mahāyāna', in Rahula (1978: 71–77).

43 *EHS* 11, Part I, Section 7 (text), p. 515, Face I, lines 4–7 (tr.), p. 517.

44 *Phra aiyakāra ājñā luang*, Section 13, in *Three Seals Law Code*, 4: 17.

45 The Pāli term *buddhaṅkura* is used as a synonym of *bodhisattva* in classical texts from Ceylon.

46 *Kham chan sansern phra kiat somdet phra phuttha chao luang prāsāt thong* (Bangkok: The Fine Arts Department, 2543 [2000]), pp. 49–56.

47 For his story, see H. Saddhatissa (1975: chapter X).

48 *Phra rājaphongsāwadān krung thonburī chabap phan chanthanumāt*, in *Prachum phongsāwadān chabap kāñcanābhiṣeka*, vol. 3 (Bangkok: The Fine Arts Department, 2542 [1999]), p. 475.

49 *Phra rājaphongsāwadān krung thonburī chabap phan chantanumāt*, p. 505.

50 Saichon, *Phutthaśāsanā*, p. 211.

51 For the politics and culture of Thonburi, see Nidhi Iaewsiwong, *Kān muang thai samai phra chao krung thonburī* (Bangkok: Matichon Press, 4th printing, 2539 [1996]). For early Ratanakosin, see the same author's *Pāk kai lae bai rua: wā duai kān suksā prawatisāt–wannakam ton ratanakosin* (2nd printing, Bangkok: Phraew Samnak Phim, 2538 [1995]).

52 *Three Seals Law Code*, 5: 326.

53 *Three Seals Law Code*, 5: 321.

54 Phra bāt somdet phra phuttha yot fā chulālok mahārāj, *Bot lakhon ruang rāmakian* (Bangkok: The Fine Arts Department, 2540 [1997] *Wannakam samai ratanakosin, muat banterngkhadī*, vol. 1, p. 1).

55 *Bot lakhon ruang rāmakian*, p. 1, line 10. The Thai form here is *śraddhādhaika* (pron. *satthātuk*), for Pāli *saddhādhika*.

56 *Saṅgītiyavaṅśa* (Bangkok: The Fine Arts Department, 2544 [2001]: *Wannakam samai ratanakosin*, vol. 3), pp. 248, 262. For the Wang Nā, see S. Phlāy Noi, *Wang nā phrayā sua: phra pavararāja prawat somdet phra bowararāj chao mahāsurasinganāt krom phra rājawang bowon nai rajakān tī 1* (3rd printing, revised, Bangkok: Silpawatthanatham, 2545 [2002]) and *Phra kiartikhun somdet phra bowararājā chao mahāsurasinghanāt (bunmā)* (Bangkok: Mūlanithi Mahāsurasinghanāt/Wat Mahāthātyuwarājarangarit, 2538 [1995]).

57 *Wannakam phrayā trang* (Bangkok: The Fine Arts Department, 2547 [2004]), pp. 248–258.

58 *Chotmaihet rajakān tī 3*, vol. 3 (Bangkok: Sahaprachaphanit, 2530 [1987]), pp. 26–27.

59 The forms 'buddha' (in Thai pronunciation *phuttha*) and 'buddhi' (in Thai pronunciation *phutthi*) are used interchangeably in our documents.

60 At this time there was no custom of making statues or portraits of living monarchs.

61 The consecutive names Rāma I, II, etc. were assigned retrospectively in 1916, during the Sixth Reign.

62 See *Phochanānukrom sap wannakhadī thai samai sukhothai traibhūmikathā chabap rājabandithayasathān* (Bangkok: The Royal Institute, 2544 [2001]), pp. 88–125; Cœdès and Archaimbault (1973: 86–111); Reynolds and Reynolds (1982: 135–172).

63 Inscription 8, in *EHS* 11, Part II, Section 10 (text), p. 555, Face I, line 13 (tr.), pp. 560–561.

64 The five *kakudhabhaṇḍa* have been defined and illustrated with a line drawing in the 'Royal Institute Dictionary' (*Phochanānukrom chabap rājabanditayasathān*) from the first edition published in BE 2493 [CE 1950] to the current edition published in 2546 [2003].

65 Inscription 2 in *EHS* 10 (text), p. 363, Face I, line 33, *khann jayasrī* (tr.), p. 381.

66 For Inscription 4, see *EHS* 11, Part I, Section 5 (text), p. 486, Face I, line 11, *makuṭa . . . khan jayaśrīy svetachatra* (tr.), p. 490. For inscription 5, see *EHS* 11, Part I, Section 6, (text), p. 502, Face I, lines 10–11, [ja]yaśrī (tr.), p. 508.

67 Cf. the phrase '*dai chāng phuek mā sū phra bāramī*'.

68 See *Phra saeng rājasastrā pracham muang* (Bangkok: The Fine Arts Department, 2539 [1996]).

69 In 2525 (1982) Queen Sirikit stood in for His Majesty, in 2585 (1985) Crown Prince Mahā Vajiralongkorn did so.

70 *Rājanitisāstra khong brāhmaṇ anantañāṇa lae brāhmaṇa gaṇamissaka* (Bangkok: 2463 [1920], 'Bān phanaek chabap luang khian nai rajakān tī 3', *plae phra rājaniti chāk phra pāḷī bhukām thawāy*.

71 *Jātaka* (PTS edition) I 260, 399; II 400; III 320; V 119, 378.

72 *Jātaka* (PTS edition) III 274.

73 *Epigraphia Indica* XVIII, p. 338.

74 *EHS* 11 Part I, Section 2 (text), p. 446, Face II, line 26 (tr.), p. 462.

75 *dasabiddha-rājadharma: EHS* 11, Part I, Section 6 (text), p. 502, Face I, line 15 (tr.), p. 508.

76 For references, see Prakong Nimmanhemindh, 'Totsabidharājadharrma', in *Sārānukrom watthanatham thai phāk klāng*, vol. 6, pp. 2448–50.

77 The concept and role of the office of 'saṅgharāja' changed radically in the late nineteenth century.

78 Ayutthaya society was graded in terms of rice fields (*nā*), although whether fields were ever actually allocated, or whether *nā* was simply a measure, remains a subject of debate. For a concise analysis of *sakdinā* and other indicators of status, see Akin Rabibhadana (1975: 93–124). See Reynolds (1987: 152), '[T]he term [*sakdinā*] refers to positions in a socio-political hierarchy underpinned by economic relations. The positions were differentiated by amounts of land allocated, e.g., from 100,000 units for the highest-ranking prince, to 10,000 units for a noble, and down to 25 units for a commoner and 5 for a slave.' By the middle of the twentieth century, *sakdinā* was used in some circles as a translation of 'feudalism'; as a result, the term has its own history in modern Thai historiography and polemics.

79 *Na tahān hua muang, Three Seals Law Code* I § 27.

80 Somdet Phra Mahāsamana Chao Krom Phra Paramānujitajinorasa, *Lilit krabuan phayuhayātrā tāng cholamāk lae sathalamāk* (Bangkok: Rong Phim Borisat Sahathammik, 2539 [1996]).

81 See *Three Seals Law Code*, vol. 4, pp. 229–257. '*Kot*' is from Pāli *kaṭikā*, a technical term for a *Vinaya* offence, and presumably related to the Pāli terms

kaṭikā and *kaṭhikāva(t)ta*, the latter used in Ceylon for royal decrees on *saṅgha* affairs. See Ratnapala (1971: 6–16), Introduction.

82 Inscription 45, *EHS* 3, pp. 67–107.

83 *EHS* 24, pp. 788–803.

84 Le Blanc, pp. 20 foll. This was a volatile period, and at least some factions in the cosmopolitan city had attempted to convert King Narai to Islam (leading to the Makassar revolt) or to Catholicism. See Hutchinson (1968), or Wyatt (1984: 101–104).

85 *nābrahma kṣatramṛdhnoti nākṣatraṃ brahma vardhate, brahma kṣatraṃ ca saṃpṛktam iha cāmutra vardhate*: Olivelle (2005: (9)322).

86 In some cases the role of brahmanism is caricatured by 'Sukhothai romanticism', which portrays Sukhothai as a sort of open society of the Thai, and Ayutthaya as an absolutist state in which the 'true Thai' values were distorted by brahmanical superstitions and Khmer despotism.

87 'Bot', abbreviated from Uposatha 'hall', came to be used for religious buildings such as churches, which are *bot khrit*.

88 The complex series of rites was last performed in BE 2477 (CE 1934).

89 See Sutthiwong Phongpaibun, 'Tamnān phrām muang nakhon si thammarat', in *Sārānukrom wathanatham thai phāk tai*, vol. 6, pp. 2670–71; Pricha Nunsuk, 'Sāsanā phrām nai phāk tai', in *Sārānukrom wathanatham thai phāk tai*, vol. 15, pp. 7347–7372. For a note on the surviving brahmanical structures in Nakhon Si Thammarat, see Munro-Hay (2001: 301–307).

90 See 'Phrām muang phattalung', in *Sārānukrom wathanatham thai phāk tai*, vol. 11, pp. 5262–69.

91 See 'Phrām muang chaiya, trakun', in *Sārānukrom wathanatham thai phāk tai*, vol. 11, pp. 5260–62.

92 *EHS* 14, p. 631.

93 For a summary of the contents of this 'exceedingly curious work', see Wyatt (1975: 52–56).

94 *Tamnān phrām muang nakhon si thammarāt* (Bangkok: Rong Phim Sophon Phiphatanakorn, 2473 [1930]), p. 20.

95 *Phra aiyākāra tamnaeng nā phonlaruan*, Section 19, in *The Three Seals Law Code* 1: 265 foll.

96 *Tamniap khā rājakān muang nakhon si thammarāt* in *Prachum phongsāwadān chabap kāñcanābhiṣeka*, vol. 5 (Bangkok: The Fine Arts Department, 2542 [1999]), pp. 161–162.

97 *Tamnān phrām muang nakhon si thammarāt*, pp. 12–14.

98 'History of the Brahmans of Nakhon Si Thammarāt', p. 22.

99 The literature on the subject for India is immense. For grants in Orissa, see Singh (1993). For the evolution from grants to individuals to grants to temples in medieval Andhra, see Talbot (2001: 88).

100 *Phra āyākān laksana wiwāt*, Section 32, in *Three Seals Law Code* (3: 199). *Buḍḍhācāriya* is *vṛddhācārya*, senior teacher.

101 For Mahārājakhrū, see *Kham chan sansern phra kiat somdet phra phuttha chao luang prasāt thong* (Bangkok: The Fine Arts Department, 2543 [2000]), Introduction.

102 Bangkok: The Fine Arts Department, 2543 [2000].

103 Another important literary figure, well beyond the range of this already inflated article, is the *rishi*. Whatever the origins of the concept, for our period the vocation is very much a part of the Thai religious imagination. Many of the *rishis* of Thai *tamnān* geography, including that of the *Cāmadevīvaṃsa*, probably have Mon or Lua ancestors, but even this ancestry is mixed with the 'isi' of Pali texts

and the 'ṛṣī' of brahmanical texts. For a dedication of a Buddha image by a *rishi* inscribed in Mon, in the cave Tham Rusi as Khao Ngū, Rājaburi province, see Cœdès, *Recueil II*, p. 19: *puñ vraḥ ṛṣi śrī samādhigupta*. See also Shorto (1971: 320), 'risi'.

104 These were not the only pressure groups in pre-modern society – there were mandarins and nobles (*khun nāng*), merchants and manufacturers, farmers and gatherers, etc. The groups discussed here are those who manufactured and enacted ideology and ritual. For the most part, our sources are elite documents – inscriptions, laws, decrees, courtly literature. There are few documents for study of grassroots ritual in the period in question – but the study should certainly be attempted.

105 One omission in studies of the political imagination in Siam is the role of China and the Chinese. Given the presence of Chinese in the region for over a millennium, and the weight of trade and political links, it is hard to imagine that Chinese conceptions of power and hierarchy did not affect Thai ideologies. They certainly did come into play in the Siamese court's self-representation to the Chinese court through embassies or 'tribute'. But did they not function closer to home? We must also ask whether court ceremonial adopted anything from Persia or contemporary courts of India.

106 Luang Phatphongphakdī (Tim Sukhayāng), *Nirāt Nong Khai* (Bangkok: Thai Wathana Phanich, 2541 [1998]), p. 3.

107 'Chao Phrayā' is Somdet Chao Phrayā Boroma Maha Si Suriyawong (Chuang Bunnag, 1808–1883). 'Chao Khun' is Chao Phrayā Mahinthornsakdamrong (Peng Phenkun), commander of the First Army and of one of the two armies sent to suppress the Ho.

108 'Jayanto' is a popular chant beginning *jayanto bodhiyā mūle, sākiyānaṃ nandivaḍḍhano*.

109 See *Phochanānukrom chabap rājabanditayasathān pho. so. 2542* (Bangkok: Nanmi Publishing, 2546 [2003]), p. 209a: '*Khlōn thawān*: a gate to the jungle (*pratū pā*), a jungle gate which is made according to brahmanical lore (*tamrā phrām*), decorated with layers of leaves, through which soldiers depart when going to war. Two brahmans sit on high platforms, one on either side of the gate, to sprinkle water charged by *devamantra*, for the success and blessings (*jayamaṅgala*) of the departing troops.' *Khlōn* is from Khmer, *thawān* is Sanskrit *dvāra*. In his *Nirāt tā din daeng*, King Rāma I refers to passing the *khlōn thawān* on his way to fight the Burmese (*Klon phleng yāo nirāt ruang rop phamā tī tā din daeng phleng yāo rop phamā tī nakhon si thammarāj lae phleng yāo ruang tī phamā*, Bangkok: Siam Press Management Ltd, 2547 [2004]), p. 29. *Khlōn thawān* is also the door to the palace, and the female troops who guard it.

110 The 'History of the Brahmans of Nakhon Si Thammarāt' includes '*khlōn thawān boek phrai*' among the twenty rites to be performed by brahmans: *Tamnān phrām muang nakhon si thammarāj*, p. 20.

111 *Tamniap khā rājakān muang nakhon si thammarāt*, in *Prachum phongsāwadān chabap kāñcanābhiṣeka*, vol. 5 (Bangkok: The Fine Arts Department, 2542 [1999]), p. 162, *phanak ngān thavāy nam sang tam khōl thawān*.

112 According to the *Tamniap khā rājakān*, op. cit., immediately following the two brahmans just mentioned, a brahman with the title Khun Phanavek had the duty to read the 'Bijaya-yātrā' (*phanak ngān ān phichai yātrā*). Can this be connected with the recitation of *Mahādibbamanta*?

113 See *Tamnān watthu sathān tāng tāng seung phra bāt somdet phra nang klao chao yū hua song sathāpanā* (first published 2472 [1929]; 6th printing, for the cremation of Nai Chamnian Nakhonprasāt, Bangkok: 2514 [1971]); Santi Leksukhum,

Chitrakam thai samai rajakān tī 3: khwām khit plian, kān sadaeng ok ko plian tām (Bangkok: Muang Boran, 2548 [2005]; *Sārānukrom phra bāt somdet phra nang klao chao yū hua rajakān tī 3*, vol. 1 (Bangkok: *Mūlanithi chalerm phra kiat phra bāt somdet phra nang klao chao yū hua*, 2545 [2002]).

114 The '*bodhisattva* monks' of pre-modern Siam require a separate study.

115 One of the best early ethnographic notes available is not on the brahmans of Siam, but on those of Cambodia: see Moura (1883: 213–219). For Siam, see Crawfurd (1987: 149–153). An interesting account of the court brahmans at Phnom Penh in the early 1920s is given by Prince Damrong Rajanubhab in his *Nirāt Nakhon Wat* (originally published 2467 [CE 1924]). For Cambodia into the post-Khmer Rouge period, see also de Bernon (1997: 33–58).

116 See, e.g., vol. 5, p. 33, 'Religion, 1. Brahmanism in Siam'.

BIBLIOGRAPHY

Agence Khmer Presse (1956) 'Inauguration de L'Hôpital des Bonzes', February 22: 2.

Akin Rabibhadana (1975) 'Clientship and Class Structure in the Early Bangkok Period', in G. William Skinner and A. Thomas Kirsch (eds) *Change and Persistence in Thai Society: Essays in Honor of Lauriston Sharp*, Ithaca and London: Cornell University Press: 93–124.

Alagappa, Muthiah (ed.) (1995) *Political Legitimacy in Southeast Asia: The Quest for Moral Authority*, Stanford: Stanford University Press.

Altbach, P. G. and Kelly, G. P. (1991) *Education and the Colonial Experience*, New York: Advent Books.

Anderson, Benedict (1983) *Imagined Communities: Reflections on the Origin and Spread of Nationalism*, London: Verso.

Archaimbault, Charles (1961) 'L'histoire de Champassak', *Journal Asiatique*, Tome CCXLIX: 519–595.

Archaimbault, Charles (1980) *Contribution à l'étude d'un cycle de légendes Lao*, Paris: Publication de l'École française d'Extrême-Orient.

Aschmoneit, Walter (1996) 'Self-Help Groups in Cambodia: Pagoda Committees and Development Cooperation in Kampong Thom Province', unpublished research report by GTZ [German Development Agency] Cambodia (Kampong Thom).

Aung San Suu Kyi (1990) *Burma and India: Some Aspects of Life under Colonialism*, Shimla: Indian Institute of Advanced Study.

Ba, Vivian (1964) 'The Beginnings of Western Education in Burma', *Journal of the Burma Research Society*, 47 (December): 287–324.

Babb, Lawrence and Wadley, Susan (eds) (1995) *Media and the Transformation of Religion in South Asia*, Philadelphia: University of Pennsylvania Press.

Bagshawe, L. E. (1976) *A Literature of School Books: A Study of the Burmese Books Approved for Use in Schools by the Education Department in 1885*, M. Phil. thesis, SOAS, London.

Bagshawe, L. E. (1981) *The Maniyadanabon of Shin Sandalinka*, Ithaca: Cornell University Press.

Bapat, P. V. (1956) *2500 Years of Buddhism*, Delhi: Government of India, The Publications Division.

Bauer, Christian (1992) 'L'epithète du maître et son origine mône', in Francois Bizot (ed.) *Le Chemin de Lankā*, Paris: École Française d'Extrême-Orient: 277–284.

Bechert, Heinz (1966–73) *Buddhismus, Staat und Gesellschaft in den Ländern des*

Theravāda Buddhismus, 3 vols, Frankfurt/Berlin: A. Metzner (vol.1, 1966); Wiesbaden: Otto Harrassowitz (vol.2, 1967; vol.3, 1973).

Bechert, Heinz (1973) 'Sangha, State, Society, "Nation": Persistence of Traditions in "Post-Traditional" Buddhist Societies', *Daedalus*, 102 (1): 85–95.

Bechert, Heinz, Daw Khin Khin Su, and Daw Tin Tin Myint (compilers) (1978–85) *Burmese Manuscripts*, Wiesbaden: Steiner.

Bečka, J. (1995) *Historical Dictionary of Burma*, London: Scarecrow Press.

Becker, A. L. and Yenogoyan, Aram A. (eds) (1979) *The Imagination of Reality: Essays in Southeast Asian Coherence Systems*. New York: Ablex

Bektimirova, Nadezda (2003) 'The Sangha in Politics: Challenges and Consequences', *Phnom Penh Post* 12/24 (21 November–4 December).

Bellah, R. and Hammond, Phillip (eds) (1980) *Varieties of Civil Religion*, San Francisco: Harper & Row.

Benda, Harry J. (1969) 'The Structure of Southeast Asian History: Some Preliminary Observations', in R. O. Tilman (ed.) *Man, State, and Society in Contemporary Southeast Asia*, New York, Washington, London: Praeger Publishers: 23–44.

Berger, Hans Georg (2000) *Het Bun Dai Bun: Luang Prabang – Sacred Rituals of Luang Prabang*, London: Westzone.

Bernon, Olivier de (1994) 'Le Buddh Daṃnāy: Note sur un texte apocalyptique khmer', *Bulletin de l'École française d'Extrême-Orient*, 81: 83–100.

Bernon, Olivier de (1997) 'À propos du retour des bakous dans le palais royal de Phnom Penh', in Catherine Clémentin-Ojha (ed.) *Renouveaux religieux en Asie*, Paris: École française d'Extrême-Orient (Études thématiques 6): 33–58.

Bernon, Olivier de (1998) 'La prediction du Bouddha', *Aséanie*, 1: 43–66.

Bernon, Olivier de (2003) 'L'inscription thaïe du Vatt Buddhaghosācāry de Phnom-Penh (K. 1213)', in *Dedications to Her Royal Highness Princess Galyani Vadhana Krom Luang Naradhiwas Rajanagarindra on her 80th Birthday*, Bangkok: The Siam Society: 137–144.

Bhikkhu Bodhi (tr.) (1978) 'A Treatise on the Paramis', in *The Discourse on the All-Embracing Net of Views: The Brahmajāla Sutta and its Commentarial Exegesis*, Kandy: Buddhist Publication Society: 254–330.

Bischoff, Roger (1997) *Buddhism in Myanmar*, Colombo: Karunaratna.

Bizot, François (1976) *Le figuier à cinq branches: Recherche sur le bouddhisme khmer*. Paris: École française d'Extrême-Orient, LXVII

Bizot, François (1980) 'La grotte de la naissance', in *Bulletin de l'École française d'Extrême Orient*, LXVII (Recherches sur le Bouddhisme Khmer, II): 222–273.

Bounleuth Sengsoulin (2004) 'The Champassak Chronicle, Vat Chitsavang Version: A Contribution to 18th–19th century Lao Historiography', MA thesis, Westphalian Wilhelms University of Münster.

Brown, MacAlister and Zasloff, Joseph J. (1999) *Cambodia Confounds the Peacemakers 1979–1998*, Ithaca and London: Cornell University Press.

Bunnag, Jane (1973) *Buddhist Monk and Buddhist Layman*, Cambridge: Cambridge University Press.

Burlingame, Eugene W. (1917) 'The Act of Truth (*Saccakiriyā*): A Hindu Spell and its Employment as a Psychic Motif in Hindu Fiction', *Journal of the Royal Asiatic Society* Vol 53 [new series], no.4.

Burma Educational Department (1892) *Report on Public Instruction in Burma, 1891–1892*, Rangoon: Superintendent, Government Printing and Stationery

Burma Educational Department (1897) *Report on Public Instruction in Burma, 1895–1896, Resolution*, Rangoon: Superintendent, Government Printing and Stationery.

Burma Educational Department (1923) *Report on Public Instruction in Burma, Quinquennial Report, 1917–1922*, Rangoon: Superintendent, Government Printing and Stationery.

Carter, John Ross (1993) 'The Origin and Development of "Buddhism" and "Religion" in the Study of the Theravāda Buddhist Tradition', in John Ross Carter (ed.) *On Understanding Buddhists: Essays on the Theravāda Tradition in Sri Lanka*, Albany, New York: State University of New York Press: 9–25.

Casanova, José (1994) *Public Religions in the Modern World*, Chicago: University of Chicago Press.

Chalermchai Kositpipat *et al.* (1987) *Mural Paintings of Wat Buddhapadipa*, London: Buddhist Temple Foundation.

Chaloermtiarana, Thak (1974) 'The Sarit Regime, 1957–1963: The Formative Years of Modern Thai Politics', PhD thesis, Ithaca, Cornell University.

Chan Htoon (1967) 'Address to the 16th IARF Conference on Buddhism – the Religion in the Age of Science, Star Island, New Hampshire, USA, August 1958', published as *Buddhism and the Age of Science*, Kandy: Wheel Publications.

Chandler, David (1983) 'Going Through the Motions: Ritual Aspects of the Reign of King Ang Duang of Cambodia (1848–1860)', in L. Gesick (ed.) *Center, Symbols, and Hierarchies: Essays of the Classical States of Southeast Asia*, New Haven: Yale University Southeast Asia Studies: 106–124.

Chandler, David (1991) *The Tragedy of Cambodian History: Politics, War and Revolution since 1945*, New Haven and London: Yale University Press, and Chiang Mai: Silkworm Books.

Chandler, David (1993) *A History of Cambodia*, 2nd edn, Chiang Mai: Silkworm Books.

Chandler, David (1996) *Facing the Cambodian Past: Selected Essays 1971–1994*, Chiang Mai: Silkworm Books.

Chatterjee, Partha (1986) *Nationalist Thought and the Colonial World: A Derivative Discourse?* London: Zed Books, for the United Nations University.

Chesterman, Simon (2005) *You, the People: The United Nations, Transitional Administration, and State-Building*, New York: Oxford University Press.

Chutintaranond, Sunait (1992) 'The Image of the Burmese Enemy in Thai Perceptions and Historical Writing', *Journal of the Siam Society*, 80 (1): 89–98.

Cœdès, George (1916) 'À propos d'une stèle sculptée d'Angkor-Vat', *Mémoires Concernant l'Asie Oriental*, 11: 117–121.

Cœdès, George (1924) *Recueil des inscriptions du Siam I, Inscriptions de Sukhodaya*, Bangkok: Bangkok Times Press/Bibliothèque Nationale Vajirañāṇa, Service Archéologique.

Cœdès, George (1929) *Recueil des inscriptions du Siam II, Inscriptions de Dvāravatī, de Crīvijaya et de Lăvo*, Bangkok: Bangkok Times Press/Institut Royal, Service Archéologique, BE 2472.

Coedès, George (1968) *The Indianized States of Southeast Asia*, 3rd edn, ed. W. F. Vella, trans. S. B. Cowing, Honolulu: University Press of Hawaii.

Cœdès, George and Archaimbault, C. (trans.) (1973) *Les trois mondes (Trabhūmi brah rvan)*, Paris: École française d'Extrême-Orient (*Publications de l'École française d'Extrême-Orient* LXXXIX).

Cœdès, George and Filliozat, Jacqueline (eds) (2001) *The Paṭhamasambodhi*, Oxford: The Pali Text Society.

Cohen, B. (1996) *Colonialism and its Forms of Knowledge: The British in India*, Princeton, NJ: Princeton University Press.

Collins, Steven (1996) 'The Lion's Roar on the Wheel-Turning King: A Response to Andrew Huxley's "The Buddha and the Social Contract" ', *Journal of Indian Philosophy* 24 (4): 421–446.

Collins, Steven (1998) *Nirvana and Other Buddhist Felicities: Utopias of the Pali Imaginaire*, Cambridge: Cambridge University Press.

Collins, William (1998) 'Grassroots Civil Society in Cambodia', a research report issued by the Centre for Advanced Study (Phnom Penh).

Comaroff, Jean (1994) 'Defying Disenchantment', in Charles Keyes, Laurell Kendal, and Helen Hardacre (eds) *Asian Visions of Authority: Religion and the Modern States of Southeast Asia*, Honolulu: University of Hawaii Press: 301–314.

Condominas, Georges (1998) *Le bouddhisme au village*, Vientiane: Édition des Cahiers de France.

Connolly, William (ed.) (1984) *Legitimacy and the State*, New York: New York University Press.

Cooper, Barry (1999) *Eric Voegelin and the Foundations of Political Science*, Columbia and London: University of Missouri Press.

Cornell, Stephen and Kalt, Joseph P. (1998) 'Sovereignty and Nation-Building: The Development Challenge in Indian Country Today', *American Indian Culture and Research Journal*, 22 (3): 187–214.

Crawfurd, John (1987) *Journal of an Embassy to the Courts of Siam and Cochin China*, Singapore: Oxford University Press.

Crystal, David (1999) *The Penguin Dictionary of Language*, 2nd edn, London: Penguin Books.

Cushing, Richard D. (2000) *The Royal Chronicles of Ayutthaya*. A synoptic translation edited by David K. Wyatt, Bangkok: The Siam Society.

Cuttriss, C. A. (1960) 'Early Newspapers in Burma', *Journal of the Burma Research Society*, Fiftieth Anniversary Publications, no. 2: 43–47.

Daube, David (1954) 'Princeps legibus solutus', in *L'Europa e il diritto Romano: Studii in memoria di Paolo Koschaker* (Milan), II: 461–465.

Delvert, Jean (1961) *La paysan cambodgien*. Paris and The Hague: Mouton.

Delvert, Jean (1979) 'La paysannerie khmère avant 1970', *Mondes en développement* (Paris) 28: 732–749.

Dhida Saraya (1982) 'The Development of the Northern Thai States from the Twelfth to the Fifteenth Centuries', PhD thesis, Sydney: University of Sydney.

Dhiravat na Pombejra (1998) 'Port, Palace, and Profit: An Overview of Siamese Crown Trade and the European Presence in Siam in the Seventeenth Century', in *Port Cities and Trade in Western Southeast Asia*, Bangkok: Institute of Asian Studies, Chulalongkorn University: 65–83.

Doré, Amphay (1987) 'Aux sources de la civilisation lao (contribution ethno-historique è la connaissance de la culture luang-phrabanaise)', mémoire présenté pour le Doctorat d'État es-Lettres et Sciences Humaines, Paris.

E Maung, (1951) 'Insolvency Jurisdiction in Early Burmese Law', *Journal of the Burma Research Society*, 34: 1–7.

Eade, J. C. (1996) *The Thai Historical Record: A Computer Analysis*, Tokyo: Centre for East Asian Cultural Studies for Unesco.

Ebihara, May (1966) 'Interrelations between Buddhism and Social Systems in Cambodian Peasant Culture', in Manning Nash *et al.* (eds) *Anthropological Studies in Theravada Buddhism*, New Haven: Yale University Southeast Asia Studies: 175–196.

Edwards, Penny (1999) 'Cambodge: The Cultivation of a Nation, 1860–1940', PhD thesis, Monash University.

Edwards, Penny (2004a) 'Making a Religion of the Nation and Its Language: The French Protectorate (1863–1954) and the Dhammakāy', in John Marston and Elizabeth Guthrie (eds) *History, Buddhism, and New Religious Movements in Cambodia*, Honolulu: University of Hawaii Press: 63–85.

Edwards, Penny (2004b) 'Relocating the Interlocutor: Taw Sein Ko (1864–1930) and the Itinerancy of Knowledge in British Burma', *South East Asia Research*, 12(3): 277–335.

Eisenbruch, Maurice (1992) 'The Ritual Space of Patients and Traditional Healers in Cambodia. *Bulletin de l'École francaise d'Extrême-Orient* 79 (2): 283–316.

Eisenbruch, Maurice (2004) 'Recovery of the Collective Spirit: The Role of the Revival of Buddhism in Cambodia', unpublished mss.

Emerson, Rupert (1955) *Representative Government in Southeast Asia*, Cambridge: Harvard University Press.

Esmein, E. (1913) 'La maxime *Princeps Legibus Solutus est* dans l'ancien droit public français', in Paul Vinogradoff (ed.) *Essays in Legal History Read Before the International Congress of Historical Studies Held in London in 1913*, London: Oxford University Press: 201–214.

Evans, Grant (1998) *Politics of Ritual and Remembrance: Laos since 1975*, Chiang Mai: Silkworm Books.

Evans, Grant (2002) *A Short History of Laos: The Land in Between*, Chiang Mai: Silkworm Books.

Evers, Hans-Dieter and Siddique, Sharon (1993) 'Religious Revivalism in Southeast Asia: An Introduction', *Sojourn* (Singapore) 8 (1): 1–10.

Fausbøll, V., Rhys Davids, T. W. and Rhys Davids, C. A. F. (eds) (1973) *Buddhist Birth-stories (Jātaka Tales): The Commentarial Introduction Entitled Nidāna-Kāthā, The Story of the Lineage*, Varanasi: Indological Book House.

Frings, Viviane (1994) 'Cambodia After Decollectivization (1989–1992)', *Journal of Contemporary Asia* (Manila), 24 (1): 50–66.

Fukuyama, Francis (1992) *The End of History and the Last Man*, New York: The Free Press.

Furnivall, J. S. (1939) 'The Fashioning of Leviathan', *Journal of the Burma Research Society*, 29: 3–137.

Furnivall, J. S. (1943) *Educational Progress in Southeast Asia*, New York: Institute of Pacific Relations.

Gagneux, Pierre-Marie (1975) 'Contribution è la connaissance de la civilisation laotienne d'après de l'épigraphie du Royaume de Vientiane (XVème-XIXème siècles)', thèse pour le doctorat de troisième cycle, Paris: École des hautes etudes en sciences sociales.

Geertz, Clifford (1973) *The Interpretation of Cultures: Selected Essays*, New York; Basic Books.

Geertz, Clifford (1993) *Local Knowledge: Further Essays in Interpretive Anthropology*, London: Fontana Press.

Geertz, Clifford (2000) *Available Light: Anthropological Reflections on Philosophical Topics*, Princeton: Princeton University Press.

Gesick, Lorraine M. (ed.) (1983) *Centers, Symbols, and Hierarchies: Essays on the Classical States of Southeast Asia*, New Haven: Yale University Southeast Asia Studies.

Gesick, Lorraine M. (1995) *In the Land of Lady White Blood: Southern Thailand and the Meaning of History*, Ithaca, New York: Southeast Asia Program, Cornell University Press.

Gethin, Rupert (1992) *The Buddhist Path to Awakening: A Study of the Bodhi-Pakkhiya Dhamma*, Leiden: Brill.

Gokhale, B. G. (1953) 'Dhammiko Dhammaraja – A Study in Buddhist Constitutional Concepts', in B. G. Gokhale (ed.) *Indica. The Indian Historical Research Institute Silver Jubilee Commemoration Volume*, Bombay: St Xavier's College: 161–166.

Gokhale, B. G. (1966) 'Early Buddhist Kingship', *Journal of Asian Studies*, 26: 15–22.

Gombrich, Richard (1988) *Theravada Buddhism: A Social History from Ancient Benares to Modern Colombo*, London and New York: Routledge.

Gombrich, Richard (1994) 'Aśoka – The Great Upāsaka', in A. Seneviratna (ed.) *King Aśoka and Buddhism. Historical and Literary Studies*, Kandy: Buddhist Publication Society: 1–14.

Gour, C. G. (1965) *Institutions constitutionelles et politiques du Cambodge*, Paris: Dalloz.

Grabowsky, Volker (2004) *The Northern Tai Polity of Lan Na (Babai-Dadian) Between the Late 14th to Mid-16th Centuries: Internal Dynamics and Relations with Her Neighbours*, Working Paper Series No. 17, Asia Research Institute, Singapore.

Gray, James (1886) *Ancient Proverbs and Maxims from Burmese Sources, or the Niti Literature of Burma*, London: Trübner & Co.

Guthrie, Elizabeth (2002) 'Buddhist Temples and Cambodian Politics', in J. Vijghen (ed.) *People and the 1998 National Elections in Cambodia: Their Voices, Roles and Impact on Democracy*, Phnom Penh: Experts for Community Research, No. 44: 59–74.

Guthrie, Elizabeth (2004) 'The History and Cult of the Buddhist Earth Deity in Mainland Southeast Asia', PhD thesis, University of Canterbury.

Hall, D. G. E. (1981) *A History of South-East Asia*, 4th edn, Basingstoke and London: Macmillan Education.

Hallisey, C. (1995) 'Roads Taken and Not Taken', in Donald S. Lopez, Jr (ed.) *Curators of the Buddha: The Study of Buddhism under Colonialism*, Chicago, Illinois: University of Chicago Press: 31–61.

Hansen, Anne (2004) 'Khmer Identity and Theravada Buddhism', in J. Marston and E. Guthrie (eds) *History, Buddhism, and New Religious Movements in Cambodia*, Honolulu: University of Hawaii Press: 40–62.

Harris, Ian (1999) 'Buddhism *in Extremis*: The Case of Cambodia', in Ian Harris (ed.) *Buddhism and Politics in Twentieth-Century Asia*, London and New York: Continuum: 54–78.

Harris, Ian (2000) 'Magician as Environmentalist: Fertility Elements in South and Southeast Asian Buddhism', *Eastern Buddhist*, 32 (22): 128–156.

Harris, Ian (2001) 'Buddhist Saṅgha Groupings in Cambodia', *Buddhist Studies Review*, 18 (1): 73–105.
Harris, Ian (2005) *Cambodian Buddhism: History and Practice*, Honolulu: University of Hawaii Press.
Harvey, G. E. (1932) *Cambridge History of India, Vol. VI: The Indian Empire 1858–1918*, Cambridge: Cambridge University Press.
Hawley, John S. and Wulff, Donna (eds) (1996) *Devi: Goddesses of India*, Berkeley: University of California Press.
Heder, Steve (2002) 'Cambodian Elections in Historical Perspective', in J. L. Vijghen (ed.) *People and the 1998 National Elections in Cambodia: Their Voices, Roles and Impact*, Phnom Penh: Experts for Community Research: 1–5.
Heine-Geldern, Robert (1956) *Conceptions of State and Kingship in Southeast Asia*, Ithaca: Cornell University Southeast Asia Program (Data Paper No. 18).
Herbert, P. (2002) 'Burmese Cosmological Manuscripts', in Alexandra Green and T. Richard Blurton (eds) *Burma: Art and Archaeology*. London: The British Museum Press: 77–97.
Hiebert, Murray (1989) 'Look, We're Buddhist: Government Leaders Court Religion as a Way of Courting Voters', *Far Eastern Economic Review*, 3 August: 36.
Hobart, Mark and Taylor, Robert H. (eds) (1986) *Context, Meaning, and Power in Southeast Asia*, Ithaca: Cornell University Studies on Southeast Asia.
Hôpital des Bonzes (1956) *Règlement intérieur*, Phnom Penh: Hôpital des Bonzes.
Hoshino, Tatsuo (1986) *Pour une histoire médievale du moyen Mékong*, Bangkok: Duang Kamol.
Hpo Hlaing, Yaw Mingyi U (Wetmasut Myoza Wungyi) (1979) *Rajadhammasangaha*, ed. U Htin Fatt (Maung Htin), Rangoon: Sape U Publishing House [trans. Euan Bagshawe in 2004 and available online at: http://www.ibiblio.org/obl/docs/THE RAJADHAMMASANGAHA.pdf]
Htin Aung (1974) 'Kinwun Mingyi's Diaries 1872–4', *Journal of the Burma Research Society*, 58: 1–190.
Hutchinson, E. W. (tr.) (1968) *1688 Revolution in Siam: The Memoir of Father de Bèze, S.J.*, Hong Kong: Hong Kong University Press.
Huxley, Andrew (1996) 'The Buddha and the Social Contract', *Journal of Indian Philosophy*, 24 (4): 407–420.
Imbert, Jean (1961) *Histoire des institutions khmères*, vol. 2, Phnom Penh: Annales de la Faculté de Droit.
Institut Bouddhique (2001 [1957]) *L'An 2500 du Bouddhisme*, Phnom Penh: Institut Bouddhique.
Ishii, Yoneo (1972) 'Ecclesiastical Examination in Thailand', *Visakhapuja*: 52–55.
Ishii, Yoneo (1986) *Sangha, State, and Society: Thai Buddhism in History*, Honolulu: University of Hawaii Press.
Jā Gān and Un' Sou (2000) 'Prawatti Bra Sakyamunīchediy', *Kambujā Suriyā*, 56 (4): 87–93.
Jackson, Karl D. (ed.) (1989) *Cambodia 1975–1978: Rendezvous with Death*, Princeton: Princeton University Press.
Jackson, Peter A. (1989) *Buddhism, Legitimation, and Conflict: The Political Functions of Urban Thai Buddhism*, Singapore: Institute of Southeast Asian Studies (Social Issues in Southeast Asia).
Jaini, Padmanabh S. (1965) 'Mahādibbamanta: A Paritta Manuscript from

Cambodia', *Bulletin of the School of Oriental and African Studies*, XXVIII.1: 61–80.

Jory, Patrick (1996) *A History of the Thet Maha Chat and its Contribution to a Thai Political Culture*, PhD thesis, Australian National University.

Jory, Patrick. (2002) 'The *Vessantara Jataka, Barami*, and the *Bodhisatta*-Kings: The Origin and Spread of a Thai Concept of Power', *Crossroads*, 16 (2): 36–78.

Kaev Sāret (1964) *Aṃbī Dānānisaṅks kñom Kār Juay Saṃgroḥ Braḥ Saṅkh âbādh*, Phnom Penh.

Kahn, Joel S. (1998) *Southeast Asian Identities: Culture and the Politics of Representation in Indonesia, Malaysia, Singapore, and Thailand*, Singapore: Institute of Southeast Asian Studies.

Kalab, M. (1976) 'Monastic Education, Social Mobility, and Village Structure in Cambodia', in D. J. Banks (ed.) *Changing Identities in Modern Southeast Asia*, The Hague/Paris: Mouton Publishers.

Kambujā Suriyā (1956) 'Bidhī Sambodh Chlaṅ Mandī Bedy Braḥ Saṅgh', *Kambujā Suriyā*, 28 (4): 382–397 and (5): 491–500.

Kamm, Henry (1998) *Cambodia: Report from a Stricken Land*, New York: Arcade Publishing.

Kapferer, Bruce (1988) *Legends of People, Myths of State: Violence, Intolerance and Political Culture in Sri Lanka and Australia*. Washington and London: Smithsonian Institution Press.

Kaung, U. (1931) '1824–1853: Roman Catholic and American Baptist Mission Schools', *Journal of the Burma Research Society*, 21: 1–12.

Kaung, U. (1960a) 'The Beginnings of Christian Missionary Education in Burma: 1600–1824', *Journal of the Burma Research Society*, Fiftieth Anniversary Publications, no. 2: 117–133.

Kaung, U. (1960b) '1824–1853: Roman Catholic and American Baptist Schools', *Journal of the Burma Research Society*, Fiftieth Anniversary Publications, no. 2: 135–147.

Kaung, U. (1963) 'A Survey of the History of Education in Burma Before the British Conquest and After', *Journal of the Burma Research Society*, 46 (December): 1–124.

Kawiwong, A. (1959) *Panha Tamnai Lok* (Riddles of World Prophecy), Khon Kaen: Khlang Nana Tham Khlang Nana Withaya Press.

Kershaw, Roger (2001) *Monarchy in Southeast Asia: The Faces of Tradition in Transition*, London and New York: Routledge.

Keyes, Charles F. (1977) 'Millenialism, Theravada Buddhism, and Thai Society', *Journal of Asian Studies*, XXXVI, 2: 283–302.

Keyes, Charles F. (1994) 'Communist Revolution and the Buddhist Past in Cambodia,' in C. Keyes et al (eds.) *Asian Visions of Authority: Religion and the Modern State of Southeast Asia*. Honolulu, University of Hawaii Press.

Khammai Dhammasami, Ven. (2004) 'Idealism and Pragmatism: A Dilemma in the Current Monastic Education Systems of Burma and Thailand', paper presented at the conference on Buddhism, Power, and Political Order in South and Southeast Asia, Oxford, 14–16 April.

Khuon Nay (1950) 'Āramgakāthā', in *Sakhāntikā Samāgam Gilān Saṅkhrāḥ caṃboḥ Braḥ Saṅkh Buddhasāsanik*.

Kiernan, Ben (1996) *The Pol Pot Regime: Race, Power, and Genocide in Cambodia under the Khmer Rouge, 1975–79*, New Haven and London: Yale University Press.

Kitthiwuttho, Bhikkhu (1976) *Khā khommunit mai bāp* (Killing Communists is Not Evil), Bangkok: Abhidhmamma Foundation of Wat Mahādhātu.

Klausner, W. J. (1973) 'Buddhist Universities under Royal Patronage: A Tribute to His Majesty, the King', *Visakhapuja*: 13–16.

Koret, Peter (1994) *Whispered So Softly It Resounds Through the Forest, Spoken So Loudly It Can Hardly Be Heard*, unpublished PhD thesis, School of Oriental and African Studies, University of London.

Koret, Peter (1996) 'Understanding the History and Social Use of Lao Traditional Literature in Relationship to the Literary Tradition of the Tai Yuan', paper presented at the Sixth International Conference on Thai Studies, Chiang Mai, October.

Koret, Peter (1999) 'Books of Search: The Invention of Lao Literature as an Academic Subject of Study', in Grant Evans (ed.) *Laos: Culture and Society*, Chiang Mai: Silkworm Press: 26–257.

Koret, Peter (2004) 'The Religious Identity of Traditional Literature', paper presented at the conference 'Revisiting History, Nation and Culture in Modern Laos' at the National University of Singapore, January.

Kulke, Hermann (1978) *The Devarāja Cult*, tr. I. W. Mabbett, Ithaca, NY: Cornell University Southeast Asia Program (Data Paper No. 108).

Kyan, Ma (1966) '*Thibaw min patomu khyain ka british myanmar naing ngan e pyinnyayay achay anay* (The State of Education in British Burma at the Fall of Thibaw)', *Journal of Burma Research Society*, XLIX, II: 236–245.

Kyaw Htun (1873) *Pakinnaka dipani kyam*, Rangoon: Gezet Pon-hneik-taik.

Kyaw Htun [Moung Kyaw Doon] (1877) *Essay on the Sources and Origins of Buddhist Law*, Rangoon: Daily News Press.

La Loubère, Simon de (1986) *The Kingdom of Siam*, Singapore: Oxford University Press.

Lao Mong Hay (2002) 'The King is More than a Mere Ceremonial Figurehead', *Phnom Penh Post*, 11/24 (22 November – 5 December).

Le Blanc, Marcel (2003) *The History of Siam, 1688*, trans. and ed. Michael Smithies, Chiang Mai: Silkworm Books.

Le Boulanger, Paul (1931) *Histoire du Laos français*, Paris: Plon.

Leclère, Adhemard (1899a) *Le Buddhisme au Cambodge*, Paris: E. Leroux (1975 reprint, New York: AMS Press).

Leclère, Adhemard (1899b) *Recherches sur les origines brahmaniques des lois cambodgiennes*, Paris: L. Larose/E. Leroux.

Leclère, Adhemard (1914) *Histoire du Cambodge*, Paris: Librairie Paul Guethner (1974 reprint, Phnom Penh: Nokor Thom Ed.).

Ledgerwood, Judy (1997) 'Rural Development in Cambodia: The View from the Village', *Asia Society Publications*, New York, (www.asiasociety.org/publications/cambodia/rural.html).

Lejosne, Jean-Claude (1993) *Le journal de voyage de Gerrit van Wuysthoff et des ses assistants au Laos (1641–1642)*, Metz: Centre de Documentation et d'Information sur le Laos.

Lester, Robert C. (1973) *Theravada Buddhism in Southeast Asia*, Ann Arbor: University of Michigan Press.

Lewis, Ivor (1991) *Sahibs, Nabobs and Boxwallahs: A Dictionary of the Words of Anglo-India*, Oxford: Oxford University Press.

Lieberman, Victor (2003) *Strange Parallels: Southeast Asia in Global Context, c. 800–1830*, Cambridge: Cambridge University Press.

Liew, Foon Ming (n.d.) *The Traditional Tai Polity of Lan Na and the Tai Polities Around: An Annotated Translation of a Collection of Records from Chinese Sources Covering the Period from the 13th to 18th Centuries*, in collaboration with V. Grabowsky, an expansion of the earlier manuscript entitled 'The Land of Eight-Hundred Daughters-in-law or Lan Na Kingdom in the Light of Official Chinese Historiography – Collected Records from Chinese Sources', unpublished manuscript.

Ling, Trevor (ed.) (1993) *Buddhist Trends in Southeast Asia*, Singapore: Institute of Southeast Asian Studies (Social Issues in Southeast Asia).

Lingat, R. (1930) 'History of Wat Mahadhātu', *Journal of the Siam Society*, XXIV (I): 1–27.

Lingat, R. (1933) 'History of Wat Pavaraniveca', *Journal of the Siam Society*, XXVI (I): 73–102.

Lizée, Pierre P. (2000) *Peace, Power and Resistance in Cambodia: Global Governance and the Failure of International Conflict Resolution*, London: Macmillan Press/New York: St Martin's Press.

Lorrillard, Michel (1995) 'Les chroniques royales du Laos: contribution è la connaissance historique des royaumes laos (1316–1887)', thèse pour le doctorat de régime unique, Paris: École pratique des hautes etudes, Ivème section (sciences historiques et philologiques).

Lorrillard, Michel (2002) 'À propos du Vat Sisaket et du Vat Ho Phra Kèo', texte d'une communication prononcée è l'occasion de la conference internationale sur le Vat Sisaket, 28 February 2003.

Lorrillard, Michel (2003) 'Insights on the Diffusion of Lao Buddhism', paper presented at the conference on Buddhist Legacy in South-East Asia: Mentalities, Interpretations and Practices to celebrate the 80th anniversary of HRH Princess Galyani Vadhana, Bangkok, 18–20 January.

Lorrillard, Michel (2004) 'Les inscriptions du That Luang de Vientiane: données nouvelles sur l'histoire d'un stupa lao', *Bulletin de l'École française d'Extrême-Orient*, 90: 289–348.

Löschmann, Heike (1991) 'Buddhismus und gesellschaftliche Entwicklung in Kambodscha seit der Niederschlagung des Pol-Pot-Regimes im Jahre 1979', *Asien*, 41: 13–27.

Lutgendorf, Philip (1994) 'My Hanuman is Bigger than Yours', *History of Religions*, 33 (3): 211–245.

Malalasekera, G. P. (1983 [1937]) *Dictionary of Pali Proper Names*, New Delhi: Munshiram Manoharlal Publishers.

Malalgoda, Kitsiri (1976) *Buddhism in Sinhalese Society, 1750–1900*, Berkeley: University of California Press.

Malalgoda, Kitsiri (1997) 'Buddhism in Post-Independence Sri Lanka' in Geoffrey A. Oddie (ed.) *Religion in South Asia: Religious Conversion and Revival Movements in South Asia in Medieval and Modern Times*. London: Curzon Press: 183–189.

Marini, G. F. de (1998) *A New and Interesting Description of the Lao Kingdom*, trs. Walter E. J. Tips and Claudio Bertuccio, Bangkok: White Lotus.

Marks, John E. (1917) *Forty Years in Burma*, London: Hutchinson.
Marston, John (2002) 'La reconstrucción de budismo "antiguo" de Camboya', *Estudios de Asia y África*, 37(2): 271–303.
Marston, John and Guthrie, Elizabeth (eds) (2004) *History, Buddhism, and New Religious Movements in Cambodia*, Honolulu: University of Hawaii Press.
Martin, Marie Alexandrine (1994) *Cambodia: A Shattered Society*, trs. Mark M. McLeod, Berkeley: University of California Press.
Marutphitakasa, Ratana (1999) *A Message from the Spoiled Earth (Truthfully Broadcast from Mae Phra Thoranee)*, Bangkok: Thoranee Publishers.
Matthews, Bruce (1999) 'The Legacy of Tradition and Authority: Buddhism and the Nation in Myanmar', in Ian Harris (ed.) *Buddhism and Politics in Twentieth-Century Asia*, London and New York: Continuum: 26–53.
Maung Maung (1980) *From Sangha to Laity: Nationalist Movements of Burma 1920–1940*, Columbia, MO: South Asia Books.
Maung Tet Pyo (1884) *Customary Law of the Chin Tribe*, Rangoon: Government Press.
Maung Tin (1914) '*Rajadhiraja Vilasani:* A Pali Historical Work Edited and Translated', *Journal of the Burma Research Society*, 4: 7–21.
Mayouri Ngaosyvathn (1996) 'An Introduction to the Laws of Khun Borom', in Andrew Huxley (ed.) *Thai Law: Buddhist Law. Essays on the Legal History of Thailand, Laos and Burma*. Bangkok: White Orchid Press: 73–80.
McCloud, Donald G. (1995) *Southeast Asia: Tradition and Modernity in the Contemporary World*, Boulder, CO: Westview Press.
McKean, Lisa (1996) 'Bhārat Mātā: Mother India and her Militant Matriarchs', in John Hawley and Donna Wulff (eds) *Devi: Goddesses of India*, Berkeley: University of California Press: 250–280.
McTernan, Oliver (2003) *Violence in God's Name: Religion in an Age of Conflict*, London: Darton, Longman and Todd.
Meddagama, Udaya (trs.) (1993) *Anagatavamsa Desana (The Sermon of the Chronicle-To-Be)*, Delhi: Motilal Banarsidass.
Mendelson, E. Michael (1975) *Sangha and State in Burma, A Study of Monastic Sectarianism and Leadership*, ed. J. P. Ferguson, Ithaca: Cornell University Press.
Miller, Terry (1985) *Traditional Music of the Lao*, Westport, Conn.: Greenwood Press.
Ministry of Information and Culture (2000). *Pavatsat lao (dükdamban-patchuban)* (History of Laos from the Early Beginnings to the Present), Vientiane.
Ministry of Welfare (1958) *Phongyi kyaung pyinnya thinkyaryay mawgun* (Records of Monastic Education), Rangoon.
Morrell, David and Samudavanija, Chai-anan (1981) *Political Conflict in Thailand: Reform, Reaction, Revolution*, Cambridge: Oelschlager, Gunn & Hain.
Moscotti, Albert D. (1974) *British Policy and the Nationalist Movement in Burma, 1917–1937*. Honolulu: University of Hawaii Press.
Moura, J. (1883) *Le royaume du Cambodge*, Tome I, Paris: Ernest Leroux.
Mulder, Niels (1996) *Inside Thai Society: Interpretations of Everyday Life*, Amsterdam: The Pepin Press.
Mulder, Niels (1997) *Inside Southeast Asia: Religion, Everyday Life, Cultural Change*, Amsterdam/Kuala Lumpur: The Pepin Press.
Mulder, Niels (2003) *Southeast Asian Images: Towards Civil Society?* Chiang Mai: Silkworm Books.

Munro-Hay, Stuart (2001) *Nakhon Sri Thammarat: The Archeology, History and Legends of a Southern Thai Town*, Bangkok: White Lotus Press.

Munson, Frederick P. *et al.* (1968) *Area Handbook for Cambodia*, Washington, DC: US Government Printing Office.

Murphy, W. T. (1991) 'The Oldest Social Science? The Epistemic Properties of the Common Law Tradition', *Modern Law Review*, 54: 182–215.

Myint-U, Thant (2000) *The Making of Modern Burma*, Cambridge: Cambridge University Press.

Népote, Jacques (1979) 'Education et développement dans le Cambodge moderne', *Mondes en développement*, Paris, 28: 767–792.

Népote, Jacques (1984) 'Pour une reconstruction de l'histoire du Cambodge', *Asie de sud-est et monde insulindienne*, Paris, 15 (1–4): 69–101.

Népote, Jacques (1990) *Pour une géographie culturelle de l'Indochine*, Geneva: Édition Olizane.

Nhouy Abhay (1959) 'Buddhism in Laos', in René de Berval (ed.) *Kingdom of Laos: The Land of the Million Elephants and the White Parasol* Saigon: France-Asie: 237–256.

Niyom Suphawut (transcriber) (1989) 'Tamnan Hin Taek', in *Wannakhadi Thaungthin Isan Jak Lek Jan Lan Thaung*, Sakon Nakhon: Sakon Nakhon Teacher's College.

Nyi Nyi (1964) 'The Development of University Education in Burma', *Journal of the Burma Research Society*, 47(June): 11–76.

Okudaira, Ryuji (1994) 'A Study on a "Mythology of Kingship" described in *Manugye dhammathat*', unpublished paper presented at the Burma Studies Conference, Dekalb, Illinois, October.

Okudaira, Ryuji and Huxley, Andrew (2001) 'Political Science in the Court of King Badon: Eleven Burmese Lists on Kingship from 1782', *Bulletin of the School of Oriental and African Studies*, 64: 248–259.

Olivelle, Patrick (ed., tr.) (2005) *Manu's Code of Law: A Critical Edition and Translation of the Mānava-Dharmaśāstra*, Oxford: Oxford University Press.

Ono Toru (1981) 'The Development of Education in Burma', *East Asian Cultural Studies*, 20 (1–4): 107–133.

Osborne, Milton (1966) 'History and Kingship in Contemporary Cambodia', *Journal of Southeast Asian History*, 7 (1): 1–14.

Osborne, Milton (1969) *The French Presence in Cochinchina and Cambodia: Rule and Response (1859–1905)*, Ithaca: Cornell University Press.

Osborne, Milton (1973) *Politics and Power in Cambodia: The Sihanouk Years*, Camberwell, Australia: Longman.

Osborne, Milton (1994) *Sihanouk, Prince of Light and Prince of Darkness*, Chiang Mai: Silkworm Books.

Osborne, Milton (1997) *Southeast Asia: An Introductory History*, 7th edn, Chiang Mai: Silkworm Books.

Oudumaphra (1984) *Samdech Phrasri Patcharindara Paramarajininaratha Phraramarajanani Phan Bei Luang*, Bangkok: Phrae Pittaya Press.

Pali-tetgatho sonsanyi kawmiti- asiyinkhanaa (1941) (Report of the Pali University Enquiry Committee), Rangoon: Government Printing and Stationery.

Pang Kāt', Ven. (1957) 'Gilānupañhānakathā', *Kambujā Suriyā*, 29(1): 1–9.

Penth, Hans (1994) *Jinakālamālī Index: An Annotated Index to the Thailand Part of*

Ratanapañña's Chronicle Jinakālamālī, Oxford: The Pali Text Society/Chiang Mai: Silkworm Books.

Pollock, Sheldon (1993) 'Rāmāyaṇa and Political Imagination in India', *The Journal of Asian Studies*, 52 (2): 261–297.

Ponchaud, François (1989) 'Social Change in the Vortex of the Revolution' in Karl D. Jackson (ed.) *Cambodia, 1975–1978: Rendezvous with Death*. Princeton: Princeton University Press.

Ponchaud, François (1990) *La cathédrale de la rizière, 450 ans d'histoire de l'Église au Cambodge*, Paris: Fayard.

Porée, Guy and Maspero, Eveline (1938) *Moeurs et coutumes des Khmers: origines, histoire, religions, croyances, rites, évolution*, Paris: Payot.

Porée-Maspero, Eveline (1962–69) *Étude sur les rites agraires des Cambodgiens*, 3 vols, Paris and The Hague: Mouton.

Pou Saveros (1991) 'Sanskrit, Pāli and Khmero-Pāli in Cambodia', in J. G. de Casparis (ed.) *Sanskrit Outside India* (in Johannes Bronkhorst (ed.) *Panels of the VIIth World Sanskrit Conference*, Vol. VII, Leiden: E. J. Brill): 13–28.

Pou Saveros (1998) 'Dieux et roi dans la pensée khmère ancienne', unpublished mss. [marked for publication in *Journal Asiatique* (Paris)].

Prapod Assavavirulhakarn (2003) 'Mahādibbamanta – A Reflection on Thai Chanting Tradition', in Olle Qvarnström (ed.) *Jainism and Early Buddhism: Essays in Honor of Padmanabh S. Jaini*, Fremont, California: Asian Humanities Press, Part II: 379–406.

Prasert Na Nagara and Griswold, A. B. (1992) *Epigraphic and Historical Studies*, Bangkok: The Historical Society.

Preschez, Philippe (1961) *Essai sur la démocratie au Cambodge*. Paris: Fondation Nationale des Sciences Politiques.

Preuss, James B. (ed. and trs.) (1976) *The Thāt Phanom Chronicle: A Shrine History and its Interpretation*, Data Paper No. 104, Ithaca, NY: Southeast Asia Program, Department of Asian Studies, Cornell University.

Pringle, James (2006) 'Mali's Unlikely Democracy', *The Wilson Quarterly*, 30 (2): 31–39.

Quaritch Wales, H. G. (1931) *Siamese State Ceremonies: Their History and Function*, London: Bernard Quaritch.

Rahula, Walpola (1956) *History of Buddhism in Ceylon*, Colombo: M. D. Gunasena.

Rahula, Walpola (1978) *Zen and the Taming of the Bull: Towards the Definition of Buddhist Thought*, London: Gordon Fraser.

Ratanapañña (1968) *The Sheaf of Garlands of the Epochs of the Conqueror*, being a translation of *Jinakālamālīpakaraṇa* (tr. N. A. Jayawickrama), London: Pali Text Society.

Ratnapala, Nandasena (1971) *The Katikāvatas: Laws on the Buddhist Order of Ceylon from the 12th Century to the 18th Century*, Munich: Münchener Studien zur Sprachenwissenschaft, Beiheft N.

Reynolds, Craig J. (1972) *The Buddhist Monkhood in Nineteenth Century Thailand*, unpublished PhD thesis, Ithaca, Cornell University.

Reynolds, Craig J. (1987) *Thai Radical Discourse: The Real Face of Thai Feudalism Today*, Ithaca, NY: Cornell University Southeast Asia Program.

Reynolds, Craig J. (2005) 'Power', in Donald S. Lopez, Jr (ed.) *Critical Terms for the Study of Buddhism*, Chicago and London: University of Chicago Press: 211–228.

Reynolds, Frank E. (1972) 'The Two Wheels of the Dhamma', in *The Two Wheels of Dhamma: Essays on the Theravāda Tradition in India and Ceylon*, Chambersburg, PA: American Academy of Religion: 6–30.

Reynolds, Frank E. (1978) 'The Holy Emerald Jewel: Some Aspects of Buddhism, Symbolism and Political Legitimation in Thailand and Laos', in Bardwell L. Smith (ed.) *Religion and Legitimation in Thailand, Laos, and Burma*, Chambersbarg, PA: Anima Books: 175–193.

Reynolds, Frank E. and Reynolds, Mani B. (trs.) (1982) *Three Worlds According to King Ruang: A Thai Buddhist Cosmology*, Berkeley: Asian Humanities Press.

Reyum (2001) 'New Khmer Architecture', *Cultures of Independence: An Introduction to Cambodian Arts and Culture in the 1950s and 1960s*, Phnom Penh: Reyum: 3–62.

Richardson, D. (1896) *The Damathat or the Laws of Menoo*, 4th edn, Rangoon: Hanthawaddy Press.

Right Documentation Unit, NCGUB (2003) *Burma Human Rights Year Book 2002–2003: Rights to Education and Health* (www.burmalibrary.org/show.php?cat=333).

Ringis, Rita (1990) *Thai Temples and Temple Murals*, Singapore: Oxford University Press.

Rives, Nang Mo Lao (1999) *The Teaching of English in Burma (Myanmar) from 1824–1988*, PhD thesis, University of Kansas.

Saddhatissa, H. (trs. and ed.) (1975) *The Birth Stories of the Ten Bodhisattas and the Dasabodhisattuppattikathā*, London: The Pali Text Society (Sacred Books of the Buddhists, Vol. XXIX).

Saeng Manavidura (1979) 'Some Observations on the Jinakālamālīpakaranam', in N. A. Jayawickrama (trs.) *The Sheaf of Garlands of the Epochs of the Conqueror, being a translation of Jinakālamālīpakaranam of Ratanapañña Thera of Thailand*, London: The Pali Text Society.

Sam, Yang (1987) *Khmer Buddhism and Politics 1954–1984*, Newington, CT: Khmer Studies Institute.

Sarkisyanz, E. (1965) *Buddhist Backgrounds of the Burmese Revolution*, The Hague: Martinus Nijhoff.

Sawing Bunjeum (transcriber) (n.d.) *Kala Nap Meu Suay*, Ubon: Moradok Isan Press.

Schaar, John H. (1984) 'Legitimacy in the Modern State', in William Connolly (ed.) *Legitimacy and the State*, New York: New York University Press.

Schober, J. (1995) 'The Theravada Buddhist Engagement with Modernity in Southeast Asia: Whither the Social Paradigm of the Galactic Polity?', *The Journal of Southeast Asian Studies*, 26 (2): 307–325.

Schober, J. (2005) 'Buddhist Visions of Moral Authority and Civil Society: The Search for the Post-Colonial State in Burma', in Monique Skidmore (ed.) *Burma at the Turn of the Twenty-First Century*, Honolulu: University of Hawaii Press: 113–133.

Scott, D. (1999) *Refashioning Futures: Criticism after Postcoloniality*, Princeton: Princeton University Press.

Sein, Daw Tin (1986) 'The Role of Christian Missions in the Relationship between Burma and the West – 17th to 19th AD', *Studies of Burmese History* [typed manuscript]: 439–444.

Sharma, Shalendra (2002) 'Thailand's Financial Crisis, part 2', *Crossroads*, 16 (2): 1–35.

Shorto, H. L (1971) *A Dictionary of the Mon Inscriptions from the Sixth to the Sixteenth Centuries*, London: Oxford University Press (London Oriental Series, Vol. 24).

Sihanouk, Norodom (1969) 'Urbanisme, Phnom Penh "Le nouvel Angkor Thom". Villes provinciales. Tourisme et industrie hôteliere. Artisanat . . .', in *Photos-Souvenirs du Cambodge: Sangkum Reastre Niyum*: 1–5, Phnom Penh: Rama Printing International.

Sihanouk, Norodom S. A. R. Samdech Preah Upayuvareach (1955) *Statut de Sangkum Reastr Niyum*, in Archives Nationales du Cambodge, 32.B.62: 395.

Sila Viravong, Maha (1964) *History of Laos*, New York: Paragon Book Reprint Corporation.

Sīlānanda, Ashin (1982) *Biography of Sayadaw Ashin Thittila*, Rangoon: Buddhasasananuggaha Ahpwe.

Simon, D. (1984) '*Princeps legibus solutus*. Die Stellung des byzantinisches Kaisers zum Gesetz', in D. Nörr and D. Simon (eds) *Gedächtnisschrift für Wolfgang Kunkel*, Frankfurt am Main: V. Klostermann: 450–459.

Singh, P. S. (1980) *Growth of Nationalism in Burma 1900–1942*, Calcutta: Firma KLM Private Ltd.

Singh, Upinder (1993) *Kings, Brāhmanas and Temples in Orissa: An Epigraphic Study*, New Delhi: Munshiram Manoharlal.

Skilling, Peter (2002) 'Three Types of Bodhisatta in Theravādin Tradition: A Bibliographical Excursion', in *Buddhist and Indian Studies in Honour of Professor Sodo Mori* (Hamamtsu: Kokusai Bukkyoto Kyokai [International Buddhist Association]: 91–102.

Skilling, Peter (2005) 'Worship and Devotional Life: Buddhist Devotional Life in Southeast Asia', in Lindsay Jones (ed.) *Encyclopedia of Religion*, 2nd edn, Detroit: Macmillan Reference USA/Thomson Gale, Vol. 14: 9826–9834.

Smith, Bardwell L. (ed.) (1978) *Religion and Legitimation of Power in Thailand, Laos, and Burma*, Chambersburg, PA: Anima Books.

Smith, Donald E. (1965) *Religion and Politics in Burma*, Princeton: Princeton University Press.

Smith, Frank (1989) *Interpretive Accounts of the Khmer Rouge Years: Personal Experience in Cambodian Peasant World View*, Occasional Paper No. 18, Madison, WI: Center for Southeast Asian Studies.

Smith, Malcolm (1947) *A Physician at the Court of Siam*, London: Country Life.

Sotthisankrām, Nathavutthi (1984) *Nāyakhwang Abhayavongsa and the Thai Democratic Party*, Bangkok: Phrae Pittaya Publishers.

Souneth Phothisane (1996) 'The Nidan Khun Borom: Annotated Translation and Analysis', PhD thesis, University of Queensland.

Spiro, M. E. (1970) *Buddhism and Society: A Great Tradition and its Burmese Vicissitudes*, New York: Harper.

Stadtner, Donald (1991) 'A Fifteenth-Century Royal Monument in Burma and the Seven Stations in Buddhist Art', *The Art Bulletin*, 73 (1): 39–52.

Stargardt, Janice (1995) 'The Oldest Known Pali Texts, 5th–6th Century: Results of the Cambridge Symposium on the Pyu Golden Pali Text from Sri Ksetra, 18–19 April 1995', *Journal of the Pali Text Society*, 21: 199–213.

Steinberg, David Joel *et al.* (eds) (1987) *In Search of Southeast Asia*, 2nd edn, Sydney, Wellington: Allen & Unwin.

Stewart, A. T. Q. (1975) *The Pagoda War: Lord Dufferin and the Fall of the Kingdom of Ava 1885–6*, London: Faber and Faber.

Stuart-Fox, Martin (1998) *The Lao Kingdom of Lān Xāng: Rise and Decline*, Bangkok: White Lotus.

Stuart-Fox, Martin and Bucknell, Rod (1982) 'The Politicization of the Buddhist Sangha in Laos', *Journal of Southeast Asian Studies*, 12(1): 60–80.

Subhadradis Diskul, M. C. (1990) *Hindu Gods at Sukhodaya* (English version by the author and A. B. Griswold), Bangkok: White Lotus.

Suksamran, Somboon (1977) *Political Buddhism in Southeast Asia: The Role of the Sangha in the Modernization of Thailand*, London: C. Hurst.

Superintendent, Government Printing and Stationery (1948) *Pondawgyi kyaung pyinnyayay sonsanyay asiyinkhansar hnint ovadacariya sayadaw mya e akyanpaykyet mya* (Report of the Enquiry Committee on the National Education in the Buddhist Monasteries and the Advice of the Advisor-Sayadaws), Rangoon.

Swearer, Donald K. (1995) *The Buddhist World of Southeast Asia*, Albany: State University of New York Press.

Swearer, Donald K. and Sommai Premchit (1978) 'The Relationship Between the Religious and Political Orders in Northern Thailand (14th–16th Centuries)', in Bardwell L. Smith (ed.) *Religion and Legitimation of Power in Thailand, Laos, and Burma*. Chambersburg, PA: Anima Books: 20–33.

Talbot, Cynthia (2001) *Precolonial India in Practice: Society, Region, and Identity in Medieval Andhra*, New York: Oxford University Press.

Tambiah, Stanley J. (1970) *Buddhism and the Spirit Cults in North-East Thailand*, Cambridge: Cambridge University Press.

Tambiah, Stanley J. (1976) *World Conquerer and World Renouncer: A Study of Buddhism and Polity in Thailand Against a Historical Background*, Cambridge: Cambridge University Press.

Tambiah, Stanley J. (1978) 'Sangha and Polity in Modern Thailand: An Overview', in Bardwell L. Smith (ed.) *Religion and Legitimation in Thailand, Laos, and Burma*, Chambersburg, PA: Anima Books: 111–133.

Taw, Sein Ko (1913a) 'Pali Examinations', in *Burmese Sketches*, Vol. I, Rangoon: British Burma Press.

Taw, Sein Ko (1913b) *Burmese Sketches*, Rangoon: British Burma Press.

Taylor, Charles (2004) *Modern Social Imaginaries*, Durham and London: Duke University Press.

Taylor, Robert H. (1987) *The State in Burma*, Honolulu: University of Hawaii Press.

Than Myint-U (2001) *The Making of Modern Burma*, Cambridge: Cambridge University Press.

Than Tun (ed.) (1984–90) *The Royal Orders of Burma AD 1598–1885, Volumes 1–10*, Kyoto: Centre of South East Asian Studies, Kyoto University.

Thein Lwin (2000) *Education in Burma (1945–2000)*, Burma Links Page UNO, Asian Virtual Library, Myanmar (Burma), htt://www.york.cuny.edu/ꞁatt/burma/

Thion, Serge (1988) 'Remodeling Broken Images: Manipulations of Identities. Towards and Beyond the Nation, an Asian Perspective', in R. Guidieri, F. Pellizzi and S. J. Tambiah (eds) *Ethnicities and Nations: Processes of Interethnic Relations in Latin America, Southeast Asia, and the Pacific*, Houston: Rothko Chapel: 229–258 (www.abbc.com/totus/1981–1990/157Cbrokim2.html).

Thion, Serge (1993a) 'The Cambodian Idea of Revolution', in Serge Thion (ed.) *Watching Cambodia*: 77–94, Bangkok: White Lotus.

Thion, Serge (1993b) *Watching Cambodia: Ten Paths to Enter the Cambodian Tangle*, Bangkok: White Lotus.

Thompson, Ashley (2004) 'The Suffering of Kings: Substitute Bodies, Healing, and Social Justice in Cambodia', in John Marston and Elizabeth Guthrie (eds) *History, Buddhism, and New Religious Movements in Cambodia*, Honolulu: University of Hawaii Press: 91–112.

Tin Ohn (1963) 'Modern Historical Writing in Burmese 1724–1942', in D. G. E. Hall (ed.) *Historians of Southeast Asia*: 85–93, London: Oxford University Press.

Tiyavanich, K. (1997) *Forest Recollections: Wandering Monks in Twentieth-Century Thailand*, Honolulu: University of Hawaii Press.

U Tin (2001) *The Royal Administration of Burma*, trs. Euan Bagshawe, Bangkok: Ava Publishing.

Vajirañāṇavarorasa, Prince (1979) *Autobiography: The Life of Prince–Patriarch Vajirañāna of Siam*, ed. and trs. Craig Reynolds, Ohio: Ohio University Press.

Van Beek, Steve (1995) *The Chao Phraya River in Transition*, Kuala Lumpur: Oxford University Press.

Vickery, Michael (1984) 'Prolegomena to Methods for Using the Ayutthayan Laws as Historical Source Material', *Journal of the Siam Society*, 72: 37–58.

Vijghen, J. L. (compiler) (1998) *People and the 1998 National Elections in Cambodia: Their Voices, Roles and Impact*, Phnom Penh: Experts for Community Research.

Voegelin, Eric (1952) *The New Science of Politics. An Introduction*, Chicago and London: University of Chicago Press.

Voegelin, Eric (2001) *The Collected Works of Eric Voegelin. Published Essays 1934–1939*, vol. 9, ed. T. W. Heilke, trs. M. J. Hanak, Columbia and London: University of Missouri Press.

Voegelin, Eric (2002) *The Collected Works of Eric Voegelin. Anamnesis: On the Theory of History and Politics*, vol. 6, ed. D. Walsh, trs. M. J. Hanak, Columbia and London: University of Missouri Press.

Wolters, O. W. (1982) *History, Culture, and Region in Southeast Asian Perspectives*, Singapore: Institute of Southeast Asian Studies.

Wyatt, David K. (1969) *The Politics of Reform in Thailand: Education under King Chulalongkorn*, New Haven: Yale University Press.

Wyatt, David K. (1975) *The Crystal Sands: The Chronicles of Nagara Śrī Dharmarāja*, Ithaca, NY: Southeast Asia Program, Cornell University, Data Paper No. 98.

Wyatt, David K. (1984) *Thailand: A Short History*, 2nd edn, New Haven and London: Yale University Press.

Wyatt, David K. (1994) 'The Buddhist Monkhood as an Avenue of Social Mobility in Traditional Thai Society', reprinted in *Studies in Thai History: Collected Articles by David K. Wyatt*, Chiang Mai: Silkworm Books: 210–222.

Wyatt, David K. and Aroonrut Wichienkeeo (1995) *The Chiang Mai Chronicle*, Chiang Mai: Silkworm Books.

Yang Sam (1987) *Khmer Buddhism and Politics 1954–1984*, Newington, CT: Khmer Studies Institute.

Yang Sam (1990) 'Buddhism in Cambodia 1795–1954', MA thesis, Cornell University.

Yule, Henry and Burnell, A. C. (1903) *Hobson-Jobson: A Glossary of Colloquial Anglo-Indian Words and Phrases, and of Kindred Terms, Etymological, Historical, Geographical and Discursive*, new edition, ed. William Crooke, John Murray: London (reprinted New Delhi: Munshiram Manoharlal, 1984).

Zack, Stephen (1977) *Buddhist Education under Prince Wachirayanwarorot*, unpublished PhD thesis, Ithaca, Cornell University.

Zadrozny, Mitchell D. (ed.) (1955) *Area Handbook on Cambodia*, Chicago: University of Chicago for the Human Relations Area Files (HRAF), preliminary edition.

Zago, Marcello (1972) *Rites et cérémonies en milieu bouddhiste lao*, Rome: Università Gregoriana Editrice.

Zago, Marcello (1976) 'Contemporary Khmer Buddhism', in H. Dumoulin and J. C. Maraldo (eds) *Buddhism in the Modern World*, New York: Collier Books: 109–119.

INDEX